GOD IN SEARCH OF MAN

GOD IN SEARCH OF MAN

■ ■ ■ ■ ■

A Philosophy of Judaism

ABRAHAM JOSHUA HESCHEL

THE NOONDAY PRESS
Farrar, Straus and Giroux / New York

The Noonday Press
A division of Farrar, Straus and Giroux
19 Union Square West, New York 10003

Library of Congress catalog card number: 55-11188

First published in 1955 by Farrar, Straus and Giroux
First Noonday paperback edition, 1976
Twentieth printing, 1998

To
SYLVIA

CONTENTS

I. God

II. Revelation

THE ELIMINATION OF ANTHROPOMORPHISM
LIKE NO OTHER EVENT

THE PARADOX OF PROPHECY
IN DEEP DARKNESS
BEYOND THE MYSTERY
THE TWO ASPECTS
WAS SINAI AN ILLUSION?
A WAY OF THINKING
AN ECSTASY OF GOD

THOUGHT AND TIME
THE GOD OF ABRAHAM
THE CATEGORY OF UNIQUENESS
THE CHOSEN DAY
THE UNIQUENESS OF HISTORY
ESCAPE TO THE TIMELESS
SEEDS OF ETERNITY
IMMUNE TO DESPAIR
EVOLUTION AND REVELATION

PROCESS AND EVENT
TO SEE THE PAST IN THE PRESENT TENSE

ATTACHMENT TO EVENTS
THE MEMORY OF A COMMITMENT
LOYALTY TO A MOMENT
A WORD OF HONOR
LIFE WITHOUT COMMITMENT
REVELATION IS A BEGINNING

III. Response

1. GOD

1 Self-understanding of Judaism

It is customary to blame secular science and anti-religious philosophy for the eclipse of religion in modern society. It would be more honest to blame religion for its own defeats. Religion declined not because it was refuted, but because it became irrelevant, dull, oppressive, insipid. When faith is completely replaced by creed, worship by discipline, love by habit; when the crisis of today is ignored because of the splendor of the past; when faith becomes an heirloom rather than a living fountain; when religion speaks only in the name of authority rather than with the voice of compassion— its message becomes meaningless.

Religion is an answer to man's ultimate questions. The moment we become oblivious to ultimate questions, religion becomes irrelevant, and its crisis sets in. The primary task of philosophy of religion is to rediscover the questions to which religion is an answer. The inquiry must proceed both by delving into the consciousness of man as well as by delving into the teachings and attitudes of the religious tradition.

There are dead thoughts and there are living thoughts. A dead thought has been compared to a stone which one may plant in the soil. Nothing will come out. A living thought is like a seed. In the process of thinking, an answer without a question is devoid of life.

3

It may enter the mind; it will not penetrate the soul. It may become a part of one's knowledge; it will not come forth as a creative force.

In our quest for forgotten questions, the method and spirit of philosophical inquiry are of greater importance than theology, which is essentially descriptive, normative, and historical. Philosophy may be defined as the art of asking the right questions. One of the marks of philosophical thinking is that, in contrast to poetry, for example, it is not a self-sufficing pouring forth of insight, but the explicit statement of a problem and the attempt to offer an answer to a problem. Theology starts with dogmas, philosophy begins with problems. Philosophy sees the problem first, theology has the answer in advance. We must not, however, disregard another important difference. Not only are the problems of philosophy not identical with the problems of religion; their status is not the same. Philosophy is, in a sense, a kind of thinking that has a beginning but no end. In it, the awareness of the problem outlives all solutions. Its answers are questions in disguise; every new answer giving rise to new questions.[1] In religion, on the other hand, the mystery of the answer hovers over all questions. Philosophy deals with problems as universal issues; to religion the universal issues are personal problems. Philosophy, then, stresses the primacy of the problem, religion stresses the primacy of the person.

The fundamentalists claim that all ultimate questions have been answered; the logical positivists maintain that all ultimate questions are meaningless. Those of us who share neither the conceit of the former nor the unconcern of the latter, and reject both specious answers and false evasions, know that an ultimate issue is at stake in our existence, the relevance of which surpasses all final formulations. It is this embarrassment that is the starting point for our thinking.

There are two types of thinking; one that deals with *concepts* and one that deals with *situations*. In our own time, the nineteenth cen tury conflict between science and religion is being replaced by a controversy between the type of thinking that has as its object particular concepts of the mind and a way of thinking that has as its object the situation of man. Conceptual thinking is an act of reasoning; situational thinking involves an inner experience; in uttering judgment about an issue, the person himself is under judgment. Conceptual thinking is adequate when we are engaged in an effort to enhance our knowledge about the world. Situational thinking is necessary when we arc engaged in an effort to understand issucs on which we stake our very existence.

One does not discuss the future of mankind in the atomic age in the same way in which one discusses the weather. It would be wrong to leave out of such a discussion the awe, the fear, the humility, the responsibility, that are or ought to be as much a part of the issue as the atom itself. What we face is not only a problem which is apart from ourselves but a situation of which we are a part and in which we are totally involved. To understand the problem we must explore the situation.

The attitude of the conceptual thinker is one of detachment: the subject facing an independent object; the attitude of the situational thinker is one of concern: the subject realizing that he is involved in a situation that is in need of understanding.

The beginning of situational thinking is not doubt, detachment, but amazement, awe, involvement. The philosopher, accordingly, is a witness, not an accountant of other people's business. Unless we are involved, the problem is not present. Unless we are in love or remember vividly what happened to us when we were in love, we are ignorant of love. Creative thinking is not stimulated by vicarious issues but by personal problems. And so, for example, the problem of religious philosophy is not how does *man* arrive at an understanding of God, but rather how can *we* arrive at an understanding of God.

In a profound sense, the philosopher is never a pure spectator. His wisdom is not a commodity that can be produced on demand. His books are not *responsa*. We should not regard them as mirrors, reflecting other people's problems, but rather as windows, allowing us to view the author's soul. Philosophers do not expend their power and passion unless they themselves are affected. The soul only communes with itself when the heart is stirred. Quandaries knocking at the heart of the philosopher provide the motive that impels him to toil for truth. All philosophy is an *apologia pro vita sua.*

RADICAL SELF-UNDERSTANDING

There are two types of philosophy. Philosophy may be pursued as a process of thinking thought, of analyzing *the content of thinking,* such as principles, assumptions, doctrines. Or it may be pursued as thinking about thinking, as *radical self-understanding,*[2] as a process of analyzing *the act of thinking,* as a process of introspection, of watching the intellectual self in action.

The action in which the intellectual self is engaged takes place on two levels: on the level of insight and on the level of translating insights into concepts and symbols. Radical self-understanding must embrace not only the fruits of thinking, namely the concepts and symbols, but also the root of thinking, the depth of insight, the moments of immediacy in the communion of the self with reality.

Correspondingly, the study of religion has two major tasks to perform. One, to understand what it means to believe; to analyze *the act of believing;* to ask what it is that necessitates our believing in God. Two, to explain and to examine *the content of believing;* to analyze that which we believe in. The first is concerned with *the problem of faith,* with concrete situations; the second with *the problem of creed,* with conceptual relations. Medieval Jewish philosophy was primarily concerned with the problem of creed. It

6

dealt, for example, more with the question: what is the *content* (and the object) of our belief in God? or at best with the nature of belief, and less with the problem: what is the *source* of our belief in God? Why believe at all? It paid more attention to the question of *what* we know about God than to the question of *how* we know about Him. Our primary concern is not to analyze concepts but to explore situations. The religious situation precedes the religious conception, and it would be a false abstraction, for example, to deal with the idea of God regardless of the situation in which such an idea occurs. Our first goal, then, is not to evolve the philosophy of a doctrine, interpretations of a dogma, but the philosophy of concrete events, acts, insights, of that which is a part of the pious man. For religion is more than a creed or an ideology and cannot be understood when detached from acts and events. It comes to light in moments when one's soul is shaken with unmitigated concern about the meaning of all meaning, about one's ultimate commitment which is integrated with one's very existence; in moments when all foregone conclusions, all life-stifling trivialities are suspended.

Thus the issue which must be discussed first is not belief, ritual or the religious experience, but the source of all these phenomena: the total situation of man; not how he experiences the supernatural, but why he experiences and accepts it.[3]

DEPTH-THEOLOGY

The theme of theology is the content of believing. The theme of the present study is the act of believing. Its purpose is to explore the depth of faith, the substratum out of which belief arises, and its method may be called *depth-theology*.

To apprehend the depth of religious faith we will try to ascertain not so much what the person is able to express as that which he is unable to express, the insights that no language can declare. We must keep in mind that "the chief danger to philosophy, apart from laziness and woolliness, is *scholasticism,* the essence of which is treating what is vague as if it were precise and trying to fit it into an exact logical category."[4] Indeed, one of the fatal errors of conceptual theology has been the separation of the acts of religious existence from the statements about it. Ideas of faith must not be studied in total separation from the moments of faith. If a plant is uprooted from its soil, removed from its native winds, sun-rays and terrestrial environment, and kept in a hothouse—will observations made of such a plant disclose its primordial nature? The growing inwardness of man that reaches and curves toward the light of God can hardly be transplanted into the shallowness of mere reflection. Torn out of its medium in human life, it wilts like a rose pressed between the pages of a book. Religion is, indeed, little more than a desiccated remnant of a once living reality when reduced to terms and definitions, to codes and catechisms. It can only be studied in its natural habitat of faith and piety, in a soul where the divine is within reach of all thoughts.

Only those will apprehend religion who can probe its depth, who can combine intuition and love with the rigor of method, who are able to find categories that mix with the unalloyed and forge the imponderable into unique expression. It is not enough to describe the given content of religious consciousness. We have to press the religious consciousness with questions, compelling man to understand and unravel the meaning of what is taking place in his life as it stands at the divine horizon. By penetrating the consciousness of the pious man, we may conceive the reality behind it.

THE SELF-UNDERSTANDING OF RELIGION

Philosophy is reflective thinking, and philosophy of religion may be defined as religion's reflection upon its basic insights and basic attitudes, as *radical self-understanding of religion in terms of its own spirit*. It is an effort at self-clarification and self-examination.

By *self-clarification* we mean the effort to remind ourselves of what we stand for, to analyze the experiences, insights, attitudes, and principles of religion; to uncover its guiding features, its ultimate

8

claims; to determine the meaning of its main teachings; to distinguish between principles and opinions.

By *self-examination* we mean the effort to scrutinize the authenticity of our position. Is our religious attitude one of conviction or a mere assertion? Is the existence of God a probability to us or a certainty? Is God a mere word to us, a name, a possibility, a hypothesis, or is He a living presence? Is the claim of the prophets a figure of speech to us or a compelling belief?

Religious thinking, believing, feeling are among the most deceptive activities of the human spirit. We often assume it is God we believe in, but in reality it may be a symbol of personal interests that we dwell upon. We may assume that we feel drawn to God, but in reality it may be a power within the world that is the object of our adoration. We may assume it is God we care for, but it may be our own ego we are concerned with. To examine our religious existence is, therefore, a task to be performed constantly.

To understand what we mean is the task of philosophy. We think in words, but to employ words is not the same as to understand what they mean. Moreover, the relation between words and their meanings is elastic. Words remain, while meanings are subject to change. The expression "our father in heaven" may evoke in some a mental picture of a bodily figure sitting on a throne, and may mean to others the maximum of all majesty, used as a figure of speech, to indicate Him who is beyond all expression.

Such self-understanding is necessary for many reasons. Original teachings of religion are not given in rational, dogmatic terms but in indicative expressions. It is therefore necessary to explicate their meanings. Moreover, since they have been expressed in an ancient language, one must carefully penetrate the genuine intent of the Biblical authors.

CRITICAL REASSESSMENT

Though the method employed in this volume is primarily one of self-understanding, there is another approach we shall have to keep in mind. Philosophy of religion has to be pursued in two ways: as radical understanding of religion in terms of its own spirit and as a *critical reassessment of religion from the point of view of philosophy.* It represents an effort of religion to justify its claims; to set forth its *validity,* not merely its *relevance.* There are false as there are true prophets; there are false as there are true religious doctrines. If a religion claims to be true, it is under obligation to offer a criterion for its validity either in terms of ideas or in terms of events.

A critical reassessment of religion is necessitated by the very situation of our thinking. We cannot continue to employ our critical faculty in all our endeavors and at the same time abstain from raising questions in regard to religion. "Our age is the age of criticism, to which everything must be subjected. The sacredness of religion, and the authority of legislation, are by many regarded as grounds of exemption from the examination of this tribunal. But, if they are exempted, they become the subject of just suspicion, and cannot lay claim to sincere respect, which reason accords only to that which has stood the test of a free public examination."[5]

Criticism of religion must extend not only to its basic claims but to all of its statements. Religion is liable to distortion from without and to corruption from within. Since it frequently absorbs ideas not indigenous to its spirit, it is necessary to distinguish between the authentic and the spurious. Furthermore, superstition, pride, self-righteousness, bias, and vulgarity, may defile the finest traditions. Faith in its zeal tends to become bigotry. The criticism of reason, the challenge, and the doubts of the unbeliever may, therefore, be more helpful to the integrity of faith than the simple reliance on one's own faith.

INTELLECTUAL HONESTY

Intellectual honesty is one of the supreme goals of philosophy of religion, just as self-deception is the chief source of corruption in religious thinking, more deadly than error. Hypocrisy rather than

A philosophy of Judaism

heresy is the cause of spiritual decay. "Thou desirest truth in the inwardness" of man (Psalms 51:8).

Rabbi Bunam of Przyscha used to give the following definition of a hasid. According to medieval sources, a hasid is he who does more than the law requires. Now, this is the law: Thou shalt not deceive thy fellow-man (Leviticus 25:17). A hasid goes beyond the law; he will not even deceive his own self.

Every king has a seal which, when attached to a document, is a guarantee of authenticity. The seal contains a symbol signifying the power and majesty of the king. What symbol is engraved on the seal of the King of kings? *"The seal of God is truth,"*[6] and truth is our only test. *A flatterer cannot come before Him* (Job 13:16).

PHILOSOPHY AS RELIGION

Philosophy of religion as criticism of religion will not fulfill its function if it acts as an antagonist or as an imitator or rival. Criticism is often guilty of forgetting that the great trends in art, for example, are appraised, but not created, by it. This applies to religion as well. The disturbing fact, however, is that philosophy remains the perpetual rival of religion. It is a power that would create religion if it could. Again and again, it has tried its talent at offering answers to ultimate questions and has failed.

Philosophy does not always produce its own themes. Its subject matter is derived from common sense, from the world of art, religion, science, and social life. Themes such as the good, the beautiful, sympathy, love, God, causality, the social order, and the state are not the invention of the speculative mind. Philosophy is more creative in symbiosis with life than in preoccupation with themes born of its own reflection. Philosophy of religion remains, accordingly, a method of clarification, examination, and validation, rather than a source of ultimate insights. It must, furthermore, elucidate the essential difference between philosophy and religion. Its task is not only to examine the claim of religion in the face of philosophy, but also to refute the claim of philosophy when it presumes to be-

11

come a substitute for religion, to prove the inadequacy of philosophy as a religion.

Philosophy, in undertaking to examine the insights of religion, will do well to remember its own limited status; the fact, namely, that it represents the limited though real point of view of one school or one period; that it is confined to the experience of only part of actuality. Indeed, without a qualifying adjective the term philosophy is somewhat of a misnomer. There is not one but many philosophies, and the divergence between Aristotle and Augustine, the Stoics and the thinkers of India is just as real as the divergence between Moses and Buddha. Those who believe in the existence of a perennial philosophy may believe in the possibility of a critical reassessment of religion from the perspective of a fixed philosophical system, the validity of which is established beyond dispute. To those who question the validity of a perennial philosophy, philosophy itself is in contant flux, in need of constant examination. Philosophy of religion would then be defined as a critical reassessment of religion from the perspective of a particular philosophical situation.

For all its limitations, philosophy is the human attempt to attain a synoptic view of things, to see the whole of the world and its parts together. Since religion tends to become self-inflated and to disregard those aspects of reality which are not immediately relevant to dogma and ritual, it is the task of philosophy of religion to place religious understanding in relation to the entire range of human knowledge. Human knowledge is continually advancing, and the eternal issues of religion find new relevance when confronted with the forces of the endless process of human inquiry.

ELLIPTIC THINKING

Philosophy of religion has two parents: philosophy and religion. It is not born of self-reflection of religion but of the encounter of the

12

two. Indeed, all philosophy of religion comes into being when both religion and philosophy claim to offer ideas about ultimate problems. Since Greek religion did not claim to be a source of such ideas, philosophy of religion did not arise in Athens but in the encounter of Judaism and Greek philosophy.[7]

Philosophy of religion is involved in a polarity; like an ellipse it revolves around two foci: philosophy and religion. Except for two points on the curve that stand in equal distance to both foci, the more closely its thought comes to one, the more distant it is from the other one. The failure to sense the profound tension of philosophical and religious categories has been the cause of much confusion.

This unique situation of being exposed to two different powers, to two competing sources of understanding, is one that must not be abandoned. It is precisely that tension, that elliptic thinking which is a source of enrichment to both philosophy and religion.

RELIGION OF PHILOSOPHY

In the desire to reconcile philosophy and science with religion, attempts have often been made not only to prove that there are no conflicts between the doctrines imparted by revelation and the ideas acquired by our own reason, but also that they are intrinsically identical. Yet such reconciliation is not a solution but a dissolution in which religion is bound to fade away. If science and religion are intrinsically identical, one of them must be superfluous. In such reconciliation, religion is little more than bad science and naive morality. Its depth gone, its majesty forgotten, its value becomes questionable. Its only justification is pedagogical, as a shortcut to philosophy, as a philosophy for the masses.

Philosophers have often mistaken the non-conformity of religion for philosophical immaturity and, instead of trying to understand religion as religion, have approached it as a rudimentary form of philosophy. In such an approach the object of inquiry became adjusted to the pattern of the inquirer, and religious categories, converted even before they were explored, were treated as if they were philosophical abstractions. The result of such an inquiry is usually a highly rarefied religion. What begins as a philosophy of religion ends as a *religion of philosophy*.

Philosophy does not begin out of nothing. It may, at best, be defined as a science with a minimum of presuppositions. But it can never dispense with all presuppositions. It is, furthermore, involved in a specific *way of thinking,* in certain modes and categories of apprehension and evaluation. The major premises of Western philosophy are derived from the Greek way of thinking.

There is more than one way of thinking. Israel and Greece not only developed divergent doctrines; they operated within different categories. The Bible, like the philosophy of Aristotle, for example, contains more than a sum of doctrines; it represents *a way of thinking,* a specific context in which general concepts possess a particular significance, a standard of evaluation, a form of orientation; not only a mental fabric but also a certain disposition or manner of interweaving and interrelating intuitions and perceptions, a unique loom of thoughts.

The human mind is one-sided. It can never grasp all of reality at once. When we look at things we see either the features which they have in common or the features that distinguish each of them. There are periods in the history of thought in which a sense for the common and universal is best developed, and there are periods in which a sense for the distinct and the individual is particularly keen. Philo's mind, for example, moved on a path which bypassed the specific and the different—in both Judaism and Hellenism. To him both offered the same message; the ecstasy that he knew from Hellenistic cults he assumed to be identical with the state in which the Hebrew prophets received revelation.[8] Following his example, many thinkers were mainly interested in pointing to the common elements in reason and revelation and desired to equalize what was

14

different in them. What they failed to see is the unique wealth of spiritual insight contained in the prophetic ideas of the divine pathos. Hebrew thinking operates within categories different from those of Plato or Aristotle, and the disagreements between their respective teachings are not merely a matter of different ways of expression but of different ways of thinking. By dwelling upon the common elements of reason and revelation, a synthesis of the two spiritual powers was attained at the price of sacrificing some of their unique insights.

Vitally important as it is for Judaism to reach out into non-Jewish cultures in order to absorb elements which it may use for the enrichment of its life and thought, it must not be done at the price of giving up its intellectual integrity. We must remember that the attempt to find a synthesis of prophetic thinking and Greek metaphysics, desirable as it may be in a particular historic situation, is not necessarily valid *sub specie aeternitatis*. Geographically and historically, Jerusalem and Athens, the age of the prophets and the age of Pericles, are not too far removed from each other. Spiritually they are worlds apart. On the other hand, had Jerusalem been located at the foot of the Himalayas, monotheistic philosophy would have been modified by the tradition of Oriental thinkers. Thus, our intellectual position situated as it is between Athens and Jerusalem is not an ultimate one. Providence may some day create a situation which would place us between the river Jordan and the river Ganges, and the problem of such an encounter will be different from that which Jewish thought underwent when meeting with Greek philosophy.

METAPHYSICS AND META-HISTORY

There is, for example, a basic difference in meaning, intention and theme between a scientific theory of the origin of the universe and what the first chapters of the Book of Genesis are trying to convey. The Book of Genesis does not intend to explain anything; the mystery of the world's coming into being is in no way made more intelligible by a statement such as *At the beginning God created*

15

heaven and earth. The Bible and science do not deal with the same problem. Scientific theory inquires: What is the cause of the universe? It thinks in the category of causality, and causality conceives of the relationship between a cause and an effect as parts of a continuous process, as changing parts of an unchanging whole. The Bible, on the other hand, conceives of the relationship of the Creator and the universe as a relationship between two essentially different and incomparable entities, and regards creation itself as an *event* rather than as a *process* (see chapter 22). Creation, then, is an idea that transcends causality; it tells us how it comes that there is causality at all. Rather than explaining the world in categories borrowed from nature, it alludes to what made nature possible, namely, an act of the freedom of God.

The Bible points to a way of understanding the world from the point of view of God. It does not deal with *being as being* but with *being as creation.* Its concern is not with ontology or *metaphysics* but with history and *meta-history;* its concern is with time rather than with space.

Science proceeds by way of equations; the Bible refers to the unique and the unprecedented. The end of science is to explore the facts and processes of nature; the end of religion is to understand nature in relation to the will of God. The intention of scientific thinking is to answer man's questions and to satisfy his need for knowledge. The ultimate intention of religious thinking is to answer a question which is not man's, and to satisfy God's need for man.

Philosophy is an attempt to find out the essence of things, the principles of being; Biblical religion is an attempt to teach about the Creator of all things and the knowledge of His will. The Bible does not intend to teach us principles of creation or redemption. It came to teach us that God is alive, that He is the Creator and Redeemer, Teacher and Lawgiver. The concern of philosophy is to analyze or to explain, the concern of religion is to purify and to sanctify. Religion is rooted in a particular tradition or in a personal insight; classical philosophy claims to have its roots in universal premises.

Speculation starts with *concepts,* Biblical religion starts with

God in search of man

events. The life of religion is given not in the mental preservation of ideas but in events· and insights, in something that happens in time.

A CHALLENGE TO PHILOSOPHY

Religion, we repeat, is a unique source of insight. This implies that the insights and demands of religion cannot be completely synchronized with the conclusions of any particular system of philosophy nor be adequately expressed in terms of science. What is meaningful in religion is not necessarily meaningful in philosophy, and vice versa. The role of religion is to be *a challenge to philosophy,* not merely an object for examination.

There is much that philosophy could learn from the Bible. To the philosopher the idea of the good is the most exalted idea. But to the Bible the idea of the good is penultimate; it cannot exist without the holy. The holy is the essence, the good is its expression. Things created in six days He considered *good,* the seventh day He made *holy.*[9]

Plato's *Euthyphro* raised an issue which, in various forms, was often debated in Christian and Mohammedan scholasticism, namely: do the gods love the good because it is good or is it good because the gods love it? Such a problem could only arise when the gods and the good were regarded as two different entities, and where it was taken for granted that the gods do not always act according to the highest standards of goodness and justice. To inquire: is a particular act holy (commanded by, or dear to God) because it is good or is it good because it is holy (commanded by or dear to God)? would be just as meaningless as to inquire: is a particular point within the circle called the center due to its equidistance from the periphery or is its equidistance from the periphery due to its being the center? The dichotomy of the holy and the good is alien to the spirit of the great prophets. To their thinking, the righteousness of God is inseparable from His being.

Wise criticism always begins with self-criticism. Philosophy, too,

17

is in need of constant examination and purification. Reason in testing religion is testing itself; examining its own premises, scope, and power; proving whether it has advanced enough to comprehend the insights of the prophets. Indeed, there are insights of the spirit to which our reason comes late, often too late, after having rejected them.

In order to succeed, philosophy of religion must keep in mind both the uniqueness and the limitations of both philosophy and religion.

Religion, as we shall see, goes beyond philosophy, and the task of philosophy of religion is to lead the mind to the summit of thinking; to create in us the understanding of why the problems of religion cannot be apprehended in terms of science; to let us realize that religion has its own scope, perspective and goal; to expose us to the majesty and mystery, in the presence of which the mind is not deaf to that which transcends the mind. One of the goals of philosophy of religion is to stimulate a *critical reassessment of philosophy from the perspective of religion.*

THE WORSHIP OF REASON

It is improper to define philosophy of religion as an attempt to supply a rational basis for religion, because such a definition implicitly identifies philosophy with rationalism. If rationalism were the sign of a philosopher, Plato, Schelling, William James, and Bergson would have to be disqualified as philosophers. Rationalism, according to Dewey, "precludes religious faith in any distinctive sense. It allows only for a belief that is unimpeachable rational inference from what we absolutely know."[10]

Extreme rationalism may be defined as the failure of reason to understand itself, its alogical essence, and its meta-logical objects. We must distinguish between ignorance and the sense of mystery, between the subrational and the super-rational. The way to truth is an act of reason; the love of truth is an act of the spirit. Every act of reasoning has a transcendent reference to spirit. We think through

18

A philosophy of Judaism

reason because we strive for spirit. We think through reason because we are certain of meaning. Reason withers without spirit, without the truth about all of life.

Reason has often been identified with scientism, but science is unable to give us all the truth about all of life. We are in need of spirit in order to know what to do with science. Science deals with relations among things within the universe, but man is endowed with the concern of the spirit, and spirit deals with the relation between the universe and God. Science seeks the truth about the universe; the spirit seeks the truth that is greater than the universe. Reason's goal is the exploration and verification of objective relations; religion's goal is the exploration and verification of ultimate personal relations.

A challenge is not the same as a clash, and divergence does not mean a conflict. It is a part of the human condition to live in polarities. It is an implication of our belief in one God to be certain that ultimately reason and revelation are both derived from the same source. Yet what is one in creation is not always one in our historic situation. It is an act of redemption when it is granted to us to discover the higher unity of reason and revelation.

The widely preached equation of Judaism and rationalism is an intellectual evasion of the profound difficulties and paradoxes of Jewish faith, belief, and observance. Man's understanding of what is reasonable is subject to change. To the Roman philosophers, it did not seem reasonable to abstain from labor one day a week. Nor did it seem unreasonable to certain plantation owners to import slaves from Africa into the New World. With what stage in the development of reason should the Bible be compatible?

For all the appreciation of reason and our thankfulness for it, man's intelligence was never regarded in Jewish tradition as being self-sufficient. "Trust in the Lord with all thy heart, and do not rely on thine own understanding" (Proverbs 3:5). "And thou has felt secure in thy wickedness, thou hast said: no one seeth me; thy wisdom and thy knowledge led thee astray, and thou hast said in thy heart: I am, and there is no one else beside me" (Isaiah 47:10).

Some of the basic presuppositions of Judaism cannot be completely justified in terms of human reason. Its conception of the nature of man as having been created in the likeness of God, its conception of God and history, of the election of Israel, of prayer and even of morality, defy some of the realizations at which we have honestly arrived at the end of our analysis and scrutiny. The demands of piety are a mystery before which man is reduced to reverence and silence.[11] Reverence, love, prayer, faith, go beyond the acts of shallow reasoning.

We must therefore not judge religion exclusively from the viewpoint of reason. Religion is not within but beyond the limits of mere reason. Its task is not to compete with reason but to aid us where reason gives only partial aid. Its meaning must be understood in terms *compatible with the sense of the ineffable.*

The sense of the ineffable is an intellectual endeavor out of the depth of reason; it is a source of cognitive insight. There is, therefore, no rivalry between religion and reason as long as we are aware of their respective tasks and areas. The employment of reason is indispensable to the understanding and worship of God, and religion withers without it. The insights of faith are general, vague, and stand in need of conceptualization in order to be communicated to the mind, integrated and brought to consistency. Without reason faith becomes blind. Without reason we would not know how to apply the insights of faith to the concrete issues of living. The worship of reason is arrogance and betrays a lack of intelligence. The rejection of reason is cowardice and betrays a lack of faith.

IDEAS AND EVENTS

The subject of a philosophy of Judaism is Judaism. But what kind of entity is Judaism? Is it a set of ideas or principles, a doctrine? To try to distill the Bible, which is bursting with life, drama, and tension, to a series of principles would be like trying to reduce a living person to a diagram. The exodus from Egypt, or the revelation at Sinai, or Miriam's slander against Moses, is an event, not an idea; a happening, not a principle. On the other hand, he who would try to reduce the Bible to a catalog of events, to a sacred history, will equally fail. *The Lord is One,* or *Justice, justice shalt thou pursue,* is an idea or a norm rather than an occurrence. A philosophy of Judaism, therefore, is a *philosophy of both ideas and events.*

Moses Maimonides (1135-1204) sums up the essence of Judaism in thirteen articles of faith: 1. The existence of God; 2. His unity; 3. His incorporeality; 4. His eternity; 5. God alone the object of worship; 6. Revelation through His Prophets; 7. The preeminence of Moses among the Prophets; 8. The entire Pentateuch was divinely given to Moses; 9. The Immutability of the Law of the Torah; 10. God's knowledge of the acts and thoughts of man; 11. Reward and punishment; 12. The coming of the Messiah; 13. Resurrection. With the exception of 6, 8, 12, 13, these articles refer to principles or to the realm of ideas, rather than to events or to the realm of history. Significantly, the form in which these articles became popular and even incorporated in many prayerbooks begins with the words, "I firmly believe that . . ."

The Maimonidean creed is based upon the premise that it is in ideas that ultimate reality comes to expression. To the Biblical man, however, it is in events, not only in ideas that ultimate reality comes to expression. The substance of Judaism is given both in history and in thought. We accept ideas and recall events. The Jew says, "I believe," and is told, "Remember!" His creed contains a summary of basic ideas as well as a summary of outstanding events.[12]

To the Jewish mind, the understanding of God is not achieved by referring in a Greek way to timeless qualities of a Supreme Being, to ideas of goodness or perfection, but rather by sensing the living acts of His concern, to His dynamic attentiveness to man. We speak not of His goodness in general but of His compassion for the individual man in a particular situation. God's goodness is not a cosmic force but a specific act of compassion. We do not know it as it *is* but as it *happens.* To mention an example, "Rabbi Meir said: When a human being suffers what does the *Shechinah* say? My head is too heavy

21

for Me; My arm is too heavy for Me. And if God is so grieved over the blood of the wicked that is shed, how much more so over the blood of the righteous."[13] This statement, quoted in the Mishnah immediately following the description of capital punishment, is intended to convey how painful it is to God when His children suffer, be it even a criminal who is punished for his crime.

Different are the problems when we accept such an approach. The problem is no longer how to reconcile the Bible with Aristotle's view of the universe and of man, but rather: what is the Biblical view of the universe and of man's position in it? How should we understand ourselves in terms of Biblical thinking? The problem is: What are the ultimate questions of existence which religion comes to answer? What are the ideas a religious man stands for?

THE PHILOSOPHY OF JUDAISM

The term Judaism in the phrase philosophy of Judaism may be used either as *an object* or as *a subject*. In the first sense, philosophy of Judaism is a critique of Judaism; Judaism as a theme or the object of our examination. In the second sense, philosophy of Judaism has a meaning comparable to the meaning of a phrase such as the philosophy of Kant or the philosophy of Plato; Judaism as a source of ideas which we are trying to understand.

Now Judaism is a reality, a drama within history, a fact, not merely a feeling or an experience. It claims that certain extraordinary events occurred in which it originated. It stands for certain basic teachings. It claims to be the commitment of a people to God. To understand the meaning of these events, teachings and commitments is the task of a philosophy of Judaism.

As already stated, our method in this book is primarily, though not exclusively, that of self-understanding, and the term Judaism in the subtitle of the book is used primarily as a subject.

22

A philosophy of Judaism

NOTES FOR CHAPTER 1

[1] A characteristic shared by philosophy and science is the fact that each answer engenders new questions. The difference seems to be that philosophy's issues are perennial, and none of its answers remains unchallenged, since each answer has to be a total answer.

[2] Self-knowledge or self-understanding has in various forms been the central concern of philosophy (the first of the three maxims inscribed on the front of the Temple of Apollo at Delphi was "Know Thyself"). Its importance has been stressed by Socrates and Plato, see *Charmides* 167B-172C; *Alcibiades* 133B; Xenophanes, *Memorabilia* IV, 2, 24. Aristotle, *Metaphysica* 1072B 20. Compare Plotinus, *Enneads*, IV, 4.2; *Theologie des Aristoteles*, translated by Dieterici, Leipzig, 1893, p. 18. All philosophy is "spiritual self-observation" (J. F. Fries, *System der Metaphysik*, 1824, p. 110), "the science of inner experience" (Th. Lipps, *Grundtatsachen des Seelenlebens*, p. 3), "the self-cognition of the human spirit" (Kuno Fisher, *Geschichte der Philosophie*, vol. I, ed, 5, p. 11); compare Max Scheler, *Die transzendentale und die psychologische Methode*, Leipzig. 1922, p. 179. In Jewish literature the definition of philosophy as self-understanding is quoted by Bahya Ibn Paquda, *The Duties of the Heart, shaar habehinah*, ch. 5, ed. Haymson, Vol. II, p. 14. Compare Joseph Ibn Saddik, *Haolam Haqaton*, ed. S. Horovitz, Breslau, 1903, beginning. See Maimonides, *The Guide of the Perplexed* 1, 53. According to Hermann Cohen, *Religion der Vernunft*, Frankfurt a. M., 1929, p. 23, the self-cognition of man is the deepest source of religion. Sayings on self-knowledge in Hebrew literature are collected in I. L. Zlotnik, *Maamarim*, Jerusalem, 1939, pp. 17-26.

[3] A. J. Heschel, *Man is Not Alone*, New York, 1951, p. 55.

[4] F. P. Ramsey, *The Foundations of Mathematics and Other Logical Essays*, New York, 1950, p. 269.

[5] Kant, *Critique of Pure Reason*, preface to the first edition, translated by J. M. D., Meikeljohn, New York, 1899, p. xl, note.

[6] *Shabbat* 51a.

[7] See Julius Guttmann, "*Religion und Wissenschaft im Mittelalterlichen und im Modernen Denken*" in *Festschrift zum 50 Jaehrigen Bestehen der Hochschule fuer die Wissenschaft des Judentums*, Berlin, 1922, p. 147f.

[8] See A. J. Heschel, *Die Prophetie*, Cracow, 1936, p. 15. The categories in which the Biblical man conceived of God, man, and the world are so different from the presuppositions of metaphysics upon which most of Western philosophy is based that certain insights that are meaningful within the Biblical mind seem to be meaningless to the Greek mind. It would be an achievement of the first magnitude to reconstruct the peculiar nature of Biblical thinking and to spell out its divergence from all other types of thinking. It would open new perspectives for the understanding of moral, social and religious issues and enrich the whole of our thinking. Biblical thinking may have a part to play in shaping our philosophical views about the world.

[9] A. J. Heschel, *The Sabbath*, New York, 1951, p. 75.

[10] Dewey, *A Common Faith*, New Haven, 1934.

[11] See A. J. Heschel, *Man's Quest for God*, New York, 1954, p. 104.

[12] See *Man is Not Alone*, p. 163.

[13] *Mishnah Sanhedrin*, VI, 5.

23

2 Ways to His Presence

In reading the works of Western philosophy it is Plato or Aristotle, the Stoics or the Neoplatonists, whom we meet again and again. The spirit of their thinking hovers over every page of philosophical writing. However, we would look in vain for the Bible in the recesses of Western metaphysics. The prophets are absent when the philosophers speak of God.

What we mean by the absence of the Bible in the history of philosophy is not references or quotations; scriptural passages have occasionally found admittance. What we mean is the spirit, the way of thinking, the mode of looking at the world, at life; the basic premises of speculation about being, about values, about meaning. Open any history of philosophy. Thales or Parmenides is there; but is Isaiah or Elijah, Job or Ecclesiastes ever represented? The result of such omission is that the basic premises of Western philosophy are derived from the Greek rather than the Hebraic thinking.

There are two approaches to the Bible that prevail in philosophical thinking. The first approach claims that the Bible is a naive book, it is poetry or mythology. Beautiful as it is, it must not be taken seriously, for in its thinking it is primitive and immature. How could you compare it with Hegel or Hobbes, John Locke or Schopenhauer? The father of the depreciation of the intellectual relevance of the Bible is Spinoza, who may be blamed for many distorted views of the Bible in subsequent philosophy and exegesis.

The second approach claims that Moses taught the same ideas as

God in search of man

Plato or Aristotle, that there is no serious disagreement between the teachings of the philosophers and the teachings of the prophets. The difference, it is claimed, is merely one of expression and style. Aristotle, for example, used unambiguous terms, while the prophets employed metaphors. The father of this approach is Philo. Theology was dominated by the theory of Philo, while general philosophy took the attitude of Spinoza.*

There is a story of a cub reporter who was sent to cover a wedding. When he came back he said dejectedly that he had no story because the bridegroom did not show up. . . .

It is true that one looks in vain for a philosophical vocabulary in the Bible. But the serious student must not look for what he already has. The categories within which philosophical reflection about religion has been operating are derived from Athens rather than from Jerusalem. Judaism is a confrontation with the Bible, and a philosophy of Judaism must be a confrontation with the thought of the Bible.

MEMORY AND INSIGHT

The Bible is not the only work in which a concern for ultimate religious problems is found. In many lands and at many ages man has searched for God. Yet the Biblical period is the grand chapter in the history of man's wrestling with God (and of God's wrestling with man). And just as in a study of moral values we cannot ignore the great tradition of moral philosophy, we must not in our wrestling with religious issues ignore the insights accumulated in the Bible. It is, therefore, the age of the Bible, a thousand years of illumination, to which we will turn for guidance.

What do we and the people of the Bible have in common? The anxieties and joys of living; the sense of wonder and the resistance to it; the awareness of the hiding God and moments of longing to find a way to Him.

The central thought of Judaism is *the living God*. It is the per-

* On the attitude of Spinoza, see p. 321 f.

25

spective from which all other issues are seen. And the supreme problem in any philosophy of Judaism is: what are the grounds for man's believing in the realness of the living God? Is man at all capable of discovering such grounds? Before attempting to deal with this problem, it is necessary to inquire: is it compatible with the spirit of Judaism to maintain that a man must seek an approach to God, that unless we seek Him we may fail to find Him? Is there a way of developing sensitivity to God and attachment to His presence?

What was the source of the faith of the people in Biblical times? Is it correct to define their faith as an act of relying upon an inherited doctrine? Is it correct to say that for more than three thousand years the Jews had access to only one source of faith, namely the records of revelation? Is it true that Judaism derived its religious vitality exclusively from loyalty to the events that occurred in the days of Moses and from obedience to Scripture in which those events are recorded? Such an assumption seems to overlook the nature of man and his faith. A great event, miraculous as it may be, if it happened only once, will hardly be able to dominate forever the mind of man. The mere remembrance of such an event is hardly powerful enough to hold in its spell the soul of man with its constant restlessness and vitality. There was wrestling for insight out of which Jewish faith drew its strength.

The Bible contains not only words of the prophets, but also words that came from non-prophetic lips. While it claims to convey words of inspiration, it also contains words of human search and concern. There is in the Bible God's word to man, but there is also man's word to Him and about Him; not only God's disclosure but man's insight. Prophetic experience is far removed from the reach of modern man. But the prophets were human, too; prophetic experiences were single moments in their lives beyond which lay the encounter with good and evil, light and darkness, life and death, love and hatred—issues which are as real today as they were three thousand years ago. These perceptions reflect human, not only prophetic thinking. It is particularly in the so-called wisdom literature, such as the books of Job, Proverbs, Ecclesiastes, as well as the

Book of Psalms, that the spontaneity of the Biblical man found its expression.

The concern for God continued throughout the ages, and in order to understand Judaism we must inquire about the way and the spirit of that concern in post-Biblical Jewish history as well.

Two sources of religious thinking are given us: *memory* (tradition) and *personal* insight. We must rely on our memory and we must strive for fresh insight. We *hear* from tradition, we also *understand* through our own seeking. The prophets appeal to the spiritual power in man: "Know, therefore, this day, and lay it to your heart, that the Lord is God in heaven above and on the earth beneath; there is no other" (Deuteronomy 4:39). The psalmist calls on us "O taste and see that the Lord is good" (34:9).[1] How does one know? How does one taste?

An allusion to the need for every man's own quest for God was seen homiletically in the Song of the Red Sea:

This is my God, and I will glorify Him;
The God of my father, and I will exalt Him.
Exodus 15:2

Out of his own insight a person must first arrive at the understanding: *This is my God, and I will glorify Him,* and subsequently he will attain the realization that He is *the God of my father, and I will exalt Him.*[2]

MAN'S QUEST FOR GOD

Burnt offerings, sacrifices are an important part of Biblical piety. And yet, "I desire mercy, and not sacrifice, *understanding (knowledge) of God,* rather than burnt offerings." (Hosea 6:6). There is a way that leads to understanding. *"Ye* will seek the Lord *thy* God, and *thou* shalt find him, if thou seek him with all thy heart and all thy soul" (Deuteronomy 4:29; Jeremiah 29:13).

"If a man says to you, I have labored and not found, do not believe him. If he says, I have not labored but still have found, do not believe him. If he says, I have labored and found, you may be-

27

lieve him."[3] It is true that in seeking Him we are assisted by Him. But the initiative and intensity of our seeking are within our power. "If thou call for understanding, and lift up thy voice for discernment; if thou seek her as silver and search for her as for hid treasures; then shalt thou understand the awe and fear of the Lord and find the knowledge of God."[4] "Everything is within the power of heaven except the awe and fear of heaven."[5]

The Bible has several words for the act of seeking God (*darash, bakkesh, shahar*). In some passages these words are used in the sense of inquiring after His will and precepts (Psalms 119:45, 94,155). Yet, in other passages these words mean more than the act of asking a question, the aim of which is to elicit information. It means addressing oneself directly to God with the aim of getting close to Him; it involves a desire for experience rather than a search for information.[6] Seeking Him includes the fact of keeping His commandments, but it goes beyond it. "Seek ye the Lord and His strength, seek His face continually" (Psalms 105:4). Indeed, to pray does not only mean to seek *help;* it also means to seek *Him*.

The commandment "is not too hard for thee, neither is it far off. It is not in heaven, that thou shouldest say: 'Who shall go up for us to heaven, and bring it unto us, that we may hear it and do it?' Neither is it beyond the sea, that thou shouldest say: 'Who shall go over the sea for us, and bring it unto us, that we may hear it and do it?' But the word is very nigh unto thee, in thy mouth and in thy heart, that thou mayest do it" (Deuteronomy 30:11-14). However, the same words cannot be said in regard to God. "Am I a God near at hand, saith the Lord, and not a God afar off?" (Jeremiah 23:23). Indeed, there are moments when He is near and may be found, and there are moments when He is far and hiding Himself from man. "Seek ye the Lord while He may be found, call ye upon Him while He is near" (Isaiah 55:6).* Not all of the people of the Bible are satisfied with *awareness* of God's power and presence. There are those *"that seek Him, that seek Thy face O God of Jacob"* (Psalms 24:6). "One thing have I asked of the Lord, that will I seek after,

* See p. 129.

28

that I may abide in the house of the Lord all the days of my life, *to behold the beauty of the Lord*" (Psalms 27:4). "As for me, the nearness of God is my good" (Psalms 73:28).

At Sinai, according to legend, Israel was not content to receive the divine words through an intermediary. They said to Moses, "We want to hear the words of our King from Himself. . . . We want to see our King."[7]

"SEEK YE MY FACE"

The craving for God has never subsided in the Jewish soul. Despite the warning, "Thou canst not see My face, for man shall not see Me and live" (Exodus 32:20), there were many who persisted in a yearning, to which Jehuda Halevi gave unforgettable utterance. "To see the face of my King is my sole desire. I fear none but Him; I revere only Him. Would that I might see Him in a dream! I would continue to sleep for all eternity. Would that I might behold His face within my heart! Mine eyes would never ask to look at anything else."[8]

> As a hart yearns for the streams of water,
> So does my soul yearn for Thee, O God.
> My soul thirsts for God, the living God,
> When shall I come and see the face of the Lord?
> Psalms 42:2f

Like Moses who pleaded, "Show me, I pray, Thy glory" (Exodus 33:18), the Psalmist prays:

> O God, Thou art my God, earnestly will I seek Thee.
> My soul thirsteth for Thee, my flesh longeth for Thee,
> In a dry and weary land, where no water is.
> So have I looked for Thee in the sanctuary,
> To see Thy strength and Thy glory.
> Psalms 63:2-3

> With my soul have I desired Thee in the night;
> Yea with my spirit within me have I sought Thee earnestly.
> Isaiah 26:9

In those days, and in that time, saith the Lord,
The children of Israel shall come,
They and the children of Judah together;
They shall go on their way weeping
And shall seek the Lord their God.

Jeremiah 50:4

God is waiting for man to seek Him. "The Lord looked forth from heaven upon the children of man, to see if there were any man of understanding that sought Him" (Psalms 14:2). "In Thy behalf my heart hath said: *'Seek ye My face'*" (Psalms 27:8). And on the Days of Awe we recall in humility: "Until the day of man's death Thou waitest for him" to return.

On the other hand, one is always faced with the possibility of failure, with the danger of being trapped in lofts without light, without motion. There are those "whose doings will not suffer them to return unto their God.... With their flocks and with their herds they shall go to seek Him, but they shall not find Him; He hath withdrawn Himself from them" (Hosea 5:4, 6).

We must go on trying to return, to care for Him, to seek Him. It is an exceptional act of divine grace that those who do not care for Him should suddenly discover that they are near Him. "I was ready to be sought by those who did not ask for Me; I was ready to be found by those who did not seek Me. I said: 'Here am I, here am I,' unto a nation that did not call on My name" (Isaiah 65:1). In his last words, David warned his son Solomon: *"If thou seek Him, He will be found of thee; but if thou forsake Him, He will cast thee off for ever"* (I Chronicles 28:9).

THREE WAYS

How does one seek Him? How does one find in this world, within one's own human existence and response to this world, ways that lead to the certainty of His presence?

Jewish literature contains many indications of an awareness of our problems, but that awareness is rarely spelled out. Usually the

A philosophy of Judaism

Jew of the past shied away from disclosing his personal religious concern and experience, and as a result his reticence has been mistaken frequently for spiritual apathy. The truth is that the soul was never silent. Up to the nineteenth century there were few outstanding Talmudists who were not stirred, for example, by the cravings and meditations of the *Zohar*. Beneath the calm surface of creed and law the souls were astir. Our task, then, is to go beneath the tranquillity of creed and tradition in order to overhear the echoes of wrestling and to recapture the living insights.

There are three starting points of contemplation about God; three trails that lead to Him. The first is the way of sensing the presence of God in the world, in things;[9] the second is the way of sensing His presence in the Bible; the third is the way of sensing His presence in sacred deeds. These three ways are intimated in three Biblical passages:

> Lift up your eyes on high and see, Who created these?
>
> Isaiah 40:26
>
> I am the Lord thy God.
>
> Exodus 20:2
>
> We shall do and we shall hear.
>
> Exodus 24:7

These three ways correspond in our tradition to the main aspects of religious existence: worship, learning, and action. The three are one, and we must go all three ways to reach the one destination. For this is what Israel discovered: the God of nature is the God of history, and the way to know Him is to do His will.

To recapture the insights found in those three ways is to go to the roots of Biblical experience of life and reality; it means to delve into the religious drama of Israel, to grasp what it was that enabled Job to say:

> As for me, I know that my Redeemer lives,
> That He will witness at the last upon the dust.
> After my skin has been destroyed,

Out of my flesh I shall see God.
My own eyes shall behold, not another's.
My heart faints within me.

Job 19:25-27

How does man reach a stage of thinking where he is able to say, "Out of my flesh I shall see God"?

Each of the three parts of this book, accordingly, is devoted to a particular way.

NOTES FOR CHAPTER 2

[1] The verb *ta'am* always means to perceive, to taste. The noun is also used in the same sense of judgment. In our passage, Targum renders the word *ta'amu* with "realize," the Septuagint with "taste." Compare Seforno's *Commentary* ad locum, "taste, namely feel with your sense and *see* with the eye of reason that God is good."

[2] See Rabbi Isaiah Horowitz, *Shne Luhot Haberith*, p. 40a. Compare also *Man is Not Alone*, p. 164, n. 2.

[3] See *Megillah* 6b.

[4] Proverbs 2:3-4

[5] *Berachot* 33b

[6] To mention but a few examples: "He sought the Lord with all his heart" (I Chronicles 22:9). "In the day of my trouble I seek the Lord" (Psalms 77:3). "I sought the Lord, and He answered me, and delivered me from all my fears" (Psalms 34:5). Seeking the Lord is not a synonym for petitioning Him or obeying His law. "Happy are they that keep His testimonies, that seek Him with the whole heart." "With my whole heart have I sought Thee; O let me not err from Thy commandments" (Psalms 119:2,10).

[7] *Mechilta* to Exodus 19:9.

[8] See *Selected Poems of Jehudah Halevi*, translated by Ninah Salaman, Philadelphia, 1928, pp. 115-166.

[9] Man is told, "Look at the heavens and see; behold the clouds which are higher than thee" (Job 35:5); see Amos 5:6, 8-9. "Meditate about the works of the Lord, for thereby you will come to know Him by whose word the world come into being." Quoted in the name of Rabbi Meir by Maimonides, *Responsa*, ed. A. Freimann, Jerusalem, 1934, 347, p. 312. See also *Wisdom of Solomon* 13:1ff; *Baruch* 54:17f. According to old legends, Abraham discovered the true faith by meditating on nature, see Louis Ginzberg, *The Legends of the Jews*, vol. V, p. 210, n. 16. Compare also p. 112 of this book. According to Bahya, *The Duties of the Heart*, ed. Moses Haymson, vol. I, p. 3, it is our duty to "meditate on the marvels as manifested in His creations, so that they may serve us as evidence of Him."

3 The Sublime

How does one find the way to an awareness of God through behold-ing the world here and now? To understand the Biblical answer, we must try to ascertain what the world means and to comprehend the categories in which the Bible sees the world: the sublime, won-der, mystery, awe, and glory.

Lift up your eys and see. How does a man lift up his eyes to see a little higher than himself? *The grand premise* of religion is that *man is able to surpass himself;* that man who is part of this world may enter into a relationship with Him who is greater than the world; that man may lift up his mind and be attached to the abso-lute; that man who is conditioned by a multiplicity of factors is capable of living with demands that are unconditioned. How does one rise above the horizon of the mind? How does one free oneself from the perspectives of ego, group, earth, and age? How does one find a way in this world that would lead to an awareness of Him who is beyond this world?

POWER, BEAUTY, GRANDEUR

Small is the world that most of us pay attention to, and limited is our concern. What do we see when we see the world? There are three aspects of nature that command our attention: its *power*, its *beauty*, and its *grandeur*. Accordingly, there are three ways in which we may relate ourselves to the world—we may exploit it, we may enjoy it, we may accept it in awe. In the history of civilization, different aspects of nature have drawn forth the talent of man; sometimes its power, sometimes its beauty and occasionally its grandeur have attracted his mind. Our age is one in which usefulness is thought to be the chief merit of nature; in which the attainment of power, the utilization of its resources is taken to be the chief purpose of man in God's creation. Man has indeed become primarily a tool-making animal, and the world is now a gigantic tool box for the satisfaction of his needs.

The Greeks learned in order to comprehend. The Hebrews learned in order to revere. The modern man learns in order to use. To Bacon we owe the formulation, *"Knowledge is power."* This is how people are urged to study: knowledge means success. We do not know any more how to justify any value except in terms of expediency. Man is willing to define himself as "a seeker after the maximum degree of comfort for the minimum expenditure of energy." He equates value with that which avails. He feels, acts, and thinks as if the sole purpose of the universe were to satisfy his needs. To the modern man everything seems calculable; everything reducible to a figure. He has supreme faith in statistics and abhors the idea of a mystery. Obstinately he ignores the fact that we are all surrounded by things which we apprehend but cannot comprehend; that even reason is a mystery to itself. He is sure of his ability to explain all mystery away. Only a generation ago he was convinced that science was on the way to solve all the enigmas of the world. In the words of a poet:

> Whatever there is to know
> That we shall know some day.

Religious knowledge is regarded as the lowest form of knowledge. The human mind, according to Comte, goes through three stages of thought: the theological, the metaphysical, and the positive. Out of the primitive religious knowledge metaphysics gradually evolved, to be succeeded by the positive, scientific method of thought. Mod-

ern man having achieved the final stage eschews all appeal to un-
observable entities. In the place of God, humanity—the *grand Être*—
becomes the supreme object of adoration. However, what is considered an achievement from the perspective of modern man may
be judged a privation by the post-modern man. "In future generations, people will find difficulty in understanding how at one time
generations existed who did not regard the idea of God as the
highest concept of which man is capable, but who, on the contrary,
were ashamed of it and considered the development of atheism a
sign of progress in the emancipation of human thought."[1]

Dazzled by the brilliant achievements of the intellect in science
and technique, we have not only become convinced that we are the
masters of the earth; we have become convinced that our needs and
interests are the ultimate standard of what is right and wrong.

Comfort, luxuries, success continually bait our appetites, impair-
ing our vision of that which is required but not always desired.
They make it easy for us to grow blind to values. Interests are the
value-blind man's dog, his pathfinder and guide.

THE DISTRUST OF FAITH

Modern man is gradually recovering from the shock of realizing
that, intellectually, he has no right to dream any more; no right to
mourn his lost craving for that which he may need but to which he
has become indifferent. He has, indeed, long since ceased to trust
his will to believe or even his grief about the loss of a desire to
believe.

A shudder stalks through our nights. There is no house in our
cities without at least one soul wailing in the midst of joy, terrified
by achievement, dismayed at the servitude to needs, at the inability
to trust what he is cherishing.

What applies to moral judgments holds true in regard to religious
beliefs. It has long been known that need and desire play a part in
the shaping of beliefs. But is it true, as modern psychology often
claims, that our religious beliefs are nothing but attempts to satisfy

subconscious wishes? That the conception of God is merely a projection of self-seeking emotions, an objectification of subjective needs, the self in disguise? Indeed, the tendency to question the genuineness of man's concern about God is a challenge no less serious than the tendency to question the existence of God. We are in greater need of a proof for the authenticity of faith than of a proof for the existence of God.

We have not only forfeited faith; we have lost our faith in the meaning of faith. All we have is a sense of horror. We are afraid of man. We are terrified at our own power. Our proud Western civilization has not withstood the stream of cruelty and crime that burst forth out of the undercurrents of evil in the human soul. We nearly drown in a stream of guilt and misery that leaves no conscience clean. What have we done with our power? What have we done to the world? The flood of wretchedness is sweeping away our monstrous conceit. Who is the Lord? We despair of ever regaining an awareness of Him, of ever regaining faith in the meaning of faith. Indeed, out of a system of ideas where knowledge is power, where values are a synonym for needs, where the pyramid of being is turned upside down—it is hard to find a way to an awareness of God. If the world is only power to us and we are all absorbed in a gold rush, then the only god we may come upon is the golden calf. Nature as a tool box is a world that does not point beyond itself. It is when nature is sensed as mystery and grandeur that it calls upon us to look beyond it.

The awareness of grandeur and the sublime is all but gone from the modern mind. Our systems of education stress the importance of enabling the student to exploit the power aspect of reality. To some degree, they try to develop his ability to appreciate beauty. But there is no education for the sublime. We teach the children how to measure, how to weigh. We fail to teach them how to revere, how to sense wonder and awe. The sense for the sublime, the sign of the inward greatness of the human soul and something which is potentially given to all men, is now a rare gift. Yet without it, the world becomes flat and the soul a vacuum. Here is where the Biblical view

36

of reality may serve us as a guide. Significantly, the theme of Biblical poetry is not the charm or beauty of nature; it is the grandeur, it is the *sublime* aspect of nature which Biblical poetry is trying to celebrate.

ON THE SUBLIME IN THE BIBLE

It has often been maintained that sublimity is a peculiar quality of the Hebrew Bible and is unknown to the Greek classical writers. Coleridge once said, "Could you ever discover anything sublime in our sense of the term in the classic Greek literature? Sublimity is Hebrew by birth." Coleridge's "contention is suggestive, but too absolute. The highest possible examples of sublimity, it may be urged, are to be found in such Hebrew writers as Isaiah. Moderns like Milton, it may be further advanced, owe much of their sub-limity, directly or indirectly, to Hebrew sources. But, on the other hand, we can hardly deny that quality, however vigorous may be our definition of it, to early Greek writers such as Homer or Aeschylus, and to the early phases of some of the more modern literatures."[2] It is clear, however, that the awareness of the sublime as a special and mysterious kind of beauty is missing in the classical period of Greek philosophy. The Greek word for sublime as a stylistic term is not traceable beyond the first century of the present era.[3]

The oldest treatise on the subject, Longinus, *On the Sublime,* was probably written after the death of Augustus. Although primarily concerned with the sublime as a quality of style, he refers also to sublimity in external nature, and, from man's ability to respond to it, he deduces *the inward greatness of the human soul.* Nature planted in the human soul an invincible love of grandeur, and a desire to emulate whatever seems to approach nearer to divinity than himself. "Hence it is, that the whole universe is not sufficient for the extensive reach and piercing speculation of the human un-derstanding. It passes the bounds of the material world, and launches forth at pleasure into endless space." Nature impels us to admire not a small river "that ministers to our necessities," but the Nile, the Ister, and the Rhine; likewise the sun and the stars "surprise" us, and "Aetna in eruption commands our wonder."[4]

In illustrating his theory Longinus refers to the Book of Genesis. "The Jewish lawgiver, no ordinary person, since he had the capacity worthily to receive the divine power and show it forth, writes at the very beginning of his legislation: 'And God said . . .' What was it God said? 'Let there be light, and there was light,' 'Let there be land, and there was land.' "[5]

THE BEAUTIFUL AND THE SUBLIME

What do we mean by the sublime? And why did Longinus maintain that man's ability to respond to it is a sign of the inward greatness of the human soul? Since the time of Edmund A. Burke (1729-1797), the sublime has been contrasted with the beautiful.[6] He identified the *sublime* with the vast, the terrible, and the obscure which arouse the feeling of pain and terror, and the *beautiful* with the smooth, the small, and the delicate which arouse a feeling of love and tenderness. "Sublime objects are vast in their dimensions, beautiful ones comparatively small; beauty should be smooth and polished . . . light and delicate; the great ought to be solid, and even massive."

According to Kant, *the beautiful* is what pleases apart from all interest, and *the sublime* is what pleases through its opposition to the interest of sense.[7] He defines the sublime as "that in comparison with which all else is small" (p. 102). It is "nature in those of its appearances, the contemplation of which brings with it the idea of infinity" (p. 109). It is "that which is beyond all comprehension great."

While disagreeing with Burke's view that the objects of sublimity arouse in us a feeling of fear and imminent danger, Kant insists that they must be fearful. The sublime is found only in nature, not in

A philosophy of Judaism

character, intellect or art, since in these "human purpose determines the form as well as the size" (p. 113).

Objects of sublime feeling, according to Kant, are "bold, overhanging, and, as it were, threatening rocks; clouds piled up in the sky, moving with lightning flashes and thunder peals; volcanoes in all their violence of destruction; hurricanes with their track of devastation; the boundless ocean in a state of tumult; the lofty waterfall of a mighty river" (p. 125).

The meaning of the sublime and its perception, we believe, was not adequately described in these theories.

The sublime is not opposed to the beautiful, and must not, furthermore, be considered an esthetic category. The sublime may be sensed in things of beauty as well as in acts of goodness and in the search for truth. The perception of beauty may be the beginning of the experience of the sublime. The sublime is that which we see and are unable to convey. It is the silent allusion of things to a meaning greater than themselves. It is that which all things ultimately stand for; "the inveterate silence of the world that remains immune to curiosity and inquisitiveness like distant foliage in the dusk." It is that which our words, our forms, our categories can never reach. This is why the sense of the sublime must be regarded as the root of man's creative activities in art, thought, and noble living. Just as no flora has ever fully displayed the hidden vitality of the earth, so has no work of art, no system of philosophy, no theory of science, ever brought to expression the depth of meaning, the sublimity of reality in the sight of which the souls of saints, artists, and philosophers live.[8]

The sublime, furthermore, is not necessarily related to the vast and the overwhelming in size. It may be sensed in every grain of sand, in every drop of water. Every flower in the summer, every snow flake in the winter, may arouse in us the sense of wonder that is our response to the sublime.

> To me the meanest flower that blows can give
> Thoughts that do often lie too deep for tears.
> William Wordsworth, "Song at the Feast of Brougham Castle"

A sense sublime
Of something far more deeply interfused,
Whose dwelling is the light of setting suns,
And the round ocean and the living air,
And the blue sky, and in the mind of man;
A motion and a spirit, that impels
All thinking things, all objects of all thought,
And rolls through all things.
  William Wordsworth, "The Old Cumberland Beggar"

THE SUBLIME IS NOT THE ULTIMATE

It is not the sublime as such of which the Biblical man is aware. To him, the sublime is but a way in which things react to the presence of God. It is never an ultimate aspect of reality, a quality meaningful in itself. It stands for something greater; it stands in relation to something beyond itself that the eye can never see.

The sublime is not simply there. It is not a thing, a quality, but rather a happening, an act of God, a marvel. Thus even a mountain is not regarded as a thing. What seems to be stone is a drama; what seems to be natural is wondrous. There are no sublime facts; there are only divine *acts*.

Moreover, the sublime in the Biblical sense is found not only in the immense and the mighty, in the "bold, overhanging, and, as it were, threatening rocks," but also in the pebbles on the road. "For the stone shall cry out of the wall" (Habakuk 2:11). "The stone which the builders rejected is become the chief cornerstone" (Psalms 118:27). A simple stone that Jacob had put under his head for the night was set up as a pillar to be "God's house" (Genesis 28:18, 22). The sublime is revealed not only in the "clouds piled up in the sky, moving with lightning flashes and thunder peals," but also in God's causing the rain "to satisfy the desolate and waste ground, and to cause the bud of the tender herb to spring forth" (Job 38:27); not only in the "volcanoes in all their violence and destruction," but also in God's "setting up on high those that are low" and in frustrating "the device of the crafty" (Job 5:11-12); not only in "the hurricanes with their track of devastation" but also in "the still small voice" (I Kings 19:12); not only in "the boundless ocean in a state of tumult" but in His setting a bar to the sea, saying, "Thus far shalt thou come, but no further; here shall thy proud waves be stayed" (Job 38:11).

HORROR AND EXALTATION

The feeling caused by the sublime is astonishment which Burke defines as "that state of the soul in which all its motions are suspended with some degree of horror," in which "the mind is so entirely filled with its object, that it cannot entertain any other, nor by consequence reason on that subject which employs it." In contrast, the Biblical man in sensing the sublime is carried away by his eagerness to exalt and to praise the Maker of the world.

> Cry out unto God, all the earth,
> Sing of the glory of His name,
> Make His praise glorious:
> Say unto God: How sublime are Thy works!
> Psalms 66:2-3

In the face of threatening sights, the Biblical man could say: "Though I walk through the valley of the shadow of death, I will fear no evil, for Thou art with me" (Psalms 23:4).

One more feature sets Biblical man's experience apart from the esthetic experience of the sublime. The most exalted objects such as heaven or the stars and he himself have a mystery in common: they all continually depend on the living God. This is why the reaction to sublime objects is not simply "terrifying astonishment" or "the stupefaction of mind and senses," as Burke described, but wonder and amazement.

NOTES FOR CHAPTER 3

[1] Walter Schubart, *Russia and Western Man*, New York, 1950, p. 62f.

[2] W. Rhys Roberts, *Longinus On Style*, Cambridge, 1899, p. 31.

[3] Roberts, loc. cit., p. 209. It is an interesting coincidence that the first treatise on the subject of the sublime known to us by name was written by Caecilius, a

Sicilian rhetorician who taught in Rome in the time of Augustus, and who was "in faith a Jew"; see W. R. Roberts, *American Journal of Philology*, XVIII, pp. 303 ff., and loc. cit., pp. 220-222. Mommsen suggested that Longinus himself was a Jew who revered Moses and Homer alike. *Roemische Geschichte*, vol. VI, p. 494. According to Pauly-Wissowa, vol. V, p. 1174 ff., Caecilius was a Jew by faith. Compare however, the statement, "Let there be land."

4 Longinus, *On the Sublime*, ch. xxxv; cf. Samuel H. Monk, *The Sublime, A Study of Critical Theories in XVIII-Century England*, New York, 1935, p. 17.

5 Longinus, loc. cit., IX, 10.

6 In *A Philosophical Inquiry into the Origin of Our Ideas of the Sublime and the Beautiful*, Part II, Section I, p. 8; III, 27.

7 "The beautiful prepares us to love something disinterestedly, even nature itself; the sublime prepares us to esteem something highly even in opposition to our own (sensible) interest." *Critique of Aesthetic Judgment*, p. 134.

8 *Man is Not Alone*, p. 4.

4 Wonder

Among the many things that religious tradition holds in store for us is *a legacy of wonder*. The surest way to suppress our ability to understand the meaning of God and the importance of worship is *to take things for granted*. Indifference to the sublime wonder of living is the root of sin.

Modern man fell into the trap of believing that everything can be explained, that reality is a simple affair which has only to be organized in order to be mastered. All enigmas can be solved, and all wonder is nothing but "the effect of novelty upon ignorance." The world, he was convinced, is its own explanation, and there is no necessity to go beyond the world in order to account for the existence of the world. This lack of wonder, this exaggeration of the claim of scientific inquiry, is more characteristic of writers of popular science books and of interpreters of science to the laymen than of the creative scientists themselves. Spencer and others "seem to be possessed with the idea that science has got the universe pretty well ciphered down to a fine point; while the Faradays and Newtons seem to themselves like children who have picked up a few pretty pebbles upon the ocean beach. But most of us find it difficult to recognize the greatness and wonder of things familiar to us. As the prophet is not without honor save [in his own country] so it is also with phenomena."[1] "The facts of the case, we venture to say, are so wonderful that from first to last no general impression of Nature reached along scientific or any other lines can be even in the direction of being true that does not sound the note of joyous appreciation and of reverent wonder."[2]

"The history of European thought, even to the present day, has been tainted by a fatal misunderstanding. It may be termed The Dogmatic Fallacy. The error consists in the persuasion that we are capable of producing notions which are adequately defined in respect to the complexity of relationship required for their illustration in the real world. Canst thou by searching describe the universe? Except perhaps for the simpler notions of arithmetic, even our most familiar ideas, seemingly obvious, are infected with this incurable vagueness. Our right understanding of the methods of intellectual progress depends on keeping in mind this characteristic of our thoughts. . . . During the medieval epoch in Europe, the theologians were the chief sinners in respect to dogmatic finality. During the last three centuries, their bad pre-eminence in this habit passed to the men of science."[3]

A TINY SCREW

When the electric streetcar made its first appearance in the city of Warsaw, some good old Jews could not believe their own eyes. A car that moves without a horse! Some of them were stupefied and frightened, and all were at a loss how to explain the amazing invention.

Once while discussing the matter in the synagogue, a man entered who in addition to studying the Talmud was reputed to know books on secular subjects, to subscribe to a newspaper, and to be well versed in worldly affairs.

—You must know you how this thing works, they all turned to him.

—Of course, I know, he said. And they were all hanging on his every word with total concentration.

—Imagine four large wheels in a vertical position in four corners of a square, connected to each other by wires. You get it?

—Yes, we get it.

—The wires are tied in a knot in the center of the square and placed within a large wheel which is placed in a horizontal position. You get it?

—Yes, we get it.

—Above the large wheel, there are several wheels, one smaller than the other. You get it?

—Yes, we get it.

—On the top of the smallest wheel there is a tiny screw which is connected by a wire to the center of the car which lies on top of the wheels. Do you get it?

—Yes, we get it.

—The machinist in the car presses the button that moves the screw that brings the horizontal wheels to move, and thus the car runs through the street.

—Ah, now we understand!

TWO KINDS OF WONDER

Wonder or radical amazement is the chief characteristic of the religious man's attitude toward history and nature. One attitude is alien to his spirit: taking things for granted, regarding events as a natural course of things. To find an approximate cause of a phenomenon is no answer to his ultimate wonder. He knows that there are laws that regulate the course of natural processes; he is aware of the regularity and pattern of things. However, such knowledge fails to mitigate his sense of perpetual surprise at the fact that there are facts at all. Looking at the world he would say, "This is the Lord's doing, it is marvelous in our eyes" (Psalms 118:23).

That "wonder is the feeling of a philosopher, and philosophy begins in wonder" was stated by Plato[4] and maintained by Aristotle: "For it is owing to their wonder that men both now begin and at first began to philosophize."[5] To this day, rational wonder is appreciated as *"semen scientiae,"* as the seed of knowledge, as some-

45

thing conducive, not indigenous to cognition.[6] Wonder is the prelude to knowledge; it ceases, once the cause of a phenomenon is explained.[7]

But does the worth of wonder merely consist in its being a stimulant to the acquisition of knowledge? Is wonder the same as curiosity? To the prophets wonder is *a form of thinking*. It is not the beginning of knowledge but an act that goes beyond knowledge; it does not come to an end when knowledge is acquired; it is an attitude that never ceases. There is no answer in the world to man's radical amazement.

"STAND STILL AND CONSIDER"

As civilization advances, the sense of wonder declines. Such decline is an alarming symptom of our state of mind. Mankind will not perish for want of information; but only for want of appreciation. The beginning of our happiness lies in the understanding that life without wonder is not worth living. What we lack is not a will to believe but a will to wonder.

Awareness of the divine begins with wonder. It is the result of what man does with his higher incomprehension. The greatest hindrance to such awareness is our adjustment to conventional notions, to mental clichés. Wonder or radical amazement, the state of maladjustment to words and notions, is therefore a prerequisite for an authentic awareness of that which is.

Radical amazement has a wider scope than any other act of man. While any act of perception or cognition has as its object a selected segment of reality, radical amazement refers to all of reality; not only to what we see, but also to the very act of seeing as well as to our own selves, to the selves that see and are amazed at their ability to see.

The grandeur or mystery of being is not a particular puzzle to the mind, as, for example, the cause of volcanic eruptions. We do not have to go to the end of reasoning to encounter it. Grandeur or

46

A philosophy of Judaism

mystery is something with which we are confronted everywhere and at all times. Even the very act of thinking baffles our thinking, just as every intelligible fact is, by virtue of its being a fact, drunk with baffling aloofness. Does not mystery reign within reasoning, within perception, within explanation? Where is the self-understanding that could unfurl the marvel of our own thinking, that could explain the grace of our emptying the concrete with charms of abstraction? What formula could explain and solve the enigma of the very fact of thinking? Ours is neither thing nor thought but only the subtle magic blending the two.

What fills us with radical amazement is not the relations in which everything is embedded but the fact that even the minimum of perception is a maximum of enigma. The most incomprehensible fact is the fact that we comprehend at all.[8]

The way to faith leads through acts of wonder and radical amazement. The words addressed to Job apply to every man:

> Hearken unto this, O Job,
> Stand still and consider the wondrous works of the Lord.
> Do you know how God lays His command upon them,
> And causes the lightning of His cloud to shine?
> Do you know the balancings of the clouds,
> The wondrous works of Him who is perfect in knowledge,
> You whose garments are hot when the earth is still
>   because of the south wind?
> Can you, like Him, spread out the skies,
> Hard as a molten mirror?
> Teach us what we shall say to Him;
> We cannot draw up our case because of darkness.
> Shall it be told Him that I would speak?
> Did a man ever wish that he would be swallowed up?
> And now men cannot look on the light
> When it is bright in the skies
> When the wind has passed and cleared them.
> Out of the north comes golden splendor;
> God is clothed with terrible majesty.
>
> Job 37:14-22

Come ye and behold the works of God,
Sublime in His dealing with the sons of men;
Psalms 66:5

The great marvels do not crush the soul; sublimity evokes humility. Looking at the star-studded sky the Psalmist exclaims:

When I behold Thy heavens, the work of Thy fingers,
The moon and the stars which Thou hast fashioned—
What is man that Thou shouldst be mindful of him?
And the son of man that Thou shouldst think of him?
Psalms 8:4-5

In radical amazement, the Biblical man faces *"the great things and unsearchable, the wondrous things without number"* (Job 5:9). He encounters them in space and in time, in nature[9] and in history;[10] not only in the uncommon but also in the common occurrences of nature.[11] Not only do the things outside of him evoke the amazement of the Biblical man; his own being fills him with awe.

I will give thanks unto Thee
For I am fearfully and marvelously made;
Wondrous are Thy works;
And that my soul knoweth exceedingly.
Psalms 139:14[12]

"FOR THY CONTINUAL MARVELS"

The profound and perpetual awareness of the wonder of being has become a part of the religious consciousness of the Jew. Three times a day we pray:

We thank Thee . . .
For Thy miracles which are daily with us,
For Thy continual marvels. . . .

In the evening liturgy we recite the words of Job (9:10):

Who does great things past finding out,
Marvelous things without number.

Every evening we recite: "He creates light and makes the dark." Twice a day we say: "He is One." What is the meaning of such

48

repetition? A scientific theory, once it is announced and accepted, does not have to be repeated twice a day. The insights of wonder must be constantly kept alive. Since there is a need for daily wonder, there is a need for daily worship.

The sense for the "miracles which are daily with us," the sense for the "continual marvels," is the source of prayer. There is no worship, no music, no love, if we take for granted the blessings or defeats of living. No routine of the social, physical, or physiological order must dull our sense of surprise at the fact that there *is* a social, a physical, or a physiological order. We are trained in maintaining our sense of wonder by uttering a prayer before the enjoyment of food. Each time we are about to drink a glass of water, we remind ourselves of the eternal mystery of creation, "Blessed be Thou . . . by Whose word all things come into being." A trivial act and a reference to the supreme miracle. Wishing to eat bread or fruit, to enjoy a pleasant fragrance or a cup of wine; on tasting fruit in season for the first time; on seeing a rainbow, or the ocean; on noticing trees when they blossom; on meeting a sage in Torah or in secular learning; on hearing good or bad tidings—we are taught to invoke His great name and our awareness of Him. Even on performing a physiological function we say "Blessed be Thou . . . who healest all flesh and *doest wonders."*

This is one of the goals of the Jewish way of living: to experience commonplace deeds as spiritual adventures, to feel the hidden love and wisdom in all things.

In the Song of the Red Sea we read:

> Who is like Thee, O Lord, among the gods?
> Who is like Thee, majestic in holiness,
> Sublime in glorious deeds, doing wonders.
>
> Exodus 15:11

The Rabbis remarked: It is not written here: *Who did wonders,* but *Who does wonders.* . . . He did and still does wonders for us in every generation, as it is said:

> Wondrous are Thy works,
> And that my soul knoweth exceedingly.
>
> Psalms 139:14[13]

Rabbi Eleazer says: "Redemption and the earning of bread may be compared to each other. There is wonder in earning bread as there is wonder in redeeming the world. And as the earning of bread takes place every day, so does redemption take place every day."[14]

Said David the king: "I shall testify to the love of the Holy One, blessed be He, and to the benefits He confers upon Israel, hour by hour, and day by day. Day by day man is sold [into slavery], and every day he is redeemed; every day the soul of man is taken from him, and delivered to the Keeper; on the morrow it is returned to him; as it is written: *Into Thy hand I commit my spirit: Thou hast redeemed me, O Lord, Thou God of truth* (Psalms 31:6). Every day miracles such as those that occurred at the Exodus come upon man; every day he experiences redemption, like those who went forth from Egypt; every day he is fed at the breasts of his mother; every day he is punished for his deeds, like a child by his master."[15]

HE ALONE KNOWS

Awareness of wonder is not the same as knowing the wonders that happen to us. Wonders happen without our being able to notice them. The Psalmist (136:3) declares:

> O give thanks . . .
> To Him who alone does great wonders.

And the Rabbis remarked: "Is there anything that He does with the aid of someone else? What is the meaning of the word alone? He alone knows what wonders He does. . . . As it is said:

> Many things hast Thou done, O Lord my God,
> Even Thy wondrous deeds and Thy thoughts toward us.
> There is none to be compared unto Thee!

A philosophy of Judaism

If I would declare and speak of them,
They are more than can be told.

Psalms 40:6

I have no right to set forth Thy praise; I am unworthy to relate Thy wonders."[16]

The belief in "the hidden miracles is the basis for the entire Torah. A man has no share in the Torah, unless he believes that all things and all events in the life of the individual as well as in the life of society are miracles. There is no such thing as the natural course of events. . . ."[17]

The sense of wonder and transcendence must not become "a cushion for the lazy intellect." It must not be a substitute for analysis where analysis is possible; it must not stifle doubt where doubt is legitimate. It must, however, remain a constant awareness if man is to remain true to the dignity of God's creation, because such awareness is the spring of all creative thinking.

Such awareness was the wellspring of Kant's basic insight. "Two things fill the mind with ever new and increasing admiration and awe, the more often and the more steadily we reflect on them: *the starry heavens above and the moral law within.* . . . The former view of a countless multitude of worlds annihilates, as it were, my importance as an *animal creature,* which after it has been for a short time provided with vital power, one knows not how, must again give back the matter of which it was formed to the planet it inhabits (a mere speck in the universe). The second, on the contrary, infinitely elevates my worth as an intelligence by my personality, in which the moral law reveals to me a life independent of animality and even of the whole sensible world—at least so far as may be inferred from the destination assigned to my existence by this law, a destination not restricted to conditions and limits of this life, but reaching into the infinite."[18]

NOTES FOR CHAPTER 4

1 Charles S. Peirce, *Collected Papers*, Cambridge, Mass., 1935, vol. V, p. 65.
2 J. Arthur Thomson, *The System of Inanimate Nature*, p. 650.
3 A. N. Whitehead, *Adventures of Ideas*, New York, 1933, p. 185.
4 *Theaetetus*, 155d.
5 *Metaphysica*, 12, 982b, 12.

6 "The special philosophical disposition consists primarily in this, that a man is capable of wonder beyond the ordinary and everyday degree . . . the lower a man stands in an intellectual regard the less of a problem is existence itself to him; everything, how it is, and that it is, appears to him rather a matter of course." Schopenhauer, *Supplements to the World as Will and Idea*, ch. xvii.

"The feeling of wonderment is the source and inexhaustible fountainhead of [the child's] desire for knowledge. It drives the child irresistibly on to solve the mystery, and if in his attempt he encounters a causal relationship, he will not tire of repeating the same experiment ten times, a hundred times, in order to taste the thrill of discovery over and over again. . . . The reason why the adult no longer wonders is not because he has solved the riddle of life, but because he has grown accustomed to the laws governing his world picture. But the problem of why these particular laws and no others hold, remains for him just as amazing and inexplicable as for the child. He who does not comprehend this situation, misconstrues its profound significance, and he who has reached the stage where he no longer wonders about anything, merely demonstrates that he has lost the art of reflective reasoning." Max Planck, *Scientific Autobiography*, New York, 1949, pp. 91-93.

7 *Mechanica*, 847a, 11.

8 See *Man is Not Alone*, pp. 11, 13f.

9 God is He "Who giveth rain upon the earth, And sends waters upon the fields. He sets up on high those that are lowly, And those who mourn are exalted to safety. He frustrates the devices of the crafty, So that their hands achieve no success. He takes the wise in their own craftiness, And the schemes of the wily are brought to a quick end. They meet with darkness in the day-time, and grope at noonday as in the night. But He saves from the sword of their mouth, Even the needy from the hand of the mighty. So the poor has hope, And iniquity shuts her mouth" (Job 5:10-16). "O Lord, Thou art my God I will exalt Thee, I will praise Thy name, For Thou hast done wondrous things. . . . For Thou hast made of a city a heap, Of a fortified city a ruin; A castle of strangers to no city, It shall never be built. . . . For Thou hast been a stronghold to the poor, A stronghold to the needy in his distress" (Isaiah 25:1-4). See Psalms 107:8.15.21.31.24; Isaiah 40:26.

10 Exodus 3:20; 34:10; Joshua 3:5; Jeremiah 21:2; Micah 7:15; Psalms 72:18; 86:10; 98:1; 106:22; 136:4; Job 9:10.

11 "God thunders wondrously with his voice; He does great things which we cannot comprehend. For to the snow he says, 'Fall on the earth'; And to the shower and the rain, 'Be strong.' He seals up the hand of every man, That all men may know his work. Then the beasts go into their lairs And remain in their dens. From its chamber comes the whirlwind, And cold from the scattering winds. By the breath of God ice is given, And the broad waters are frozen fast. He loads the thick cloud with moisture; The clouds scatter his lightning. They turn round and round by his guidance. To accomplish all that he

commands them On the face of the habitable world. Whether for correction, or for his land, Or for love, he causes it to happen" (Job 37:5-13).

[12] "Didst Thou not pour me out like milk, And curdle me like cheese? Thou didst clothe me with skin and flesh, And knit me together with bones and sinews, Thou hast granted me life and steadfast love; And Thy care has preserved my spirit. Yet these things Thou didst hide in Thy heart; I know that this is with Thee" (Job 10:10-13).

[13] *Mechilta* on Exodus 15:11.

[14] Says Rabbi Samuel bar Nahmani: "The earning of bread is an even greater wonder than redemption, for redemption is done through an angel, and the earning of bread is made possible through the Holy One, blessed be He. In regard to the first we read, *The angel who has redeemed me from all evil'* (Genesis 48:16), while in regard to the second we read, *Thou openest Thy hand, thou satisfiest* every living thing' (Psalms 145:16)." Rabbi Joshua ben Levi says: "The earning of bread is a greater wonder than the division of the Red Sea." *Genesis Rabba,* ch. 20, 22. See *Pesahim* 118a.

[15] *Seder Eliyahu Rabba,* ch. 2, ed. Friedmann, p. 8 (in Nahum N. Glatzer, *In Time and Eternity,* p. 22f.) : "Just as the Holy One, Blessed be He, wrought many miracles in order to redeem Israel from Egypt, so He does concerning a piece of bread which a man puts in his mouth." *Pesikta Rabbati,* ed. M. Friedmann, ch. 33, p. 152a. "Greater is the miracle that occurs when a sick person escapes from perilous disease than that which happened when Hananiah, Mishael, and Azariah escaped from the fiery furnace. For Hananiah, Mishael, and Azariah escaped a fire kindled by man, which all men can extinguish, whilst a sick person escapes a heavenly fire, and who can extinguish that?" *Nedarim,* 41a.

[16] *Midrash Tehillim* 136, 4. "Miracles happen at all times. However, since they come to us not because we deserve to be saved but because of His great mercy and grace, they remain unnoticed. Only a generation that serves Him wholeheartedly is worthy of knowing the miracles that happen to it." Rabbi Eliezer of Tarnegrod, *Amaroth Tehorot,* Warsaw, 1838, on Psalms 136:4.

[17] Nahmanides, *Commentary* on Exodus 13:16.

[18] Kant, *Critique of Practical Reason,* translated by Abbott, London, 1889, p. 260.

5 The Sense of Mystery

"FAR OFF AND DEEP"

In the Book of Ecclesiastes we read the account of a man who sought wisdom, who searched for insight into the world and its meaning. "I said, I will be wise" (7:23), and "I applied my mind to know wisdom and to see what is done on earth" (8:16). Did he succeed? He claims, "I have acquired great wisdom, surpassing all who were over Jerusalem before me" (1:16). But he ultimately realized "that *man cannot find out* the work that is done under the sun. However much man may toil in seeking, he will not find it out; even though a wise man claims to know, he cannot find it out" (8:17).

"I said, I will be wise, but it was *far from me*. That which *is, is far off and deep, exceedingly deep*. Who can find it out?" (7:23-24). Ecclesiastes is not only saying that the world's wise are not wise enough, but something more radical. What *is,* is more than what you see; what *is,* is "far off and deep, exceedingly deep." *Being is mysterious.*

This is one of Ecclesiastes' central insights: "I have seen the task that God has given to the sons of men. . . . He has made all things beautiful in its time; but he has also *implanted in the hearts of men the mystery,* so that man cannot find out what God has done from the beginning to the end" (3:10-11).[1]

Wisdom is beyond our reach. We are unable to attain insight into the ultimate meaning and purpose of things. Man does not know the thoughts of his own mind nor is he able to understand the meaning of his own dreams (see Daniel 2:27).

54

A philosophy of Judaism

In awe and amazement the prophets stand before the mystery of the universe:

> Who has measured the waters in the hollow of his hand,
> And marked off the heavens with a span,
> Enclosed the dust of the earth in a measure,
> And weighed the mountains in scales,
> And the hills in a balance?
>
> Isaiah 40:12

An even deeper sense of humility is expressed in the words of Agur:

> Surely I am too stupid to be a man.
> I have not the understanding of a man.
> I have not learned wisdom,
> Nor have I knowledge of the Holy One.
> Who has ascended to heaven and come down?
> Who has gathered the wind in his fists?
> Who has wrapped up the waters in a garment?
> Who has established all the ends of the earth?
> What is his name, and what is his son's name,
> If thou knowest?
>
> Proverbs 30:2-4

"WHERE SHALL WISDOM BE FOUND?"

Philosophy is the love and quest of wisdom. To attain wisdom is one of the highest aspirations.

> But where shall wisdom be found?
> Where is the place of understanding?
> Man does not know the way to it;
> It is not found in the land of the living.
> The deep says, "It is not in me";
> The sea says, "It is not with me . . ."
> Whence then comes wisdom?

And where is the place of understanding?
It is hidden from the eyes of all living;
And concealed from the birds of the air.
Destruction and Death say:
"We have heard a rumor of it with our ears."
                                                    Job 28:12-14. 20-22

What have Job, Agur, Ecclesiastes discovered in their search?
They have discovered that the existence of the world is a mysterious
fact. Referring not to miracles or startling phenomena, but to the
natural order of things, they insist that the world of the known is
a world unknown; hiddenness, mystery. What stirred their souls
was neither the hidden nor the apparent, but the hidden in the
apparent; not the order but the mystery of the order that prevails
in the universe.

We live on the fringe of reality and hardly know how to reach the
core. What is our wisdom? What we take account of cannot be
accounted for. We explore the ways of being but do not know what,
why or wherefore being is. Neither the world nor our thinking or
anxiety about the world are accounted for. Sensations, ideas are
forced upon us, coming we know not whence. Every sensation is
anchored in mystery; every new thought is a signal we do not quite
identify. We may succeed in solving many riddles; yet the mind
itself remains a sphinx. The secret is at the core of the apparent;
the known is but the obvious aspect of the unknown. No fact in
the world is detached from universal context. Nothing here is final.
The mystery is not only beyond and away from us. We are involved in it. It is our destiny, and "the fate of the world depends
upon the mystery."[2]

TWO KINDS OF IGNORANCE

There are two kinds of ignorance. The one is "dull, unfeeling, barren," the result of indolence; the other is keen, penetrating, re-
splendent; the one leads to conceit and complacency, the other leads

to humility. From the one we seek to escape, in the other the mind finds repose.

The deeper we search the nearer we arrive at knowing that we do not know. What do we truly know about life and death, about the soul or society, about history or nature? "We have become increasingly and painfully aware of our abysmal ignorance. No scientist, fifty years ago, could have realized that he was as ignorant as all first-rate scientists now know themselves to be."[3] "Can we not see that exact laws, like all the other ultimates and absolutes, are as fabulous as the crock of gold at the rainbow's end?"[4] "Beware lest we say, we have found wisdom" (Job 32:13).[5] "They who travel in pursuit of wisdom, walk only in a circle; and after all their labor, at last return to their pristine ignorance."[6] "No illumination," remarks Joseph Conrad in *The Arrow of Gold,* "can sweep all mystery out of the world. After the departed darkness the shadows remain."

WE APPREHEND AND CANNOT COMPREHEND

The mystery is an ontological category. What it stands for is to most people most obviously given in the experience of exceptional events. However, it is a dimension of all existence and may be experienced everywhere and at all times. In using the term mystery we do not mean any particular esoteric quality that may be revealed to the initiated, but the essential mystery of being as being, the nature of being as God's creation out of nothing, and, therefore, something which stands beyond the scope of human comprehension. We do not come upon it only at the climax of thinking or in observing strange, extraordinary facts but in the startling fact that there are facts at all: being, the universe, the unfolding of time. We may face it at every turn, in a grain of sand, in an atom, as well as in the stellar space. Everything holds the great secret. For it is the inescapable situation of all being to be involved in the infinite mystery. We may continue to disregard the mystery, but we can neither deny nor escape it. The world is something *we apprehend but cannot comprehend*.

Significantly, the Hebrew word *'olam* that in post-Biblical times came to denote "world" is, according to some scholars, derived from the root *'alam* which means to hide, to conceal.[7] The world is itself hiddenness; its essence is a mystery.

Such awareness continued to be a part of the religious consciousness of the Jew. It found expression in numerous ways. The following passage is a striking formulation.

"HIDDEN ARE THE THINGS THAT WE SEE"

"[A Psalm] of the sons of Korah; upon 'Alamot. A Song (Psalm 46:1). This is meant in the verse: 'He does great things past finding out, marvels without number' (Job 9:10). It is beyond the power of man to recount the marvels and wonders of the Holy One, blessed be He. It is said: 'To Him who alone does great wonders' (Psalm 136:4). What is the meaning of the word 'alone'? It is He alone who knows what He does for you. It is in this sense that the sons of Korah said a song upon 'Alamot': *hidden are the things that we see; we do not know what we see.*" ("*'alam,*" as said above, means to hide, to conceal).[8]

Inaccessible to us are the insights into the nature of ultimate reality. Even what is revealed is incomplete and in disguise. Of Moses, the greatest of prophets, we are told that God has given in his charge all "fifty gates of wisdom except one."[9] He was neither perfect nor omniscient. There were things which were difficult for him to understand[10]; and there were problems of the law which he was unable to solve.[11] And though he ascended to heaven and received the Torah without an intermediary, the mystery of God remained unfathomable to him.[12]

According to legend, God had revealed to Moses the treasures of the Torah, of wisdom and knowledge, and the whole world's future.[13] And yet, there were intimations in the Torah which were not disclosed to Moses. These intimations are contained in "the crowns" or the three little strokes written on top of seven letters of the Hebrew alphabet whenever they occur in the Torah.[14] Of these allusions which are not expressed by either letters or words it is said, "things not revealed to Moses were known to Rabbi Akiba" (martyred about the year 132).[15]

The Torah, we are told, is both concealed and revealed,[16] and so is the nature of all reality. All things are both known and unknown, plain and enigmatic, transparent and impenetrable. "Hidden are the things that we see; we do not know what we see." The world is both open and concealed, a matter of fact and a mystery. We know and do not know—this is our condition.

Strange are the words which conclude the Pentateuch. After telling us all the details about where Moses was buried:

> And he was buried in the valley
> in the land of Moab
> over against Bet Peor

the Torah concludes

> And no one knows of his grave unto this day.

The Torah, the Rabbis said, teaches us the way of faith. Though we know the site of Moses' grave and all the signs of its geographic location, we must realize that we know nothing at all about its whereabouts.[17]

NOTES FOR CHAPTER 5

[1] The difficult word here is *ha'olam* which has been rendered by the Septuagint with "eternity," by the Vulgate with "world," and by others with "knowledge" (on the basis of the Arabic cognate). Rashi, following rabbinic sources (*Kohelet Rabba* 3, 15; *Tanhuma*, Kedoshim, 8; *Midrash Tehillim* 9, 1), explains it as "hiddenness" or mystery.

[2] Zohar, vol. III, p. 128a.

[3] Abraham Flexner, *Universities*, New York, 1930, p. 17.

[4] Gilbert N. Lewis, *The Anatomy of Science*, New Haven, 1926, p. 154.

[5] According to Socrates, "God only is wise," and the man who claimed actual possession of wisdom was guilty of presumption, if not blasphemy. He called himself a lover of wisdom. *Apology*, 20ff.

[6] Oliver Goldsmith, *The Citizen of the World*, letter 37.

[7] The etymology is generally questioned by modern scholars. Compare the

reference in Brown-Driver-Briggs, *A Hebrew and English Lexicon of the Old Testament*, Oxford, 1906, p. 761.

[8] *Midrash Tehillim* 46, 1; *Yalkut Shimoni*, II, 751. Significantly, *Midrash Tehillim* 45, 4 derives the idea of silent prayer—"My heart overflows with a goodly matter" (Psalms 45:2; see *Or Zarua*, p. 112)—from the sons of Korah who, when the earth yawned to swallow Korah and his company, repented in silence and did not die (Numbers 26:11). They later received the prophetic gift and composed psalms. According to one legend they entered into paradise alive. See Louis Ginsberg, *Legends of the Jews*, vol. VI, p. 104. Compare also *Genesis Rabba* 12, 1.

[9] *Rosh Hashanah* 21b.

[10] *Mechilta* to Exodus 12:2; *Yalkut Shimoni* I, 764.

[11] *Sifre* Numbers, p. 68.

[12] *Midrash Tehillim* to 106, 2.

[13] *Yalkut Shimoni* I, 173.

[14] *Yalkut Reubeni* to Exodus 19, 2.

[15] *Numbers Rabba*, 19, 5.

[16] Zohar, vol. III, p. 159a. Compare the remark on "Let there be light" in vol. I, 140a.

[17] See *Ecclesiastes Rabba* to 12:9.

6 The Enigma is Not Solved

The mystery of God remains for ever sealed to man. *Thou canst not see My face, for man shall not see Me and live.* Even the seraphim cover their faces with their wings in the presence of God (Isaiah 6:2). Solomon, who built the great Temple in Jerusalem, knew that the Lord who fixed the sun in the heavens decided *"to dwell in deep darkness"* ('arafel) (I Kings 8:12).[1]

He made darkness His hiding place (Psalms 18:12). "God is great, beyond our knowledge" (Job 36:26). "God thunders marvelously with His voice; He does great things which we cannot understand" (Job 37:5). Not only His essence; His ways are deep, mysterious, and inscrutable. His righteousness, "like the mighty mountains," is beyond our comprehension, and His judgments are as deep as "the great abyss" (Psalms 36:7). "For My thoughts are not your thoughts, neither are your ways My ways, says the Lord. For as the heavens are higher than the earth, so are My ways higher than your ways, and My thoughts than your thoughts" (Isaiah 55:8-9).

The mysteries of nature and history challenged and often startled the Biblical man. But he knew that it was beyond his power to penetrate them. "The mysteries belong to God" (Deuteronomy 29:28). "God is in heaven and thou upon earth; therefore let thy words be few" (Ecclesiastes 5:1).

All we have is an awareness of the presence of the mystery, but it is a presence that the mind can never penetrate. Such an attitude may be contrasted with Hegel's characterization of the transition of the Egyptian to the Greek religion. "The enigma is solved; the Egyptian sphinx, according to a deeply significant and admirable myth, was slain by a Greek, and thus the enigma has been solved."[2]

To the Jewish mind the ultimate enigmas remain inscrutable. "It is the glory of God to conceal things" (Proverbs 25:2). Man's royal privilege is to explore the world of time and space; but it is futile for him to try to explore what is beyond the world of time and space. "Whosoever gives his mind to four things, it were better for him if he had not come into the world: what is above? what is beneath? what was beforetime? and what will be hereafter?"[3] "What is too wonderful for you, do not seek, nor search after what is hidden from you. Meditate upon that which is permitted to you. Do not occupy yourself with mysteries."[4] Occultism is presumption. Magic, divination, necromancy are forbidden by law. "The hidden things belong to the Lord," and from Him alone must come the knowledge and the answer.

There have been men who like the author of the medieval "Hymn of Glory" confessed, "My soul desired in Thy shelter to know all Thy mystery." Yet the Psalmist avers, "I have stilled and quieted my soul, like a weaned child with his mother." "Lord, my heart is not haughty, nor mine eyes lofty; neither do I exercise myself in things too great or in things too marvelous for me" (Psalms 131:1-2).

With awe and trepidation the priests and the Levites must "approach unto the most holy things." Only "Aaron and his sons shall go in, and appoint them every one to his service and to his burden; but *they shall not go in to see the holy things* as they are being covered, lest they die" (Numbers 4:20).[5]

A LOAF OF BREAD

We have said above that the root of worship lies in the sense of the "miracles that are daily with us." There is neither worship nor ritual without a sense of mystery. For worship and ritual imply the

A philosophy of Judaism

ability to address ourselves to God—an implication that cannot be integrated into any system of pure naturalism—and are only meaningful as a mystery we are convinced of, without being able to analyze it or to submit it to experiment. What is more, all worship and ritual are essentially attempts to remove our callousness to the mystery of our own existence and pursuits.

Let us take a loaf of bread. It is the product of climate, soil and the work of the farmer, merchant and baker. If it were our intention to extol the forces that concurred in producing a loaf of bread, we would have to give praise to the sun and the rain, to the soil and to the intelligence of man. However, it is not these we praise before breaking bread. We say, "Blessed be Thou, O Lord our God, King of the Universe, who brings forth bread from the earth." Empirically speaking, would it not be more correct to give credit to the farmer, the merchant and the baker? To our eyes, it is they who bring forth the bread.

Just as we pass over the mystery of vegetation, we go beyond the miracle of cultivation. We bless Him who makes possible both nature and civilization. It is not important to dwell each time on what bread is empirically, namely "an article of food made of the flour of grain, mixed with water, to which yeast is commonly added to produce fermentation, the mixture being kneaded and baked in loaves." It is important to dwell each time on what bread is ultimately.

Firm and abiding are the laws of nature. And yet, we are told that a farmer scattering the seeds in the earth for the purpose of growth must do so by faith in God, not by faith in nature.[6] For this is the essence of faith: even what appears to us as a natural necessity is an act of God.[7]

Jewish observance is a constant reminder, an intense appeal, to be attentive to Him who is beyond nature, even while we are engaged in dealing with nature. The awareness of mystery, not often expressed, is always implied. A classical example of that awareness is the attitude toward the *Ineffable Name*.

63

The true name of God is a mystery. It is stated in the Talmud, *"And God said unto Moses . . . This is My name for ever* (Exodus 3:15). The Hebrew word 'for ever' *(leolam)* is written here in a way that it may be read *lealem* which means 'to conceal.' The name of God is to be concealed."[8]

Throughout the ages the Jews shrank from uttering, and, to some degree, even from writing out in full the four-lettered Holy Name of God (the Tetragrammaton).[9] Except in the Bible, the name is usually not written out in full. Even when the portion of the Pentateuch is read during the service, the Name is never pronounced as it is written. The true name is the *Ineffable Name*. It is rendered by the Jews as *Adonai* (literally, "My Lord"),[10] by the Samaritans as *Hashem,* and by the translators of the Bible into Greek by the word "Lord" *(kyrios)*. According to Abba Saul, he who pronounces the Ineffable Name is among those who have no share in the life to come.[11] "No one may utter the mystery of Thy name."[12]

Only once a year, on the Day of Atonement, was the Ineffable Name uttered by the High Priest at the Temple in Jerusalem. And when the name came out of his mouth, "in holiness and purity," "those who stood near him prostrated themselves, and those who stood afar said, 'Blessed be the name . . . for ever and ever.' " The name was pronounced ten times during the worship, and yet even before the people had left the Temple, all of them would forget the pronunciation.[13] According to a medieval source, the name escaped even the High Priest himself as soon as he left the Temple.[14]

To this day the priests close their eyes when pronouncing the blessing, because when the Temple was in existence, they would utter the Ineffable Name . . . and the *Shechinah* would rest on their eyes. In remembrance thereof they close their eyes.[15]

The Decalogue does not contain any commandment to worship God. It tells us "honor thy father and thy mother," it does not tell us, "honor thy God, worship Him, offer sacrifice to Him." The only reference to worship is indirect and negative: *Thou shalt not take My name in vain.*

The sense of the ineffable, the awareness of the grandeur and mystery of living, is shared by all men, and It is in the depth of such awareness that acts and thoughts of religion are full of meaning. The ideas of religion are *an answer,* when the mystery is *a problem.* When brought to the level of utilitarian thinking, when their meaning is taken literally as solutions to scientific problems, they are bound to be meaningless. Thus the basic *ideas* in Judaism have more than one dimension; what they refer to is a mystery, and they become distorted when taken as matter-of-fact descriptions. The idea of man as a being created in the likeness of God, the idea of creation, of divine knowledge, the election of Israel, the problem of evil, messianism, the belief in the resurrection or faith in revelation become caricatures when transposed into categories of pedestrian thinking.[16]

When Moses was about to depart from this world, he said, "Master of the Universe, I ask of Thee one favor before I die, that all the gates of both heaven and the abyss be opened, and people shall see that there is none beside Thee."[17] Moses' request was not granted, and the gates remain closed.

THE MYSTERY IS NOT GOD

Is this the meaning of the human situation: to be tied to the stake and to stand the course? Job is not told to kiss the rod, to submit to necessity. He is not told, there is neither justice nor wisdom but only the darkness of mystery. In his search for meaning he is told:

> God understands the way to it,
> He knows its place.
> For He looks to the ends of the earth,
> And sees everything under the heavens.
> When He gave to the wind its weight,
> And meted out the waters by measure.
> When He made a decree for the rain,

And a way for the lightning of the thunder;
Then He saw it and declared it;
He established it, and searched it out.
And he said to man
"Behold, the fear of the Lord, that is wisdom;
And to depart from evil is understanding."
Job 28:23-28

God's power is not arbitrary. "The Almighty—whom we cannot find out is great in power, yet to justice and abundant righteousness He does not violate." What is mysterious to us is eternally meaningful as seen by God. Nature is subject to His purposive will, and man who was given a share in His wisdom is called to responsible living and to be a partner of God in the redemption of the world.

The extreme hiddenness of God is a fact of constant awareness. Yet His concern, His guidance, His will, His commandment, are revealed to man and capable of being experienced by him.

God is a mystery, but the mystery is not God.[18] He is a *revealer of mysteries* (Daniel 2:47). "He reveals deep and mysterious things; He knows what is in the darkness and the light dwells with Him" (Daniel 2:22). In the words of the liturgy of the Days of Awe: "Thou knowest eternal mysteries and the ultimate secrets of all living." The certainty that there is meaning beyond the mystery is the reason for ultimate rejoicing.

The Lord reigns; let the earth rejoice;
Let the many coastlands be glad!
Clouds and thick darkness are round about him;
Righteousness and justice are the foundation of his throne.
Psalms 97:1-2

We do not deify the mystery; we worship Him who in His wisdom surpasses all mysteries. As said above, it is not our task to break the barriers, to penetrate the mysteries. Any attempt to fathom the mysteries by means of the occult arts, by necromancy or by recourse to oracles, is forbidden by law.[19]

A philosophy of Judaism

When the great moment arrived and the voice of God became audible at Sinai, what mysteries did it disclose? In apocalyptic visions one is shown "the treasuries of the stars," mountains of gold, seas of glass, cities of jasper. Did Israel learn anything at Sinai about the enigmas of the universe? About the condition of the departed souls? About demons, angels, heaven? The voice they perceive said: Remember the seventh day to keep it holy. . . . Honor thy father and thy mother. . . .

When in response to Moses' request, the Lord appeared to tell him what He is, did He say: I am the all-wise, the perfect, and of infinite beauty? He did say: I am full of love and compassion. Where in the history of religion prior to the age of Moses, was the Supreme Being celebrated for His being sensitive to the suffering of men? Have not philosophers agreed, as Nietzsche remarked, in the deprecation of pity?

THREE ATTITUDES

There are three attitudes toward the mystery: the fatalist, the positivist, and the Biblical.

To the fatalist, mystery is the supreme power controlling all reality. He believes that the world is controlled by an irrational, absolutely inscrutable and blind power that is devoid of either justice or purpose. The Maat of the Egyptian, Pta and Asha among the Indians and Persians, and the Moira among the Greeks signify a power set over the gods. The stern decrees of Moira are feared even by Zeus. To the notion of fate history is an impenetrable mystery, and man is in dark uncertainty with regard to the future. A tragic doom is hanging over the world, to which gods and men alike are subject, and the only attitude one may take is that of resignation. It is a view that is found in various forms and degrees in nearly all pagan religions, in many modern philosophies of history (history as a cycle of becoming and decay), as well as in popular thinking.

The positivist has a matter-of-fact orientation. To him the mystery does not exist; what is regarded as such is simply that which we do not know yet, but shall be able to explain some day. The logical positivist maintains that all assertions about the nature of reality or about a realm of values transcending the familiar world are meaningless and that, on the other hand, all meaningful questions are in principle answerable.

The awareness of mystery was common to all men of antiquity. It was the beginning of a new era when man was told that the mystery is *not* the ultimate; that not a demonic, blind force but a God of righteousness rules the world. In Greek tragedy man is invariably the victim of some unseen power which foredooms him to disaster. "Awful is the mysterious power of fate." "Pray not at all, since there is no release for mortals from predestined calamity."[20] In contrast, Abraham stands before God, arguing for the salvation of Sodom: "Far be it from Thee to do such a thing, to slay the righteous with the wicked, so that the righteous fare as the wicked! Far be it from Thee! Shall not the judge of all the earth do right?"[21]

The theology of fate knows only a one-sided dependence upon the ultimate power. That power has neither concern for man nor need of him. History runs its course as a monologue. To Jewish religion, on the other hand, history is determined by the covenant: God is in need of man.[22] The ultimate is not a law but a judge, not a power but a father.

GOD IS NOT ETERNALLY SILENT

The Jewish attitude toward the mystery may be compared with the following statement by Plotinus.

"If a man were to inquire of Nature, 'Wherefore dost thou bring forth creatures?' and she were willing to give ear and to answer, she would say, 'Ask me not, but understand in silence, even as I am silent.'"[23]

68

God in search of man

The Jew will not accept that answer. He will continue to pray, "O God, do not keep silence, do not hold Thy peace or be still, O God" (Psalms 83:2). "Why dost Thou hide Thy face? Why dost Thou forget our affliction and oppression?" (Psalms 44.25). God is not always silent, and Israel is waiting for the word. "He is our God; He is our Father; He is our King; He is our Deliverer. He will again in His mercy proclaim to us in the presence of all living . . . to be your God—I am the Lord your God."[24]

The most vexing issue in Jewish thinking, furthermore, is not, "wherefore dost Thou bring forth creatures?" but rather, "where is Thy mercy?" "Where is Thy zeal and Thy might? The yearning of Thy heart and Thy compassion are withheld from me." "Look down from heaven and see, even from Thy holy and glorious habitation."[25]

A Talmudic legend reflects two problems that baffled the Rabbis: the election of Israel and the suffering of Israel. Both problems were raised by Moses and exemplified in the life of Rabbi Akiba. The first problem: why was Moses chosen of all men to bring the word of God to the world, though a man like Rabbi Akiba was not inferior to him in intellectual power?[26] The second problem: why did Rabbi Akiba suffer martyrdom?

When Moses ascended to heaven, he found the Holy One, blessed be He, engaged in attaching crowns to the letters of the Torah (see above, p. 58 f). Said Moses, Lord of the universe, who stays Thy hand to reveal in words what is merely to be indicated in the crowns? He answered, There will arise a man at the end of many generations, Akiba ben Joseph by name, who will expound upon each little dot heaps and heaps of laws. Lord of the universe, said Moses, permit me to see him. Turn back and see, the Lord replied. Moses went and sat behind eight ranks and there he could hear the discussions of Rabbi Akiba with his disciples. But Moses was unable to understand the discussions, and he was very much grieved. But then he heard the disciples asking the master, in regard to a certain subject, How do you know that? and the latter replied, It is a law given unto Moses at Sinai, and Moses was comforted. Thereupon Moses returned to the Holy One, blessed be He, and said, Lord of the universe, Thou has such a man and Thou givest the Torah to Israel through me! But God replied, *Be silent,* for such is My decree. Then said Moses, Lord of the universe, Thou hast permitted me to behold his learning, let me I pray behold the reward which he is destined to receive. Turn back and see, said the Lord, and Moses turned around and saw how the Romans were selling the flesh of the martyr Akiba at the market place. Lord of the universe, cried Moses, is this the reward for such learning? And the Lord replied, *Be silent, for such is My decree.*[27]

NOTES FOR CHAPTER 6

[1] In the Septuagint the paradox is made explicit by a few additional words. The verse reads: "The sun He made manifest in heaven. The Lord said, He would dwell in darkness."
[2] Hegel, *The Philosophy of Religion,* vol. II, p. 122. Hegel's characterization is hardly valid.
[3] *Mishnah Hagigah,* 2, 2.
[4] *Sirach* 3: 21f. See Jerushalmi Hagigah 77c; *Genesis Rabba* 8, 2. "The great mysteries of the world are known to God alone." Maimonides in his letter to Rabbi Hisdai, in *Kobets,* ed. Lichtenberg, vol. II, p. 24d. The first words of the Lord that Moses heard in his life were: *Moses, Moses, draw not nigh hither.* Moses had turned aside to *see* the "great sight" of the burning bush, but when the voice reached his soul, he "hid his face, for he was afraid to look upon God" (Exodus 3:3, 5f). And the Rabbis remarked: as a reward for "And Moses hid his face," "The Lord spoke unto Moses face to face" (Exodus 33: 11), and because he feared to look, we read "and the similitude of the Lord does he behold" (Numbers 12:8). But Nadab and Abihu, who uncovered their heads and fed their eyes on the luster of the *Shechinah,* did they not receive [the death penalty] for what they had done? (*Exodus Rabba,* Exodus 3. 1.)
[5] The reason for this statement is that since the Holy of Holies is the abode of "the glory which sitteth upon the cherubim, the Levites are charged lest they break through unto the Lord to gaze. They must wait until the priests bring down the veil. Then the glory will be revealed in the hiding of its power and return to its abode." Nahmanides, *Commentary* on Numbers 4:20; see Rabbi Eliezer of Mayence, *Yereyim,* 352.
[6] *Shabbat* 31a, see the comment in *Tosafot,* referring to Isaiah 36:6.
[7] Rabbi Isaac Meir Alter of Ger, quoted in *Sefat Emet,* vol. III, p. 81a.
[8] *Kiddushin* 71a.
[9] K. Kohler, in *Jewish Encyclopedia,* vol. I, pp. 202-203, s. v. "Adonai"; W. Bacher, ibid., vol. XI, pp. 262-264, s. v. "Shem Hameforash"; L. Blau, ibid., vol. XII, p. 119-120, s. v. "Tetragrammaton." The meaning of the Hebrew equivalent for the Ineffable Name, "Shem Hameforash" (also "Shem Hameyuhad"), is obscure. On "The Substitutes for the Tetragrammaton," see Jacob Z.

A philosophy of Judaism

Lauterbach, *Proceedings of the American Academy for Jewish Research*, 1931, vol. II, pp. 39-67.

[10] A Babylonian Amora paraphrased Exodus 3:15 as follows: I am not read, says God, as I am written; I am written as the Tetragrammaton and pronounced as "Adonai."

[11] *Mishnah Sanhedrin* X, 1.

[12] In the Musaf liturgy for the Days of Awe.

[13] *Jerushalmi Yoma* III, 7, 40d; *Bab. Yoma*, 39b; *Ecclesiastes Rabba* 3, 15.

[14] *Otzar Hegeonim, Kiddushin* 71a.

[15] *Sefer Hasidim*, ed. Wistinetzki, Frankfurt a. M., 1924, pp. 388, 1588.

[16] In the verse in Psalms 9:1, the great Massorah reads *al mut* as one word, in the sense of "hiddenness"; see Rashi's *Commentary*. *Midrash Tehillim* seems to have had the same reading (see S. Buber's remark ad locum), and consequently lists several "hidden" themes such as the paradox that the ashes of the Red Heifer purify the unclean and make unclean the pure; the reward for good deeds; the end of days. Thus the first chapter in the Book of Genesis was not intended to supply us with information about how the universe came into being. The human language has no words which are capable of conveying such information. "Since it is impossible to express the mystery of creation, Scripture *concealed it* in the words *In the beginning God created heaven and earth.*" *Batei Midrashot*, ed. Wertheimer, Jerusalem, 1950, vol. 1, p. 251; Maimonides, *The Guide of the Perplexed*, Introduction; Nahmanides, *Commentary* on Genesis 1:1. Of the mystery of the divine knowledge, Maimonides says, "This is something which is beyond the power of any mouth to utter, beyond the capacity of any ear to hear nor is it possible for the heart of any man to grasp its significance." *Mishneh Torah, Yesode Hatorah*, 2, 10. Similarly, "the end of days" is something no man can fathom. Should a man tell you when the day of redemption will occur, reply to him, the Lord said, "it is in My heart." "If the heart has not revealed the secret to the mouth, to whom could my mouth have revealed it!" *Ecclesiastes Rabba* to 12:9; compare *Sanhedrin* 99a and Maharsha's comment. Even to the prophets, "the world to come" remained a mystery. "No one has heard or perceived by the ear, no eye has seen." It is "wine preserved in the grapes since the days of creation" (*Berachot* 34b and Isaiah 64:4).

[17]*Deuteronomy Rabba* 11, 8. Usually every new section (*sedrah*) in the Pentateuch is separated from the previous one by the space of nine letters. However the section in the Book of Genesis in which the last days of Jacob are described is "closed"; it is separated from the previous one by the space of one letter only. The reason given is that "Jacob wished to reveal the end (when the Messiah would come) but it was hidden (closed) from him" (*Genesis Rabba*, 96, 1). While the sons were standing around the golden bed wherein Jacob lay, the Shechinah visited him for a moment and departed as quickly, and with her departed all trace of the knowledge of the great mystery from the mind of Jacob. Jacob wished to reveal the end to his sons, and said to them: *Gather yourselves together, that I may tell you that which shall befall you in the end of days* (Genesis 49:2). Said God to Him, *It is the glory of God to conceal a thing* (Proverbs 25:2). Such actions are not for the wise. *He that goes about as a talebearer reveals secrets; but he who is of a faithful spirit conceals a matter* (Proverbs 11:13). *Genesis Rabba*, ch. 96 (new version).

The language of the Bible is particularly rich in words that express the concept of "hiding" or "being hidden." That abundance is strikingly impressive when compared with the Greek language. The Greek translators of the Bible could find only one word *krypto* (in addition to *kalypto*) with which to render the numerous Hebrew synonyms. *Theologisches Wœrterbuch zum Neuen Testament,* vol. III, p. 967.

[18] "For the Lord is a God of knowledge" (I Samuel 2:3).

[19] "Let lying lips be made dumb that speak arrogantly against the righteous with pride and contempt" (Psalms 31:19). These words were explained by the Rabbis in the following way. "Let them be bound! *Let them be made dumb!* Let them be silenced! the lying lips *that speak arrogantly against* (the will) of *the Righteous One,* who is the life of all worlds, on matters which He has withheld from His creatures, *with pride,* in order to boast and say, I discourse on (the mystery of) creation, and *contempt,* to think that he contemns My glory." *Genesis Rabba,* 1, 5.

[20] Sophocles, *Antigone,* 951 and 133ff.

[21] Genesis 18:25

[22] *Man is Not Alone,* p. 241ff.

[23] Plotinus, *Enneads,* III, 8.4.

[24] The Musaf liturgy for Sabbath.

[25] Isaiah 63:15; see Psalms 89:50, and *Yoma,* 69b.

[26] Compare Maimonides, *The Guide of the Perplexed,* vol. II, ch. 25.

[27] *Menahot,* 29b.

7 Awe

The awe and humility sensed in the face of the mystery and grandeur of nature and history affected the Biblical understanding of the character, scope, and worth of human knowledge and wisdom. Since all reality is involved in the will and thought of God, he who wants to understand the world must seek to understand God. Yet what is the way of understanding Him?

> Canst thou by searching find out God?
> Canst thou find out the purpose of the Almighty?
> It is as high as heaven; what canst thou do?
> Deeper than the nether-world; what canst thou know?
> The measure thereof is longer than the earth,
> And broader than the earth.
>
> Job 11:7-9

Much has been said in praise of wisdom and the wise: "The teaching of the wise is a fountain of life" (Proverbs 13:14). "The tongue of the wise brings healing" (Proverbs 12:14). "Wisdom preserves the life of him who has it" (Ecclesiastes 7:12). Human wisdom, however, is not our ultimate security.

Human wisdom is contingent, not absolute. It is given to us by God and may be taken away by Him. "For the Lord gives wisdom" (Proverbs 2:6), but He also *turns wise men back and makes their knowledge foolish* (Isaiah 44:25).

The practical wisdom which man can achieve and which was so sincerely appreciated and celebrated becomes ignorance when we are confronted with the mysteries of nature and history.

The message that the Bible conveys is not that of despair or agnosticism. Job does not simply say, "We do not know," but rather that God knows, that "God understands the way to it," He knows where wisdom is. What is unknown and concealed from us is known and open to God. This, then, is the specific meaning of mystery in our sense. It is not a *synonym for the unknown* but rather a name for a *meaning which stands in relation to God.*

THE BEGINNING OF WISDOM IS AWE

Ultimate meaning and ultimate wisdom are not found within the world but in God, and the only way to wisdom is, as said above, through our relationship to God. That relationship is *awe.* Awe, in this sense, is more than an emotion; it is a way of understanding. Awe is itself an act of insight into a meaning greater than ourselves.

The question, therefore, *where shall wisdom be found?* is answered by the Psalmist: *the awe of God is the beginning of wisdom.*[1] The Bible does not preach awe as a form of intellectual resignation; it does not say, awe is the end of wisdom. Its intention seems to be that awe is a way to wisdom. In Job we encounter a complete equation: *the awe of God is wisdom.*[2]

The beginning of awe is wonder, and the beginning of wisdom is awe.

THE MEANING OF AWE

Awe is a way of being in rapport with the mystery of all reality. The awe that we sense or ought to sense when standing in the presence of a human being is a moment of intuition for the likeness of God which is concealed in his essence. Not only man; even inanimate things stand in a relation to the Creator. The secret of every being is the divine care and concern that are invested in it. Something sacred is at stake in every event.[3]

74

A philosophy of Judaism

Awe is an intuition for the creaturely dignity of all things and their preciousness to God; a realization that things not only are what they are but also stand, however remotely, for something absolute. Awe is a sense for the transcendence, for the reference everywhere to Him who is beyond all things. It is an insight better conveyed in attitudes than in words. The more eager we are to express it, the less remains of it.

The meaning of awe is to realize that life takes place under wide horizons, horizons that range beyond the span of an individual life or even the life of a nation, a generation, or an era. Awe enables us to perceive in the world intimations of the divine, to sense in small things the beginning of infinite significance, to sense the ultimate in the common and the simple; to feel in the rush of the passing the stillness of the eternal.

In analyzing or evaluating an object, we think and judge from a particular point of view. The psychologist, economist, and chemist pay attention to different aspects of the same object. Such is the limitation of the mind that it can never see three sides of a building at the same time. The danger begins when, completely caught in one perspective, we attempt to consider a part as the whole. In the twilight of such perspectivism, even the sight of the part is distorted. What we cannot comprehend by analysis, we become aware of in awe. When we "stand still and consider," we face and witness what is immune to analysis.

Knowledge is fostered by curiosity; wisdom is fostered by awe. True wisdom is participation in the wisdom of God. Some people may regard as wisdom "an uncommon degree of common sense." To us, wisdom is the ability to look at all things from the point of view of God, sympathy with the divine pathos, the identification of the will with the will of God. "Thus says the Lord: Let not the wise man glory in his wisdom, let not the mighty man glory in his might, let not the rich man glory in his riches; but let him who glories glory in this, that he understands and knows Me, that I am the Lord who practises kindness, justice, and righteousness on the earth; for in these things I delight, says the Lord" (Jeremiah 9:22-23).

There are, of course, moments of higher or lower intensity of awe. When a person becomes alive to the fact that God "is the great ruler, the rock and foundation of all worlds, before Whom all existing things are as nought, as it has been said, all the inhabitants of the earth are as nought" (Daniel 4:32),[4] he will be overwhelmed by a sense of the holiness of God. Such awe is reflected in the exhortation of the prophets: "Enter into the rock, hide thee in the dust, from before the terror of the Lord, from the splendor of His majesty" (Isaiah 2:10).

We find a classical expression of the meaning and expression of awe in Maimonides:

When a man is in the presence of a mighty king, he will not sit, move, and behave in the same way as he would when he is alone in his own house; nor will he speak in the king's audience chamber in the same easy-going manner as he would in his own family circle or among his relatives. Therefore any man who is keen on attaining human perfection and wishes to be a true "man of God" must awake to the fact that the great King who constantly protects him and is near to him is mightier than any human individual, even if it were David or Solomon. That King and constant guardian is the spirit emanated upon us which is the bond between us and God. Just as we perceive Him in that light which He emanates upon us—as it is said: *In thy light we see light* (Psalm 36:9)—so God looks down upon us by the same light. Because of it God is perpetually with us looking down upon us from above, *Can any hide himself in secret places that I shall not see him, saith the Lord* (Jeremiah 23:24).[5]

AWE AND FEAR

According to the Bible the principal religious virtue is *yirah*. What is the nature of *yirah?* The word has two meanings: *fear* and *awe*. There is the man who fears the Lord lest he be punished in his body, family, or in his possessions. Another man fears the Lord because he is afraid of punishment in the life to come. Both types are considered inferior in Jewish tradition.[6] Job, who said, "Though He slay me, yet will I trust in Him," was not motivated in his piety by fear but rather by awe, by the realization of the grandeur of His eternal love.

Fear is the anticipation and expectation of evil or pain, as contrasted with hope which is the anticipation of good. Awe, on the other hand, is the sense of wonder and humility inspired by the sublime or felt in the presence of mystery. Fear is "a surrender of the succors which reason offers";[7] awe is the acquisition of insights which the world holds in store for us. Awe, unlike fear, does not make us shrink from the awe-inspiring object, but, on the contrary, draws us near to it. This is why awe is compatible with both love[8] and joy.[9]

In a sense, awe is the antithesis of fear. To feel "The Lord is my light and my salvation" is to feel "Whom shall I fear?" (Psalms 27:1).[10] "God is my refuge and my strength. A very present help in trouble. Therefore will we not fear, though the earth do change, and though the mountains be moved into the heart of the seas" (Psalms 46:2-3).

AWE PRECEDES FAITH

Awe precedes faith; it is at the root of faith. We must grow in awe in order to reach faith. We must be guided by awe to be worthy of faith. Awe rather than faith is the cardinal attitude of the religious Jew. It is "the beginning and gateway of faith, the first precept of all, and upon it the whole world is established."[11] In Judaism, *yirat hashem,* the awe of God, or *yirat shamayim,* the "awe of heaven," is almost equivalent to the word "religion." In Biblical language the religious man is not called "believer," as he is for example in Islam *(mu'min),* but *yare hashem.*

77

There is thus only one way to wisdom: awe. Forfeit your sense of awe, let your conceit diminish your ability to revere, and the universe becomes a market place for you. The loss of awe is the great block to insight. A return to reverence is the first prerequisite for a revival of wisdom, for the discovery of the world as an allusion to God. Wisdom comes from awe rather than from shrewdness. It is evoked not in moments of calculation but in moments of being in rapport with the mystery of reality. The greatest insights happen to us in moments of awe.

A moment of awe is a moment of self-consecration. They who sense the wonder share in the wonder. They who keep holy the things that are holy shall themselves become holy.[12]

NOTES FOR CHAPTER 7

[1] Psalms 111:10; Proverbs 9:10; see Proverbs 1:7; 15:33; Ecclesiastes 12:13; Sirach 25:12-13; and *The Sayings of the Fathers,* III, 21:

> Where there is no wisdom, there is no awe;
> Where there is no awe, there is no wisdom.

[2] Job 28:28.

[3] See *Man is Not Alone,* p. 286.

[4] *Zohar,* vol. I, 11b. In the opening paragraph of the *Shulchan Aruch,* the Code of Laws, the word of the Psalmist, *I keep the Lord always before me* (16:8) is described as *"the basic principle of the Torah"* (according to Rabbi Moshe Isserles). It was a requirement in Jewish piety to be constantly aware of His presence. As an aid to such remembrance, it was suggested that one constantly keep before the inner eye the four letters of the Ineffable Name. Paraphrasing the verse in Psalms 32:2, it was said, that blessed is he to whom not to think of God for one moment is a sin.

[5] Maimonides, *The Guide of the Perplexed,* vol. III, ch. 52. Translated by Ch. Rabin, London, 1952.

[6] In regard to God, *yirah* is used in the Bible primarily in the sense of awe. See Gesenius-Driver-Briggs, *Hebrew and English Lexicon of the Old Testament,* Oxford, 1906, p. 431. Compare also "Ye shall fear every man his mother and his father" (Leviticus 19:3), corresponding to the words in the Decalogue, "Revere" or "Honor thy father and mother" (Exodus 20:12); see Hosea 3:5. See also Robert H. Pfeiffer, The Fear of God, in *Eretz Israel,* vol. III, p. 59f. In some places, *yirah* does indeed mean dread of God's punishment in consequence of sin. See Abraham Ibn Daud, *Emunah Ramah,* Frankfurt a.M., 1852, p. 100, and Joseph Albo, *Ikkarim,* ed. Husik, Philadelphia, 1930, vol. III, ch. 34.

A philosophy of Judaism

According to Louis Finkelstein, *Mabo le-Massektot Abot ve-Abot d'Rabbi Natan*, New York, 1950, p. 33 f, the School of Shammai held an opposite view of the relation of fear and love.

[7] The Wisdom of Solomon 17:12.

[8] See Albo, *Ikkarim*, ed. Husik, Philadelphia, 1930, vol. III, ch. 32.

[9] Deuteronomy 10:12; see Psalms 2:11. Compare *Seder Eliahu Rabba*, ch. 3: "I feared in my joy, I rejoiced in my fear, and my love prevailed over all."

[10] See also Psalms 23:1,4; 102:26-29; 112:7.

[11] *Zohar*, vol. I, p. 11b. See *Shabbat* 31b. Compare *Man is Not Alone*, p. 146.

[12] See *Wisdom* 6:10.

8 Glory

THE GLORY IS THE INEFFABLE

In his great vision Isaiah perceives the voice of the seraphim even *before* he hears the voice of the Lord. What is it that the seraphim reveal to Isaiah: "Holy, holy, holy is the Lord of hosts; *the whole earth is full of His glory"* (6:3). It is proclaimed not as a messianic promise but as a fact. *Man* may not sense it, but *the seraphim* announce it. It is the first utterance which Isaiah perceived as a prophet. Ezekiel, too, when the heavens were opened by the river Chebar, hears the voice of a great rushing, "Blessed be the glory of the Lord from His place" (3:12). And when again "the hand of the Lord was upon Ezekiel," he saw: "The glory of the God of Israel came from the way of the east; and His voice was like the sound of many waters; and the earth did shine with His glory" (43:2). In the Pentateuch the fact that the glory of God pervades the world is expressed in the name of God. "And the Lord said . . . in very deed, as I live—and as *the earth is filled with the glory of the Lord . . ."* (Numbers 14:21).

Is the presence of the glory in the world a divine secret, something known to God and the seraphim alone? According to the Psalmist, *"The heavens declare the glory of God"* (19:2). How do they declare it? How do they reveal it? *"Day unto day utters speech, and night unto night reveals knowledge."* Speech? Knowledge? What is the language, what are the words in which the heavens express the glory? *"There is no speech, there are no words, neither*

80

is their voice heard." And yet, "Their radiation goes out through all the earth, and their words to the end of the world" (Psalms 19:4-5). The song of the heavens is *ineffable.*

The glory is concealed, yet there are moments in which it is revealed, particularly to the prophets. During the sojourn in the wilderness it happened more than once that "the glory of the Lord appeared unto all the people" (Leviticus 9:23; Numbers 16:19, 17:7, 20:6), so that the Book of Deuteronomy could acknowledge that "the Lord our God hath shown us His glory" (Deuteronomy 5:21).[1]

THE GLORY IS NOT A THING

What is the nature and meaning of the glory or, as it was frequently called in later times, the *Shechinah?* Since the glory was often revealed in a cloud and its appearance compared with a devouring fire (Exodus 24:17), it was sometimes characterized as a purely external manifestation, entirely divested of inner content; an exhibition of power, never of the spirit.[2] Yet such a conception is erroneous. Is it possible to substitute fire or cloud for glory in the prophecy of Haggai (2:7): "I will fill this house with glory"? Or in the words of the Psalmist (85:10): "Surely His salvation is nigh them that fear Him, that [His] glory may dwell in our land"? Is it, moreover, conceivable that this is what the seraphim proclaim: the whole earth is full of fire or cloud?

It is true that the glory as a prophetic manifestation does not appear undisguised. A sublime phenomenon such as storm, fire, cloud, or lightning (Exodus 24:15ff; 40:34ff; I Kings 8:11) provides a "setting for the glory; it is not the glory itself."[3]

Nor is the glory the same as the essence or existence of God. The Psalmist's prayer, "May the glory of God be for ever" (104:31) cannot be taken to mean, "May the existence of God continue for ever"; this would be blasphemous.

81

What, then, is the nature of the glory? Perhaps this was what Moses was anxious to know when he prayed, "Show me, I pray Thee, Thy glory." His prayer was granted, and the Lord said, "I will make all My goodness pass before thee" (Exodus 33:18-19). The glory, then, is not a physical phenomenon. It is equated with the goodness of God.

And this is how the glory was revealed. Moses stood alone on the top of the mount, the glory passed by, "the Lord descended in the cloud," and the great answer was revealed:

> The Lord, the Lord, God, merciful and gracious,
> long-suffering, and abundant in goodness and
> truth; keeping mercy unto the thousandth
> generation, forgiving iniquity and transgression
> and sin; and that will by no means clear the
> guilty; visiting the iniquity of the fathers
> upon the children and upon the children's children
> unto the third and unto the fourth generation.
> Exodus 34:6-7

The glory is the presence, not the essence of God; an act rather than a quality; a process not a substance. Mainly the glory manifests itself as a power overwhelming the world. Demanding homage, it is a power that descends to guide, to remind. The glory reflects abundance of good and truth, the power that acts in nature and history.

The whole earth is full of His glory. It does not mean that the glory fills the earth in the way in which the ether fills space or water fills the ocean. It means that the whole earth is full of His presence.[4]

THE LIVING PRESENCE

In English the phrase that a person "has presence" is hard to define. There are people whose being here and now is felt, even though they do not display themselves in action or speech. They have "presence." There are other people who may be here all the time, and no one will be aware of their presence. Of a person whose outwardness communicates something of his indwelling power or greatness, whose soul is radiant and conveys itself without words, we say he has presence.

The whole earth is full of His glory. The outwardness of the world communicates something of the indwelling greatness of God, which is radiant and conveys itself without words. *"There is no speech, there are no words, neither is their voice heard."* And yet, *"their radiation goes out through all the earth and their words to the end of the world"* (Psalms 19:4-5).

The glory is neither an esthetic nor a physical category. It is sensed in grandeur, but it is more than grandeur. It is, as we said, a living presence or *the effulgence of a living presence.*

THE KNOWLEDGE OF THE GLORY

Is the glory something that is seen, heard, or clearly apprehended? In the same vision in which the ubiquity of the glory is revealed to Isaiah, an intimation of man's *suspended sensibility* is proclaimed:

> Go, and say to the people:
> "Hear and hear, but do not understand;
> See and see, but do not perceive."
> Make the heart of this people fat,
> and their ears heavy
> and shut their eyes;
> Lest they see with their eyes,
> and hear with their ears,
> And understand with their hearts,
> and turn and be healed.
> Isaiah 6:9-10

The whole earth is full of His glory, but we do not perceive it; it is within our reach but beyond our grasp.

Lo, He passes by me, and I see Him not;
He moves on, but I do not perceive Him.
Job 9:11

The earth is filled with the glory; it is not filled with knowledge of the glory. In the time to come, "the earth shall *be filled with the knowledge of the glory of the Lord,* as the waters cover the sea" (Habakuk 2:14). Now the glory is *concealed;* in the time to come *"The glory of the Lord shall be revealed,* and all flesh shall see it together" (Isaiah 40:5). It is in this messianic sense that the Psalmist prays, "Let the whole world be filled with His glory. Amen and Amen" (72:19).[5] And still, the glory is not entirely unknown to us. That not only the heavens are able to declare it, may be seen from the fact that we are all called upon: "Declare His glory among the nations, His marvels among all the peoples" (I Chronicles 16:24; see also Psalms 145:5). We have no words to describe the glory; we have no adequate way of knowing it. Yet what is decisive is not our knowing it but our awareness of *being known* by it.

Thou compasseth my path and my lying down,
Thou art acquainted with all my ways.
For there is not a word in my tongue,
But lo, O Lord, Thou knowest it altogether.

Whither shall I go from Thy spirit?
Or whither shall I flee from Thy presence?
If I ascend up into heaven, Thou art there;
If I make my bed in the netherworld, behold Thou art there.
If I take the wings of the morning,
And dwell in the uttermost parts of the sea;
Even there would Thy hand lead me,
And Thy right hand would hold me.
And if I say: "Surely the darkness shall envelop me,
And the light about me shall be night";
Even the night shineth as the day;
The darkness is even as the light.
Psalms 139:3-4, 7-12

Standing face to face with the world, we often sense a spirit which surpasses our ability to comprehend. The world is too much for us. It is crammed with marvel. The glory is not an exception but an aura that lies about all being, a spiritual setting of reality.

To the religious man it is as if things stood with their backs to him, their faces turned to God, as if the glory of things consisted in their being an object of divine thought.[6]

BLINDNESS TO THE WONDER

The perception of the glory is a rare occurrence in our lives. We fail to wonder, we fail to respond to the presence. This is the tragedy of every man: "to dim all wonder by indifference." Life is routine, and routine is resistance to the wonder. "Replete is the world with a spiritual radiance, replete with sublime and marvelous secrets. But a small hand held against the eye hides it all," said the Baal Shem. "Just as a small coin held over the face can block out the sight of a mountain, so can the vanities of living block out the sight of the infinite light."[7]

The wonders are daily with us,* and yet "the miracle is not recognized by him who experiences it."[8] Its apprehension is not a matter of physical perception. "Of what avail is an open eye, if the heart is blind?"[9] One may see many things without observing them —"his ears are open, but he does not hear."[10]

"The word of the Lord came to me: 'Son of man, you dwell in the midst of a rebellious house, who have eyes to see, but see not, who have ears to hear but hear not.' "[11]

"Alas for people that they see but do not know what they see, they stand and do not know on what they stand."[12]

HARDNESS OF HEART

In the Bible, callousness is the root of sin. There are many words to express it: "stubbornness of heart," "hardness of heart" (Deuter-

* See above, p. 48 f.

onomy 29:18; Lamentations 3:65); "brazen-faced and stiff-hearted" (Ezekiel 2:4); "stout-hearted" (Isaiah 46:12); "uncircumcised in the heart" (Jeremiah 9:25). "The heart [of the godless] is gross like fat," exclaims the Psalmist (119:70).

The prophets continually reproach Israel for lack of sensib lity:

> He sees many things but does not observe them;
> His ears are open, but he does not hear.
>
> Isaiah 42:20

In a mood of bitterness the prophet complains that callousness has been the permanent condition of the people:

> You have never heard, you have never known,
> From of old your ear has not been opened.
> For I knew that you would deal very treacherously,
> And that from birth you were called a rebel.
>
> Isaiah 48:8

> Our fathers, when they were in Egypt did not consider
>   Thy wonderful works;
> They did not remember the abundance of Thy steadfast love,
> But rebelled against the Most High at the Red Sea.
>
> Psalms 106:7

NOTES FOR CHAPTER 8

1 See also Exodus 16:6, 7, 10; 24:16f.

2 See I. Abrahams, *The Glory of God*, Oxford, 1925, p. 17, in refutation of A. Von Gall, *Die Herrlichkeit Gottes*, Giessen, 1900.

3 I. Abrahams, op. cit., p. 24f.

4 *Kavod*, the Hebrew word for glory, means in its root "heaviness," the fact of being heavy, then wealth, strength, honor, fame, dignity, and worth. But it also means *the higher soul* as evidenced in Psalms 30:13; 16:9; 57:9; 7:6; and Genesis 49:6. Thus the psalmist says: "My heart is steadfast; I will sing and give praise even with my glory." (108:2). Compare Qimhi, *Sefer ha-Sherashim*, Berlin, 1847, p. 311; cf. I. Abrahams, *The Glory of God*, p. 18 and Pedersen, *Israel*, I-II, index, under *kabhodh*. In our study we are only concerned with *kavod* as applied to God. It would, of course, be meaningless to assume that in the most sublime prophetic vision the seraphim would proclaim, "Holy, holy, holy is the Lord of hosts. The whole earth is full of His fame."

5 See also Isaiah 59:19; 60:1-3; 66:18; Psalms 97:1, 4-6.

6 *Man is Not Alone*, p. 63f.

A philosophy of Judaism

[7] *Likkute Maharan,* I, 133. "Rabbi Helbo said: The wine of Perugitha (a place in northern Israel famous for its wine) and the water of Diomsith cut off the ten tribes from Israel (they were so much preoccupied with these pleasures that they neglected learning and lost faith, which ultimately led to their exile and disappearance)." "Rabbi Eleazar ben Arak visited that place and was attracted to [its inhabitants and their luxurious life] and [in consequence] his learning vanished. When he returned to [his home town], he arose to read in the Scroll [of the Torah]. He wished to read, *Hahodesh hazeh lakem* [*This month shall be unto you a beginning*] (Exodus 12:2), [instead of which he read] *haharesh hayah libbam* (which means, their heart was silent or callous). He misread one letter in each word of the text." *Shabbat* 147a.

[8] See *Niddah,* 31a.

[9] Ibn Gabirol, *A Choice of Pearls,* ed. Ascher, London, 1859, p. 82.

[10] Isaiah 42:20.

[11] Ezekiel 12:1; see Jeremiah 5:21.

[12] *Hagigah,* 12b. To the wicked, the spiritual light that is hidden from the eyes of the body is indistinguishable from darkness. This is due to their blindness. *If they were wise, they would understand this, they would discern* (Deuteronomy 32:29). *Yet they know not, neither do they understand; they go about in darkness.* They do not even know that they walk in the darkness. They are like him who gropes at noonday "as the blind gropes in the darkness." It is a double darkness: they are blind and they are not aware of their blindness. Rabbi Phinehas Horowitz, *Hamakneh,* preface.

9 The World

No one is without a sense of awe, a need to adore, an urge to worship. The question only is what to adore, or more specifically, what object is worthy of our supreme worship. "The starry heavens above ... fill the mind with ever new and increasing admiration and awe." Indeed, it is hard to live under a sky full of stars and not be struck by its mystery. The sun is endowed with power and beauty, for all eyes to see. Who could refrain from extolling its grandeur? Who could go beyond the realization: nature is the ultimate mystery; and mystery is the end?

The Greeks regarded the elemental powers of nature as holy. Expressions such as "the holy rain" or "the holy light" are characteristic of their attitude.[1] "O Nature, how we worship thee even against our wills," Seneca confesses.[2] In *King Lear* Edmund exclaims, "Thou, nature, art my goddess; to thy law my services are bound."[3] Belarius says, "Stoop boys: this gate instructs you how to *adore the heavens,* and bows you to a morning's holy office."[4]

The religion of nature, the worship of the grandeur of the given, has always had its votaries. Despite the injunction, "Beware lest you lift up your eyes to heaven, and when you see the sun and the moon and the stars, all the host of heaven, you be drawn away and worship them" (Deuteronomy 4:19), there were, even in the times of the Babylonian Exile, those who turned their faces to the east and worshiped the sun.[5]

Indeed, the beauty of nature may become a menace to our spiritual understanding; there is a deadly risk of being enchanted by its power.

> If I have looked at the sun when it shone,
> Or the moon moving in splendor,
> And my heart has been secretly enticed,
> And my mouth has kissed my hand;
> This also would be an iniquity to be punished by the judges,
> For I should have been false to God above.
>
> Job 31:26-28

THE DISILLUSIONMENT

It was in the romantic movement that a new religious enthusias.n for nature began, which lingers on in many minds to this very day. Nature assumed ultimate significance and became the supreme object of adoration, the only source of comfort and salvation, and the final arbiter of values. To love her, to hold communion with her, to expose oneself to her healing sympathy was the highest form of religious experience. The god Pan was resurrected. But soon he died again, when the post-romantic man discovered that nature could not save him; nature is herself in need of salvation. Pitiless is the silence of the sky. Nature is deaf to our cries and indifferent to our values. Her laws know no mercy, no forbearance. They are inexorable, implacable, ruthless.

The Greeks would address earth and air and sun, unburdening their woes. "But of belief in the power of nature to comfort the heart, to subdue the passions, and to speak peace to the souls of men we find no trace in Greek poetry. Greek sentiment does not endorse the words of Cowper—'The spleen is seldom felt when Flora reigns.' The Greeks did not take nature medicinally. Inert matter having no moral life of its own could give no moral impulse."[6]

"To commune with the heart of Nature—this has been the accredited mode since the days of Wordsworth. Nature, Coleridge assures us, has ministrations by which she heals her erring and distempered child. . . .

"I do not believe that Nature has a heart; and I suspect that, like many another beauty, she has been credited with a heart because of her face. . . . What, indeed, does she want with a heart or brain? She knows that she is beautiful, and she is placidly content with the knowledge; she was made to be gazed on, and she fulfills the end of her creation. . . . She cannot give what she does not need; and if we were but similarly organized, we should be independent of sympathy. A man cannot go straight to his objects, because he has a heart; he cannot eat, drink, sleep, make money, and be satisfied, because he has a heart. It is a mischievous thing, and wise men accordingly take the earliest opportunity of giving it away.

"Yet the thing is, after all, too deep for jest. What is this heart of Nature, if it exist at all? Is it, according to the conventional doctrine derived from Wordsworth and Shelley, a heart of love, according with the heart of man, and stealing out to him through a thousand avenues of mute sympathy? No; in this sense I repeat seriously what I said lightly: Nature has no heart."[7]

The gradual decline of naturalism in contemporary art and philosophy is in a sense a movement of spiritual iconoclasm. At the same time, nature, once the object of ultimate adoration, threatens to become a source of ultimate despair. To Judaism, the adoration of nature is as absurd as the alienation from nature is unnecessary.

THE DESANCTIFICATION OF NATURE

Biblical thinking succeeded in subduing the universal tendency of ancient man to endow nature with a mysterious potency like mana and orenda by stressing the indication in all nature of the wisdom and goodness of the Creator.

One of the great achievements of the prophets was the repudiation of nature as an object of adoration. They tried to teach us that neither nature's beauty nor grandeur, neither power nor the state, neither money nor things of space are worthy of our supreme

A philosophy of Judaism

adoration, love, sacrifice, or self-dedication. Yet the *desanctification of nature* did not in any way bring about an alienation of nature. It brought man together with all things in a fellowship of praise. The Biblical man could say that he was "In league with the stones of the field" (Job 5:23).

WHAT IS GIVEN IS NOT THE ULTIMATE

What then is the ultimate? What object is worthy of our supreme worship? These questions are involved in all problems which man continues to struggle with to this very day. The Western man must choose between the worship of God and the worship of nature. The Bible asserts that for all her power and preciousness, beauty and grandeur, nature is not everything. It calls upon us to remember that what is given is not the ultimate. It calls upon us not to let the world stand as a wall between us and God.

To the Greek mind the universe is the sum and substance of all there is; even the gods are a part of, rather than the cause of, the universe. "The world (cosmos), the same for all, was not made by any god or man but was always, and is, and shall be."[8] The universe to Plato is "a visible living being . . . a perceptible god . . . the greatest, best, fairest, most perfect."[9] "O Nature, from thee are all things, in thee are all things, to thee all things return."[10]

In contrast, the Biblical mind is deeply aware that the ultimate, God, is beyond the given. What is given is not ultimate but created by Him Who is not given. Nowhere in the Bible is the reality of the universe questioned, but at the same time a certainty prevails that for all its greatness the universe is as nothing compared with its Maker. "The heaven is My throne, and the earth is My footstool" (Isaiah 66:1). "All the nations are as nothing before Him; they are accounted by Him as things of nought, and vanity" (Isaiah 40:17). Perhaps it was such an awareness that made possible the famous words: "Vanity of vanities, says Koheleth, vanity of vanities, all is vanity. What profit has man of all his labor, wherein he laboreth under the sun?" (Ecclesiastes 1:2-3).

To the Greeks as to many other peoples, the earth is generally known as *Mother Earth*. She is the mother who sends up fruits, the giver of children, and to her men return at death. Greek poetry and drama exalt the divinity of the earth, and according to Plutarch, "The name of *Ge* is dear and precious to every Hellene, and it is our tradition to honor her like any other god." The adoration of the beauty and abundance of the earth in Greek literature is tinged with a sense of gratefulness to the earth for her gifts to man.

Such a concept is alien to the Biblical man.[11] He recognizes only one parent: God as his father. The earth is his sister rather than his mother. Man and earth are equally the creations of God. The prophets and the Psalmist do not honor or exalt the earth, though dwelling upon her grandeur and abundance. They utter praise to Him who created her.

THE CONTINGENCY OF NATURE

To the Biblical man, the power of God is behind all phenomena,[12] and he is more concerned to know the will of God who governed nature than to know the order of nature itself. Important and impressive as nature is to him, God is vastly more so. That is why Psalm 104 is a hymn to God rather than an ode to the cosmos.

The idea of the cosmos is one of the outstanding contributions of Greek philosophy, and we can well understand why a similar conception did not emerge in Hebrew thinking. For the idea of a cosmos, of a totality of things, complete in itself, implies the concept of an immanent norm of nature, of an order which has its foundation in nature.

But what are the foundations of nature? To the Greeks who take the world for granted Nature, Order is the answer. To the Biblical mind in its radical amazement nature, order are not an answer but a problem: why is there order, being, at all?

What are the foundations of the earth? There are no natural foundations. The foundations of the world are not of this world. The earth continues to exist because of Him

God in search of man

That sits above the circle of the earth
And the inhabitants thereof are as grasshoppers . . .
That brings princes to nothing.
He makes the judges of the earth as a thing of naught,
Scarce are they planted
Scarce are they sown
Scarce has their stock taken root in the earth;
When He blows upon them, they wither,
And the whirlwind takes them away as stubble.

Isaiah 40:22-24

Now the Biblical man, of course, is conscious of an order of nature which could be relied upon in daily life. But that order is one which was invested in nature by the will of God and remains constantly dependent upon Him. It is not an immanent law but a divine decree that dominates everything. God had given His decree to the sea; He had appointed the foundations of the earth (Proverbs 8:29); and He continued to rule the world from without. Nature is the object of His perpetual care, but this very dependence of nature on divine care is an expression of its contingency. Biblical man does not take anything for granted, and to him the laws of nature are as much in need of derivation as the processes ruled by these laws. The continued existence of the world is guaranteed by God's faithfulness to this covenant. "Thus says the Lord: if My covenant be not with day and night . . ." (Jeremiah 33:25). The world is not an ontological necessity. Indeed, heaven and earth may not last for ever:

Of old Thou didst lay the foundation of the earth;
And the heavens are the work of Thy hands.
They shall perish, but Thou shalt endure;
Yea, all of them shall wax like a garment;
As a vesture shalt Thou change them, and they shall pass away;
But Thou are the selfsame,
And Thy years shall have no end.

Psalms 102:26-28[13]

93

The world is not the *all* to the Bible, and so the *all* could never come to denote the world. Biblical man is not enchanted by the given. He realizes the alternative, namely the annihilation of the given. He is not enchanted by the order, because he has a vision of a new order. He is not lost to the here and now, nor to the beyond. He senses the non-given with the given, the past and future with the present. He is taught that "the mountains may depart, the hills be removed, but My kindness shall not depart from thee . . ." (Isaiah 54:10). The Hebrew conception has been rightly characterized by A. N. Whitehead as the doctrine of the *imposed* law, as contrasted with the doctrine of the *immanent* law developed in Greek philosophy. According to the doctrine of the *imposed* law, there is imposed on each existent the necessity of entering into relationships with the other constituents of nature. These imposed behavior patterns are the laws of nature. Newton, for example, clearly states that the correlated modes of behavior of the bodies forming the solar system require God for the imposition of the principles on which all depend.

The doctrine of the imposed law leads to the monotheistic conception of God as essentially transcendent and only accidentally immanent; while the doctrine of the immanent law leads to the pantheistic doctrine of God as essentially immanent and in no way transcendent. "Subsequent speculation," Whitehead points out,[14] "wavers between these two extremes, seeking their reconciliation. In this, as in most other matters, the history of Western thought consists in the attempted fusion of ideas which in their origin are predominantly Hellenic, with ideas which in their origin are predominantly Semitic."

In a profound sense, the question: what is reality? what is the world to the Biblical man? is best answered by another question: what is the world to God? To him the subject matter of the question—the world—is too wondrous to be fully comprehended in relation to man. The world in its ultimate significance must be understood in relation to God, and the answer to the question is: all things are His servants.

A philosophy of Judaism

For ever, O Lord,
Thy word stands fast in heaven.
Thy faithfulness is unto all generations;
Thou hast established the earth, and it stands,
They stand this day according to Thine ordinances;
For all things are Thy servants.

Psalm 119:89-91

THE FALLACY OF ISOLATION

The prophets attacked what may be called the fallacy of isolation. Things and events, man and the world, cannot be treated apart from the will of God but only as inseparable parts of an occasion in which the divine is at stake. Paraphrasing the verse, "that thou canst not stir a flower without troubling a star," a prophet might say, "thou canst not offend a human being without affecting the living God." We are taught to believe that where man loves man His name is sanctified; that in the harmony of husband and wife dwells the presence of God.

To the Biblical man, the sublime is but a form in which the presence of God strikes forth. Things do not always stand still. The stars sing; the mountains tremble in His presence.[15] To think of God man must hear the world. Man is not alone in celebrating God. To praise Him is to join all things in their song to Him. Our kinship with nature is a kinship of praise. All beings praise God. We live in a community of praise.

NATURE IN ADORATION OF GOD

Few are the songs in the Bible that celebrate the beauty of nature, and these songs are ample testimony to the fact that the Biblical man was highly sensitive to form, color, force and motion. However, since the link between the world and God was not broken in his mind, the beauty of the universe was not the supreme object of his adoration. To the Biblical man, the beauty of the world issued from the grandeur of God; His majesty towered beyond the breath-

95

taking mystery of the universe. Rather than being crushed by the mystery, he was inspired to praise the majesty. And rather than praise the world for its beauty, he called upon the world to praise its Creator.

What the Psalmist felt in meeting the world is succinctly expressed in the exclamation:

> Sing unto the Lord a new song;
> Sing unto the Lord, all the earth.
>
> Psalms 96:1

> Praise Him, sun and moon,
> Praise Him, all you shining stars!
> Praise Him, you highest heavens,
> And you waters above the heavens . . .
> Praise the Lord from the earth,
> You sea-monsters and all deeps,
> Fire and hail, snow and frost,
> Stormy wind fulfilling His command!
> Mountains and all hills,
> Fruit trees and all cedars!
> Beasts and all cattle,
> Creeping things and flying birds!
>
> Psalms 148:3-9

The Egyptian priest could not call upon the stars to praise the gods. He believed that the soul of Isis sparkled in Sirius, the soul of Horus in Orion, and the soul of Typhon in the Great Bear;[16] it was beyond his scope to conceive that all beings stand in awe and worship God. To the Biblical mind, the whole of creation was called into being by God unto His glory, and each creature has its own hymn of praise with which to extol the Creator. "All Thy works praise Thee" (Psalms 145:10). It is a belief that is repeatedly avowed in Jewish liturgy.

There is a small Hebrew book, written in the Middle Ages, called *The Chapter of Song,* which contains eighty-four songs that the heavenly and earthly beings utter in praise of God. Stars and clouds, wind and rain, springs and rivers, trees and vegetables, beasts and birds—every creature has its own song.[17]

A THING THROUGH GOD

According to the Bible, the "inner" life of nature is closed to man. The Bible does not claim that things speak to man; it only claims that things speak to God. Inanimate objects are dead in relation to man; they are alive in relation to God. They sing to God. The mountains melt like wax, the waters tremble at the presence of the Lord (Psalms 77:17; 97:5). "Tremble, O earth, at the presence of the Lord, at the presence of the God of Jacob" (Psalms 114:7).

Whose ear has heard the trees sing to God? Has our reason ever thought of calling upon the sun to praise the Lord? And yet, what the ear fails to perceive, what reason fails to conceive, the Bible makes clear to our souls. It is a higher truth, to be grasped by the spirit.

Modern man dwells upon the order and power of nature; the prophets dwell upon the grandeur and creation of nature. The former directs his attention to the manageable and intelligible aspect of the universe; the latter to its mystery and marvel. What the prophets sense in nature is not a direct reflection of God but an allusion to Him. Nature is not a part of God but rather a fulfillment of His will.

Lift up your eyes on high and see who created these. There is a higher form of seeing. We must learn how to lift up our eyes on high in order to see that the world is more a question than an answer. The world's beauty and power are as naught compared to Him. The grandeur of nature is only the beginning. *Beyond the grandeur is God.*

The Biblical man does not see nature in isolation but in relation to God. "At the beginning God created heaven and earth"—these few words set forth the contingency and absolute dependence of all of reality. What, then, is reality? To the Western man, it is *a thing in itself;* to the Biblical Man, it is *a thing through God.* Looking at

97

a thing his eyes see not so much form, color, force and motion as an act of God. The world is a gate, not a wall.

Greek philosophy began in a world without God. It could not accept the gods or the example of their conduct. Plato had to break with the gods and to ask: What is good? Thus the problem of values was born. And it was the idea of values that took the place of God. Plato lets Socrates ask: What is good? But Moses' question was: What does God require of thee?

There is no word in Biblical Hebrew for doubt; there are many expressions of wonder. Just as in dealing with judgments our starting point is doubt, wonder is the Biblical starting point in facing reality. The Biblical man's sense for the mind-surpassing grandeur of reality prevented the power of doubt from setting up its own independent dynasty. Doubt is an act in which the mind inspects its own ideas; wonder is an act in which the mind confronts the universe. Radical skepticism is the outgrowth of subtle conceit and self-reliance. Yet there was no conceit in the prophets and no self-reliance in the Psalmist.

And so the Biblical man never asks: Is there a God? To ask such a question, in which doubt is expressed as to which of two possible attitudes is true, means to accept the power and validity of a third attitude, namely the attitude of doubt. The Bible does not know doubt as an absolute attitude. For there is no doubt in which faith is not involved. The questions advanced in the Bible are of a different kind.

Lift up your eyes on high and see, Who created thee?

This does not reflect a process of thinking that is neatly arranged in the order of doubt first, and faith second; first the question, then the answer. It reflects a situation in which the mind stands *face to face* with the mystery rather than with its own concepts.

98

A philosophy of Judaism

A question is an interrogative sentence calling for either a positive or a negative answer. But the sentence *Who created these?* is a question that contains the impossibility of giving a negative answer; it is an answer in disguise; a question of amusement, not of curiosity. This, then, is the prophet's thesis: there is a way of asking the great question which can only elicit an affirmative answer. What is the way?

"At the end of the days I, Nebuchadnezzar, lifted my eyes to heaven, and my power of knowledge returned to me." This confession of the king of Babylon reported in the Book of Daniel (4:31), gives us an inkling of how to recover one's ability to ask the ultimate question: *to lift the eyes to heaven.* It is the same expression that Isaiah used: "Lift up your eyes on high and see, Who created these?"

The following parable was told by Rabbi Nahman of Bratslav.

There was a prince who lived far away from his father the king, and he was very, very homesick for his father. Once he received a letter from his father, and he was overjoyed and treasured it. Yet, the joy and the delight that the letter gave him increased his longing even more. He would sit and complain: "Oh, oh, if I could only touch his hand! If he would extend his hand to me, how I would embrace it. I would kiss every finger in my great longing for my father, my teacher, my light. Merciful father, how I would love to touch at least your little finger!" And while he was complaining, feeling and longing for a touch of his father, a thought flashed in his mind: Don't I have my father's letter, written in his own hand! Is not the handwriting of the king comparable to his hand? And a great joy burst forth in him.

When I look at the heavens, the work of Thy fingers.
Psalms 8:4

NOTES FOR CHAPTER 9

[1] Sophocles, *Oedipus Tyrannus*, 1424-1429; *Electra*, 86-95.
[2] *Hippolitus*, Act IV, 1116.
[3] *King Lear*, Act I, Scene 2, 1-2.

99

4 *Cymbeline,* Act III, Scene 3, 2-7.
5 Ezekiel 8:16; compare II Kings 17:16; 21:3.
6 G. Soutar, *Nature in Greek Poetry,* London, 1939, pp. 178-191.
7 *The Works of Francis Thompson,* vol. III, pp. 80-81. See Will Herberg, *Judaism and Modern Man,* New York, 1951, p. 34.
8 Diels, *Die Fragmente der Vorsokratiker,* Heracleitus, fr. 30.
9 *Timaeus,* end.
10 Marcus Aurelius, *Meditations,* IV, 23.
11 The phrase in *Sirach* 40:1, referring to earth as "the mother of all living" has often been misinterpreted as expressing the conceptions of the earth as the mother of man. The true meaning, it seems to us, is a reference to the recesses of the earth as the realm of the life after death. Compare Ezekiel 26:20; 32:32; Job 1:21; Psalms 116:9. In Psalms 139:15, reference is not to the earth but to the recesses of the earth. God is He who formed man; the recesses of the earth were the place of that formation. Compare IV *Ezra* 5:28.
12 Every occurrence in nature was regarded as an act of divine providence; cp. Isaiah 40:26; Job 27:4-6.
13 Compare Abravanal, *Mifalot Elohim,* VII, 3. Following Saadia, Abravanal supports his thesis of the destructibility of the universe with references from rabbinic literature. Maimonides, *The Guide of the Perplexed,* II, ch. 27 and 29; Gersonides, *Milhamot Hashem,* VI, 1.16, and, in modern times, Hermann Cohen, *Ethik des reinen Willens,* p. 387ff, maintain the thesis of the indestructibility.
14 *Adventures of Ideas,* p. 154.
15 Job 38:7; Psalms 114:4.
16 J. G. Frazer, *The Dying God,* p. 5.
17 See Louis Ginsberg, *The Legends of the Jews,* vol. I, p. 44 and vol. V, p. 60 n. 194.

10 A Question
Addressed to Us

The ideals we strive after, the values we try to fulfill, have they any significance in the realm of natural processes? The sun spends its rays upon the just and the wicked, upon flowers and snakes alike. The heart beats normally within those who torture and kill. Is all goodness and striving for veracity but a fiction of the mind to which nothing corresponds in reality? Where are the spirit's values valid? Within the inner life of man? But the spirit is a stranger in the soul. A demand such as "love thy neighbor as thyself" is not at home in the self.

We have in common a terrible loneliness. Day after day a question goes up desperately in our minds: Are we *alone* in the wilderness of the self, alone in this silent universe, of which we are a part, and in which we feel at the same time like strangers?

It is such a situation that makes us ready to search for a voice of God in the world of man: the taste of utter loneliness; the discovery that unless God has a voice, the life of the spirit is a freak; that the world without God is a torso; that a soul without faith is a stump.

NOT A SCIENTIFIC PROBLEM

What are the grounds for our certainty of the realness of God? It is clear that we cannot submit religion to scientific logic. Science is not the only way to truth, and its methods do not represent all of human thinking. Indeed, they are out of place in that dimension of human existence in which God is a burning issue.

God is not a scientific problem, and scientific methods are not capable of solving it. The reason why scientific methods are often thought to be capable of solving it is the success of their application in positive sciences. The fallacy involved in this analogy is that of treating God as if He were a phenomenon within the order of nature. The truth, however, is that the problem of God is not only related to phenomena within nature but to nature itself; not only to concepts within thinking but to thinking itself. It is a problem that refers to what surpasses nature, to what lies beyond all things and all concepts.

The moment we utter the name of God we leave the level of scientific thinking and enter the realm of the ineffable. Such a step is one which we cannot take scientifically, since it transcends the boundaries of all that is given. It is in spite of all warnings that man has never ceased to be stirred by ultimate questions. Science cannot silence him, because scientific terms are meaningless to the spirit that raises these questions, meaningless to the concern for a truth greater than the world that science is engaged in exploring.

God is not the only problem which is inaccessible to science. The problem of the origin of reality remains immune to it. There are aspects of given reality which are congruous with the categories of scientific logic, while there are aspects of reality which are inaccessible to this logic. Even some aspects and concepts of our own thinking are impregnable to analysis.

BEYOND DEFINITIONS

One of the earliest dialogues of Plato, the *Charmides,* is devoted to the examination of the question, what is temperance? Several definitions are offered but they all prove inadequate. Socrates then admits that temperance cannot be defined: "I have been utterly defeated, and have failed to discover what that is to which the

A philosophy of Judaism

imposer of names gave this name of temperance." There is a possibility of a man "knowing in a sort of way that which he does not know at all."

The deepest doctrines "do not admit of verbal expression like other studies." They can only be understood "as a result of continued application to the subject itself and communion therewith." Such understanding is "brought to birth in the soul on a sudden, as light that is kindled by a leaping spark, and thereafter it nourishes itself."[1]

It is impossible to define "goodness," or "fact," not because they stand for something irrational or meaningless, but because they stand for ideas that surpass the limits of any definition; they are super-rational rather than subrational. We cannot define "the holy" or utter in words what we mean in saying "blessed be He." What the "holy" refers to, what we mean by "blessed be He," lies beyond the reach of words. "The best part of beauty is that which a picture cannot express."[2]

If our basic concepts are impregnable to analysis, then we must not be surprised that the ultimate answers are not attainable by reason alone. If it is impossible to define "goodness," "value," or "fact," how should we ever succeed in defining what we mean by God? Every religious act and judgment involves the acceptance of the ineffable, the acknowledgement of the inconceivable. When the basic issues of religion, such as God, revelation, prayer, holiness, commandments, are dissolved into pedestrian categories and deprived of sublime relevance, they come close to being meaningless.

The categories of religious thinking, as said above, are unique and represent a way of thinking on a level that is deeper than the level of concepts, utterances, symbols. It is immediate, ineffable, metasymbolic. Teachers of religion have always attempted to raise their insights to the level of utterance, dogma, creed. Yet such utterances must be taken as indications, as attempts to convey what cannot be adequately expressed, if they are not to stand in the way of authentic faith.

The object of science is to explain the processes of nature. Every scientific explanation of a natural phenomenon rests upon the assumption that things behave in a way which is fundamentally rational and intelligible to the human reason.[3] Through the advancement of science, more and more phenomena are shown to be intelligible, thus confirming the assumption of the rationality of the way in which things behave and their compatibility with human reason. Many phenomena unapprehended today will in all probability be explained as scientific investigation continues to advance.

However, the essence of reality remains incompatible with our categories. Nature, being *as* being, and even the very act of thinking, lie beyond the scope of apprehension. The essence of things is ineffable and thus incompatible with the human mind, and it is precisely this *incompatibility* that is the source of all creative thinking in art, religion, and moral living. We may, therefore, suggest that just as the discovery of reality's compatibility with the human mind is the root of science, so the discovery of the world's incompatibility with the human mind is the root of artistic and religious insight. It is the realm of the ineffable, where the mystery is within reach of all thoughts, in which the ultimate problems of religion are born.

THE DIMENSION OF THE INEFFABLE

By the ineffable we do not mean the unknown as such; things unknown today may be known a thousand years from now. By the ineffable we mean that aspect of reality which by its very nature lies beyond our comprehension, and is acknowledged by the mind to be beyond the scope of the mind. Nor does the ineffable refer to a realm detached from the perceptible and the known. It refers to the correlation of the known and the unknown, of the knowable and the unknowable, upon which the mind comes in all its acts of thinking and feeling.

God in search of man

The sense of the ineffable is a sense for transcendence, a sense for the allusiveness of reality to a super-rational meaning. The ineffable, then, is a synonym for hidden meaning rather than for absence of meaning. It stands for a dimension which in the Bible is called glory, a dimension so real and sublime that it stuns our ability to adore it, and fills us with awe rather than curiosity.

The universe with its millions upon millions of bodies, the farthest of which is an incomprehensible distance away from the globe, is without any reference to the needs of life as we comprehend it. From the point of view of man, the universe seems to be without aim or purpose, and it would appear meaningless if man were the measure of meaning. But here we are guilty of a contradiction. How could man be a measure of meaning if ultimately there is no meaning? Faced with the mind-surpassing grandeur of the universe, we cannot but admit that there is meaning which is greater than man. There seem to be two courses of human thinking: one begins with man and his needs and ends in assuming that the universe is a meaningless display or a waste of energy; the other begins in amazement, in awe and humility and ends in the assumption that the universe is full of a glory that surpasses man and his mind, but is of eternal meaning to Him who made being possible.

Let us recall what was said elsewhere[4] in answer to the question: What may we legitimately assert about the endless sweep of mystery in which our souls are caught? Is it unknown and out of consonance with our categories because of its being void of sense? We have suggested that unless our insights of awe are signs of madness, and scorn for the grandeur and mystery of the universe the only valid attitude of the soul, it would be an act of callousness to defy our intuitive sense for the mystery and to assert that the ultimate enigmas are the brink of chaos rather than the shore of endless meaning.

Confined in our own study rooms, we may entertain any idea that comes to our minds. Under such circumstances it is even plausible to say that the world is worthless and all meaning a dream or fiction. And yet, no one can sneer at the stars, mock the dawn, ridicule the outburst of the spring, or scoff at the totality of being.

105

Away from the immense, cloistered in our own concepts, we may scorn and revile everything. But standing between heaven and earth, we are silenced.

THE AWARENESS OF TRANSCENDENT MEANING

We are conditioned by the structure of nature and by the structure of our minds. And more important than the feeling of awe is the validity and requiredness of awe which remain unchallenged by the mind of man. Awe is the awareness of *transcendent meaning,* of a spiritual suggestiveness of reality, an allusiveness to transcendent meaning. The world in its grandeur is full of a spiritual radiance, for which we have neither name nor concept.

We are struck with an awareness of the immense preciousness of being; a preciousness which is not an object of analysis but a cause of wonder; it is inexplicable, nameless, and cannot be specified or put in one of our categories. Yet we have a certainty without knowledge: it is real without being expressible. It cannot be communicated to others; every man has to find it by himself. In moments of sensing the ineffable we are as certain of the value of the world as we are of its existence. There must be a value which was worth the world's coming into existence. We may be skeptical as to whether the world is perfect. However, even if we admit its imperfection, the preciousness of its grandeur is beyond question.

Awe, then, is more than a feeling. It is an answer of the heart and mind to the presence of mystery in all things, *an intuition for a meaning that is beyond the mystery,* an awareness of the *transcendent worth of the universe.*

In asserting that there is a transcendent meaning to the universe independent of our comprehension, we do not endow a mere idea with existence, any more than we do so in asserting "This is an ocean," when we are carried away by its waves. The mystery and grandeur we face are overwhelmingly real. What they stand for is so sublime that it stuns our ability to adore it. The imperative of awe is its certificate of evidence, a universal certificate which we all

106

seal with tremor and fascination, *not* because we desire to, but because we are stunned and cannot brave it. There is so much more meaning in reality than the soul can take in. To our sense of mystery and wonder the world is too incredible, too meaningful for us, and its existence the most unlikely, the most unbelievable fact, contrary to all reasonable expectations. Even our ability to wonder fills us with amazement.

This, then, is an insight we gain in acts of wonder: not to measure meaning in terms of our own mind, but to sense a meaning infinitely greater than ourselves.

On the certainty of ultimate meaning we stake our very lives. In every judgment we make, in every act we perform, we assume that the world is meaningful. Life would come to naught if we acted as if there were no ultimate meaning. Indeed, its negation would involve a self-contradiction, because if there were no ultimate meaning the very act of negating it would be meaningless; in a world not governed by meaning the difference between affirmation and negation would be meaningless.

THE SENSE OF WONDER IS INSUFFICIENT

Our statement must be qualified. Not all speculation leads to awe. Kepler could experience God in the mathematical laws of nature. As he discovered the order and harmony of nature, he could exclaim, "I think Thy thoughts after Thee, O God!" Yet we have moved a long way from the approach of the early scientists. Before we can ascertain whether our loss of awe is irretrievable, we must try to understand how the loss came about.

The modern scientist does not deal with nature; he deals with figures, formulations and instruments. "If he would understand the structure of an atomic nucleus, he must spend half a million pounds on some tremendous piece of engineering equipment and while the experiment is in progress he must be prepared to be screened off from what is happening by thick layers of concrete." "Looking back, for example, over the controversy between Goethe and Newton as to the nature of light, it can now be seen that what Goethe missed in Newton's approach was an attitude of reverence. No one can move among the scientists today without feeling much the same: there is respect and excitement, sometimes astonishment, but all too seldom reverence."[5]

The heavens declare the glory of God. Man is confronted with a world that alludes to something beyond itself, to a truth beyond experience. It is the allusiveness to a meaning which is not of this world, and it is that allusiveness which conveys to us the awareness of a spiritual dimension of reality, the relatedness of being to transcendent meaning.

True, the mystery of meaning is silent. There is no speech, there are no words, the voice is not heard. Yet beyond our reasoning and beyond our believing, there is a *preconceptual* faculty that senses the glory, the presence of the Divine. We do not perceive it. We have no knowledge; we only have an awareness. We witness it. And to witness is more than to give an account. We have no concept, nor can we develop a theory. All we have is an awareness of something that can be neither conceptualized nor symbolized.

The answer to the ultimate question is not found in the notion that the foundations of the world lie amid impenetrable fog. Fog is no substitute for light, and the totally unknown God is not a god but a name for the cosmic darkness. The God whose presence in the world we sense is anonymous, mysterious. We may sense that He is, not what He is. What is His name, His will, His hope for me? How should I serve Him, how should I worship Him? The sense of wonder, awe, and mystery is necessary, but not sufficient to find the way from wonder to worship, from willingness to realization, from awe to action.

THE ARGUMENT FROM DESIGN

Of the various ways in which the existence of a supreme intelligence has been demonstrated, the teleological proof or the argument from design is one which according to Kant "must always be mentioned with respect." It claims that the order and arrangement of the universe cannot be adequately explained without assuming the activity of an intelligent God.[6]

The argument from design infers the existence of a divine power from the purposeful structure of nature. Order implies intelligence. That intelligence is God. A classic formulation is found in a familiar passage in Paley's *Natural Theology* (1803), ch. 1. "Suppose I had found a watch upon the ground. . . . The mechanism being observed . . . the inference we think is inevitable that the watch must have a maker; that there must have existed, at some time, and at some place or other, an artificer or artificers, who formed it for the purpose which we find it actually to answer; who comprehended its construction, and designed its use." The universe stands to God in the relation in which a watch is related to the mechanic who constructed it. The heavens are the works of His hands, just as the watch is the work of the watchmaker.

This comparison regards the universe as it does the watch as a separate, independent and absolute entity. Nature is a thing in itself, complete and self-sufficient at this present moment. The problem thus faced concerns not the existence of the universe but its cause; not its present, but its past. Since the ultimate structure and order of nature were thought of in mechanical terms, its origin or creation was also conceived of as a mechanical process, comparable to the process of constructing a watch.

The shortcomings of this view lie in its taking both the watch and all of reality for granted. The ultimate problem is not only how it came into being, but also how is it that it is. The problem extends furthermore not only to the substance of the question, but to the act of asking that question. We cannot take the existence of the watch as a safe starting point and merely ask the question of who brought it into being. *Is not the watch itself a mystery? Is not the act of my perceiving the watch and of my comprehending its design a most incomprehensible fact?*

The value of the proof from design lies in its being an answer to a speculative problem; its weakness lies in its failure to answer the religious problem. The first problem comes out of the quest of those who are sure of what they know (the fact of the design of the universe); the latter problem comes out of the amazement of those who know that they do not know. The speculative mind seeks to explain the known; the religious mind seeks a way by which to account for the unknown. If the world is taken for granted, then all we need is to know its cause; but if the world is a mystery, then the most pressing problem is, what does it stand for? What is its meaning? All reference to ideas that are analogous to this-worldly acts becomes utterly inadequate.

There is no answer in the world for man's ultimate wonder at the world. There is no answer in the self to man's ultimate wonder at the self. The question, Who created these? cannot be answered by referring to a cause or a power, since the question would remain, who created the power or the cause? There is nothing in the world to deserve the name God. The world is a mystery, a question, not an answer. Only an idea that is greater than the world, an idea not borrowed from either experience or speculation, is adequate and worthy to be related to the religious problem. The mystery of creation rather than the concept of design; a God that stands above the mystery rather than a designer or a master mind; a God in relation to Whom the world here and now may gain meaning—these are answers that are adequate to the religious problem. The admission that we do not comprehend the origin of the universe is more honest than the acceptance of a designer.

A QUESTION ADDRESSED TO US

There is another essential difference between the issue of God in speculation and the issue of God in religion. The first is a question *about* God; the second is a question *from* God. The first is concerned with a solution to the problem, whether there is a God and, if there is a God, what is His nature? The second is concerned with our personal answer to the problem that is addressed to us in the facts and events of the world and our own experience. Unlike questions of science which we may if we wish leave to others, the ultimate question gives us no rest. Every one of us is called upon to answer.

To the speculative mind, the world is an enigma; to the religious mind, the world is a challenge. The speculative problem is impersonal; the religious problem is a problem addressed to the person. The first is concerned with finding an answer to the question: what is the cause of being? The second, with giving an answer to the question: what is asked of us?

Thinking is not an isolated phenomenon: it affects all of one's life and is in turn affected by all one knows, feels, values, utters, and does. The act of thinking about God is affected by one's awe and arrogance, humility and egotism, sensitivity and callousness.

We do not think in a vacuum. To think means first of all to reflect upon what is present to the mind. What is present to us in religious thinking is not a hypothesis, but the sublime, the marvel, the mystery, the challenge. To think about God does not mean simply to theorize or to conjecture about something that is inane and unknown. We do not conjure up the meaning of God out of nothing. It is not a vacuum we face, but the sublime, the marvel, the mystery, the challenge.

There is no concern for God in the absence of awe, and it is only in moments of awe that God is sensed as an issue. In moments of indifference and self-assertion, He may be a concept, but not a concern, and it is only *a concern* that initiates religious thinking.

"A PALACE FULL OF LIGHT"

Lift up your eyes on high. Religion is the result of what man does with his ultimate wonder, with the moments of awe, with the sense of mystery.

111

How did Abraham arrive at his certainty that there is a God who is concerned with the world? According to the Rabbis, Abraham may be "compared to a man who was traveling from place to place when he saw *a palace full of light.*⁷ 'Is it possible that there is no one who cares for the palace?' he wondered. Until the owner of the palace looked at him and said, 'I am the owner of the palace.' Similarly, Abraham our father wondered, 'Is it conceivable that the world is without a guide?' The Holy One, blessed be He, looked out and said, 'I am the Guide, the Sovereign of the world.'"⁸ It was in wonder that Abraham's quest for God began.

WHAT TO DO WITH WONDER

Thus it is not a feeling for the mystery of living, or a sense of awe, wonder, or fear, which is the root of religion; but rather the question *what to do* with the feeling for the mystery of living, what to do with awe, wonder, or fear. Thinking about God begins when we do not know any more how to wonder, how to fear, how to be in awe. For wonder is not a state of esthetic enjoyment. Endless wonder is endless tension, a situation in which we are shocked at the inadequacy of our awe, at the weakness of our shock, as well as the state of being asked the ultimate question.

The soul is endowed with a sense of indebtedness, and wonder, awe, and fear unlock that sense of indebtedness. Wonder is the state of our being asked.

In spite of our pride, in spite of our acquisitiveness, we are driven by an awareness that something is asked of us; that we are asked to wonder, to revere, to think and to live in a way that is compatible with the grandeur and mystery of living.

What gives birth to religion is not intellectual curiosity but the fact and experience of our being asked.

All that is left to us is a choice—to answer or to refuse to answer. Yet the more deeply we listen, the more we become stripped of the arrogance and callousness which alone would enable us to refuse. We carry a load of marvel, wishing to exchange it for the simplicity

112

of knowing what to live for, a load which we can never lay down nor continue to carry not knowing where.[9]

If awe is rare, if wonder is dead, and the sense of mystery defunct, then the problem what to do with awe, wonder and mystery does not exist, and one does not sense being asked. The awareness of being asked is easily repressed, for it is an echo of the intimation that is small and still. It will not, however, remain forever subdued. The day comes when the still small intimation becomes "like the wind and storm, fulfilling His word" (Psalms 148:8).

Indeed, the dead emptiness in the heart is unbearable to the living man. We cannot survive unless we know what is asked of us. But to whom does man in his priceless and unbridled freedom owe anything? Where does the asking come from? To whom is he accountable?

NOTES FOR CHAPTER 10

[1] Plato, *Epistles*, VII, 341.

[2] Bacon, *Apothegms*, 64.

[3] See p. 288 f.

[4] *Man is Not Alone*, p. 28ff.

[5] C. A. Coulson, "Science and Religion: A Changing Relationship" (pamphlet), Cambridge, 1954.

[6] An impressive restatement of the teleological argument is found in Frederick Robert Tennant's *Philosophical Theology, Cambridge*, 1929-30, vol. II, pp. 78ff. Compare also Frederick J. E. Woodbridge, *Nature and Mind*, New York, 1937, pp. 29-36.

[7] The word *doleket* is ambiguous. It may mean "illumined," "full of light," or it may mean "in flames." In the first sense it is understood by the "Rashi" Commentary on *Genesis Rabba*, in the second by *Yede Moshe* and the commentaries of Rabbi David Luria and Rabbi Zev Einhorn. The parable is significant in both senses. See p. 367.

[8] *Genesis Rabba*, ch. 39.

[9] *Man is Not Alone*, p. 69.

11 An Ontological Presupposition

But how can we ever reach an understanding of Him who is beyond the mystery? How do we go from the intimations of the divine to a sense for the realness of God? Certainty of the realness of God comes about

As a response of the whole person to the mystery and transcendence of living.

As a response, it is an act of raising from the depths of the mind an *ontological presupposition* which makes that response intellectually understandable.

The meaning and verification of the ontological presupposition are attained in rare *moments of insight.*

THE ENCOUNTER WITH THE UNKNOWN

It is the mystery that evokes our religious concern, and it is the mystery where religious thinking must begin. The way of thinking about God in traditional speculation has been *via eminentiae,* a way of proceeding from the known to the unknown. Our starting point is not the known, the finite, the order, but *the unknown within the known,* the infinite with the finite, *the mystery within the order.*

All creative thinking comes out of *an encounter with the un-*

known. We do not embark upon an investigation of what is definitely known, unless we suddenly discover that what we have long regarded as known is actually an enigma. Thus the mind must stand beyond its shell of knowledge in order to sense that which drives us toward knowledge. It is when we begin to comprehend or to assimilate and to adjust reality to our thought that the mind returns to its shell.

Indeed, knowledge does not come into being only as the fruit of thinking. Only an extreme rationalist or solipsist would claim that knowledge is produced exclusively through the combination of concepts. Any genuine encounter with reality is an encounter with the unknown, is an intuition in which an awareness of the object is won, a rudimentary, *preconceptual* knowledge. Indeed, no object is truly known, unless it was first experienced in its unknown-ness.

It is a fact of profound significance that we sense more than we can say. When we stand face to face with the grandeur of the world, any formulation of thought appears as an anticlimax. It is in the awareness that the mystery which we face is incomparably deeper than what we know that all creative thinking begins.

PRECONCEPTUAL THINKING

The encounter with reality does not take place on the level of concepts through the channels of logical categories; concepts are second thoughts. All conceptualization is symbolization, an act of accomodation of reality to the human mind. The living encounter with reality takes places on a level that precedes conceptualization, on a level that is responsive, *immediate, preconceptual,* and *presymbolic.*[1] Theory, speculation, generalization, and hypothesis, are efforts to clarify and to validate the insights which preconceptual experience provides. "To suppose that knowledge comes upon the scene only as the fruit of reflection, that is generated in and through the symbols and sign manipulations, is, in principle, to revert to that very idol of sheer rationalism against which the whole vigorous movement of modern empiricism has lodged such effective and necessary protest."[2]

All insight stands between two realms, the realm of objective reality and the realm of conceptual and verbal cognition. Conceptual cognition must stand the test of a double reference, of the reference to our system of concepts and the reference to the insights from which it is derived.

Particularly in religious and artistic thinking, the disparity between that which we encounter and that which is expressed in words and symbols, no words and symbols can adequately convey. In our religious situation we do not comprehend the transcendent; we are present at it, we witness it. Whatever we know is inadequate; whatever we say is an understatement. We have an awareness that is deeper than our concepts; we possess insights that are not accessible to the power of expression.

Knowledge is not the same as awareness, and expression is not the same as experience. By proceeding from awareness to knowledge we gain in clarity and lose in immediacy. What we gain in distinctness by going from experience to expression we lose in genuineness. The difference becomes a divergence when our preconceptual insights are lost in our conceptualizations, when the encounter with the ineffable is forfeited in our symbolizations, when the dogmatic formulation becomes more important than the religious situation.

The entire range of religious thought and expression is a sublimation of a presymbolic knowledge which the awareness of the ineffable provides. That awareness can only partly be sublimated into rational symbols.

Philosophy of religion must be an effort to recall and to keep alive *the meta-symbolic relevance of religious terms.* Religious thinking is in perpetual danger of giving primacy to concepts and dogmas and to forfeit the immediacy of insights, to forget that the known is but a reminder of God, that the dogma is a token of His will, the expression the inexpressible at its minimum. Concepts, words must not become screens; they must be regarded as windows.

116

God in search of man

The roots of ultimate insights are found, as said above, not on the level of discursive thinking, but on the level of wonder and radical amazement, in the depth of awe, in our sensitivity to the mystery, in our awareness of the ineffable. It is the level on which the great things happen to the soul, where the unique insights of art, religion, and philosophy come into being.

It is not from experience but *from our inability to experience* what is given to our mind that certainty of the realness of God is derived. It is not the order of being but the transcendent in the contingency of all order, the allusions to transcendence in all acts and all things that challenge our deepest understanding.

Our certainty is the result of wonder and radical amazement, of awe before the mystery and meaning of the totality of life beyond our rational discerning. Faith is *the response* to the mystery, shot through with meaning; the response to a challenge which no one can for ever ignore. "The heaven" is a challenge. When you "lift up your eyes on high," you are faced with the question. Faith is an act of man who *transcending himself* responds to Him who *transcends the world.*

TO RISE ABOVE OUR WISDOM

Such response is a sign of man's essential dignity. For the essence and greatness of man do not lie in his ability to please his ego, to satisfy his needs, but rather in his ability to stand above his ego, to ignore his own needs; to sacrifice his own interests for the sake of the holy. The soul's urge to judge its own judgments, to look for meaning beyond the scope of the tangible and finite—in short, the soul's urge *to rise above its own wisdom*—is the root of religious faith.

God is the great mystery, but our faith in Him conveys to us more understanding of Him than either reason or perception is able to grasp.

117

Rabbi Mendel of Kotsk was told of a great saint who lived in his time and who claimed that during the seven days of the Feast of Booths his eyes would see Abraham, Isaac, Jacob, Joseph, Moses, Aaron, and David come to the booth. Said Rabbi Mendel: "I do not see the heavenly guests; I only have faith that they are present in the booth, and to have faith is greater than to see."

This, indeed, is the greatness of man: to be able to have faith. For faith is an act of freedom, of independence of our own limited faculties, whether of reason or sense-perception. It is *an act of spiritual ecstasy,* of rising above our own wisdom.

In this sense, the urge of faith is the reverse of the artistic act in which we try to capture the intangible in the tangible. In faith, we do not seek to decipher, to articulate in our own terms, but to rise above our own wisdom, to think of the world in the terms of God, to live in accord with what is relevant to God.

To have faith is not to capitulate but to rise to a higher plane of thinking. To have faith is not to defy human reason but rather to share divine wisdom.

Lift up your eyes on high and see: Who created these. One must rise to a higher plane of thinking in order to see, in order to sense the allusions, the glory, the presence. One must rise to a higher plane of living and learn to sense the urgency of the ultimate question, the supreme relevance of eternity. He who has not arrived at the highest realm, the realm of the mystery; he who does not realize he is living at the edge of the mystery; he who has only a sense for the obvious and apparent, will not be able to lift up his eyes, for whatever is apparent is not attached to the highest realm; what is highest is hidden. Faith, believing in God, is attachment to the highest realm, the realm of the mystery. This is its essence. Our faith is capable of reaching the realm of the mystery.[3]

ULTIMATE CONCERN IS AN ACT OF WORSHIP

The sense of wonder, awe, and mystery does not give us a knowledge of God. It only leads to a plane where the question about God

118

becomes an inescapable concern, to a situation in which we discover that we can neither place our anxiety in the safe deposit of opinions nor delegate to others the urgent task of answering the ultimate question.

Such ultimate concern is *an act of worship,* an act of acknowledging in the most intense manner the supremacy of the issue. It is not an act of choice, something that we can for ever ignore. It is the manifestation of a fundamental fact of human existence, the fact of worship.

Every one of us is bound to have an ultimate object of worship, yet he is free to chose the object of his worship. He cannot live without it; it may be either a fictitious or a real object, God or an idol.

It is a characteristic inversion to speak of the "problem of God." At stake in the discussion about the problem of God is the problem of man. *Man is the problem.* His physical and mental reality is beyond dispute; his meaning, his spiritual relevance, is a question that cries for an answer. And worship is an answer. For worship is an act of man's relating himself to ultimate meaning. Unless man is capable of entering a relation to ultimate meaning, worship is an illusion. And if worship is meaningless, human existence is an absurdity.

Since our concern with the question about God is an act of worship, and since worship posits the realness of its object, our very concern involves by implication the acceptance of His realness.

Just as supreme worship of an ultimate object is indigenous to human existence, so is explicit denial of the realness of an ultimate object absurd. Let man proclaim his denial over a loud-speaker that would bring his voice to the Milky Way a hundred million light-years from now and how ludicrous he would be.

There can be no honest denial of the existence of God. There can only be faith or the honest confession of inability to believe—or arrogance. Man could maintain inability to believe or suspend his judgment, if he were not driven by the pressure of existence into a situation in which he must decide between yes and no; in which he must decide what or whom to worship. He is driven toward some sort of affirmation. In whatever decision he makes he implicitly accepts either the realness of God or the absurdity of denying Him.

WE PRAISE BEFORE WE PROVE

Understanding God is not attained by calling into session all arguments for and against Him, in order to debate whether He is a reality or a figment of the mind. God cannot be sensed as a second thought, as an explanation of the origin of the universe. He is either the first and the last, or just another concept.

Speculation does not precede faith. The antecedents of faith are the premise of wonder and the premise of praise. Worship of God precedes affirmation of His realness. We *praise* before we *prove*. We respond before we question.

Proofs for the existence of God may add strength to our belief; they do not generate it. Human existence implies the realness of God. There is a certainty without knowledge in the depth of our being that accounts for our asking the ultimate question, a preconceptual certainty that lies beyond all formulation or verbalization.

AN ONTOLOGICAL PRESUPPOSITION

It is *the assertion* that God is real, independent of our preconceptual awareness, that presents the major difficulty. Subjective awareness is not always an index of truth. What is subjectively true is not necessarily trans-subjectively real. All we have is the awareness of allusions to His concern, intimations of His presence. To speak of His reality is to transcend awareness, to surpass the limits of thinking. It is like springing clear of the ground. Are we intellectually justified in inferring from our awareness a reality that lies beyond it? Are we entitled to rise from the realm of this world to a realm that is beyond this world?

We are often guilty of misunderstanding the nature of an assertion such as "God is." Such an assertion would constitute a leap if the assertion constituted an addition to our ineffable awareness of

120

God. The truth, however, is that to say "God is" means less than what our immediate awareness contains. *The statement "God is" is an understatement.*

Thus, the certainty of the realness of God does not come about as a corollary of logical premises, as a leap from the realm of logic to the realm of ontology, from an assumption to a fact. It is, on the contrary, a transition from an immediate apprehension to a thought, from a preconceptual awareness to a definite assurance, from being overwhelmed by the presence of God to an awareness of His existence. What we attempt to do in the act of reflection is to raise that preconceptual awareness to the level of understanding.

In sensing the spiritual dimension of all being, we become aware of the absolute reality of the divine. In formulating a creed, in asserting: God is, we merely bring down overpowering reality to the level of thought. Our thought is but an after-belief.

In other words, our belief in the reality of God is not a case of first possessing an idea and then postulating the ontal counterpart of it; or, to use a Kantian phrase, of first having the idea of a hundred dollars and then claiming to possess them on the basis of the idea. What obtains here is first the actual possession of the dollars and then the attempt to count the sum. There are possibilities of error in counting the notes, but the notes themselves are here.[4]

In other words, our belief in His reality is not a leap over a missing link in a syllogism but rather *a regaining,* giving up a view rather than adding one, going behind self-consciousness and questioning the self and all its cognitive pretensions. *It is an ontological presupposition.*

In the depth of human thinking we all presuppose some ultimate reality which on the level of discursive thinking is crystallized into the concept of a power, a principle or a structure. This, then, is the order in our thinking and existence: The ultimate or God comes first and our reasoning about Him second. Metaphysical speculation has reversed the order: reasoning comes first and the question about His reality second; either He is proved or He is not real.

However, just as there is no thinking about the world without the premise of the reality of the world, there can be no thinking about God without the premise of the realness of God.

THE DISPARITY OF EXPERIENCE AND EXPRESSION

Certain assertions, particularly those that intend to describe the functional aspects of reality, the aspect of power, do not suffer from the incongruity and inadequacy of expression. What can be measured, weighed, or calculated can be exactly formulated. But assertions that intend to convey the essence of reality or the aspect of mystery and grandeur are always understatements; inadequacy is their distinct feature. Thus we have no adequate words or symbols to describe God or the mystery of existence.

The divergence between what we think and what we say is due to the necessity of the adjustment of insight to the common categories of thought and language. Thus, more serious than the problem of how should the religious man justify his creed in terms of philosophical thinking is the problem of how should the religious man justify his concepts, his creed in terms of religious insight and experience? There is a profound disparity between man and reality, between experience and expression, between awareness and conception, between mind and mystery. Thus the disparity of faith and creed is a major problem of the philosophy of religion.

Maimonides urges the reader of his *Guide of the Perplexed* to acquire an adequate understanding for the "unity of God" and to become one of those "who have a notion of, and apprehend the truth, even though they do not utter it, as is recommended to the pious, *Commune with your own heart upon your bed and be still perpetually* (Psalms 4:5)."[5] Why should one be "still perpetually"? Why is silence preferable? The reason, we believe, lies in Maimonides' experience of the inadequacy of all our categories. Following the statement that God's unity is not something superadded to His essence ("He is One without unity"), Maimonides says: "These subtle concepts, which almost pass the comprehension of our minds, are not readily expressed by words. Words are altogether one of the

122

A philosophy of Judaism

main causes of error, because whatever language we employ, we find the restrictions it imposes on our expression extremely disturbing. We cannot even picture this concept by using inaccurate language."[6] And all language is inaccurate.

In order to speak we must make concessions and compromises. We must therefore remember that ultimate ideas can never be expressed. "Since it is a well-known fact that even that knowledge of God that is accessible to man cannot be attained except by the way of negations, and that negations do not convey a true idea of the Being to which they refer, all men . . . declared that God cannot be the object of human comprehension, that none but Himself comprehends what He is, and that our knowledge consists in knowing that we are unable truly to comprehend Him. . . . The idea is best expressed in the book of Psalms: *Silence is praise to Thee* (65:2). It is a very expressive remark on this subject; for whatever we utter with the intention of extolling and praising Him, contains something that cannot be applied to God, and includes derogatory expressions. It is, therefore, more becoming to be silent, and to be content with intellectual reflection. . . . Commune with your own heart upon your bed, and be still (Psalms 4:4)."[7]

Silence is preferable to speech. Words are not indispensible to cognition. They are only necessary when we wish to communicate our ideas to others or to prove to them that we have attained cognition.[8]

In concluding his discussion of the nature and attributes of God, Maimonides writes: "Praise be to Him who is such that when our minds try to visualize His essence, their power of apprehending becomes imbecility; when they study the connection between His works and His will, their knowledge becomes ignorance; and when our tongues desire to declare His greatness by descriptive terms, all eloquence becomes impotence and imbecility."[9]

We said that God is an ontological presupposition, and that all statements about Him are understatements. But what is the meaning and content of that ontological presupposition? We believe that there is another source of certainty of God's existence and one which is more capable of giving us an understanding that goes beyond our mere awareness. To explore that source of certainty is the object of the following inquiry.

NOTES FOR CHAPTER 11

[1] W. von Humboldt's celebrated statement that "man lives with his objects chiefly . . . as language presents them to him" (see Ernst Cassirer, *Language and Myth*, New York, 1946, p. 9) does not apply to creative thinking. Intuition and expression must not be equated. Thought contains elements that cannot be reduced to verbal expression and are beyond the level of verbalization. Non-objective art may be characterized as an attempt to convey a preconceptual, pre-symbolic encounter with reality. Compare also Philip Wheelwright, *The Burning Fountain*, Bloomington, 1954, p. 18f. For an analysis and critique of symbolism in religion and theology, see A. J. Heschel, *Man's Quest for God*, pp. 117-144.

[2] George P. Adams, "The Range of Mind" in *The Nature of Mind*, Berkeley, Cal., 1936, p. 149. Compare J. Loewenberg, "The Discernment of Mind," ibid., p. 90f.

[3] Rabbi Loew of Prague, *Netivot Olam*, netiv haavodah, ch. 2.

[4] See *Man is Not Alone*, p. 84f.

[5] *The Guide of the Perplexed*, vol. I, p. 50.

[6] Ibid., p. 57.

[7] Ibid., p. 59.

[8] Ibid., Book II, p. 5.

[9] Ibid., Book I, p. 58. *Lift up your eyes on high and see: who created these?* "Are we to imagine from this that by lifting his eyes upward a man can know and see what is not permitted to know and see? No, the true meaning of the passage is that whoever desires to reflect on and to obtain a knowledge of the works of the Holy One, let him lift his eyes upwards and gaze on the myriads of hosts and legions of existence there, each different from the other, each mightier than the other. Then will he, while gazing, ask: who *(mi)* created these? 'Who created these?' amounts to saying that the whole of creation springs from a region that remains an everlasting *who?* in that it remains undisclosed." *Zohar*, vol. II, 231b.

12 About the Meaning of God

In undertaking an inquiry, we must from the beginning possess a minimum of knowledge of the meaning of that about which we are trying to inquire. No inquiry starts out of nothing. In asking the first question, we must anticipate something of the nature of that which we ask about, because otherwise we would not know in what direction to proceed or whether the result of our inquiry will be an answer to the question we ask.

We ask about God. But what is the minimum of meaning that the word God holds for us? It is first the idea of *ultimacy*. God is a Being beyond which no other exists or is possible. It means further One, unique, eternal. However, all these adjectives are auxiliary to the noun to which they are attached. In themselves they do not express the essence. We proclaim, God is One; it would be intellectual idolatry to say, the One is God. What, then, is the meaning of the noun to which ultimacy or oneness is attached? Is it the concept of the absolute? Is it the concept of a first cause?

To say that our search for God is a search for the idea of the absolute is to eliminate the problem which we are trying to explore. A first cause or an idea of the absolute—devoid of life, devoid of freedom—is an issue for science or metaphysics rather than a concern of the soul or the conscience. An affirmation of such a cause or such an idea would be an answer unrelated to our question. The living soul is not concerned with a dead cause but with a living God.

Our goal is to ascertain the existence of a Being to whom we may confess our sins, of a God who loves, of a God who is not above concern with our inquiry and search for Him; a father, not an absolute.

We must see clearly from the beginning that the minimum of meaning we associate with the word God is that He is alive, or, to put it negatively, He is not inferior to us in the order of being. A being that lacks the attributes of personal existence is not our problem.

This, then, is the minimum of meaning which the word God holds for us: *God is alive.* To assume the opposite, namely that the word God means a Being devoid of life and freedom—inferior to us in the order of being and more finite than ourselves—would immediately invalidate the problem we are concerned with in the same way as the premise that the universe is more finite than our own body would invalidate any effort to explore the meaning of the universe.

Indeed, there are essentially only two ways to begin: to think of God in terms of free and spontaneous being or in terms of inanimate being; either He is alive or devoid of life. Both premises are beyond demonstration, and yet the second premise in the form of saying, God is the great unknown, appears to most people to be more respectable. Let us examine the latter premise.

The statement "God is the great unknown," meaning that He has never become known and can never become known, is an absolute assertion based upon the theory that God remains eternally mysterious. Such a theory, however, is a dogma entailing a contradiction. For by attributing eternal mysteriousness to the ultimate being, we definitely claim to know it. Thus the ultimate being is not an unknown but a known God. In other words: a God whom we know but one who does not know, the great Unknower. We proclaim the ignorance of God together with our knowledge of His being ignorant!

This seems to be a part of our pagan heritage: to say, the Supreme Being is a total mystery, and even having accepted the idea of a first cause and its power of bringing the universe into being, we still cling to the assumption that the power that can make possible the world's coming into being has never been able to make itself known. Yet why should we assume that the absolute power is absolutely powerless? Why should we *a priori* exclude life and freedom from the ultimate being?

Thinking of God as a speculative problem may perhaps start out with the premise of God's absolute mysteriousness. Thinking of God as a religious problem which begins with wonder, awe, praise, fear, trembling and radical amazement cannot proceed one step if tied to the assumption that God is devoid of life. We cannot utter words and deny at the same time that there are words, and we cannot in religious thinking say God and deny at the same time that He is alive. If God is dead, then worship is madness.

The problem of religious thinking is not only whether God is dead or alive, but also whether we are dead or alive to His realness. A search for God involves a search of our own measure, a test of our own spiritual potential. To be sure, there are levels of thinking where we can comfortably maintain that God is not alive: on the level of conceit and callousness to the grandeur and mystery of living. In moments when we carry the load of radical amazement we know that to say God is alive is an understandment.

Yet there seems to be a third possibility: God is neither alive nor devoid of life but a *symbol*. If God is defined "as a name for that which concerns man ultimately," then He is but a symbol of man's concern, the objectification of a subjective state of mind. But as such God would be little more than a projection of our imagination.

As the acceptance of God and the rejection of idols are indicated in the first two of the Ten Commandments, the rejection of the symbol is implied in the third commandment: "Thou shalt not take the name of God in vain."

Certainly God is more than "a name for that which concerns man ultimately." Only saints are ultimately concerned with God. What concerns most of us ultimately is our ego. The Biblical consciousness begins not with man's but with *God's concern*. The supreme fact in the eyes of the prophets is the presence of God's concern for man and the absence of man's concern for God. It is God's concern for man that cries out behind every word of their message. But how do we become aware of His concern?

The assumption that God is not to be thought of in terms of lifeless being has two important corollaries. The one concerns *His part* in the process of our understanding Him, and the other concerns *the role of time* in such understanding.

My attempts to become acquainted with a stone or a plant are almost entirely dependent upon my will and intelligence; the plant or the stone has no voice in the process of inquiry and is at all times at my disposal. In contrast, my attempts to become acquainted with another person depend not only upon me but also upon the willingness of the person to be seen and to be understood by me. There may be people whom the person would consider worthy of becoming his acquaintance and others whom he would keep at a distance. And he may treat the same people differently at different times.

Now if we assume God is not a passive object but a Being endowed with at least as much life and will as ourselves, understanding Him cannot be a process that goes on regardless of His agreement. If God is alive, we must assume that He plays a part in our acts of trying to understand Him; that our understanding of God depends not only on man's readiness to approach Him but also on God's willingness to be approached.[1]

GOD'S PART IN HUMAN INSIGHT

There is a common misunderstanding of the meaning of divine assistance in Judaism. Admittedly, the hope for it is an integral part of the religious consciousness. Yet we usually restrict it to the practical realm, as if God were expected to assist us in our material but not in our spiritual endeavors. The truth is that for all our aspirations we remain spiritually blind unless we are assisted.

God in search of man

God is not a pearl at the bottom of the ocean, the discovery of which depends upon the skill and intelligence of man. The initiative must be ours, yet the achievement depends on Him, not only on us. Without his love, without His aid, man is unable to come close to Him.[2]

And yet, "everything is in the hands of heaven, except the fear of heaven."[3] Man is free to seek Him and free to ignore Him. Only he who endeavors to purify himself, is assisted from above.[4] Only he who sanctifies himself a little, is endowed with greater sanctity from above.[5]

THE ROLE OF TIME

Furthermore, if God is not thought of in terms of inanimate being, in terms of a Being that is not endowed with either will or freedom, then we must assume that He is not at all times at our disposal. There are times when He goes out to meet us, and there moments when He hides His face from us.[6]

Leopold von Ranke, the historian, maintained that every age is equally near to God. To a person who thinks in Biblical terms, this statement amounts to saying that every age is equally distant from God. Jewish tradition claims that there is a hierarchy of moments within time, that all ages are not alike. Man may pray to God equally at all places, but God does not speak to man equally at all times. Sinai does not happen every day, and prophecy is not a perpetual process. There are ages when men are chosen to be prophets, and there are ages when the voice of prophecy is subdued.

And yet this does not mean that God is utterly silent in our age. The divine voice has not died away "to an echo from the Judean hills." It may break forth to pierce the dreadful silence in our day. There are many ways and many levels on which the will of God communicates itself to man.

The role of time is also necessitated by the human situation. Since our understanding of God involves the whole person, his mind and his heart, his intelligence and his concern, his experiences and his attachments, it cannot be regarded as unchangeable, timeless, and universal. Man is not the same at all times. It is only at certain moments that he becomes aware of the heart-breaking inconceivability of the world in which he lives and which he ignores. At such moments, he wonders: what is my place in the midst of the terrifying immensity of time and space? what is my task? what is my situation?

THE RELIGIOUS SITUATION

We cannot succeed in understanding the reasons that force us to attach ourselves to a certainty of God's realness, unless we understand the situation in which we are concerned with the ultimate question.

A legitimate question represents more than what it says. It represents a radical situation which accounts for its coming into being, a *raison d'être* for the presence of the question in the mind. Now the question about God does not always occupy our minds. At times we are pursued by it, at others it seems irrelevant to us. There are times when wonder is dead, when the ultimate question is meaningless; there are times when there is only wonder and the mystery is within reach of all thoughts.

We must, therefore, not deal with the ultimate question, apart from the situation in which it exists, apart from the insights in which it is evoked and in which it is involved. Apart from its human and personal setting it withers to a mere speculative issue. Yet it is as a religious concern that we are dealing with it here.

The ultimate question, moreover, is a question that arises on the level of the ineffable. It is phrased not in *concepts* but in *acts,* and no abstract formulation is capable of conveying it. It is, therefore, necessary to understand the inner logic of the situation, the spiritual climate in which it exists, in order to comprehend what the ultimate question implies. It is a situation in which we are challenged, aroused, stirred by the sublime, the marvel, the mystery and the Presence. We do not choose to raise the question, we are compelled.

130

A philosophy of Judaism

The question breaks forth with the realization that it is man who is the problem; that more than God is a problem to man, man is a problem to God. The question: Is there a personal God? is a symptom of the uncertainty: Is there a personal man?

In moments in which the soul undergoes the unmitigated realization of the mystery that vibrates between its precarious existence and its inscrutable meaning, we find it unbearably absurd to define the essence of man by what he knows or by what he is able to bring about. To the sense of the ineffable the essence of man lies in his being a means of higher expression, in his being an intimation of ineffable meaning.

MOMENTS

Thus, unlike scientific thinking, understanding for the realness of God does not come about by way of syllogism, by a series of abstractions, by a thinking that proceeds from concept to concept, but by way of insights. The ultimate insight is the outcome of *moments* when we are stirred beyond words, of instants of wonder, awe, praise, fear, trembling and radical amazement; of awareness of grandeur, of perceptions we can grasp but are unable to convey, of discoveries of the unknown, of moments in which we abandon the pretense of being acquainted with the world, of *knowledge by inacquaintance*. It is at the climax of such moments that we attain the certainty that life has meaning, that time is more than evanescence, that beyond all being there is someone who cares.

To repeat, it is only in such moments, in moments lived on the level of the ineffable, that the categories and acts of religion are adequately meaningful. Acts of love are only meaningful to a person who is in love, and not to him whose heart and mind are sour. The same applies to the categories of religion. For ultimate insight takes place on the presymbolic, preconceptual level of thinking. It is difficult, indeed, to transpose insights phrased in the presymbolic language of inner events into the symbolic language of concepts.[7]

In conceptual thinking, what is clear and evident at one moment

131

remains clear and evident at all other moments. Ultimate insights, on the other hand, are events, rather than a permanent state of mind; what is clear at one moment may subsequently be obscured. Concepts we acquire and retain. We have learned that two plus two equals four, and once we become convinced of the validity of this equation, the certainty will not leave us. In contrast, the life of the spirit is not always at its zenith, and the mercy of God does not at all times bestow upon man the supreme blessings. Flashes of insight "come and go, penetrate and retreat, come forth and withdraw." For this is the way all emanation proceeds—"the light flows out of Him and the light streams back perpetually, from the uppermost heights to the nethermost depths."

The immediate certainty that we attain in moments of insight does not retain its intensity after the moments are gone. Moreover, such experiences or inspirations are rare events. To some people they are like shooting stars, passing and unremembered. In others they kindle a light that is never quenched. The remembrance of that experience and the loyalty to the response of that moment are the forces that sustain our faith. In this sense, *faith is faithfulness*, loyalty to an event, loyalty to our response.[8]

AN ANSWER IN DISGUISE

The ultimate question, bursting forth in our souls, is too startling, too heavily laden with unutterable wonder to be an academic question, to be equally suspended between yes and no. We can no longer ask: Is there a God? In humility and contrition we realize the presumption of such asking. The more deeply we meditate, the more clearly we realize that the question we ask is a question we are being asked; that *man's question about God is God's question of man*.

He who has never been caught in such a radical situation will fail to understand the certainty it engenders. He who absconds, who is always absent when God is present, should explain the reasons for his alibi, and abstain from bearing witness. He who has ever gone

God in search of man

through a moment of radical insight cannot be a witness to God's non-existence without laying perjury upon his soul.

NOTES FOR CHAPTER 12

[1] "For the palace will be forsaken, the populous city deserted; the hill and the watchtower will become dens for ever, a joy of wild asses, a pasture of flocks; *until the spirit is poured upon from on high* and the wilderness becomes a fruitful field, and the fruitful field is deemed a forest" (Isaiah 32:14-15).

[2] In the story of Hagar we read: "And God opened her eyes, and she saw a well of water" (Genesis 21:19). "All men are blind until God opens their eyes" *(Genesis Rabba* 53, 13). When Hagar wandered with her child in the wilderness of Beersheba and could find no water, she cast the child under one of the bushes and went away, saying, "Let me not look upon the death of the child." She did not see what was in front of her, until "God opened her eyes, and she saw a well of water." When Balaam went to Moab to curse the people of Israel, he did not see what his ass perceived, until "the Lord opened the eyes of Balaam, and he saw the angel of the Lord standing in the way" (Numbers 22:31). "It is beyond the power of man to see many things, unless God wants him to see" *(Lekah Tov* to Numbers 22:31). This applies to individuals as well as to the whole people. "They know not, nor do they discern, for He has shut their eyes, so that they cannot see; and their minds, so that they cannot understand" (Isaiah 44:18).

"I will give them a heart to know Me, that I am the Lord" (Jeremiah 24:7). "I will make him draw near and he shall approach Me. For who would dare of himself to approach Me? says the Lord" (Jeremiah 30:21). This is why the Psalmist says: "Blessed is he whom Thou dost choose and bring near" (65:5). God is the Teacher, not only the Creator; the giver of wisdom, not only the giver of life. "I am the Lord thy God who teaches thee for thy profit, leading thee in the way thou shouldest go" (Isaiah 48:17). We must search for truth with all our might; we must also pray for His guidance in all our search. "From the end of the earth will I call unto Thee, when my heart faints: Lead me to a rock that is too high for me" (Psalms 61:3). "Lead me where I cannot ascend myself" (Rabbi David Kimchi). We must not despond when our efforts fail. "For the Lord will be with you where your wisdom ends, and will keep thy foot from being caught" (Proverbs 3:26 According to *Jerushalmi Peah* 1, 1). "It is not the great that are wise, nor the aged that understand what is right" (Job 32:9). "Not everybody who studies the Torah becomes wise. Unless God endows man with spirit, he will not be at home in what he knows." *Tanhuma,* ed. Buber, I, p. 193. "He who toils in the Torah, the Torah toils for him." *Sanhedrin* 99b. See also *Megillah* 6b, concerning remembrance.

[3] *Berachot* 33b.

[4] *Shabbat* 104a.

[5] *Yoma,* 39a. To the life of the individual the principle has been applied that "blessings from above descend only where there is some substance and not mere emptiness." The verse, "I am my beloved's and toward me is His desire" (The Song of Songs 7:11) was taken to refer to the relation between God and man: first I must become His, and then, in consequence, His desire is toward me; first I prepared for Him a place, and then His desire is toward me. Only "if

133

man endeavors to purify himself and to draw near to God, then the *Shechinah* rests upon him." *Zohar* vol. I, p. 88a-b. For "the stirring above is produced only in response to an impulse from below, and depends upon the longing of that below." *Zohar,* vol. I 86b; see III, 132b. "How may one recognize a person with whom the Holy One is pleased and in whom He has His abode? When we observe that a man endeavors to serve the Holy One in joy, with his heart, soul and will, then we can be quite sure that the *Shechinah* has her abode in Him." *Zohar* vol. II, 128b. "Even the things perceived by our senses we cannot know except through the loving kindness which comes from thee. For light itself we cannot see; our vision is dimmed by it. It is the divine light which gives us the power to perceive light partially and enables our vision to pass from potentiality to actuality. . . . The grace of understanding is more properly bestowed upon those who know Him than upon others." Albo, *Ikkarim,* II, ch. 15, ed. Husik, p. 97f.

⁶ The role of time in religious understanding is often expressed in Jewish literature. Commenting on Isaiah 55:6, *Seek the Lord while He may be found,* the Rabbis pondered the question, what are the times when He may be found? The answer given was: *the ten days of return,* from the Day of the New Year to the Day of Atonement, *Rosh Hashanah* 18a. Maimonides, *Mishneh Torah, teshuvah* 2,6.

Isaiah (55:6) said "Seek the Lord while He may be found, call upon Him while He is near," and David said "Seek the Lord and His strength, seek His presence continually" (1 Chronicles 16:10). Why did David tell us to seek His presence continually? In order to teach us that God is sometimes seen and sometimes not seen, that He sometimes hearkens and sometimes does not hearken, that He is sometimes available and sometimes not available, sometimes found and sometimes not found, sometimes near and sometimes not near. He was once seen, as it is written, "the Lord spoke to Moses face to face" (Exodus 33:11); and then was not seen, as it is written, "Moses prayed, show me then Thy glory" (Exodus 33:18). So also He was seen at Sinai, as it is written, "And they saw the God of Israel" (Exodus 24:10), and "the appearance of the glory of the Lord was like a devouring flame" (Exodus 24:17), but then He was not seen, as it is written, "You saw no form on the day that the Lord spoke to you at Horeb" (Deuteronomy 4:15), and "You heard the sound of words but saw no form" (Deuteronomy 4:12). When Israel was in Egypt, it is written, "And God heard their groaning" (Exodus 2:24), but when Israel sinned it is written, "And the Lord did not hearken to your voice or give ear to you" (Deuteronomy 1:15). He answered the cry of Samuel at Mitspah, as it is written, "And Samuel cried unto the Lord and the Lord answered him" (1 Samuel 7:9), but again He did not answer him, as it is written, "How long will you grieve over Saul, seeing that I have rejected him?" (1 Samuel 16:17). He answered David as it is written, "I sought the Lord and He answered me" (Psalms 34:5), but again he did not answer him, as it is written, "David besought the Lord for the child" (II Samuel 12:16). When Israel repents, He is available to them, as it is written, "But from there you will seek the Lord and you will find Him" (Deuteronomy 4:29), but when Israel does not repent, He is not available to them, as it is written, "With their flocks and herds they shall go to seek the Lord but they will not find Him" (Hosea 5:6). He is sometimes close, as it is written, "The Lord is close to those who call upon Him" (Psalms 145:18) and sometimes far, as it is written,

A philosophy of Judaism

"The Lord is far from the wicked" (Proverbs 15:29). *Pesikta de Rav Kahana,* XXIV, ed. Buber, Lyck 1868, p. 156a. See also *Jerushalmi Makkot,* 2, 31d.

"There are times when God is propitious and ready to dispense blessing to those that pray to Him, and times when He is not propitious and judgment is let loose on the world, and times when judgment is held in suspense. There are seasons in the year when grace is in the ascendant, and seasons when judgment is in the ascendant, and seasons when judgment is in the ascendant but held in suspense. Similarly with the months and similarly with the days of the week, and even with the parts of each day and each hour. Therefore it is written: 'There is a time for every purpose' (Ecclesiastes 3:1) and again, 'My prayer is unto thee, O Lord, in an acceptable time' (Psalm 69:14). Hence it says here: 'Let him not come at every time to the Sanctuary.' Rabbi Simeon said: 'This interpretation of the word "time" is quite correct, and here God warned Aaron not to make the same mistake as his sons and try to associate a wrong "time" with the King, even if he should see that the control of the world has been committed for the time to the hands of another, and though he has the power to unify with it and bring it near to Holiness.' " *Zohar,* vol. III, 58a.

7 It must be clearly understood that when one of those who have attained deeper insights "wishes to tell, by word of mouth or in writing, anything of the mysteries which he has grasped, it is not possible for him to expound clearly and systematically whatever he has comprehended, as he would have done in any other science which has an established method of instruction. When he tries to teach others, he has to contend with the same difficulty which faced him in his own study, namely, that matters become clear for a moment and then recede into obscurity. It appears that this is the nature of this subject, be one's share of it large or small. For this reason when any metaphysician and theologian, in possession of some truth, intends to impart of his science, he will not do so except in similes and riddles. The writers on this subject have used many different similes, varying not only in details but in their essential character." Maimonides, *The Guide of the Perplexed,* introduction, ed. J. Ibn Shmuel, p. 7.

8 *Man's Quest for God,* New York, 1954, p. 74; *Man is Not Alone,* p. 165.

13 God in Search of Man

"WHERE ART THOU?"

Most theories of religion start out with defining the religious situation as man's search for God and maintain the axiom that God is silent, hidden and unconcerned with man's search for Him. Now, in adopting that axiom, the answer is given before the question is asked. To Biblical thinking, the definition is incomplete and the axiom false. The Bible speaks not only of man's search for God but also of *God's search for man.* "Thou dost hunt me like a lion," exclaimed Job (10:16).

"From the very first Thou didst single out man and consider him worthy to stand in Thy presence."[1] This is the mysterious paradox of Biblical faith: *God is pursuing man.*[2] It is as if God were unwilling to be alone, and He had chosen man to serve Him. Our seeking Him is not only man's but also His concern, and must not be considered an exclusively human affair. His will is involved in our yearnings. All of human history as described in the Bible may be summarized in one phrase: *God is in search of man.* Faith in God is a response to God's question.

> Lord, where shall I find Thee?
> High and hidden in Thy place;
> And where shall I not find Thee?
> The world is full of Thy glory.
>
> I have sought Thy nearness;
> With all my heart have I called Thee,

God in search of man

And going out to meet Thee
I found Thee coming toward me.

Even as, in the wonder of Thy might,
In holiness I have beheld Thee,
Who shall say he hath not seen Thee?
Lo, the heavens and their hosts
Declare the awe of Thee,
Though their voice be not heard.[3]

When Adam and Eve hid from His presence, the Lord called: *Where art thou* (Genesis 3:9). It is a call that goes out again and again. It is a still small echo of a still small voice, not uttered in words, not conveyed in categories of the mind, but ineffable and mysterious, as ineffable and mysterious as the glory that fills the whole world. It is wrapped in silence; concealed and subdued, yet it is as if all things were the frozen echo of the question: *Where art thou?*

Faith comes out of awe, out of an awareness that we are exposed to His presence, out of anxiety to answer the challenge of God, out of an awareness of our being called upon. Religion consists of *God's question and man's answer*. The way *to* faith is the way *of* faith. The way to God is a way of God. Unless God asks the question, all our inquiries are in vain.

The answer lasts a moment, the commitment continues. Unless the awareness of the ineffable mystery of existence becomes a permanent state of mind, all that remains is a commitment without faith. To strengthen our alertness, to refine our appreciation of the mystery is the meaning of worship and observance. For faith does not remain stationary. We must continue to pray, continue to obey to be able to believe and to remain attached to His presence.

Recondite is the dimension where God and man meet, and yet not entirely impenetrable. He placed within man something of His spirit (see Isaiah 63:10), and "it is the spirit in a man, the breath of the Almighty, that makes him understand" (Job 32:8).

137

Men have often tried to give itemized accounts of why they must believe that God exists. Such accounts are like ripe fruit we gather from the trees. Yet it is beyond all reasons, beneath the ground, where a seed starts to become a tree, that the act of faith takes place.

The soul rarely knows how to raise its deeper secrets to discursive levels of the mind. We must not, therefore, equate the act of faith with its expression. The expression of faith is an affirmation of truth, a definite judgment, a conviction, while faith itself is *an event,* something that happens rather than something that is stored away; it is *a moment* in which the soul of man communes with the glory of God.[4]

Man's walled mind has no access to a ladder upon which he can, on his own strength, rise to knowledge of God. Yet his soul is endowed with translucent windows that open to the beyond. And if he rises to reach out to Him, it is a reflection of the divine light in him that gives him the power for such yearning. We are at times ablaze against and beyond our own power, and unless man's soul is dismissed as an insane asylum, the spectrum analysis of that ray is evidence for the truth of his insight.

For God is not always silent, and man is not always blind. His glory fills the world; His spirit hovers above the waters. There are moments in which, to use a Talmudic phrase, heaven and earth kiss each other; in which there is a lifting of the veil at the horizon of the known, opening a vision of what is eternal in time. Some of us have at least once experienced the momentous realness of God. Some of us have at least caught a glimpse of the beauty, peace, and power that flow through the souls of those who are devoted to Him. There may come a moment like a thunder in the soul, when man is not only aided, not only guided by God's mysterious hand, but also taught how to aid, how to guide other beings. The voice of Sinai goes on for ever: "These words the Lord spoke unto all your assembly in the mount out of the midst of the fire, of the cloud, and of the thick darkness, with *a great voice that goes on for ever.*"[5]

A philosophy of Judaism

The fact that ultimately the living certainty of faith is a conclusion derived from acts rather than from logical premises is stated by Maimonides:

"Do not imagine that these great mysteries are completely and thoroughly known to any of us. By no means: sometimes truth flashes up before us with daylight brightness, but soon it is obscured by the limitations of our material nature and social habits, and we fall back into a darkness almost as black as that in which we were before. We are thus like a person whose surroundings are from time to time lit up by lightning, while in the intervals he is plunged into pitch-dark night. Some of us experience such flashes of illumination frequently, until they are in almost perpetual brightness, so that the night turns for them into daylight. That was the prerogative of the greatest of all prophets (Moses), to whom God said: *But as for thee, stand thou here by Me* (Deuteronomy 5:28), and concerning whom Scripture said: *the skin of his face sent forth beams* (Exodus 32:39). Some see a single flash of light in the entire night of their lives. That was the state of those concerning whom it is said: *they prophesied that time and never again* (Numbers 11:25). With others again there are long or short intermissions between the flashes of illumination, and lastly there are those who are not granted that their darkness be illuminated by a flash of lightning, but only, as it were, by the gleam of some polished object or the like of it, such as the stones and [phosphorescent] substances which shine in the dark night; and even that sparse light which illuminates us is not continuous but flashes and disappears as if it were the *gleam of the ever-turning sword* (Genesis 3:24). The degrees of perfection in men vary according to these distinctions. Those who have never for a moment seen the light but grope about in their night are those concerning whom it is said: *They know not, neither will they understand; they walk on in darkness* (Psalms 82:5). The Truth is completely hidden from them in spite of its powerful brightness, as it is also said of them:

And now men see not the light which is bright in the skies (Job 37:21). These are the great mass of mankind. . . ."[6]

Only those who have gone through days on which words were of no avail, on which the most brilliant theories jarred the ear like mere slang; only those who have experienced ultimate not-knowing, the voicelessness of a soul struck by wonder, total muteness, are able to enter the meaning of God, a meaning greater than the mind.

There is a loneliness in us that hears. When the soul parts from the company of the ego and its retinue of petty conceits; when we cease to exploit all things but instead pray the world's cry, the world's sigh, our loneliness may hear the living grace beyond all power.

We must first peer into the darkness, feel strangled and entombed in the hopelessness of living without God, before we are ready to feel the presence of His living light.

"And it shall come to pass, when I bring a cloud over the earth, that the bow shall be seen in the cloud" (Genesis 9:14). When ignorance and confusion blot out all thoughts, the light of God may suddenly burst forth in the mind like a rainbow in the sky. Our understanding of the greatness of God comes about as an act of illumination. As the Baal Shem said, "like a lightning that all of a sudden illumines the whole world, God illumines the mind of man, enabling him to understand the greatness of our Creator." This is what is meant by the words of the Psalmist: "He sent out His arrows and scattered [the clouds]; He shot forth lightnings and discomfited them." The darkness retreats, "The channels of water appeared, the foundations of the world were laid bare" (Psalms 18: 15-16).[7]

The essence of Jewish religious thinking does not lie in entertaining a concept of God but in the ability to articulate a memory of moments of illumination by His presence. Israel is not a people of definers but a people of witnesses: "Ye are My witnesses" (Isaiah 43:10). Reminders of what has been disclosed to us are hanging over our souls like stars, remote and of mind-surpassing grandeur.

140

God in search of man

They shine through dark and dangerous ages, and their reflection can be seen in the lives of those who guard the path of conscience and memory in the wilderness of careless living.

Since those perennial reminders have moved into our minds, wonder has never left us. Heedfully we stare through the telescope of ancient rites lest we lose the perpetual brightness beckoning to our souls. Our mind has not kindled the flame, has not produced these principles. Still our thoughts glow with their light. What is the nature of this glow, of our faith, and how is it perceived?

RETURN TO GOD IS AN ANSWER TO HIM

We do not have to discover the world of faith; we only have to recover it. It is not a *terra incognita,* an unknown land; it is a forgotten land, and our relation to God is a palimpsest rather than a *tabula rasa.* There is no one who has no faith. Every one of us stood at the foot of Sinai and beheld the voice that proclaimed, *I am the Lord thy God.*[8] Every one of us participated in saying, *We shall do and we shall hear.* However, it is the evil in man and the evil in society silencing the depth of the soul that block and hamper our faith. "It is apparent and known before Thee that it is our will to do Thy will. But what stands in the way? The leaven that is in the dough (the evil impulse) and the servitude of the kingdoms."[9]

In the spirit of Judaism, our quest for God is a return to God; our thinking of Him is a recall, an attempt to draw out the depth of our suppressed attachment. The Hebrew word for repentance, *teshuvah,* means *return.* Yet it also means *answer.* Return to God is an answer to Him. For God is not silent. "Return O faithless children, says the Lord" (Jeremiah 3:14).[10] According to the understanding of the Rabbis, daily, at all times, "A Voice cries: in the wilderness prepare the way of the Lord, make straight in the desert a highway for our God" (Isaiah 40:3). "The voice of the Lord cries to the city" (Micah 6:9).[11]

"Morning by morning He wakens my ear to hear as those who are taught" (Isaiah 50:4). The stirring in man to turn to God is

141

actually a "reminder by God to man."[12] It is a call that man's physical sense does not capture, yet the "spiritual soul" in him perceives the call.[13] The most precious gifts come to us unawares and remain unnoted. God's grace resounds in our lives like a staccato. Only by retaining the seemingly disconnected notes do we acquire the ability to grasp the theme.

Is it possible to define the content of such experiences? It is not a perception of a thing, of anything physical; nor is it always a disclosure of ideas hitherto unknown. It is primarily, it seems, an enhancement of the soul, a sharpening of one's spiritual sense, an endowment with a new sensibility. It is a discovery of what is in time, rather than anything in space.

Just as clairvoyants may see the future, the religious man comes to sense the present moment. And this is an extreme achievement. For the present is the presence of God. Things have a past and a future, but only God is pure presence.

A SPIRITUAL EVENT

But if insights are not physical events, in what sense are they real?

The underlying assumption of modern man's outlook is that objective reality is physical: all non-material phenomena can be reduced to material phenomena and explained in physical terms. Thus, only those types of human experiences which acquaint us with the quantitative aspects of material phenomena refer to the real world. None of the other types of our experience, such as prayer or the awareness of the presence of God, has any objective counterpart. They are illusory in the sense that they do not acquaint us with the nature of the objective world.

In modern society, he who refuses to accept the equation of the real and the physical is considered a mystic. However, since God is not an object of a physical experience, the equation implies the impossibility of His existence. Either God is but a word not designating anything real or He is at least as real as the man I see in front of me.

142

A philosophy of Judaism

This is the premise of faith: Spiritual events are real. Ultimately all creative events are caused by spiritual acts. The God who creates heaven and earth is the God who communicates His will to the mind of man.

"In Thy light we shall see light" (Psalms 36:10). There is a divine light in every soul, it is dormant and eclipsed by the follies of this world. We must first awaken this light, then the upper light will come upon us. In Thy light which is within us will we see light (Rabbi Aaron of Karlin).

We must not wait passively for insights. In the darkest moments we must try to let our inner light go forth. "And she rises while it is yet night" (Proverbs 31:15).

NOTES FOR CHAPTER 13

[1] The liturgy of the Day of Atonement.

[2] "Said Rabbi Yose: Judah used to expound, *The Lord came from Sinai* (Deuteronomy 33:2). Do not read thus, but read, *The Lord came to Sinai.* I, however, do not accept this interpretation, but, *The Lord came from Sinai,* to welcome Israel as a bridegroom goes forth to meet the bride." *Mechilta, Bahodesh* to 19:17. God's covenant with Israel was an act of grace. "It was He who initiated our delivery from Egypt in order that we should become His people and He our King," *Kuzari* II, 50. "The first man would never have known God, if He had not addressed, rewarded and punished him. . . . By this he was convinced that He was the Creator of the world, and he characterized Him by words and attributes and called Him *the Lord.* Had it not been for this experience, he would have been satisfied with the name *God;* he would not have perceived what God was, whether He is one or many, whether He knows individuals or not." *Kuzari,* IV, 3.

[3] See *Selected Poems of Jehudah Halevi,* translated by N. Salamon, Philadelphia, 1928, pp. 134-135.

[4] *Man is Not Alone,* p. 87f.

[5] Deuteronomy 5:19, according to the Aramaic translation of Onkelos and Jonathan ben Uzziel and to the interpretation of *Sanhedrin,* 17b; Sotah, 10b; and to the first interpretation of Rashi.

[6] *More Nebuchim,* introduction, ed. J. Ibn Shmuel, Jerusalem, 1947, pp. 6-7. *The Guide of the Perplexed,* translated by Ch. Rabin, London, 1952, p. 43f. In a somewhat similar vein, we read in the *Zohar,* the Torah reveals a thought "for an instant and then straightway clothes it with another garment, so that it is hidden there and does not show itself. The wise, whose wisdom makes them full of eyes, pierce through the garment to the very essence of the word that is hidden thereby. Thus when the word is momentarily revealed in that first instant those whose eyes are wise can see it, though it is soon hidden again." *Zohar,* vol. II, p. 98b. See also Plato, *Epistles,* VII, 341.

7 Rabbi Yaakov Yosef of Ostrog, *Rav Yevi*, Ostrog, 1808, p. 43b.

8 *Tanhuma*, Yitzo, I. The words, according to the Rabbis, were not heard by Israel alone, but by the inhabitants of all the earth. The divine voice divided itself into "the seventy tongues" of man, so that all might understand it. *Exodus Rabba*, 5, 9.

9 *Berachot*, 17a.

10 According to Rabbi Jonathan, "Three and a half years the *Shechinah* abode upon the Mount of Olives hoping that Israel would return, but they did not, while a voice from heaven issued announcing, Return, O faithless sons." *Lamentations Rabba*, proemium 25.

11 According to *Masechet Kallah*, ch. 5, ed. M. Higger, New York, 1936, p. 283, these passages refer to a perpetual voice.

12 "This call of God comes to him who has taken the Torah as a light of his path, attained intellectual maturity and capacity for clear apprehension, yearns to gain the Almighty's favor, and to rise to the spiritual heights of the saints, and turns his heart away from worldly cares and anxieties." Bahya, *The Duties of the Heart, Avodat Elohim*, ch. 5 (vol. II, p. 55).

13 Rabbi Mordecai Azulai, *Or Hachamah*, Przemysl, 1897, vol. III, p. 42b.

14 Insight

The voice of God is not always inaudible. "In every generation didst Thou make plain parts of the mystery of Thy name."[1]

"Every day a heavenly voice resounds from Mount Horeb, proclaiming: 'Woe unto the people for their disregard of the Torah.' "[2] "Every day a voice goes forth saying: 'How long will scoffers delight in their scoffing and fools hate knowledge?' 'Return, O faithless sons, I will heal your faithlessness' (Jeremiah 3:22). But there is no one who inclines his ear. The Torah calls on man, and none pay regard."[3]

The Baal Shem raised the question: What is the purpose of the voice? If no one ever hears it, of what avail is it? If there is always one who hears it, would he presume to admit it? And would anybody believe him? This is how the Baal Shem explained it: The voice that goes forth from above does not reach the physical ear of man. "There is no speech, there are no words, the voice is not heard."[4] It is uttered not in sounds but in thoughts, in signs that man must learn to perceive. "A man who does not understand what he is being shown by gesture is not worthy to converse in signs before the king."[5] All the longings to return to God that come to man, as well as all his inner awakenings of either joy or fear are due to that voice.[6]

"Bless the Lord, ye angels of His, ye mighty in strength, that fulfill His word, hearkening unto the voice of His word" (Psalms 103:

145

20). "By the angels are meant the saints of this world who are as esteemed by the Holy One, blessed be He, as the supernal angels in heaven. . . . They hear the voice of the Lord, they are privileged to hear daily the voice from above."[7]

Hear, O Israel. . . . "Every day a voice goes out of Mount Horeb which the righteous men perceive. This is meant by *Hear, O Israel*: Israel, thou, hear the voice that proclaims all the time, at every moment: The Lord is our God, the Lord is One." "The acts of God are eternal and continue for ever. Every day he who is worthy receives the Torah standing at Sinai; he hears the Torah from the mouth of the Lord as Israel did when they stood at Sinai. Every Israelite is able to attain that level, the level of standing at Sinai."[8]

THE INITIATIVE OF MAN

"I sleep but my heart waketh, it is the voice of my beloved that knocketh: Open to me, my sister, my love, my dove" (The Song of Songs, 5:2). "The voice of my beloved, the Holy One, Blessed be He, is calling: Open to Me an opening no bigger than the eye of a needle, and I will open to thee the supernal gates. Open to Me, my sister, because thou art the door through which there is entrance to Me; if thou openest not, I am closed."[9]

Again and again His call goes out to the soul: Open to Me, my sister, my love, my dove; but the call is usually lost in the confusion of the heart, in the ambiguity of the world. Yet, God tries in many ways to reach the soul. "Thou turnest man to contrition and sayest: 'Return, ye children of man' " (Psalms 90:3).

Without God's aid, man cannot find Him. Without man's seeking, His aid is not granted. "The Community of Israel spoke before the Holy One, blessed be He:

—Lord of the Universe, it depends upon Thee, so turn Thou us unto Thee.

He said to them:

—It depends upon you, as it is said, *Return unto Me and I will return unto you, saith the Lord of hosts* (Malachai 3:7).

146

A philosophy of Judaism

The Community spoke before Him:

—Lord of the universe, it depends upon Thee, as it is said, *Restore us, O God of our salvation* (Psalms 85:5).

And therefore the Book of Lamentations concludes with the words, *"Turn Thou us unto Thee, O Lord, and we shall be turned."*

It is within man's power to seek Him; it is not within his power to find Him. All Abraham had was wonder, and all he could achieve on his own was readiness to perceive. The answer was disclosed to him; it was not found by him.[10]

But the initiative, we believe, is with man. The great insight is not given unless we are ready to receive. God concludes but we commence.

"Whoever sets out to purify himself is assisted from above."[11] The *Shechinah,* the presence of God, is not found in the company of sinners; but when a man makes an effort to purify himself and to draw near to God, then the *Shechinah* rests upon him. When man is ready to say, "I am my beloved's," then "His desire is toward me."[12]

In the flame which rises from a burning coal or candle there are two lights: one white and luminous, and the other black or blue. The white light is the higher of the two and rises steadily. The two are inseparably connected, the white resting and being enthroned upon the black. The blue or black base is in turn attached to something beneath it, which keeps it in flame and impels it to cling to the white light above. It is a connecting link between the white light to which it is attached above and the concrete body to which it is attached below. The impulse through which this blue is set aflame comes only from man.[13] The blue light is not caught up by the white light until it has first begun to mount; but when it does so, forthwith the white light rests upon it. In regard to the white light, it is said: "O Lord, keep Thou not silence, hold not Thy peace and be not still, O Lord" (Psalms 83:2). In regard to the blue light, it is said, "Ye that stir the Lord to remember, take no rest" (Isaiah 62:6).[14]

147

In his great code that begins with the words, "The principle of all principles and the pillar upon which all science rests is to know that there is a First Being who brought every existing thing into being," Maimonides does not offer a speculative proof for the existence of God. He states that the source of our knowledge of God is the inner eye, *"the eye of the heart,"* a medieval name for intuition.[15]

To Jewish thinkers of the past, the evidence for their certainty of the existence of God was neither a syllogism derived from abstract premises nor any physical experience but *an insight.* The eye of the body is not that of the soul, and the soul, it was believed, does at times attain higher insights.[16]

Bahya Ibn Paquda believed that to him whose mind is always alive to God, He will reveal "mysteries of His wisdom." Such a person will "see without eyes, hear without ears, speak without the tongue, perceive things which his sense cannot perceive, and comprehend things without reasoning."[17]

Moses Ibn Ezra tells us, "My thoughts arouse me to behold Thee, and enable me to behold Thy wonders *with the eye of my heart.*"[18]

Yehuda Halevi maintains that just as the Lord gave all of us a bodily eye to perceive external things, he endowed some people with "an inner eye" or "inner sense."[19] In his poems he speaks of himself having seen God *with the heart* (rather than with the bodily eye).[20] "My heart saw Thee and believed Thee."[21] "I have seen Thee with the eye of the heart."[22]

> The Creator who discovereth all from nothing,
> Is revealed to the heart, but not to the eye;
> Therefore ask not how and where—
> For He filleth heaven and earth.
> Remove lust from the midst of Thee;
> Thou will find Thy God within thy bosom,
> Walking gently in thine heart—
> He that bringeth low and that lifteth up.[23]

"DOORS FOR THE SOUL"

In the *Zohar* we read the following discourse on the verse: *Her husband* is known in the gates, when he sitteth amor.g the elders of the land* (Proverbs 31:23). "The Holy One, blessed be He, is transcendent in His glory, He is hidden and removed far beyond all ken; there is no one in the world, nor has there ever been one, whom His wisdom and essence do not elude, since He is recondite and hidden and beyond all ken, so that neither the supernal nor the lower beings are able to commune with Him until they utter the words 'Blessed be the glory of the Lord from his place' (Ezekiel 3: 12). The creatures of the earth think of Him as being on high, declaring, 'His glory is above the heavens' (Psalms 113:4), while the heavenly beings think of Him as being below, declaring, 'His glory is over all the earth' (Psalms 57:12), until they both, in heaven and on earth concur in declaring, 'Blessed be the glory of the Lord from his place,' because He is unknowable and no one can truly understand Him. This being so, how can you say, 'Her husband is known in the gates'? But of a truth the Holy One makes Himself known to every one according to the insight of his heart and his capacity to attach himself to the spirit of divine wisdom; and thus 'Her husband is known', not 'in the gates' *(bishe 'arim)*, but, as we may also translate, 'by insight,' though a full knowledge is beyond the reach of any being. . . . According to another interpretation, the gates mentioned in this passage are the same as the gates in the passage, 'Lift up your heads, O ye gates' (Psalms 24:7), and refer to the supernal grades by and through which alone a knowledge of the Almighty is possible to man, and but for which man could not commune with God. Similarly, man's soul cannot be known directly, save through the members of the body, which are the grades forming the instruments of the soul. The soul is thus known and unknown. So it is with the Holy One, blessed be He, since He is the Soul of souls, the Spirit of spirits, covered and veiled

---

* "Husband" or "master" is taken to be a synonym for God.

from anyone; nevertheless, through those gates, which are doors for the soul, the Holy One makes Himself known. For there is door within door, grade behind grade, through which the glory of the Holy One is made known."[24]

NOTES FOR CHAPTER 14

[1] *Siddur Saadia*, p. 379. According to *The Wisdom of Solomon* (7:25, 27), the wisdom by which the world was created is "a breath of the power of God, a clear effluence of the glory of the Almighty. Therefore can nothing defiled find entrance into her. . . . From generation to generation passing into holy souls, she makes them friends of God and prophets." *And God said, Let there be light, and there was light.* (Genesis 1:3). According to an ancient view, that light, had it remained in the world, would have enabled man to see the world at a glance from one end to the other. Anticipating the wickedness of the sinful generations of the Deluge and the Tower of Babel, who were unworthy to enjoy the blessings of such light, God concealed it. In the world to come it will appear to the pious in all its pristine glory *(Hagigah* 12a.) But had it been hidden away altogether, the world, according to another view, "would not have been able to exist for one moment. But it was only hidden like a seed which generates others, seeds and fruits, and the world is sustained by it. There is not a day that something does not emanate from that light to sustain all things, for it is with this that the Holy One nourishes the world." *Zohar,* vol. II, p. 149a. See vol. II, pp. 166b-167a. On the whole problem compare my studies, "Did Maimonides Strive for Prophetic Inspiration?" in *Louis Ginzberg Jubilee Volume,* the Hebrew volume, New York, 1945, pp. 159-188; "Inspiration in the Middle Ages," in *Alexander Marx Jubilee Volume,* the Hebrew volume, New York, 1950, pp. 175-208.

[2] *Abot* 6, 2.

[3] *Zohar,* vol. III, pp. 126a, 52b, 58a; Vol. I, pp. 78a, 90a, 124a, 193a; vol. II, pp. 5a; see *Hagigah* 15b, and *Pirke de Rabbi Eliezer,* ch. 15.

[4] According to Psalms 19:3.

[5] *Hagigah* 5b.

[6] *Toldot Yaakov Yosef,* Lemberg, 1863, p. 172a; see the sources mentioned in *Sefer Baal Shem Tov,* vol. II, p. 167, and Rabbi Eliezer Azkari, *Haredim,* Venice, 1601, p. 81a.

[7] Rabbi Levi Yitzhak of Berditshev, *Kedushat Levi,* Lublin 1927, p. 186b; see p. 28a. Compare *Lekkute Yekarim,* Mesyrov, 1797, p. 2d.

[8] *Zohar,* vol. I, p. 90a.

[9] *Midrash Rabba,* The Song of Songs, 5,2, and *Zohar,* vol. III, p. 95a.

[10] According to *Numbers Rabba* 14, 7, the verse "Whoso has anticipated Me, I will repay him" (Job 41:3), refers to Abraham who, of himself, achieved knowledge of the existence of God. "There was no man who taught him how to obtain a knowledge of the Holy One, blessed be He." He was one of the four people who of themselves learned to know God. The other three were Job, Hezekiah, and the Messiah. However, the intention of this passage is to stress that Abraham was unaided by any man. It does not refer to divine aid. Moreover, the fact that four men are singled out is an exception that proves the rule.

[11] *Yoma* 38b.

[12] *Zohar*, vol. I, p. 88b.

[13] *Zohar*, vol. I, p. 51a.

[14] *Zohar*, vol. I, p. 77b.

[15] "You can never see matter without form, or form without matter. . . . Forms devoid of matter cannot be perceived by the eyes of the body but only by the eye of the heart. In the same way we know the Lord of the universe without physical vision." *Mishne Torah, Yesode Hatorah*, IV, 7. See *The Duties of the Heart*, vol. II, p. 55. The chosen ones are endowed with "an inner eye which sees things as they really are" *(Kuzari* IV, 3); see Ibn Ezra, *Commentary* on Exodus 7:89. The term is also used by Gazzali, see David Kaufmann, *Geschichte der Attributenlehre*, Gotha, 1877, p. 202, n. 180; and J. Obermann, *Der philosophische und religioese Subjektivismus Ghazalis, Wien*, 1921, p. 27. Compare Aristotle, *De Mundo*, 391: "by the divine eye of the soul apprehending things divine and interpreting them to mankind."

[16] The concept of insight seems to be contained in the Talmudic expression, *ovanta deliba*. It is an act in which a perception of the mysteries of the Merkaba is attained, see *Megillah* 24a, and *Tosafot, Avoda Zara*, 28b.

[17] *The Duties of the Heart, heshbon hanefesh*, ch. 3, par. 10. Bahya refers to "the inward science" which he describes as the light of hearts and the radiance of souls. Concerning this science Scripture says, Behold Thou desirest Truth in the inward being; teach me, therefore, wisdom in my inmost heart (Psalms 51:8). *The Duties of the Heart*, Vol. I, p. 7.

[18] *Selected Poems of Moshes Ibn Esra*, edited by Heinrich Brody and translated by Solomon Solis-Cohen, Philadelphia, 1945, p. 124. The expression also occurs in Bahya, ibidem, *Avodat Elohim*, ch. 5.

[19] *Kusari*, IV, 3.

[20] *Shirim Nivharim*, ed; Shirman, poem 4, line 22.

[21] Shirman, ibid., poem 2, line 5.

[22] *Selected Poems of Jehudah Halevi*, Philadelphia, 1928, p. 94.

[23] *Diwan des . . . Jehuda ha-Levi*, edited by H. Brody, Gottesdienstliche Poesie, Berlin, 1911, p. 159.

[24] *Zohar*, vol. I, p. 103a-b; see Vol. II, p. 116b. See Rabbenu Hananel's view, quoted in *Commentar zum Sepher Jezira* by R. Jehuda G. Barsilai aus Barcelona, ed. Halberstam, Berlin, 1885, p. 32. The *Zohar* relates *bishe'arim* to the verb *Lesha'er*, to estimate. See Proverbs 23:7, and Rashi on Sotah 38b.

15 Faith

Thinking about the ultimate, climbing toward the invisible, leads along a path with countless chasms and very few ledges. For all our faith, we are easily lost in misgivings which we cannot fully dispel. What could counteract the apprehension that it is utter futility to crave for understanding of God?

Man in his spontaneity may reach out for the hidden God and with his mind try to pierce the darkness of His distance. But how will he know whether it is God he is reaching out for or some value personified? How will he know where or when God is found? In moments of meditation we may encounter His presence. But does God encounter us? We may deeply, wholeheartedly adore His glory. But how do we know that He takes notice of our adoration?

"Canst thou by searching find out God?" (Job 11:7). Job admits freely: "God is great, beyond our knowledge" (36:26).[1] "The Almighty—we cannot find Him; He is great in power and justice, and abundant righteousness He will not violate" (37:23). All Abraham could achieve by his own power was wonder and amazement; the knowledge that there is a living God was given him by God.

There is no substitute for faith, no alternative for prophecy, no surrogate for tradition.

NO FAITH AT FIRST SIGHT

There is no faith at first sight. A faith that comes into being like a butterfly is ephemeral. He who is swift to believe is swift to forget.

Faith does not come into being out of nothing, inadvertently, unprepared, as an unearned surprise. Faith is preceded by awe, by acts of amazement at things that we apprehend but cannot comprehend. In the story of the Red Sea we read. "Israel *saw* the great works which the Lord did . . . and the people *feared* the Lord . . . and they *believed in the Lord*" (Exodus 14:31). We must learn how to see "the miracles which are daily with us"; we must learn how to live in awe, in order to attain the insights of faith.

"The thoughtless believes every word, but the prudent looks where he is going" (Proverbs 14:15). The will to believe may be the will to power in disguise, yet the will to power and the will to believe are mutually exclusive. For in our striving for power we arrogate to ourselves what belongs to God and suppress the claim of His presence. We must learn how to let His will prevail. We must understand that our faith is not only our concern but also His; that more important than our will to believe is His will that we believe.

It is not easy to attain faith. A decision of the will, the desire to believe, will not secure it. All the days of our lives we must continue to deepen our sense of mystery in order to be worthy of attaining faith. Callousness to the mystery is our greatest obstacle. In the artificial light of pride and self-contentment we shall never see the splendor. Only *in His light shall we see light.*

Man's quest for God is not a quest for mere information. In terms of information little was attained by those countless men who strained their minds to find an answer. Only in terms of responsiveness, as an answer to Him who asked, much was achieved and much can be achieved by every one of us. In the realm of science, a question may be asked and an answer given by one man for all men. In the realm of religion, the question must be faced and the answer given by every individual soul.

God is of no importance unless He is of supreme importance.[2] We cannot leave it uncertain whether or not there is a living God who is concerned with the integrity of man. We cannot leave it uncertain whether or not we know what He requires of us. The answer to these questions cannot be found off-hand. According to

Maimonides, "It is well known and quite evident that the love of God cannot strike deep root in the heart of man unless it occupies his mind constantly so that nothing in the world matters to him but this love of God."[3] What applies to the love of God applies to some degree to faith in God.

FAITH IS ATTACHMENT

Faith is not the same as belief, not the same as the attitude of regarding something as true.[4] When the people of Israel worshiped a golden calf, forty days after Sinai, their belief in the event was surely present. Faith is an act of the whole person, of mind, will, and heart. Faith is *sensitivity, understanding, engagement,* and *attachment;* not something achieved once and for all, but an attitude one may gain and lose.

The generation that went out of Egypt and witnessed the marvels at the Red Sea and Sinai did not attain faith completely. At the end of forty years in the wilderness Moses summoned all Israel and said to them: *"You have seen* all that the Lord did before your eyes in the land of Egypt, to Pharaoh and to all his servants and to all his land; the great trials which *your eyes saw,* the signs, and those great wonders. But to this day *the Lord has not given you a mind to understand or eyes to see, or ears to hear"* (Deuteronomy 29: 1-3).

"Marvelous things did He in the sight" of Israel. "For all this they sinned still, and believed not in His wondrous works" (Psalms 78: 14-32).

THE EMBARRASSMENT OF FAITH

Faith in the living God is, we repeat, not easily attained. Had it been possible to prove His existence beyond dispute, atheism would have been refuted as an error long ago. Had it been possible to awaken in every man the power to answer His ultimate question, the great prophets would have achieved it long ago. Tragic is the embarrassment of the man of faith. "My tears have been my food day and

154

A philosophy of Judaism

night, while they say unto me all the day, where is thy God?" (Psalms 42:4). "Where are all His marvelous works which our father told us of?" (Nehemiah 6:13; see Psalms 44:2). "How long, O Lord, wilt Thou hide Thyself perpetually?" (Psalms 89:47). "My God, my God, why hast Thou forsaken me?" (Psalms 22:2).

Why, we often ask in our prayers, hast Thou made it so difficult to find Thee? Why must we encounter so much anguish and travail before we can catch a glance of Thy presence? What a sad spectacle are the honest efforts of the great minds to prove Thy existence! And why dost Thou permit faith to blend so easily with bigotry, arrogance, cruelty, folly and superstition?

> O Lord, why dost Thou make us err from thy ways
> And harden our heart, so that we fear Thee not?
> Isaiah 63:17

There must be a profound reason for this fact, for man's supreme misery. The reason, perhaps, is that God in His relation to us follows not only the path of compassion but also the path of justice, and that His compassion is concealed by His justice, as His justice is concealed by His compassion.

FAITH INCLUDES FAITHFULNESS

Faith includes *faithfulness,* strength of waiting, the acceptance of His concealment, defiance of history.

> O Lord our God,
> Other lords besides Thee have had dominion over us,
> But Thy name alone we acknowledge.
> Isaiah 26:13

No moment in human history was as sad as the moment in which the Lord said unto Moses, *and I will surely hide My face in that day on account of all the evil which they have done, because they have turned to other Gods* (Deuteronomy 31:18).[5]

"Who is like unto Thee in silence!" Who is as silent as Thou

155

"who seest the insult heaped upon Thy children, yet keepest silence?"[6]

The failure of perception, the inability to apprehend Him directly is the sad paradox of our religious existence. It was an extraordinary moment when man was ready to exclaim:

> This is my God, I will glorify Him;
> The God of my father, I will exalt Him.
> Exodus 15:2

The normal situation is expressed in the words of Job:

> Lo, He goes by me, and I see Him not;
> He passes on also, but I perceive Him not.
> Job 9:11

However, God is not indifferent to man's quest of Him. He is in need of man, in need of man's share in redemption. God who created the world is not at home in the world, in its dark alleys of misery, callousness and defiance.

Of Noah it is said, *Noah walked with God* (Genesis 6:9), and to Abraham the Lord said, Walk before *Me* (Genesis 17:1). Said the Midrash: "Noah might be compared to a king's friend who was plunging about in the dark alleys, and when the king looked out and saw him, he said to him, Instead of plunging about in dark alleys, come and walk with me. But Abraham's case is rather to be compared to that of *a king who was sinking in dark alleys,* and when his friend saw him he shone a light for him through the window. Said he to him, Instead of lighting me through the window, come and show a *light before me.*"[7] The world was covered with darkness, but Abraham gave the light that illumined His presence.

The words, "I am a stranger on earth" (Psalms 119:19), were interpreted to refer to God. God is a stranger in the world. The *Shechinah,* the presence of God, is in exile. Our task is to bring God back into the world, into our lives. To worship is to expand the presence of God in the world. To have faith in God is to reveal what is concealed.

[1] *Lift up your eyes on high.* "By doing so, you will know it is the mysterious Ancient One whose essence can be sought but not found, who created these. . . . He is ever to be sought, though mysterious and unrevealable. . . . But after a man by means of inquiry and reflection has reached the utmost limit of knowledge . . . he stops, as if to say, what knowest thou? what have thy searchings achieved?" *Zohar*, vol. 1, p. 1b.

[2] *Man is Not Alone*, p. 92.

[3] *Mishnah Torah, teshuvah*, x, 6.

[4] A thief while breaking into a home in order to steal calls upon God to help him, reminds Rabbi Shneur Zalman of Ladi; see *Berachot* 63a.

[5] *Jerushalmi Sanhedrin*, x, 2, 28b.

[6] *Mechilta* to Exodus 15:11. According to the legend in *Gittin* 56b, Titus is supposed to have said blasphemously, "Even the silent ones speak at times, but Thou art silent for ever," see *Arugat Habosem*, vol. 1, p. 26.

[7] *Genesis Rabba*, 30, 10.

16 Beyond Insight

What is the cognitive value of our insights? What is disclosed and what is retained out of such moments? When a person is hit by a bullet, he feels the pain, not the bullet. When a person is called to return, he feels his being called rather than the call. The guiding hand is hidden; what he may sense is his being *an object of concern.* There would be no call to man without a concern for man.

This is the certainty which overwhelms us in such moments: man lives not only in time and space but also in the dimension of God's attentiveness. God is concern, not only power. God is He *to whom we are accountable.*

In the wake of religious insight we retain an awareness that the transcendent God is *He to Whom our conscience is open.* In spite of some ambiguity in the specific demands, we retain a contact that is immediate and one that may remain uninterrupted. We are exposed to the challenge of a power that, not born of our will nor installed by it, robs us of independence by its judgment of the rectitude or depravity of our actions, by its gnawing at our heart when we offend against its injunctions. It is as if there were no privacy within ourselves, no possibility of either retreat or escape, no place in us in which to bury the remains of guilt-feelings. There is a voice that reaches everywhere, knowing no mercy, digging in the burial-places of charitable forgetfulness.

Is the God of this awareness the God *to whom we are accountable?* Is this awareness artificially produced by fears and illusions, and gradually developed as an attitude toward laws that regulated primitive society? Even those who would assume that this was so should not make the mistake of evaluating things by the way in which they came into existence. Some of the most relevant and essential institutions of humanity have started in an incidental manner. It may well be that the art of making tools or the discovery of fermentation originated in magic and superstition. Whatever the origin of conscience may have been, there are few things in the realm of human life that are of such fundamental significance. It is as bold and as far reaching as reason. For just as reason assumes that the processes in nature are intelligible, that there is a rational relationship between events, thus assuming that human intelligence and the natural order are compatible, so does our conscience, our moral sense claim that there is a moral relationship between God and human.

Our sense of what is right and wrong may at times be uncertain. What is indubitably certain is our sense of obligation to answer for our conduct. A unique feature of the conscience is that, unlike reason, its main awareness does not lie in conceiving something but in being related to, in being accountable, in being judged as well as in judging. Accountability means to be accountable *to* someone. Who is that someone? That someone cannot be an abstract law or a blind force; in violating a physical law we never feel any guilt. Nor can it be our own self; the essential admission of the soul is that the self is not its final authority. We have not the power to forgive ourselves the wrongs we have committed. We are open and communicative to someone who transcends us and is concerned with our life.

GOD IS THE SUBJECT

The sense for the realness of God will not be found in insipid concepts; in opinions that are astute, arid, timid; in love that is scant, erratic. Sensitivity to God is given to a broken heart, to a mind that rises above its own wisdom. It is a sensitivity that bursts all abstractions. It is not a mere playing with a notion. There is no conviction without contrition; no affirmation without self-engagement. Consciousness of God is a response, and God is a challenge rather than a notion. We do not think Him, we are stirred by Him. We can never describe Him, we can only return to Him. We may address ourselves to Him; we cannot comprehend Him. We can sense His presence; we cannot grasp His essence.

His is the call, ours the paraphrase; His is the creation, ours a reflection. He is not an object to be comprehended, a thesis to be endorsed; neither the sum of all that is (facts) nor a digest of all that ought to be (ideals). He is the ultimate subject.

The trembling sense for the hereness of God is the assumption of our being accountable to Him. God-awareness is not an act of God being known to man; it is the awareness of man's being known by God. In thinking about Him we are thought by him.[1]

ADVERBS

If we begin with entertaining an opinion of God as the absolute, His realness remains barred behind the abstraction. But opinions are oversimplifications, conclusions. Instead of testifying to an impact they formulate an inference from premises. Even the impact of a thing upon the mind cannot be expressed in the form of an opinion or a conclusion. To conclude means to bring to an end. But who can bring to an end the impact of the sky upon the soul?

We should eschew nouns in speaking of the nature of God. A noun presupposes comprehension. But even the world we encounter is one we apprehend and cannot comprehend.

God seems to be remote, but nothing is as close as He is.[2] When we think He is close, then He is remote; when we think He is remote, then He is near (the Baal Shem). The bridge to God is awe.

In awe our question is not, what is His essence? But rather, what is His relation to man? If God is derived from abstractions, then His indifference to man and man's irrelevance to Him remain compatible with His greatness. But if our awareness of God is an answer to His search for man, or a return, then indeed His realness and His concern dawn upon us together. God's question to man is an act of His concern.

We have no nouns by which to describe His essence; we have only *adverbs* by which to indicate the ways in which He acts toward us.

ONENESS IS THE STANDARD

Everywhere we encounter the mystery: in the rock and in the bee, in the cloud and in the sea; it is as if all things were thoroughfares. But, do all ways lead to *one* goal, to *one* God? How do we know whether all men experience at all times and at all places one and the same reality? Do not the manifold experiences of mystery testify to a multiplicity of deities rather than to one God?

For all its preciousness and intensity, religious insight is susceptible to doubt. What gives us the certainty that the substance of our insight is not a projection of our own soul? Is not the soul a breeding place for illusions? How do we know that our interpretation of what is given to us in moments of religious insight is correct? How do we know that it is a living God, the creator of heaven and earth, whose concern reached the soul? What is the standard by which to test the veracity of religious insights?

Such a standard would have to be an idea, not an event. It would have to be an ultimate idea, worthy of serving as an identification of the divine and at the same time the supreme idea in human thinking, a universal idea. Such an idea is *oneness* or *love,* which is an expression of oneness.

All knowledge and understanding in science, art, ethics, as well as in religion, rest upon its validity.[3] Oneness is the norm, the standard and the goal. If in the afterglow of a religious insight we can see a way to gather up our scattered lives, to unite what lies in strife—we know it is a guidepost on His way.

If a thought generates pride, separation from other people's suffering, unawareness of the dangers of evil—we know it is a deviation from His way.

An insight is not meaningful to one man unless it is capable of becoming meaningful to all men. He who has made that which is at all times, illumines man with thoughts that ought to be valid at all times.

Only that which is good for all men is good for every man. No one is truly inspired for his own sake. He who is blessed, is a blessing for others.

There are many ways but only *one* goal. If there is one source of all, there must be one goal for all. The yearnings are our own, but the answer is *His*.

Beyond all mystery is the mercy of God. It is a love, a mercy that transcends the world, its value and merit. To live by such a love, to reflect it, however numbly, is the test of religious existence.

To summarize: the power of religious truth is a moment of insight, and its content is oneness or love. Source and content may be conveyed in one word: *transcendence*.

Transcendence is the test of religious truth. A genuine insight rends the enclosure of the heart and bestows on man the power to rise above himself.

FROM INSIGHT TO ACTION

How can we be sure that oneness is really a way of God? How do we presume to know what is beyond the mystery? The certainty of being exposed to a presence not of the world is a fact of human existence. But such certainty does not find its fulfillment in esthetic contemplation; it is astir with a demand to live in a way that is worthy of that presence.

The beginning of faith is, as said above, not a feeling for the mystery of living or a sense of awe, wonder and amazement. The root of religion is the question what to do with the feeling for the mystery of living, what to do with awe, wonder and amazement. Religion begins with a consciousness that something is asked of us. It is in that tense, eternal asking in which the soul is caught and in which man's answer is elicited.

A philosophy of Judaism

Something is asked of us. But what? The ultimate question that stirs our soul is anonymous, mysterious, powerful, yet ineffable. Who will put into words, who will teach us the way of God? How shall we know that the way we choose is the way He wants us to pursue?

In moments of insight we are called to return. But how does one return? What is the way to Him? We all sense the grandeur and the mystery. But who will tell us how to answer the mystery? Who will tell us how to live in a way that is compatible with the grandeur, the mystery, and the glory? All we have is a perception but neither words nor deeds in which to phrase or to form an answer.

Man does not live by insight alone; he is in need of a creed, of dogma, of expression, of a way of living. Insights are not a secure possession; they are vague and sporadic. They are like divine sparks, flashing up before us and becoming obscure again, and we fall back into a darkness "almost as black as that in which we were before." The problem is: How to communicate those rare moments of insight to all hours of our life? How to commit intuition to concepts, the ineffable to words, insight to rational understanding? How to convey our insights to others and to unite in a fellowship of faith?

Moments of insight are not experienced with sufficient intensity by all men. Those sparks are powerful enough to light up a soul, but not enough to illumine the world. Has God never said, Let there be light, for all the world to see? In moments of insight God addresses himself to a single soul. Has He never addressed the world, a people, or a community? Has He left Himself without a trace in history for those who do not have the strength to seek Him constantly?

ONLY INSIGHTS AND NOTHING ELSE?

In thinking about the world, we cannot proceed without guidance, supplied by logic and scientific method. In thinking about the living God we must look to the prophets for guidance.

Those who share in the heritage of Israel believe that God is not

163

always evasive. He confided Himself at rare moments to those who were chosen to be guides. We cannot express God, yet God expresses His will to us. It is through His word that we know that God is not beyond good and evil. Our own thinking would leave us in a state of bewilderment if it were not for the guidance we receive.

It is not right for us to be waiting for God, as if he had never entered history. In his quest for God, the man who lives after the age of Sinai must learn to understand the realness of God's search for man. He must not forget the prophets' world, God's waiting for man.

What a sculptor does to a block of marble, the Bible does to our finest intuitions. It is like raising the mystery to expression.

Private insights and inspirations prepare us to accept what the prophets convey. They enable us to understand the question to which revelation is an answer. For our faith does not derive its full substance from private insights. Our faith is faith by virtue of being a part of the community of Israel, by virtue of our having a share in the faith of the prophets. From their words we derive the norms by which to test the veracity of our own insights.

It is through the prophets that we may be able to encounter Him as a Being who is beyond the mystery. In the prophets the ineffable became a voice, disclosing that God is not a being that is apart and away from ourselves, as ancient man believed, that He is not an enigma, but justice, mercy; not only a power to which we are accountable, but also a pattern for our lives. He is not the Unknown; He is the Father, the God of Abraham; out of the endless ages come compassion and guidance. Even the individual who feels forsaken remembers Him as the God of his fathers.

NOTES FOR CHAPTER 16

[1] *Man is Not Alone*, p. 74.
[2] *Jerushalmi Berachot*, 9, 1.
[3] For a detailed analysis, see *Man is Not Alone*, pp. 102-123.

2. REVELATION

17 The Idea of Revelation

We have never been the same since the day on which the voice of God overwhelmed us at Sinai. It is for ever impossible for us to retreat into an age that predates the Sinaitic event. Something unprecedented happened. God revealed His name to us, and we are named after Him. "All the peoples of the earth shall see that you are called by the name of the Lord" (Deuteronomy 28:10). There are two Hebrew names for Jew: *Yehudi*, the first three letters of which are the first three letters of the Ineffable Name, and *Israel*, the end of which, *el*, means God in Hebrew.

If other religions may be characterized as a relation between man and God, Judaism must be described as a relation between *man with Torah* and *God*. The Jew is never alone in the face of God; the Torah is always with him. A Jew without the Torah is obsolete.

The Torah is not the wisdom but the destiny of Israel; not our literature but our essence. It is said to have come into being neither by way of speculation nor by way of poetic inspiration but by way of prophecy or revelation.

It is easy to say prophecy, revelation. But do we sense what we say? Do we understand what these words mean? Do we refer to a certainty or a fantasy, an idea or a fact, a myth or a mystery when we speak of prophecy or revelation? Did it ever happen that God disclosed His will to some men for the benefit of all men?

It is not historical curiosity that excites our interest in the problem of revelation. As an event of the past which subsequently affected the course of civilization, revelation would not engage the modern mind any more than the Battle of Marathon or the Congress of Vienna. If it concerns us, it is not because of the impact it had upon past generations but as something which may or may not be of perpetual, unabating relevance. In entering this discourse, we do not conjure up the shadow of an archaic phenomenon, but attempt to debate the question whether to believe that there is a voice in the world that pleads with us in the name of God.

Thus, it is not only a personal issue, but one that concerns the history of all men from the beginning of time to the end of days. No one who has, at least once in his life, sensed the terrifying seriousness of human history or the earnestness of individual existence can afford to ignore that problem. He must decide, he must choose between yes and no.

WE FORGOT THE QUESTION

The most serious obstacle which modern men encounter in entering a discussion about revelation does not arise from their doubts as to whether the accounts of the prophets about their experiences are authentic. The most critical vindication of these accounts, even if it were possible, would be of little relevance. The most serious problem is *the absence of the problem*. An answer to be meaningful presupposes the awareness of a question, but the climate in which we live today is not congenial to the continued growth of questions which have taken centuries to cultivate. The Bible is an answer to the supreme question: *what does God demand of us?* Yet the question has gone out of the world. God is portrayed as a mass of vagueness behind a veil of enigmas, and His voice has become alien to our minds, to our hearts, to our souls. We have learned to listen to every "I" except the "I" of God. The man of our time may

168

proudly declare: nothing animal is alien to me but everything divine is. This is the status of the Bible in modern life: it is a sublime answer, but we do not know the question any more. Unless we recover the question, there is no hope of understanding the Bible.

THE DOGMA OF MAN'S SELF-SUFFICIENCY

Resistance to revelation in our time came from two diametrically opposed conceptions of man: one maintained that man was too great to be in need of divine guidance, and the other maintained that man was too small to be worthy of divine guidance. The first conception came from social science, and the second from natural science.

Since the days of the Deists, the idea of man's self-sufficiency has been used as an argument to discredit the belief in revelation. The certainty of man's capacity to find peace, perfection, and the meaning of existence, gained increasing momentum with the advancement of technology. Man's fate, we were told, depended solely upon the development of his social awareness and the utilization of his own power. The course of history was regarded as a perpetual progress in cooperation, an increasing harmonization of interests. Man is too good to be in need of supernatural guidance.

The idea of man's self-sufficiency, man's exaggerated consciousness of himself, was based upon a generalization; from the fact that technology could solve some problems it was deduced that technology could solve all problems. This proved to be a fallacy. Social reforms, it was thought, would cure all ills and eliminate all evils from our world. Yet we have finally discovered what prophets and saints have always known: bread and power alone will not save humanity. There is a passion and drive for cruel deeds which only the awe and fear of God can soothe; there is a suffocating selfishness in man which only holiness can ventilate.

Man is meaningless without God, and any attempt to establish a system of values on the basis of the dogma of man's self-sufficiency is doomed to failure.

Our understanding of man and his liberty has undergone profound change in our time. The problem of man is more grave than we were able to realize a generation ago. What we used to sense in our worst fears turned out to have been a utopia compared with what has happened in our own days. We have discovered that reason may be perverse, that science is no security.

Is liberty alone, regardless of what we do with it, regardless of good and evil, of kindness and cruelty, the highest good? Is liberty an empty concept—the ability to do what we please? Is not the meaning of liberty contingent upon its compatibility with righteousness? There is no freedom except the freedom bestowed upon us by God; there is no freedom without sanctity.

THE IDEA OF MAN'S UNWORTHINESS

The advancement in both natural and social sciences has compelled us to realize how insignificantly small man is in relation to the universe and how abortive are his attempts to establish a universally valid system of values. It is in such humility that modern man finds it preposterous to assume that the infinite spirit should come down to commune with the feeble, finite mind of man; that man could be an ear to God. With the concept of the absolute so far removed from the grasp of his mind, man is, at best, bewildered at the claims of the prophets. With his relative sense of values, with his mind conditioned by circumstances and reduced to the grasp of the piecemeal, constantly stumbling in his efforts to establish a system of universally integrated ideas, how can he conceive that man was ever able to grasp the unconditioned?

It is, furthermore, hard for the mind to believe that any member of a species who can organize or even witness the murder of millions and feel no regret should ever be endowed with the ability to receive a thought of God. If man can remain callous to the horror of exterminating millions of men, women, and children; if man can be bloodstained and self-righteous, distort what his conscience tells,

A philosophy of Judaism

make soap of human flesh, then how can we assume that he is worthy of being approached and guided by the infinite God?

Man rarely comprehends how dangerously mighty he is. In our own days it is becoming obvious to many of us that unless man attaches himself to a source of spiritual power—a match for the source of energy that he is now able to exploit—a few men may throw all men into final disaster. There is only one source: the will and wisdom of the living God.

The realization of the dangerous greatness of man, of his immense power and ability to destroy all life on earth, must completely change our conception of man's place and role in the divine scheme. If this great world of ours is not a trifle in the eyes of God, if the Creator is at all concerned with His creation, then man—who has the power to devise both culture and crime, but who is also able to be a proxy for divine justice—is important enough to be the recipient of spiritual light at the rare dawns of his history.

Unless history is a vagary of nonsense, there must be a counterpart to the immense power of man to destroy, there must be a voice that says NO to man, a voice not vague, faint and inward, like qualms of conscience, but equal in spiritual might to man's power to destroy.

The voice speaks to the spirit of prophetic men in singular moments of their lives and cries to the masses through the horror of history. The prophets respond, the masses despair.

The Bible, speaking in the name of a Being that combines justice with omnipotence, is the never-ceasing outcry of "No" to humanity. In the midst of our applauding the feats of civilization, the Bible flings itself like a knife slashing our complacency, reminding us that God, too, has a voice in history. Only those who are satisfied with the state of affairs or those who choose the easy path of escaping from society, rather than to stay within it and to keep themselves clean of the mud of specious glories, will resent its attack on human independence.

Resistance to revelation came also from the conception of God. Of one thing we seem to be sure: God dwells at an absolute distance from man, abiding in deep silence. Is it meaningful, then, to speak of communication between God and man?

Patient, pliant, and submissive to our minds is the world of nature, but obstinately silent. We adore her wealth and tacit wisdom, we tediously decipher her signs, but she never speaks to us. Or do we expect the stars to understand us or the sea to be persuaded? Communication is an act contingent upon so many intricate and complex conditions that the idea of nature addressing herself to man is inconceivable. Communication would not only presuppose her being endowed with a soul, but also man's possessing a mental capacity to understand her specific signs of communication. Still, the prophetic claim that the eternal God addressed Himself to a mortal mind is not inimical to reason. The very structure of matter is made possible by the way in which the endless crystallizes in the smallest. If the stream of energy that is stored up in the sun and the soil can be channeled into a blade of grass, why should it be *a priori* excluded that the spirit of God reached into the minds of men?

There is such a distance between the sun and a flower. Can a flower, worlds away from the source of energy, attain a perception of its origin? Can a drop of water ever soar to behold, even for a moment, the stream's distant source? In prophecy it is as if the sun communed with the flower, as if the source sent out a current to reach a drop.

Let us pause for a moment to consider the constant *interaction* that exists between the somatic and the psychic. A touch of the finger tips is translated into a concept, while an intention of the mind is communicated to the body. How this interaction takes place remains indescribable. Are we, then, because of the indescribability of revelation, justified in rejecting *a priori* as untrue the assertion of the prophets that, at certain hours in Israel's history, the divine came in touch with a few chosen souls? That the creative source of our own selves addressed itself to man?

If there are moments in which genius speaks for all men, why should we deny that there are moments in which a voice speaks for God? that the source of goodness communicates its way to the human mind?

True, it seems incredible that we should hold in our gaze words containing a breath of God. What we forget is that at this moment we breathe what God is creating, that right in front of us we behold works that reflect His infinite wisdom, His infinite goodness.

THE DOGMA OF GOD'S TOTAL SILENCE

In many minds, not knowing God is an abyss, with a rumor floating over it about an ultimate being, of which they only know it is an immense unconscious mass of mystery. It is from the perspective of such knowledge that the prophets' claim seems preposterous.

Let us examine that perspective. In attributing eternal mysteriousness to the ultimate being, we definitely claim to know it. Thus, the ultimate being is not an unknown but a known God. In other words: a God whom we know but one who does not know, the great Unknower. We proclaim the ignorance of God as well as our knowledge of His being ignorant!

This seems to be a part of our pagan heritage: to say, the Supreme Being is a total mystery, and even having accepted the God of creation we still cling to the assumption that He who has the power to create a world is never able to utter a word. Yet why should we assume that God is forever imprisoned in silence? Why should we *a priori* exclude the power of expression from the absolute being? If the world is the work of God, isn't it conceivable that there would be within His work signs of His expression?

We do not cease to proclaim *the dogma of God's total silence* and act as if God had never spoken and if He did man was too deaf to hear. But at times, some of us shudder: is not that dogma a frightful slur?

True, the claim of the prophets is staggering, almost incredible. But to us, living in this horribly beautiful world, God's thick silence is incomparably more staggering and totally incredible.

THE PERSONAL ANALOGY

In our own lives many of us have found that there are channels of knowledge other than those of speculation and observation. When living true to the wonder of the steadily unfolding wisdom, we feel at times as if the echo of an echo of a voice were piercing the silence, trying in vain to reach our attention. We feel at times called upon, not knowing by whom, against our will, terrified at the power invested in our words, in our deeds, in our thoughts.

In our own lives the voice of God speaks slowly, a syllable at a time. Reaching the peak of years, dispelling some of our intimate illusions and learning how to spell the meaning of life-experiences backwards, some of us discover how the scattered syllables form a single phrase. Those who know that this life of ours takes place in a world that is not all to be explained in human terms; that every moment is a carefully concealed act of His creation, cannot but ask: is there anything wherein His voice is not suppressed? Is there anything wherein His creation is not concealed?

Behind the radiant cloud of living, perplexing the unacquainted souls, some men have sensed the sound of *Let There Be,* in the fullness of being. In others not only a song but a voice, lifting the curtain of unknowableness, reached the mind. Those who know that the grace of guidance may be ultimately bestowed upon those who pray for it, that in spite of their unworthiness and lowliness they may be enlightened by a spark that comes unexpectedly but in far-reaching wisdom, undeserved, yet saving, will not feel alien to the minds that perceived not a spark but a flame.

The idea of revelation remains an absurdity as long as we are

174

A philosophy of Judaism

unable to comprehend the impact with which the realness of God is pursuing man, every man. However, collecting the memories of the sparks of illuminations we have perceived, the installments of insight that have been bestowed upon us throughout the years, we will find it impossible to remain certain of the impossibility of revelation.

18 The Prophetic Understatement

THE IDEA, THE CLAIM, THE RESULT

In the previous chapter we discussed *the idea* of revelation and the major reasons for man's resistance to it. We attempted to indicate its importance to the human situation and suggested that it is impossible to remain certain of the impossibility of revelation. However, *an idea,* even when proved to be plausible, may still not be a fact. Is it not conceivable that God did not meet our expectation? What gives us the assurance that our belief in revelation is not a compromise with wishful thinking? Should we not resign ourselves to the belief that there is a God but He has no voice?

A clarification of this question will depend on our dealing with another question, namely, why do we turn to the Bible in our search for the voice of God in the world? It is because the Bible does more than posit the idea or the possibility of revelation. In the Bible we are confronted with *a claim,* with prophets who claim to convey the will of God; a fact that has dominated the history of Israel. Thus, in approaching the Bible, it is not a principle, a general idea, or a metaphysical possibility which we discuss, but specific prophetic acts which, according to the Bible, happened in the life of the people of Israel between the time of Moses and the time of Malachi.

Had the Bible been lost, had the words of the prophets disappeared, and all that was left was a remembrance of men who

176

claimed to have been prophets, the only object of exploration would be their claim. However, the Bible is with us to this very day, and what we encounter is not only human beings who claimed to have had extraordinary experiences: we encounter extraordinary words. Thus it is not that claim alone, or even primarily, that draws us to the Bible. It is *what* the prophets say that is a challenge to our life, to our thinking, and that drives us in our efforts to understand the meaning of that claim.

It is, therefore, necessary to distinguish between three aspects of the problem of revelation: *the idea, the claim,* and *the result.* The idea of revelation we discussed in the previous chapter. It is the claim to which we will turn now before we discuss the words or the result.

At stake in our discussion is not only the belief that the will of God may reach the mind of man, but also the question of either accepting or rejecting the Bible's formidable claim that God really is such as the prophets proclaim; that His will really is such as the prophets maintain.

WHAT IS PROPHETIC INSPIRATION?

The prophets' consciousness of being inspired; the unshakable conviction that the message they brought to the people was not the product of their own hearts is the starting-point of our inquiry.

In a moment of crisis Moses stakes his entire authority on the claim of being inspired by God.[1] In a variety of ways the prophets maintain that their words did not come out of "their own heart" (Ezekiel 13:2); that their prophecies were inspirations, not inventions; that it was God who sent them to the people (Isaiah 48:16). It is our task to deal with two questions: what is the meaning of prophetic inspiration and what is the truth about prophetic inspiration? The first question inquires: what kind of act is described by prophetic inspiration? The second question inquires: is it true? Did it really happen?

Our inquiry must begin with the first question, for it is obvi-

177

ously necessary to know what prophetic inspiration is before attempting to prove or disprove its having taken place. What kind of fact is described by the term prophecy? What does it signify?

Today it is possible to imagine a great orator whose broadcast would eventually become the focus of mankind's attention. But it surpasses our imagination to conceive of a human being who could become the focus of attention of heaven and earth and be addressed by the entire universe. Even if we assume that there is a spirit which animates all existence, its mysteriousness essentially outstrips the scope of the human mind. The experience of having been spoken to by Him, who is more than heaven and earth, has a grandeur in comparison to which all words lose their weight. An examination of the psychic and historic circumstances would be of little relevance. Whatever answer may be found to the question— How did prophecy happen? Was it an inner or an external experience? What was its historic background?—will revolve around the adventitious, just as a discussion of colons and semicolons will hardly bring out the content of a sentence. The words and their meaning have to be grasped first.

Adequate understanding of a phrase depends upon its being compatible with the meaning intended by the author of the phrase. Our question then is: What did the prophet mean by the phrase, "God spoke"? To understand the statements of the prophet about his experience we must keep in mind the following principles about the nature of these statements: (1) things and words have many meanings. (2) the prophet's statements are understatements. (3) the language of the prophet is the language of grandeur and mystery. (4) there is a distinction between descriptive and indicative words. (5) the statements of the prophet must be taken responsively.

WORDS HAVE MANY MEANINGS

The surest way of misunderstanding revelation is to take it literally, to imagine that God spoke to the prophet on a long-distance telephone. Yet most of us succumb to such fancy, forgetting that the

A philosophy of Judaism

cardinal sin in thinking about ultimate issues is *literal-mindedness.*

The error of literal-mindedness is in assuming that things and words have only one meaning. The truth is that things and words stand for different meanings in different situations. Gold means wealth to the merchant, a means of adornment to the jeweler, "a non-rusting malleable ductile metal of high specific gravity" to the engineer, and kindness to the rhetorician ("a golden heart"). Light is a form of energy to the physicist, a medium of loveliness to the artist, an expression of grandeur in the first chapter of the Bible. *Ruah,* the Hebrew word for spirit, signifies also breath, wind, direction. And he who thinks only of breath, forfeits the deeper meaning of the term. God is called father, but he who takes this name physiologically distorts the meaning of God.

The language of faith employs only a few words coined in its own spirit; most of its terms are borrowed from the general sphere of human experience and endowed with new meaning. Consequently, in taking these terms literally we miss the unique connotations which they assumed in the religious usage.

The meaning of words in scientific language must be clear, distinct, unambiguous, conveying the same concept to all people. In poetry, however, words that have only one meaning are considered flat. The right word is often one that evokes a plurality of meanings and one that must be understood on more than one level. What is a virtue in scientific language is a failure in poetic expression.

Is it correct to insist that Biblical words must be understood exclusively according to one literal meaning? It often seems as if the intention of the prophets was to be understood not in one way, on one level, but in many ways, on many levels, according to the situation in which we find ourselves. And if such was their intention, we must not restrict our understanding to one meaning.

THE PROPHETIC UNDERSTATEMENT

It is usually assumed that the Biblical writers had a bent for lofty, swelling language, a preference for extravagant exaggeration of statement. However, pondering about the substance of what they were trying to express, it dawns upon us that what sounds to us as *grand eloquence* is *understatement* and *modesty of expression*. Indeed, their words must not be taken literally, because a literal understanding would be a partial, shallow understanding; because the literal meaning is but a *minimum of meaning*.[2]

"God spoke." Is it to be taken symbolically: He did not speak, yet it was as if He did? The truth is that *what is literally true to us is a metaphor compared with what is metaphysically real to God.* A thousand years to us are a day to Him. And when applied to Him our mightiest words are feeble understatements.

And yet, that "God spoke" is not a symbol. A symbol does not raise a world out of nothing. Nor does a symbol call a Bible into being. The speech of God is not less but more than literally real.

THE LANGUAGE OF GRANDEUR AND MYSTERY

The modern student of the Bible is tempted to interpret the Bible in the context of his own world outlook. To understand the authentic meaning of the Bible we must remember its basic conception of the world. The Biblical man is primarily attentive to the aspect of *grandeur,* and his language for revelation is that of grandeur and mystery.

"The word of God," "God spoke"—what should it be compared with? Should it be compared with the articulate utterance in the voice of a human being? Now, to be perceived by man the word of God must be conveyed by a voice; yet to be divine it must be conveyed by something far greater than a voice. There are many voices in the world; what was the divine quality of that utterance? If God is He who created the world, how could His utterance be compared with a phenomenon which means so little even within the world?

To say that to the Biblical man the word of God is as great as the cosmic power, as the power that holds all the elements and forces together would be an understatement. The word of God is the power of creation. He said *Let there be, and it was.*

> By the word of the Lord the heavens were made,
> And all their host by the breath of His mouth.
> For He spoke, and it came to be,
> He commanded, and it stood forth.
>
> Psalms 33:6,9

Sublime, magnificent is the world. Yet if it were not for His word, there would be no world, no sublimity and no magnificence.

What is the word of God to the prophets? A combination of sounds conveying a conventional idea and capable of serving as a part of a sentence?

> Is not my word like fire, says the Lord, and like a hammer which breaks the rock in pieces?
>
> Jeremiah 23:29

The extraordinary quality of the divine word is in its mystery of omnipotence. Out of God went the mystery of His utterance, and a word, a sound, reached the ear of man. The spirit of His creative power brought a material world into being; the spirit of His revealing power brought the Bible into being.

DESCRIPTIVE AND INDICATIVE WORDS

The human mind is a repository of a variety of ideas, some of which are definite and expressive while others resist definition and remain ineffable. Correspondingly, there are two kinds of words: *descriptive* words which stand in a fixed relation to conventional and definite meanings, such as the concrete nouns, chair, table, or the terms of science; and *indicative* words which stand in a fluid relation to ineffable meanings and, instead of describing, merely intimate something which we intuit but cannot fully comprehend. The content of words such as God, time, beauty, eternity cannot be faithfully imagined or reproduced in our minds. Still they convey a wealth of meaning to our sense of the ineffable. Their function is not to call up a definition in our minds but to introduce us to a reality which they signify.

The function of descriptive words is to evoke an idea which we already possess in our minds, to evoke *preconceived meanings.* Indicative words have another function. What they call forth is not so much a memory but a *response,* ideas unheard of, meanings not fully realized before.

A great number of words serve both a descriptive and an indicative function. To the captain of a boat the words "wind" and "dawn" have definite meanings: a mass of air in motion of a particular direction and velocity; a moment definable in terms of a clock. But when reading in a poem of *"the wind that sighs before the dawn,"* do we try to ascertain the *exact* moment of time the poet had in mind? Do we ask what was the direction or velocity of the wind? And yet there is no doubt that the poet refers to the same wind and the same dawn which the captain has to deal with. He refers to another aspect of the same phenomenon.

It is equally true that in reading of "the wind that sighs" no one will inquire about the physiology of the wind's inhaling and expelling air. And yet there is a type of reader who, when you talk to him of Jacob's ladder, would ask the number of the steps.

RESPONSIVE INTERPRETATION

The wind in the line quoted above is not a figure of speech. To take it *figuratively,* to regard it as referring to something else than a wind, is to misunderstand the poet's experience and intention. Yet to take it *literally* in the same sense in which the meteorologist knows it is to cling to a level of meaning different than the level on which the poet sensed it. It is the wind on the metasymbolic level of meaning that the poet is referring to. Words used in this sense must neither be taken literally nor figuratively but *responsively*.

To take a word literally means to reproduce in our mind an idea

A philosophy of Judaism

which the word denotes and with which it is definitely associated in our memory. It is apparent that only descriptive words can be taken literally. To take a descriptive word figuratively is to assume that the author is speaking double talk; saying one thing, he means another. It is apparent that only metaphoric expressions must be taken figuratively. Indicative words must be taken responsively. In order to understand them we must part with preconceived meanings; clichés are of no avail. They are not portraits but *clues,* serving us as guides, suggesting a line of thinking.

This indeed is our situation in regard to a statement such as "God spoke." It refers to an idea that is not at home in the mind, and the only way to understand its meaning is by *responding* to it. We must adapt our minds to a meaning unheard of before. The word is but a clue; the real burden of understanding is upon the mind and soul of the reader.

NOTES FOR CHAPTER 18

[1] "And Moses said: Hereby shall ye know that the Lord has sent me to do all these works, and that I have not done them of my own mind" (Numbers 16:28).

[2] The prophets adjusted their words to the capacity of human understanding; see *Mechilta* to Exodus 19:18; compare *The Mishnah of Rabbi Eliezer,* rule 14, ed. Enelow, New York, 1933, p. 25.

19 The Mystery of Revelation

If revelation was a moment in which God succeeded in reaching man, then to try to describe it exclusively in terms of optics or acoustics, or to inquire was it a vision or was it a sound? was it forte or piano? would be even more ludicrous than to ask about the velocity of "the wind that sighs before the dawn." Of course, the prophets claimed to have seen, to have heard. But that kind of seeing and hearing cannot be subjected to psychological or physiological analysis. An analysis of the poet's ability to hear the wind sigh would have no relevance to our understanding of the poem. Did the prophet claim to have encountered God in the way in which he met one of his contemporaries or in the way in which Aristotle met Alexander the Great?

If revelation were *only* a psycho-physical act, then it would be little more than a human experience, an event in the life of man. Yet just as a work of sculpture is more than the stone in which it is carved, so is revelation *more* than a human experience. True, a revelation that did not become known by experience would be like a figure carved in the air. Still its being a human experience is but a part of what really happened in revelation, and we must, therefore, not equate the event of revelation with man's experience of revelation.

THE MYSTERY OF REVELATION

The nature of revelation, being an event in the realm of the ineffable, is something which words cannot spell, which human lan-

184

guage will never be able to portray. Our categories are not applicable to that which is both within and beyond the realm of matter and mind. In speaking about revelation, the more descriptive the terms, the less adequate is the description. The words in which the prophets attempted to relate their experiences were not photographs but illustrations, not descriptions but songs. A psychological reconstruction of the prophetic act is, therefore, no more possible than the attempt to paint a photographic likeness of a face on the basis of a song. The word "revelation" is like an exclamation; it is an *indicative* rather than a descriptive term. Like all terms that express the ultimate, it points to its meaning rather than fully rendering it. "It is very difficult to have a true conception of the events at Sinai, for there has never been before nor will there ever be again anything like it."[1] "We believe," says Maimonides, "that the Torah has reached Moses from God in a manner which is described in Scripture figuratively by the term 'word,' and that nobody has ever known how that took place except Moses himself to whom that word reached."[2]

We must not try to read chapters in the Bible dealing with the event at Sinai as if they were texts in systematic theology. Its intention is to celebrate the mystery, to introduce us to it rather than to penetrate or to explain it. As a report about revelation the Bible itself is *a midrash*.

To convey what the prophets experienced, the Bible could use either terms of description or terms of indication. Any description of the act of revelation in empirical categories would have produced a caricature. This is why all the Bible does is to state *that* revelation happened; *how* it happened is something they could only convey in words that are evocative and suggestive.

The same word may be used in either way. The sound is the same, but the spirit is different. "And God said: Let there be light" is different in spirit from a statement such as "And Smith said: Let us turn on the light." The second statement conveys a definite meaning; the first statement evokes an inner response to an ineffable meaning. The statement, man speaks, describes a physiological and psychological act; the statement, God speaks, conveys a mystery. It calls upon our sense of wonder and amazement to respond to a mystery that surpasses our power of comprehension.

There are spiritual facts which are wholly irreducible to verbal expression and completely beyond the range of either imagination or definition.

It was not essential that His will be transmitted as sound; it was essential that it be made known to us. The sound or sight is to the transcendent event what a metaphor is to an abstract principle.

THE NEGATIVE THEOLOGY OF REVELATION

When challenged, the prophets could only deny that what they said was their own: "Not out of my heart" (Numbers 16:28; compare Ezekiel, ch. 13). Revelation can only be described *via negationis;* we can only say what it is not. Perhaps the oldest example of negative theology was applied to the understanding of revelation. We read that Elijah was told (I Kings 19:11-12):

> Go forth, and stand upon the mount before the Lord.
> And behold, the Lord passed by,
> And a great strong wind rent the mountains
> And broke in pieces the rocks before the Lord;
> But the Lord was not in the wind;
> And after the wind an earthquake;
> But the Lord was not in the earthquake;
> And after the earthquake a fire;
> But the Lord was not in the fire;
> And after the fire a still small voice.

Literally: *a voice of silence.* Only upon hearing the almost inaudible did the passionate fiery Elijah wrap his face in his mantle; he went out and stood in the entrance of the cave, to listen to the voice.

The voice he perceived was almost stillness.

A philosophy of Judaism

TO IMAGINE IS TO PERVERT

For us, therefore, to imagine revelation, namely, to conceive it as if it were a psychic or physical process, is to pervert its essence and to wreck its mystery. It is just as improper to conceive revelation as a psycho-physical act as it is to conceive God as a corporeal being. Few of us are able to think in a way which is never crossed by the path of imagination, and it is usually at the crossroads of thought and imagination that the great sweep of the spirit swerves into the blind alley of a parabolic image.

A hasid, it is told, after listening to the discourse of one who lectured to him about the lofty concept of God according to the philosophers, said: "If God were the way you imagine Him, I would not believe in Him." However subtle and noble our concepts may be, as soon as they become descriptive, namely, definite, they confine Him and force Him into the triteness of our minds. Never is our mind so inadequate as in trying to describe God. The same applies to the idea of revelation. When defined, described, it completely eludes us.

THE ELIMINATION OF ANTHROPOMORPHISM

It is a depressing sight to see how the truth recedes through awkward formulations; how many of our conceptions of Him and His acts tend to confine and to distort Him. We are inclined to ascribe to God a human shape, and we are inclined to think of prophecy as a psycho-physical act. Yet this is the axiom of Biblical thinking: God who created the world is unlike the world. To form an image of Him or His acts is to deny His existence. Not all reality is material; not all real acts are perceptible to our bodily senses. It is not only by his ear that man can hear. It is not only the physical sound that can reach the spirit of man.

The leading exponents of Jewish thought exhort us not to imagine that God speaks, or that a sound is produced by Him through organs of speech.

"The perception by the senses, especially by hearing and seeing, is best known to us; we have no idea or notion of any other mode of communication between the soul of one man and that of another man except by means of speaking, namely by the sounds produced by lips, tongue, and other organs of speech. When, therefore, we are to be informed that God has a knowledge of things, and that communication is made by Him to the prophets who convey it to us, they represent Him to us . . . as speaking, namely, that communications from Him reach the prophets."[3] However, in being "told that God addressed the prophets and spoke to them, our minds are merely to receive a notion that there is a divine knowledge to which the prophets attain; we are to be impressed with the idea that the things which the prophets communicate to us come from the Lord and are not *altogether* the product of their own conceptions and ideas. . . . We must not suppose that in speaking God employed voice or sound."[4]

"Every intelligent person knows" that when the Bible asserts that the people saw or heard the voice at Sinai, it does not refer to a "perception by the eye" or "a perception by the ear," but to a spiritual perception.[5] "There was neither a physical voice nor a physical perception but rather a spiritual voice. . . . Is it conceivable that the words spoken by God should be in the manner of human speech? These words were audible to Moses but not to the people. Is it natural that one and the same voice should be heard by one person but not by the other?"[6]

LIKE NO OTHER EVENT

Vain would be any attempt to reconstruct the hidden circumstances under which a word of God alarmed a prophet's soul. Who could uncover the divine data or piece together the strange perceptions of a Moses? The prophet did not leave information behind. All we have is the prophet's certainty, endless awe and appreciation. All we have is a Book, and all we can do is to try to sense the unworded across its words.

God in search of man

What actually transpired is as unimaginable to us as it was unbelievable to those who witnessed it. We cannot comprehend it. We can only answer it. Or refuse to answer.

Some of us approach the Bible stalking on the stilts of a definition. But who are we to speak of the mystery without knowledge and to state what it means that His spirit burst forth from its hiddenness? Who has fathomed the depth of the Bible? Have we entered the springs of its wisdom or walked in the recesses of its innermost meaning? Have the gates of its holiness ever been open to us, and have we ever comprehended the expanse of its word? Where were we when the word was set as a limit, and God said: Thus far shall my wisdom be disclosed and no farther?

Souls are not introduced to a range of mountains through the courtesy of a definition. Our goal, then, must not be to find a definition, but to learn how to sense, how to intuit the will of God in the words. The essence of intuition is not in grasping what is describable but in sensing what is ineffable. The goal is to train the reason for the appreciation of that which lies beyond reason. It is only through our sense of the ineffable that we may intuit the mystery of revelation.

The dogmatic theologian who tries to understand the act of revelation in terms of his own generalizations takes himself too seriously and is guilty of oversimplification. Revelation is a mystery for which reason has no concepts. To ignore its mysterious nature is an oversight of fatal consequence. Out of the darkness came the voice to Moses; and out of the darkness comes the Word to us. The issue is baffling.

And if you ask: what was it like when the people stood at Sinai, hearing God's voice? the answer will be: Like no other event in the history of man. There are countless legends, myths, reports, but none of them tells of a whole people witnessing an event such as Sinai.

189

NOTES FOR CHAPTER 19

1 Maimonides, *The Guide of the Perplexed,* Book II, ch. 33.
2 Introduction to his *Commentary on Mishnah Sanhedrin,* ch. X, Principle 8.
3 Maimonides, *The Guide of the Perplexed,* I, 65.
4 *Ibid.,* I, 41.
5 Rabbi Shlomo ibn Adret, *Maamar Al Ishmael* in J. Perles, R. *Salomo b. Abraham b. Aderath,* Breslau, 1863 (Hebrew), p. 12.
6 Rabbi Loew of Prague, *Tiferet Israel,* ch. 43.

20 The Paradox of Sinai

To us today the great puzzle is: how is revelation possible? how to conceive that the eternally hidden should become revealed? While to the Biblical man the great puzzle is: how is the experience of revelation possible? how is it possible for man to endure the shattering presence of God?

God to the Biblical man is a Being whose manifestation is more than flesh and blood can bear. One cannot see Him, one cannot hear Him and remain alive (Exodus 33:20; Deuteronomy 4:33). "A dread, a great darkness" fell upon Abraham (Genesis 15:12). To perceive Him is to be crushed by His majesty. In His sight, seraphim cover their faces and a prophet cries "I am undone" (Isaiah 6:5). When aflame with His presence, the world is consumed.

Then the startling moment occurred: God appeared to Moses "in a flame of fire out of the bush; and he looked, and lo, the bush was burning, yet it was not consumed" (Exodus 3:2). In the face of that startling fact, Moses said: "I will turn aside and see this great sight, *why* the bush is not burnt." The question "why" was never answered. How indeed is it possible for the world to bear the divine?

Perhaps this is the meaning of the burning bush. A new element was brought into being: fire that burns but does not consume. It indicated a new order in God's relation to man, namely, that *to reveal He must conceal,* that to impart His *wisdom* He must hide His *power*. It made revelation possible.

191

The bush was the precedent for Sinai that was not crushed, for Israel that was not consumed. When the Lord was about to utter His word:

> Mount Sinai was wrapped in smoke,
> because the Lord descended upon it in fire;
> the smoke of it went up like the smoke of a kiln,
> the whole mountain trembled greatly.
>
> Exodus 19:18

> The mountain burned with fire up to the heart of heaven,
> darkness, cloud and thick darkness.
>
> Deuteronomy 4:11

The mountain burned with fire and was not consumed.

To the Biblical man, the miracle of revelation was not only in the fact of God speaking but also in the fact of man being able to endure it.

"For ask now of the days that are past, which were before you, since the day that God created man upon the earth, and ask from one end of heaven to the other, whether such a great thing as this has ever happened or was ever heard of. Did any people ever hear the voice of a god speaking out of the midst of the fire, as you have heard *and still live?*" (Deuteronomy 4:32 f).

At the foot of Sinai, the people implored Moses, "Speak thou with us, and we will hear, but let not God speak to us, lest we die" (Exodus 20:19).

IN DEEP DARKNESS

The content of the Decalogue is utterly plain, utterly simple: Thou shalt not kill. . . . Thou shalt not steal. . . . Yet the manner in which these words were proclaimed is shrouded in mystery. "These words (namely the Decalogue) the Lord spoke to all your assembly *out of the midst of the fire (esh), the cloud ('anan) and the deep darkness* ('arafel)" (Deuteronomy 5:19). In order to understand what is articulated here we must first of all ascertain whether "fire," "cloud" and "deep darkness" are empty platitudes or distinct terms, words expressing a definite conception.

"Deep darkness" ('*arafel*) is where God dwells. Solomon who built the great Temple in Jerusalem knew that the Lord who fixed the sun in the heavens decided to dwell in "deep darkness."[1]

With amazing consistency the Bible records that the theophanies witnessed by Moses occurred in a cloud. Again and again we hear that the Lord "called to Moses out of the midst of the cloud" (Exodus 24:16); that the Lord appeared and spoke to him "in the pillar of a cloud" (Numbers 12:4; Deuteronomy 12:5; Psalms 99:7); the "Lord descended in the cloud" (Exodus 34:5; Numbers 11:25); "the glory of the Lord appeared in the cloud" (Exodus 16:10); "I will appear in the cloud" (Leviticus 16:2).

We must neither willfully ignore nor abuse by allegorization these important terms. Whatever specific fact it may denote, it unequivocally conveys to the mind the fundamental truth that God was *concealed* even when He *revealed,* that even while his voice became manifest His essence remained hidden.

In the divine words which for the first time announced to Moses that the unparalleled theophany at Sinai is about to happen before the eyes of the whole people, an unparalleled phrase is found, one that occurs nowhere else in the Bible and one that expresses what the theophany was like: "Lo, I am coming to you *in the thickness of a cloud*" (Exodus 19:9). It was in the most obscure or most hidden part of a cloud, or in a hiddenness deeper than the one Moses himself had known, that the theophany at Sinai occurred.

BEYOND THE MYSTERY

The mystery stands between God and the people. The people at Sinai are overawed; they tremble and stand far off.[2] But beyond the mystery is meaning, beyond "the deep darkness" is light, this is why Moses was able to draw near "to the deep darkness where God was," able to enter "the cloud" (Exodus 20:21; 24:18).

The extreme hiddenness of God was a fact of constant awareness to the Biblical man. It is this awareness that makes clear the transcendent meaning of the Divine word: The clear unambiguous will of God is not lower but higher than the mystery. There is *meaning beyond the mystery*. This is our reason for ultimate rejoicing:

> The Lord reigns; let the earth rejoice;
> let many coastlands be glad.
> *Cloud and deep darkness* are round
> *about Him;*
> *righteousness and justice are the*
> *foundation* of His throne.
>
> Psalms 97:1-2

THE TWO ASPECTS

What happened on Sinai? The Bible tries to say it in two ways. What it says in one is something words can hardly bear: "The Lord came down upon Mount Sinai" (Exodus 19:20). No sentence in the world has ever said more: He who is beyond, hidden and exalted above space and time was humbly here, for all of Israel to sense. But the Bible also speaks in another way: "I have talked to you from heaven" (Exodus 20:22). He did not descend upon the earth; all that happened was that His word welled "from heaven." These passages do not contradict each other; they refer not to one but to two events. For *revelation was both an event to God and an event to man*. Indeed, in the second passage it is God who speaks (in the first person); the first passage conveys what the people experienced (it speaks of God in the third person). The same act had two aspects. God did and did not descend upon the earth. The voice came out of heaven but man heard it out of Sinai.

Scant and meager are the records about the event if all they convey is what they literally describe, namely, a natural phenomenon. To us today fire is a physical phenomenon conveying no message, containing no reference to God who creates the world and the force of fire. Sinai was a moment in which the fire that does not consume was a witness to God.

A philosophy of Judaism

And yet, the perception of fire, thunder and lightning was a perception on the periphery. They perceived the awesome sight, yet they did not dare to enter it.

"And all the people perceived the thunderings and the lightnings, the sound of the trumpet and the mountain smoking, and the people were afraid and they trembled, and they stood far off . . . but Moses drew near the thick darkness where God was" (Exodus 20:18-21).

When the sainted master, Rabbi Isaac Jacob, the Seer of Lublin, was about to recite the blessing over the four plants on *Sukkot,* the crowd thronged after him into the *sukkah.* In preparing to recite the blessing, the master went into a state of contemplation that lasted almost an hour, all the time swaying in fear and trembling. The crowd that watched his every motion was carried away by what they saw, and swayed with him and trembled. There was one hasid present who stood on the side and did not spend himself on preparatory ecstasies. But when all the swaying and trembling was over, and the master began to utter the words of the blessing, the hasid drew near to absorb what he heard.

So it was at Sinai. The masses perceived the external: they saw the sound of the trumpet and the thundering and lightning, and the mountain on fire and they trembled at the sight of these—but they remained far off. Moses, however, paid no attention to all these phenomena, instead "he drew near to the thick darkness where God was."[3]

WAS SINAI AN ILLUSION?

How did Israel know that what their eye and ear perceived in the desert of Sinai was not a phantom? Mirages are a common phenomenon in the desert. What is a mirage? It denotes an optical illusion whereby something known from previous experience is seen where it is not present. Owing to atmospheric conditions, travelers who have previously seen a *real* pool of water may see an *apparent* pool of water on a highway on a hot day. Now where and when, prior to the moment on Sinai, have the people of Israel or any other people in the world heard a voice out of the atmosphere saying:

I am the Lord your God who brought you out of the land of Egypt, out of the house of bondage.

Indeed, there is no perception that may not be suspected of being a delusion. But there are perceptions which are so staggering as to render meaningless the raising of such a suspicion.

A cosmic fear enveloped all those who stood at Sinai, a moment more staggering than the heart could feel. The earth reacted more violently than the human heart: "The people trembled . . . the mountain trembled greatly" (Exodus 19:17f). Was that perception an illusion? *What* we see may be an illusion; *that* we see can never be questioned. The thunder and lightning at Sinai may have been merely an impression; but to have suddenly been endowed with the power of seeing the whole world struck with an overwhelming awe of God was a new sort of perception.

At that moment the people of Israel not only were able to entertain a feeling but also to share in an awe that overtook the world. Only in moments when we are able to share in the spirit of awe that fills the world are we able to understand what happened to Israel at Sinai. This is said to have been the purpose of that event: "that the fear of Him may be before our eyes, that you may not sin" (Exodus 20:20). It is God's prayer: "Oh that the people had a spirit such as they have today on all days to come: to fear me" (Deuteronomy 5:26).

Just as important as the problem of the *origin,* or immediate *authorship,* is the problem of the *relevance* of the Bible: whether the norms it stands for are only a concern to man or also to God. Revelation means that the thick silence which fills the endless distance between God and the human mind was pierced, and man was told that God is concerned with the affairs of man; that not only does man need God, God is also in need of man. It is such knowledge that makes the soul of Israel immune to despair. Here truth is not timeless and detached from the world but a way of living and

196

involved in all acts of God and man. The word of God is not an object of contemplation. The word of God must become history.

Thus the word of God entered the world of man; not an "ought to," an idea suspended between being and non-being, a shadow of the will, a concession of the mind, but a perpetual event, a demand of God more real than a mountain, more powerful than all thunders.

A WAY OF THINKING

The spirit of philosophy has often been characterized as *the quest of values,* as a search for that which is of greatest value. What is the spirit of the Bible? Its concern is not with the abstract concept of disembodied values, detached from concrete existence. Its concern is with man and his relation to the will of God. The Bible is the *quest for the righteous man,* for a righteous people.

> The Lord looks down from heaven upon the children of man,
> to see if there are any that act wisely, that seek after God.
> They have all gone astray, they are all alike corrupt;
> there is none that does good, no, not one.
> Psalms 14:2-3

The incidents recorded in the Bible to the discerning eye are episodes of one great drama: the quest of God for man; His search for man, and man's flight from Him.

Judaism is *a way of thinking,* not only a way of living. And this is one of its cardinal premises: the source of truth is found not in "a process for ever unfolded in the heart of man" but in unique events that happened at particular moments in history. There are no substitutes for revelation, for prophetic events. Jewish thought is not guided by abstract ideas, by a generalized morality. At Sinai we have learned that spiritual values are not only aspirations in us but a response to a transcendent appeal addressed to us.

197

Despite all vagueness one feature clearly stands out. To the mind of the prophet revelation was not merely an event that happened to him only. The prophetic act is *an experience of an act of God* which was both beyond and for the sake of man.

Unlike the mystic act, revelation is not the result of a quest for esoteric experience. What characterizes the prophet is, on the contrary, an effort to escape such experience. Never does he relish his vision as one relishes the attainment of a goal longed for. Revelation is not an act of his seeking, but of his being sought after, an act in God's search of man. The prophet did not grope for God. God's search of man, not man's quest for God, was conceived to have been the main event in Israel's history. This is at the core of all Biblical thoughts: God is not a being detached from man to be sought after, but a power that seeks, pursues and calls upon man. The way to God is a way of God. Israel's religion originated in the initiative of God rather than in the efforts of man. It was not an invention of man but a creation of God; not a product of civilization, but a realm of its own. Man would not have known Him if He had not approached man. God's relation to man precedes man's relation to Him.

The mystic experience is man's turning toward God; the prophetic act is God's turning toward man. The former is first of all an event in the life of man, contingent on the aspiration and initiative of man; the latter is first of all an event in the life of God, contingent on the pathos and initiative of God. From the mystic experience we may gain an insight of man into the life of God; from the prophetic act we learn of an insight of God into the life of man.

Therefore, to characterize revelation as a prophetic insight or experience is to reduce a reality to a perception. Seen from man's aspect, to receive a revelation is *to witness how God is turning toward man*. It is not an act of gazing at the divine reality, a static and eternal mystery. The prophet is in the midst of a divine event, of an event in the life of God, for in addressing the prophet, God comes

A philosophy of Judaism

out of His imperceptibility to become audible to man. The full intensity of the event is not in the fact that "man hears" but in the "fact" that "God speaks" to man. The mystic experience is an ecstasy of man; revelation is *an ecstasy of God*.

As described by the prophets in terms of time and space, the act of revelation represents the image of a transcendent event as reflected in the restricted terms of human experience. Its indigenous quality is to be found in the creative fact of how the divine was carried into the concrete experience of man. Imbued with a sense of the crushing marvel of God's reality, compared with which mankind appeared to be less than nothingness,[4] the prophets must have been more astounded about their experience than any one of us to whom the transcendence of God is only a vague concept, of which we occasionally become aware in calm speculation.

To sum up, revelation is a moment in which God succeeded in reaching man; an event to God and an event to man. To receive a revelation is to witness how God is turning toward man.

NOTES FOR CHAPTER 20

For a phenomenological analysis of the prophetic event as reflected in the consciousness of the prophets, and for a comparison of Biblical prophecy with analogous phenomena in other religions, compare my book *Die Prophetie*, soon to be published in English.

[1] I Kings 8:12. "Deep darkness was under His feet"; Psalms 18:10; II Samuel 22:10.

[2] Twice the Bible says, "The people stood far off"; Exodus 20:18, 21.

[3] Rabbi Yehudah of Zakilkov, *Lekute Maharil*, Lublin, 1899, p. 47a.

[4] Isaiah 40:17; see also Daniel 4:32.

21 A Religion of Time

Little is recorded or remembered either about the life and character of Euclid or about the way in which his *Elements* came into being. The laws of his geometry are timeless, and the moment in which they first dawned upon the human mind seems to have no bearing upon their meaning and validity. Time and thought, act and content, author and teaching, are not related to each other.

In contrast, the words of the Bible are not suspended; they do not dangle in an air of timelessness. Here time and thought, act and content, author and teaching, are profoundly related to each other.

The Bible is not only a system of norms but also a record of happenings in history. Indeed, some of the Biblical maxims and principles may be found or could have been conceived elsewhere. Without parallel in the world are the events it tells about and the fact of taking these events as the points where God and man meet. Events are among the basic categories by which the Biblical man lives; they are to his existence what axioms are to measuring and weighing.

Judaism is *a religion of history, a religion of time.* The God of Israel was not found primarily in the facts of nature. He spoke through events in history. While the deities of other peoples were associated with places or things, the God of the prophets was the God of events: the Redeemer from slavery, the Revealer of the Torah, manifesting Himself in events of history rather than in things or places.[1]

200

God in search of man

The events from which the religion of Israel is derived, the particular moments in time in which God and man met are as fundamental to Judaism as the eternity of Divine justice and compassion and the general truth that God and man stand at all times in relation to each other. To maintain that the exodus from Egypt is a symbol only, that the essential point is the general idea of liberty which the story signifies is to disregard the heart of Jewish faith.

Judaism demands the acceptance of some basic thoughts or norms as well as attachment to some decisive events. Its ideas and its events are inseparable from each other. The spirit manifests itself through God's presence in history, and the acts of manifestation are verified through basic thoughts or norms.

THE GOD OF ABRAHAM

The term "God of Abraham, Isaac, and Jacob" is semantically different from a term such as "the God of truth, goodness and beauty." Abraham, Isaac, and Jacob do not signify ideas, principles or abstract values. Nor do they stand for teachers or thinkers, and the term is not to be understood like that of "the God of Kant, Hegel, and Schelling." Abraham, Isaac, and Jacob are not principles to be comprehended but lives to be continued. The life of him who joins the covenant of Abraham continues the life of Abraham. For the present is not apart from the past. "Abraham is still standing before God" (Genesis 18:22). Abraham endures for ever. We are Abraham, Isaac, Jacob.

THE CATEGORY OF UNIQUENESS

To most of us the idea of revelation is unacceptable, not because it cannot be proved or explained, but because it is *unprecedented*. We do not even reject it, it simply does not enter our minds; we possess no form or category in which that idea could take hold. Trained in seeking to explain all that happens as a manifestation of a general law, every phenomenon as an example of a type, we find it hard to

201

believe in the extraordinary, in the absolutely singular; we find it hard to believe that an event which does not happen *all the time* or from time to time should have happened only *once, at one time.* It is taken for granted in science that in the realm of space a process which happened once can happen all the time, but we have not the power to understand that in the realm of time certain events do not happen again and again. Now, revelation is an event that does not happen all the time but at a particular time, at a unique moment of time.

No other deficiency makes the soul more barren than the lack of a sense for the unique. The creative man is he who succeeds in capturing the exceptional and instantaneous before it becomes stagnant in his mind. In the language of creative thinking, whatever is alive is unique. And true insight is a moment of perceiving a situation before it freezes into similarity with something else.

Only genius knows how to communicate to others the sense of the instantaneous and unique, and even so the poetry of all ages has captured a mere fraction of the endless music of the incomparable. There is more discernment in sensing the ineffable uniqueness of an event than in trying to explain it away by our stereotyped doubts.

Just as there are ideas which are true, though only a few men are able to corroborate or verify them, there are experiences which are real, though only a few men are able to attain them. Many things occur between God and man which escape the attention even of those to whom they happen.

THE CHOSEN DAY

Unless we learn how to appreciate and distinguish moments of time as we do things of space, unless we become sensitive to the uniqueness of individual events, the meaning of revelation will remain obscure. Indeed, uniqueness is a category that belongs more to the realm of time than to the realm of space. Two stones, two things in space may be alike; two hours in a person's life or two ages in human history are never alike. What happened once will never happen again in the same sense. The age of Pericles or the period of the Renaissance were never duplicated. It is ignorance of time, unawareness of the depth of events that leads to the claim that history repeats itself. It is because of his profound sense of time that the Biblical man was able to comprehend that at Sinai he witnessed an event without parallel in human history.

> "For ask now of the days that are past, which were before you, since the day that God created man upon the earth, and ask from one end of heaven to the other, whether such a great thing as this has ever happened or was ever heard of. Did any people ever hear the voice of a god speaking out of the midst of the fire, as you have heard, and still live? Or has any god ever attempted to go and take a nation for himself from the midst of another nation, by trials, by signs, by wonders, and by war, by a mighty hand and an outstretched arm, and by great terrors, according to all that the Lord your God did for you in Egypt before your eyes?"
>
> Deuteronomy 4:32-34

Important to the Biblical understanding of history is not only the concept of a chosen people but also the concept of a *chosen time;* the election of a day, not only of a people. Israel accepted the sovereignty of that chosen moment. This moment changed the world for us. Referring to that moment, a Talmudic sage exclaimed: "If not for that day . . .!"[2]

Much has happened since the day on which an obscure group of slaves went out of Egypt. Empires came into being; wars were fought that shook the world; conquests, discoveries, revolutions, catastrophies and triumphs. Why should the exodus still be celebrated? Why should it be more memorable than even the French Revolution?

"It seems absurd to subordinate philosophy to certain historical events in Palestine—more and more absurd to me," exclaimed Sir Walter Raleigh, an Oxford professor of political science. And absurd it must be to all those who have no sense for the uniqueness that is in time, for the uniqueness of what happens in time. Why, indeed, should one hour out of an infinite number of hours be of particular importance to the history of man? Why, indeed, should the significance of Sinai transcend the importance of all subsequent events?

On the other hand, a prophet might have said: "It seems absurd to subordinate history to abstract laws—more and more absurd to me."

The lack of realism, the insistence upon generalizations at the price of a total disregard of the particular and concrete is something which would be alien to prophetic thinking. Prophetic words are never detached from the concrete, historic situation. Theirs is not a timeless, abstract message; it always refers to an actual situation. The general is given in the particular, and the verification of the abstract is in the concrete.

Judaism does not seek to subordinate philosophy to events, timeless verities to a particular history. It tries to point to a level of reality where the events are the manifestations of divine norms, where history is understood as the fulfillment of truth.

The meaning of history is our profound concern. It is difficult to remain immune to the anxiety of the question, whence we come, where we are, and whither we are going.

THE UNIQUENESS OF HISTORY

The uniqueness of history is something which is hard to comprehend. This is why we often apply categories and methods of natural science to the understanding of history, such as the ancient theory that history follows the same cyclic order as heavenly bodies, expressed in the principle of the eternal recurrence of the same; or Spengler's theory that every civilization passes through the same succession of ages as organic life. These theories treat events as if they were processes. We all have a keen sense for what things have in common and a poor sense for what is incomparable and peculiar. Unique categories are necessary for the understanding of history, since that which is individual cannot be comprehended in terms of generalities. The category of the general is the key to the knowledge of the world of space; the category of the individual is the key to the understanding of the world of time.

At night—in the soul—all moments look alike. Most of us appreciate and distinguish things, places, but are callous to the uniqueness of individual events. Accordingly the idea of the sacred place is not only indigenous to almost all religions; it has retained its appeal to men of all ages, religious, secular, or superstitious. We are all willing to admit that certain things are sacred; no one would condone the desecration of a national or religious shrine. Everyone will admit that the Grand Canyon is more awe-inspiring than a trench. Everyone knows the difference between a worm and an eagle. But how many of us have a similar sense of discretion for the diversity of time? The historian Ranke claimed that every age is equally near to God. Yet Jewish tradition claims that there is a hierarchy of moments within time, that all ages are not alike. Man may pray to God equally at all places, but God does not speak to man equally at all times. At a certain moment, for example, the spirit of prophecy departed from Israel.[3]

ESCAPE TO THE TIMELESS

Contempt for time seems to be characteristic of human thought almost everywhere. To the Hindu as well as to the Greek mind, time, compared with eternity, appears empty, irrelevant and essentially unreal. Things that happen in history are of little significance; only the timeless is truly relevant. "The Mahayanist believer is warned—precisely as the worshiper of Krishna is warned . . . that the Krishna Lila is not a history, but a process unfolded for ever in the heart of man—that matters of historical fact are without religious significance." History is moving in cycles without ever changing. A hen may be defined as "an egg's way of making another egg," and history may be conceived as an act of Brahma who is "emitting, sustaining and reabsorbing the universe, apparently with no special motive beyond the release of surplus energy."[4]

According to Meister Eckhart, "Time is what keeps the light from reaching us. There is no greater obstacle to God than time. And not only temporalities, not only temporal things but temporal affections; not only temporal affections but the very taint and smell of time."[5]

It was the glory of Greece to have discovered the idea of cosmos, the world of space; it was the achievement of Israel to have experienced history, the world of time. Judaism claims that time is exceedingly relevant. Elusive as it may be, it is pregnant with the seeds of eternity. Significant to God and decisive for the destiny of man are the things that happen in time, in history. Biblical history is the triumph of time over space. Israel did not grow into being through a series of accidents. Nature itself did not evolve out of a process, by necessity; it was called into being by an event, an act of God. History is the supreme witness for God.

This was a new insight. The non-prophetic religious man was impressed by the processes of nature; there he sensed Divine mystery and there he found reason for reverence and adoration. Events did not convey to him any lasting religious significance or involve him in any spiritual commitment. Time for the non-prophetic man is the dark destroyer, and history is at bottom meaningless, a monotonous repetition of hatred, bloodshed and armistice.

In the light of the Bible, history is not a mere succession of *faits accomplis,* things done and no longer worth arguing against. Though events do not run according to a predestined plan, and though the ultimate goal can never be expressed in one word or in words at all, we believe that history as a whole has a meaning that transcends that of its parts. We must remember that God is involved in our doings, that meaning is given not only in the timeless but primarily in the timely, in that task given here and now. Great are man's possibilities. For time is but a little lower than eternity, and

A philosophy of Judaism

history is a drama in which both man and God have a stake. In its happenings we hear the voice as well as the silence of God.

EVOLUTION AND REVELATION

There is an aspect of prophetic experience that is related to a universal problem of philosophy, namely: whether all the ideas, visions, and aspirations of the mind originated in the soul of man, or whether they were ultimately derived from a source outside of man.

We have a shallow consciousness of drawing the reins of our minds. But how did we get the reins and the mind? To the naked eye, thinking appears to be a purely human affair, self-induced with nothing perceptible beyond it. Yet, that perception may well be like the blue of the sky, not real but an illusion. Skillful masters that we are in drawing from the well of thought, we are certainly not the well itself. We do not know where the force of thought comes from, what is behind all certainty. The mind can only grasp what is reducible to a mental object; it cannot reach beyond itself and sense the origin. Being always in motion, it would have to be unmoved in order to grasp that which brought it into motion. In acts of prophecy a new motion sets in and man is placed at the source of all thinking.

We are today conditioned to conceive the origin of things in terms of their development, and lack the ability to grasp suddenness, pure events, creativeness. Thus even those who assert that human consciousness goes back in its essence to a universal consciousness, are inclined to conceive such derivation in terms of evolution.

The Bible asserts that man has given himself neither his existence nor his wisdom; that both are derived from the will of God. It teaches us also that certain insights come to us not by the slow process of evolution but by His direct, *sudden grant*.

Not all mental phenomena are derivatives of more primitive instinctual ones, however much they may be colored and conditioned in their emergence and direction by instinctual functions. Human life is inconceivable without its containing a spiritual drive.

207

The assumption that there is a drive in the soul for searching after a moral and spiritual mode of living implies our possessing such a drive without our being aware of its origin. Prophecy proclaims the belief in a particular *act of communication*—one that took place not beyond, but within the consciousness of man, not prior to, but within the realm of his historic existence—teaching us what to yearn after, what to pursue, what to expect.

NOTES FOR CHAPTER 21

[1] A. J. Heschel, *The Sabbath,* New York, 1951, p. 7f.
[2] *Pesahim,* 68b.
[3] *The Sabbath* p. 96.
[4] Ananda K. Coomaraswamy, quoted by Aldous Huxley, *The Perennial Philosophy,* New York, 1945, p. 51. Compare p. 53; "The vast numbers of Buddhas and Bodhisattvas, of whom the Mahayanist theologians speak, are commensurate with the vastness of their cosmology. Time, for them, is beginningless, and the innumerable universes, every one of them supporting sentient beings of every possible variety, are born, evolve, decay and die, only to repeat the same cycle—again and again, until the final inconceivably remote consummation, when every sentient being in all the worlds shall have won to deliverance out of time into eternal Suchness or Buddhahood."
[5] Quoted by Huxley, *Ibid.,* p. 189.

22 Process and Event

PROCESS AND EVENT

"It is more or less clearly seen that a vital religious faith must find expression in the world in which modern man must live. To rest religion on events which cannot be repeated means to isolate it from the daily experience of man today."[1] It is in such a spirit that Martineau declared, "revelation signifies not some particular historical disclosure authenticated by miracles, but the progressive self-revelation which God makes of His existence and of His character in the divinest experiences of the human soul."[2]

Now, we must admit that revelation is remote from "the daily experience of modern man today"; even the thought of it is intellectually embarrassing. But to identify it with our own intellectual preference is to distort it before attempting to explore it. We must be ready to go beyond the categories of our own experience, even though such a procedure may upset our mental routine and ease.

Prophetic inspiration must be understood as *an event,* not as *a process.* What is the difference between process and event? A process happens regularly, following a relatively permanent pattern; an event is extraordinary, irregular. A process may be continuous, steady, uniform; events happen suddenly, intermittently, occasionally. Processes are typical; events are unique. A process follows a law, events create a precedent.

A process occurs in the physical order. But not all events are reducible to physical terms. The life of Beethoven left music behind; yet valued in physical terms its effects on the world were felt less than the effect of a normal rain storm or an earthquake.

Man lives in an order of events, not only in an order of processes. It is a spiritual order. Moments of insight, moments of decision, moments of prayer—may be insignificant in the world of space, yet they put life into focus.

Nature is made up of processes—organic life, for example, may be described as consisting of the processes of birth, growth, maturity and decay; history consists primarily of events. What lends human, historical character to the life of Pericles or Aristotle are not the organic processes through which they went but the extraordinary, surprising and unpredictable acts, achievements or events which distinguished them from all other human beings.

An event is a happening that cannot be reduced to a part of a process. It is something we can neither predict nor fully explain. To speak of events is to imply that there are happenings *in the world* that are beyond the reach of our explanations. What the consciousness of events implies, the belief in revelation claims explicitly, namely, that a voice of God *enters the world* which pleads with man to do His will.

What do we mean by "the world"? If we mean an ultimate, closed, fixed and self-sufficient system of phenomena behaving in accord with the laws known to us, then such a concept would exclude the possibility of admitting any super-mundane intervention or penetration by a voice not accounted for by these laws. Indeed, if the world as described by natural science is regarded as the ultimate, then there is no sense in searching for the Divine which is by definition the ultimate. How could there be one ultimate within the other?

The claim of the Bible is absurd, unless we are ready to comprehend that the world as scrutinized and depicted by science is but a thin surface of the profoundly unknown. Order is only one of the aspects of nature; its reality is a mystery given but not known. Countless relations that determine our life in history are neither

210

A philosophy of Judaism

known nor predictable. What history does with the laws of nature cannot be expressed by a law of nature.

One of many difficulties is this: there would have to be a flaw in the perfect mechanism of mind and matter to let the spirit of God penetrate its structure. To assume that the world for all its immense grandeur is a little cymbal in the hand of God, on which at certain times only one soul vibrates though all are struck; in other words: to assume that the entire complex of natural laws is transcended by the freedom of God, would presuppose the metaphysical understanding that the laws of nature are derived not from a blind necessity but from freedom, that the ultimate is not fate but God. Revelation is not an act of interfering with the normal course of natural processes but the act of instilling a new creative moment into the course of history.

The chain of causality and of discursive reasoning, in which things and thoughts are fettered, is fixed in the space of endless possibilities like the tongue hanging in a silent bell. It is as if all the universe were fixed to a single point. In revelation the bell rings, and words vibrate through the world.

TO SEE THE PAST IN THE PRESENT TENSE

A process has no future. It becomes obsolete and is always replaced by its own effects. We do not ponder about last year's snow. An event, on the other hand, retains its significance even after it has passed; it remains as a lasting motive because and regardless of its effects. Great events, just as great works of art, are significant in themselves. Our interest in them endures long after they are gone.

It is, indeed, one of the peculiar features of human existence that the past does not altogether vanish, that some events of hoary antiquity may hold us in their spell to this very day. Events which are dead, things which are gone, can neither be sensed nor told. There is a liberation from what is definitely past. On the other hand, there are events which never become past. Sacred history may be described as an attempt to overcome the dividing line of past and present, as an attempt *to see the past in the present tense.*

Such understanding of time is not peculiar to historians. It is shared unknowingly by all men and is essential to civilized living.

NOTES FOR CHAPTER 22

[1] G. B. Smith, *Religious Thought in the Last Quarter-Century,* Chicago, 1927, p. 103f.

[2] Quoted in H. McLachlan, *The Religious Opinions of Milton, Locke, and Newton,* Manchester, 1941, p. 98.

23 Israel's Commitment

The God of the philosopher is a concept derived from abstract ideas; the God of the prophets is derived from acts and events. The root of Jewish faith is, therefore, not a comprehension of abstract principles but an inner *attachment to sacred events;* to believe is to remember, not merely to accept the truth of a set of dogmas. Our attachment is expressed by our way of celebrating them, by weekly reading of the Pentateuch rather than by the recital of a creed. To ignore these events and only to pay attention to what Israel was taught in these events is to miss an essential aspect.

THE MEMORY OF A COMMITMENT

An esthetic experience leaves behind the memory of a perception and enjoyment; a prophetic experience leaves behind *the memory of a commitment.* Revelation was not an act of enjoyment. God spoke and man not only perceived but also accepted the will of God. Revelation lasts a moment, acceptance continues.

This, then, is given to us in Jewish tradition: not an idea of, but a commitment to revelation. Our task is to examine our attitude to that commitment. Is there any meaning to our being loyal to events that happened more than three thousand years ago?

LOYALTY TO A MOMENT

It is a supreme necessity for human beings to live in more or less permanent and dependable relations to each other. There is a variety

213

of such relations, as, for example, marriage, friendship, professional organizations and international conventions. With some exceptions, such as those which grow out of parenthood and the like, social relations are not given naturally; they do not originate in a process; they are initiated in an act or in an event *at a definite moment of time*. These relations can only endure if we remain loyal to the promise we have made or to the agreements into which we have entered. They collapse when our loyalty ceases.

The paradoxical nature of such loyalty is obvious. Why should a person be bound all his life by what he did or said at one single moment? And yet civilized men have never failed to admit that their promise had some force to affect their future acts. People believe in the passing away of time; they claim that the past is dead for ever. Indeed, the moment in which a promise is made is quickly gone: gone from our calendar, gone from our clocks. And yet we are willing to regard it as if it were immortal. In other words, we accept events that happened at moments gone by, as if those moments were still present, as if those events were happening now.

A WORD OF HONOR

Sinai, the decisive moment in Israel's history, initiated a new relationship between God and man: God became engaged to a people. Israel accepted the new relationship; it became engaged to God. It was an event to which both were partners. God gave His word to Israel, and Israel gave its word of honor to God.

A pledge goes on for ever. In making a pledge our entire future is invested as a pawn. It is a moment that does not vanish; it is a moment that determines all other moments.

Remember His covenant for ever, the word
which He pledged for a thousand generations.
I Chronicles 16:15

Israel accepted the covenant: Israel gave its word of honor to stand by it.

214

A philosophy of Judaism

In what sense does the acceptance affect our lives? Does one generation have the right to commit all other generations to a covenant? Why must we feel committed, and to what?[1]

Sinai is both an event that happened once and for all, and an event that happens all the time. What God does, happens both in time and in eternity. Seen from our vantage-point, it happened once; seen from His vantage-point, it happens all the time. Monuments of stone are destined to disappear; days of spirit never pass away. About the arrival of the people at Sinai we read in the Book of Exodus: "In the third month after the children of Israel were gone forth out of the land of Egypt, on this day they came into the wilderness of Sinai" (19:1). Here was an expression that puzzled the ancient rabbis: on *this* day? It should have been said: on *that* day. This can only mean that the day of giving the Torah can never become past; that day is this day, every day. The Torah, whenever we study it, must be to us "as if it were given us today."[2]

Every one of us has heard the Voice; every one of us has received the divine gift of freedom at Sinai. This is why no one has the right to sell himself into slavery. The ear of him who becomes a slave voluntarily is to be bored (Exodus 21:1-6). "The Holy One, blessed be He, said: This ear, which heard My voice on Mount Sinai when I proclaimed, *For unto Me the children of Israel are servants, they are My servants* (Leviticus 25:55), and not servants of servants, and yet this man went and acquired a master for himself—let it be bored."[3]

"I keep the King's command because of the oath of loyalty" (Ecclesiastes 8:2). Said Rabbi Yose, "I keep the command of the King of Kings who told *me* at Sinai, I am the Lord thy God."[4] All generations of Israel, we are told, were present at Sinai (see above, p. 141).

Nor is it with you only that I make this sworn covenant, but with him who is not here with us this day as well as with him who stands here with us this day before the Lord our God.

Deuteronomy 29:13-14

It was an act of transcending the present, *history in reverse*: think-ing of the future in the present tense. It was a prophetic foresight, for to be a prophet is to be ahead of other people's time, to speak of the future in the present tense.

The contemporaries of Moses succeeded in transcending the pres-ent and committed the subsequent generations to the word of God because of their ability to think of life in terms of time.

They had no space, they had no land; all they had was time and the promise of a land. Their future depended upon God's loyalty to His own promise, and their loyalty to the prophetic events was the essence of their future.

LIFE WITHOUT COMMITMENT

Some of us may think: how unwise of our ancestors to have com-mitted all future generations to a covenant with God. Yet the life of a historic people is not unlike the life of an individual. As we have seen, there is no civilized living without acts of entering upon social relations, and such acts imply the acceptance of a commitment, the making of a promise or the taking of a pledge. To enter a relation with God the people had to accept a commitment.

Socrates taught us that a life without thinking is not worth living. Now, thinking is a noble effort, but the finest thinking may end in futility. In thinking, man is left to himself; he may soar into astral space and proclaim the finest thoughts; yet what will be the echo and what its meaning for the soul?

The Bible taught us that life without commitment is not worth living; that thinking without roots will bear flowers but no fruits. Our commitment is to God, and our roots are in the prophetic events of Israel.

The dignity of man stands in proportion to his obligations as well as to his rights. The dignity of being a Jew is in the sense of com-mitment, and the meaning of Jewish history revolves around the faithfulness of Israel to the covenant.

216

REVELATION IS A BEGINNING

And yet mere attachment to events does not fully express the essence of Jewish living. Event is a formal category, describing the fact of pure happening. However, to speak of a pure event, of an event in and by itself, is to speak of an artificial abstraction that exists nowhere except in the minds of some theologians. The moment of revelation must not be separated from the content or substance of revelation. Loyalty to the norms and thoughts conveyed in the event is as essential as the reality of the event. Acceptance was not complete, the fulfillment has not occurred. The decisive moment is yet to come. The event must be fulfilled, not only believed in. What was expected at Sinai comes about in the moment of a good deed. A commandment is a foresight, a deed is a fulfillment. The deed completes the event. Revelation is but a beginning, our deeds must continue, our lives must complete it.

We must not idolize the moment or the event. The will of God is eternal, transcending all moments, all events, including acts of revelation. The significance of time depends upon what is done in time in relation to His will. The moment at Sinai depends for its fulfillment upon this present moment, upon all moments. Had Israel been disloyal subsequent to Sinai, that great moment would have been deprived of all meaning. The Tablets are broken whenever the golden calf is called into being. We believe that every hour is endowed with the power to lend meaning to—or withhold meaning from—all other hours.[5]

NOTES FOR CHAPTER 23

[1] The phrase *rebus sic stantibus* expresses the limitation understood in the case of agreements. Circumstances must remain fundamentally the same if the obligation undertaken is to be morally operative.

[2] *Tanhuma,* ed. Buber, II, 76; *Sifre* to Deuteronomy 11:13; *Berachot,* 63b; Rashi to Exodus 19:1; Deuteronomy 11:13 and 26:16.

[3] *Kiddushin* 22b.

[4] *Jerushalmi Sanhedrin,* IV, 21b.

[5] "If one keeps but one Sabbath properly, it is regarded as if he had observed all the Sabbaths from the day on which God created His world to the time of the resurrection of the dead." *Mechilta* to Exodus 31:16.

24 An Examination of the Prophets

The result of our discussion has been to show what it is that necessitates our raising the question about revelation, to clarify its meaning, as well as to establish the possibility and likelihood of its having taken place. Yet, as said above, what is possible and likely is not necessarily actual and certain. The problem concerning us most is whether revelation has ever taken place; whether there are any compelling reasons for accepting the Bible as an expression of the will of God.

Our major aim is to find an answer to the question: Is revelation a fact? Did it actually take place? Such an answer will obviously depend upon our ability to find evidence either to refute or to confirm the claim of the prophets. Now, before starting an inquiry it is important to know exactly what to look for. In our case, we must make clear to ourselves what sort of evidence we should like to find.

At first thought, the ideal attainment of an inquiry into this problem would be the archeological discovery of impartial evidence such as, for example, contemporary Egyptians who accompanied the Israelites on their march through the wilderness and wrote about what happened at Sinai; or Assyrians who visited Palestine and watched and interviewed Amos or Isaiah. Modern man would be inclined to consider such testimonies more reliable

218

A philosophy of Judaism

than the Biblical records. To him who would argue that a great
many Biblical records have proved to be accurate and that hence the
records about revelation should likewise be trusted, others will re-
tort that the experience of revelation is in a class by itself. If this is
the case, how could the Egyptians or the Assyrians be expected to
report about that which constituted the essence of prophetic experience? What would be gained by possessing another report about
the external circumstances in which the event at Sinai took place?
A show of thunder and lightning with a mysterious voice coming
through the clouds would, indeed, be susceptible of impartial recording by shorthand or photography. Yet the physical aspect, what
the eye or ear could perceive, is of little relevance. Thunder and
lightning may be more striking to the senses than a soft whisper,
but Elijah trusted only "the still small voice." The essence of what
happened at Sinai, the inspiration and spiritual elevation of an entire
people, never could have been perceived, recorded or verified by
impartial reporters.

What is true about the Egyptian contemporaries of Moses holds
true of the Egyptians till this day. And every one of us is an Egyptian, asking at one time or another: "Who is the Lord that I should
hearken unto His voice?" (Exodus 5:2).

What makes one receptive and responsive to that which is beyond the reach of the soul? Were the prophets endowed with a
separate faculty, a special sense? Nothing of this sort could be
traced in their utterances. The great prophets had one feature in
common: revelation came to them as a surprise, as a sudden burst.
They were more startled *that* they heard, than *at what* they heard.
Their perceptiveness came into being with revelation itself. It is
revelation that makes man capable of receiving a revelation. He
becomes expert with the experience.

THE MISTAKEN NOTION

Many people reject the Bible because of a mistaken notion that
revelation has been proved to be scientifically impossible. It is all so

very simple: there is no source of thought other than the human mind. The Bible is a book like any other book, and the prophets had no access to sources inaccessible to us. The Bible is but the national literature of the Jewish people. To the average mind, therefore, revelation is a sort of mental outcast, not qualified to be an issue for debate. At best, it is regarded as a fairy tale, on a par with the conception that lightning and thunder are signs of anger of sundry gods and demons, rather than the result of a sudden expansion of the air in the path of an electric discharge. Indeed, has not the issue been settled long ago by psychology and anthropology as primitive man's mistaking an illusion for a supernatural event?

The truth is that revelation is a problem that eludes scientific inquiry; that no scholar has ever devised a lens to pierce its mystery. Biblical criticism may have succeeded in finding spots in the sun and in compelling us to modify our conception of how the text was transmitted, but the act of revelation remains beyond its scope. The intellectual adolescence of those who proclaimed Moses has never lived, and if he did he was not a monotheist, is of great interest to a psychologist as an example of iconoclastic tendencies but is of little interest to those who look for spiritual truth. The relatively minor discrepancies within the Bible may only prove that its words were written in and for many different situations, that its text is an organism rather than monolithic stone. Yet, we must not "disturb the foundation of the temple in order to repair a petty breach or rat-hole in the wall, or fasten a loose stone or two in the outer court" (Coleridge).

IS REVELATION EXPLAINABLE?

The claim of the prophets could be verified, were we able to repeat and put their perceptions to a test. Yet, the prophets themselves could only relate, but not reproduce, what happened to them. They endeavored to vindicate their own reliability by forecast or persuasion; the act itself could not be displayed to others. However, the fact of our inability to share an experience does not deny its authen-

220

ticity. Many of our own experiences, the most precious and singular, can hardly be shared by anybody else. Much of what a person goes through cannot be communicated, and what is not communicable is not sharable. All communication is an attempt to make something understandable to others by conveying it into universal and typical terms. But the spark of the singular is extinguished in the atmosphere of generalities. Particularly, the impact of the transcendent upon the human mind can be as little described in general terms as my perception of beauty can be told in terms of pounds and ounces. How could we expect it to be explainable?

Is it worthwhile, even if it were possible, to let our whisper try to imitate thunder? It is essential to revelation that it elude our inquiries. To explain, to make it intelligible, transparent, would be to ignore it; in proving it, it would be reduced to insignificance. There is a partner to revelation with whose ways the mind's categories are incongruous.

Revelation should not be rejected because of its being incomprehensible. It is not the only fact that is impervious to exploration, unverifiable by experience. That which is incomprehensible must not be considered unreal. Can we explain how being came into being? Can we describe exactly how the tense power of a spirit glides on the strings of a violin, creating a world of delicacy out of nothing? Is the cry and anguish of six million martyrs theoretically comprehensible?

There is, indeed, no way of explaining how thoughts of the infinite God move along the narrow path of a human mind. All explaining or proving operates by means of analogy. We explain something that is doubtful by comparing it with things that are possible or certain. The strength of a proof or an explanation depends upon how complete is the resemblance between those things. Yet, the authenticity of revelation is shown in its being *different* from all other events and experiences. Its truth is in its *uniqueness*. Only as something incomparable can it be trusted. This is perhaps why the book of Deuteronomy emphasizes that the event at Sinai was unprecedented (4:32-37).

All we can do is to analyze our own reasons for accepting it and to eliminate the probability of having been subject to an illusion or the probability of our faith being nothing but a rationalization, namely the fabrication of rational arguments to justify something which deep in our hearts we do not consider to be correct.

For the sake of intellectual convenience we would like to be in possession of some spectacular evidence that the prophets were neither psychopaths nor liars. Yet, how odd and unworthy of God if, in giving man what is priceless, He were to secure man's trivial testimonies to the authenticity of His gift! Must the sun be labeled with a mark of identification in order to be acknowledged?

Our inability to prove that the record of the prophet contains an exact description of what he has actually experienced does not preclude the legitimacy of asserting the truthfulness of that record. In investigating historical documents man is never able to confront the record with the fact; he can inquire, however, whether a particular record is consistent with his knowledge and conception of the period to which it is ascribed. With what knowledge or with what facts is revelation to be in accord?

ARE THE PROPHETS RELIABLE?

Not having witnessed the act of revelation, we have no knowledge of it except that conveyed to us by the prophets. Thus our attitude will depend on whether we are ready to take the word of the prophets seriously. This, then, is decisive: are the prophets reliable? Is their testimony trustworthy?

In calling upon the prophets to stand before the bar of our critical judgment, we are like dwarfs undertaking to measure the heights of giants. How could our spiritual attainments be a yardstick with which to measure what they achieved, if their strivings were so completely above our own? Are we as open to God as they were? Do we care as intensely, as exclusively for what God has to say as they did?

An aspiring composer would not compare Beethoven with himself but compare himself with Beethoven. That which transcends us is not something we judge but something by which we are judged, and to be a prophet is to represent that which is spiritually transcendent.

Our situation is somewhat like that of a person who, when faced with overwhelming beauty, is called upon to say what he thinks about it. Actually, it is his intelligence which is on trial, though seemingly it is the quality of beauty which he has to probe.

There are only three ways of judging the prophets: they told the truth, deliberately invented a tale, or were victims of an illusion. In other words, revelation is either a fact or the product of insanity, self-delusion, or a pedagogical invention, the product of a mental confusion, of wishful thinking, or a subconscious activity.

A PRODUCT OF INSANITY

Should we maintain that men such as Moses, Samuel, Nathan, Elijah, Amos, Micah, Isaiah, Jeremiah, were mentally deranged, victims of hallucinations? This, indeed, has often been asserted. Yet on what basis? Frantic efforts have been made to prove the pathological nature of the prophets. Yet no trace or symptom of abnormality or frenzy has been detected in either Moses or Isaiah, in either Amos or Jeremiah.[1] On the other hand, the manner in which the prophets dealt with the issues of their own time and the fact that the solutions they propounded seem to be relevant for all times have compelled people in every generation to repeat a commonplace: the prophets were among the wisest of all men. Their message being ages ahead of human thinking, it would be hard to believe in the normalcy of our own minds, if we questioned theirs. Indeed, if such is insanity, then we ought to feel ashamed of being sane.

And granted, unlikely as it is, that signs of sickness should be traced in the life of the prophets, as indeed Nietzsche stated in his famous generalization, "It does not seem possible to be an artist and not to be sick,"[2] it would still be absurd to reject their claim. Is it not more meaningful to maintain that a person has to be sick in

223

order to see what those who are benighted by their robustness and complacency fail to perceive? Biological normalcy is no prerequisite of spiritual insight.

Were the prophets victims of self-delusion? Was revelation a mockery, a snare? Self-delusion is usually the attainment of a specious goal which comes about when one fails to attain a genuine goal striven for. But the gift of prophecy was not a goal for which the prophets strove.

Unlike the mystic experience which is attained as the result of craving for communion with God, revelation occurred against the will of the prophet. It was not a favor to him, but a burden of terror. To Isaiah (6:5) the perception of God is a venture fraught with shock, peril and dismay, something which is more than his soul can bear:

> Woe is me!
> I am undone!
> . . . For mine eyes have seen the King."

Moses hid his face; he was afraid to look upon God (Exodus 3:6). When called, the prophets recoiled, resisted, and pleaded to be left alone. "O Lord, send, I pray Thee, someone else," was Moses' response to the mission. It is such incredible resistance that enables a prophet honestly to say *Not I, but God*: "Thus saith the Lord." Is not the experience of resistance to the experience a mark of truthfulness, authenticity—or is this, too, a part of self-deception?

None of the prophets had any vested interests to protect or cherished the desire to gain power or prestige. None of them was enamored of being a prophet or even prided himself on his attainment. Was it the quest for happiness that drove Jeremiah to being a prophet? Here is his answer:

> Cursed be the day
> Wherein I was born . . .
> Because He slew me not from the womb;

224

God in search of man

And so my mother would have been my grave . . .
Wherefore came I forth from the womb
To see labor and sorrow,
That my days should be consumed in shame.

20;14,17,18

Over the life of a prophet words are invisibly inscribed: All flattery abandon, ye who enter here. But flattery is that which people love to hear. He who carries the torch of hope kindles enthusiasm and wins acclaim. Yet almost every true prophet begins with a message of doom, and only after long periods of misery and darkness is he able to speak of the dawn and to proclaim a message of hope.

Bitter is the taste of the divine word to the prophet's soul; no reward is promised him and no reward could temper it. In the very hour when the call first came to Ezekiel, he was told what to expect: it will be as though briars and thorns were with him, as though he dwelt among scorpions. "Be not afraid, be not dismayed" (Ezekiel 2:6).

Loneliness and misery were only part of the reward that prophecy brought to Jeremiah: "I sat alone because of Thy hand" (15:17). Mocked, reproached and persecuted, he would think of casting away his task:

If I say, I will not make mention of Him, nor speak any more in His name, then there is my heart as it were a burning fire, shut up in my bones. I am weary with forbearing, and I cannot contain.

Jeremiah 20:9

How little ado they made about themselves. The prophets considered themselves servants, not masters, and in their eyes the act of receiving a revelation was not glorified as a fact significant in itself. Unlike the mystic experience, the significance of prophecy lay not in those who perceived it but in those to whom the word was to be conveyed. The experience itself was a beginning, a means, rather than a goal. The purpose was not in the perception of the voice but in bringing it to bear upon the reality of the people's life. Conse-

225

quently, the substance of prophecy was in the content rather than in the act, and revelation was a prelude to action.

Out of the field went Amos to Beth El to predict in public that the king of Israel would die by the sword and that the people of Israel would be led away captive out of his land. The priest, outraged at the terrible message, said unto Amos: go, flee away and never prophesy again in Beth El, for it is the king's sanctuary and a royal house. But the prophet retorted:

I was no prophet nor the disciple of a prophet; I was a herdman and a dresser of sycamore trees. And the Lord took me from following the flock and said unto me: Go prophesy unto my people Israel. Now therefore hear thou the word of the Lord:

Thou sayest: Prophesy not against Israel
And preach not against the house of Isaac;
Therefore thus saith the Lord:
Thy wife shall be a harlot in the city,
And thy sons and thy daughters shall fall by the sword,
And thy land shall be divided by line;
And thou thyself shalt die in an unclean land,
And Israel shall surely be led away captive out of his land.
Amos 7:14-17

The prophet did not volunteer for his rightful mission; it was forced upon him. How could he resist the power of God? "The hand of God came upon him" (Ezekiel 3:22). He was seduced, he was overwhelmed (Jeremiah 20:7). There was no choice.

The lion hath roared,
Who will not fear?
The Lord God hath spoken,
Who can but prophesy?
Amos 3:8

As for me, I am filled with power,
with the spirit of the Lord,
with justice, with might,

226

A philosophy of Judaism

To declare to Jacob his transgression,
to Israel his sin.

Micah 3:8

And this, too, is a theory. The prophets, just as the philosophers of Greece, arrived at their insights by speculation or intuition, but in their desire to impress the people with their authority, they invented a story about revelation. Perhaps they were not interested in attaining personal prestige, but, out of a desire to bring about a moral or spiritual improvement of the conditions of their people, they might have been willing to use a lie, thinking that a good purpose justified evil means.

No one acquainted with the spiritual rigorism and lack of self-righteousness of the prophets could conceivably ascribe to them such a way of thinking. Could a man like Isaiah, who felt shattered by the overwhelming power of God's holiness, have fabricated a story like the one of his vision (chapter 6)? The fear of God was too constricting to allow the prophets to take the name of God in vain. Is this not the gist of all their thoughts: Above all, God abhors deceit?

Is it conceivable that men who placed God's demand for righteousness even above the interests of their own country and above the glory of their own sanctuary—and who condemned the lie as a fundamental evil—should have lived by a lie?

Moreover, prophecy was not an episode in the life of a few individuals, and it would be most fantastic to assume that, generation after generation, men of highest passion for truth, of deepest contempt for sham, all schemed and conspired to deceive the people of Israel. Did Moses pray for a people of connivers when he said, "Would that all the people were prophets"?

Should we perhaps say the prophets' lofty claims were the result of their inability to analyze their inner life correctly, of their mistaking a feeling born in the heart for an idea bestowed upon them from without? Was prophecy, then, the result of mental confusion? Now, the prophets asserted that many of their experiences were not moments of passive receptivity, or mere listening to a Voice, but dialogues with God, and in recording their experiences they clearly distinguished between the words they heard and the words they uttered.[3] Does not this fact testify to their ability for discernment?

Moreover, circumstances did compel the prophets clearly to discern between the voice of the heart and the voice of God. Something happened:

> An appalling and horrible thing
> has come to pass in the land:
> The prophets prophesy falsely,
> and the priests rule at their beck.
> And my people love to have it so.
>
> Jeremiah 5:31

Jeremiah, for example, did not question the sincerity of all the so-called "false prophets." He condemned them for mistaking "a dream" for a divine message. For thus says the Lord:

> I have heard what "the prophets" have said,
> Those who prophesy lies in My name, saying,
> "I have dreamed, I have dreamed."
> How long shall this be. . . ?
> The prophet who has a dream, let him
> tell a dream;
> And he who has a word, let him
> speak my word,
> Faithfully,
> Says the Lord.
> What has the chaff in common with the wheat?
> Says the Lord.

God in search of man

Is not My word as fire?
Says the Lord;
And like a hammer that breaks the rock
in pieces?
Jeremiah 23.25-29

It is beyond doubt that in their condemning "the false prophets who prophesy out of their own heart" (Ezekiel 13:17), calling upon them in the name of God: "you say: the Lord saith, and I have not spoken" (Ezekiel 13:7), "the prophets prophesy lies in My name: I sent them not, neither have I commanded them, neither spoke I unto them: they prophesy unto you a lying vision, divination, a thing of nought, the deceit of their own heart" (Jeremiah 14:14)—men like Jeremiah and Ezekiel manifested a critical attitude toward prophecy as such. Since they argued not only against the ideas but primarily against the false prophets' claim that they had received the word of God, they must have had a criterion for distinguishing between experience and illusion. There are always imitators, but the worth of the genuine is never impaired by the abundance of imitation and forgery.

The word of the prophets was not proclaimed to a gullible, primitive society. The people of Israel, whose country felt the impact of the great neighboring civilizations of Egypt and Babylonia, knew of the world and wisdom of other nations. They were far from being predisposed to accept the prophetic claim. The story of the prophets' activity is one of encountering constant rivalry, opposition and disbelief. Had the story of prophecy been an invention of the Biblical writer, it would have been a story of a people swept into faith by the power of prophecy. Instead, the opposition to the prophets is recorded with reckless honesty.

What gave the prophets the certainty that they witnessed a divine event and not a figment of their own imagination? The mark of authenticity of the divine character of revelation was not in outward signs, visible or sonorous; revelation did not hinge upon a particular sense-perception, upon hearing a voice or seeing a light. A thunder out of a blue sky, a voice coming from nowhere, an effect without a visible cause, would not have been enough to identify a perception as a divine communication. Immense chunks of natural reality, showers of light thrust upon the mind, would, even if they were not phantasmagorial, only manifest a force of nature, not God.

This, it seems, was the mark of authenticity: the fact that prophetic revelation was not merely an act of experience but an act of *being experienced,* of being exposed to, called upon, overwhelmed and taken over by Him who seeks out those whom He sends to mankind. It is not God who is an experience of man; it is man who is an experience of God.

THE SPIRIT OF THE AGE

There is still another way of explaining prophecy. History has shown us how men are influenced in their thinking and feeling by "the spirit of the age" in which they live. In the age in which the prophets lived, the belief was common that the deities revealed themselves to men. It might have been easy to fall victim to an illusion. Yet, why did "the spirit of the age" produce no prophets in Assyria and Babylonia, among the Phoenicians or Canaanites? Knowing the old Oriental literature as we do today, it is easy to imagine how the life and letters of ancient Israel might have been without divine inspiration.

When the northern neighbors of Israel, the Moabites, were engaged in a war and their king Mesha saw that the battle was going against him, "he took his eldest son who was to reign in his stead, and offered him for a burnt offering upon the wall" (II Kings 3:27). Israel's kings, Ahaz and Manasseh, too, burned their sons as offerings "according to the abominable practices of the nations" (II Kings 16:3; see 21:6). If the prophets were inspired by "the spirit of the age," why did they express horror at such acts of "supreme piety"? Why was not the worship of the God of Israel like the worship of Baal or Tammuz?

Religion and piety are found among all nations. But the prophets

A philosophy of Judaism

were those who in the name of God stood up against that which most people to this very day call religion.

Indeed, the nature of the Bible is precisely something which is not consistent with everything else we know about the historical circumstances under which it took place. It would have been more consistent with our general understanding, if the great religious insights had been given to the sages of Egypt or Athens rather than to a homeless people roaming and starving in the wilderness of the Sinai peninsula. The wonder of the Bible is against all human expectations, and if it had not been for its apparent spiritual glory, or for the inexplicable power of human faith, it would have been rejected as absurd and unlikely.

THE SUBCONSCIOUS

Was it the subconscious that acted as a prompter in the experiences of the prophets? Did the Bible arise from the vortex of psychic power, generated by yearning and imagination? Such a view, while not questioning the integrity or sanity of the prophets, would stamp them as deceived deceivers; while not bringing us closer to an understanding of what really took place, it would merely substitute an enigma for the mystery. The subconscious is a hypothesis so wide and so vague that it is hardly more positively known to us than the idea of the supernatural. How strange that the cunning demon of the subconscious, in spite of its omnipresence and relentless vitality, has not produced elsewhere works of such sublime power! The paths of imagination opened by mythologies were certainly unbounded, but where did they lead to? Where else did a divine idea sanctify history? Where else did a history of a people become sacred scripture?

To assume that prophetic revelation was the expression of an urge, hidden in the heart of the prophet, of which he not only was unaware but which he resisted, would presuppose the action of a spiritual power so wise and so holy, that there would be no other name for it but God.

231

Revelation can be either doubted or affirmed but neither denied nor proved. All that is given to us are the records of the prophets, and none of us can probe beyond their words or directly scrutinize their experiences. There are no scientific grounds which would compel us to regard revelation as a subjective experience, while, on the other hand, the prophets themselves who were the first critics of the so-called false prophets, emphatically asserted the non-subjective character of their experiences.

And if beyond all answers and assurances, doubt continues to quiver: is not even genius subject to error? Is not the knowledge of the prophet of his encounter with God too thin, too inward, too subjective to be built upon? Why should humanity stake its most important decisions on the reliability of a handful of men? Have not "false prophets," too, been certain of having been recipients of revelation?

It is, in fact, not the opinion of the prophet concerning his experience, his wisdom, or self-consciousness that is the ultimate sign of evidence. How significant that Moses was not praised for wisdom or heroism; he was not, like Solomon, the wisest, but rather the humblest of men (Numbers 11:3); nor was he ingenious or infallible. "My servant Moses is not so: he is trusted in all my house" (Numbers 12:7).

To convey in words the will of God was easier than to put in words the act of revelation. Had a prophet tried to go beyond hints in describing his experience, he would have told us as much about it as a great poet could tell a polar bear about the spring in Italy. More communicative than description is the paucity of description and the inability to say much more than *Thus saith the Lord*. The light with which a prophet is aglow casts into the shade his own power of vision and self-awareness.

When Moses came down from Mount Sinai, the two Tablets in his hands, the whole people of Israel saw that his face sent forth beams; and they were afraid to come nigh unto him. Only Moses did not know that his face sent forth beams. . . .

232

God in search of man

"I say that there is a limit to human reason and as long as the soul resides within the body, it cannot grasp what is above nature, for nothing that is immersed in nature can see above it. Reason is limited to the sphere of nature and it is unable to understand that which is above its limits. . . . Know that there is a level of knowledge which is higher than all philosophy, namely prophecy. Prophecy is a different source and category of knowledge. Proof and examination are inapplicable to it. If prophecy is genuine then it cannot and need not depend on the validation of reason. The only test ever asked of a prophet in the Scriptures is concerning the genuineness of his claim to have prophecy, but no one ever asked for proofs or reasons or validations above prophecy itself. . . . Reason and proof cannot aspire to the level of insight at which prophecy exists—how then can they ever prove or disprove it? . . . No one can demand validations from reason or proofs from logic for the Torah, unless he first denies the authenticity of Moses's claim to prophecy. Our faith is based on the principle that the words of Moses are prophecy and therefore are beyond the domain of speculation, validation, argument, or proof. Reason is inherently unable to pass judgment in the area from which prophecy originates. It would be like trying to put all the water in the world into a little cup."[4]

There are no proofs for demonstrating the beauty of music to a man who is both deaf and insensitive, and there are no proofs for the veracity of the prophet's claim to a man who is spiritually deaf and without faith and wisdom. Proofs may aid in protecting but not in initiating certainty; essentially they are explications of what is already intuitively clear to us.[5]

The goal of our "examination" of the prophets was not to furnish the prophets with a letter of recommendation, but rather to point to the difficulty of an outright rejection of their claim. Proofs cannot open the gates of mystery for all men to behold. The only thing we can do is to open the gates of our own soul for God to behold us, to open the gates of our minds and to respond to the words of the prophets. It is their word that gives force to their claim; it is history that gives force to their word.

NOTES FOR CHAPTER 24

[1] See A. J. Heschel, *Die Prophetie*, Cracow, 1936, pp. 8-40.
[2] *Wille zur Macht*, 811.
[3] Amos 7:2-9, 15; 8:1,2; Micah 7:1-10; 18-20; Isaiah 6:5-12; 16:9-11; 21:2-10; 22:4-14; 25:1-5; 26:8-19; 29:11-12; 40:6; 49:3-6; 50:4-9; 64:6-12; Jeremiah 1:6-14; 4:10, 19-21; 5:3-6; 10:19-25; 12:1-6; 14:7-9, 13-14, 18-22; 15:10-21; 17:15-18; 18:18-23; 20:7-18; 32:16-25.
[4] Maimonides in a letter to Rabbi Hisdai, in *Kobets Teshubot Harambam Weiggerotav*, ed. Lichtenberg, Leipzig, 1859, II, pp. 23a-23b.
[5] *Man is Not Alone*, p. 83.

25 The Bible and the World

IS THE BIBLE AN ILLUSION?

We have discussed the idea of prophecy; we have dealt with the claim of the prophets. We must now turn to the Bible itself. The Bible is not an abstract idea, a spiritual possibility. It is more than a claim made by men who lived once upon a time. The Bible is an ever present reality, and it is in the presence of the Bible that we raise again the problem of prophetic inspiration.

At what source did the prophets find that stream of insight which has been channeled into the books of the Bible? Who has done unto them what they are able to do unto us? Did their own heart radiate a conceit which is able to illumine the world's spiritual gloom?

The prophet's answer is consistently the same: It was a word of God that scorched my tongue. Is it right for us to ignore, belittle or traduce that claim?

We are confronted with a stubborn fact. A galaxy of men such as Moses, Nathan, Elijah, Amos, Isaiah, Jeremiah, claim to have perceived a word of God. If their claim is false, are we not compelled to condemn them as impostors who have confused the minds of men for more than three thousand years?

The character of the Bible is a most embarrassing issue; it is too important to be ignored. More disquieting than the personal problem, namely, whether we are ready to believe, is the objective question: is Biblical prophecy an illusion? The affirmation of this

235

question is fraught with grave implications. The issue, then, is not only whether we can believe in revelation, but also whether we can believe in the negation of revelation.

IS GOD ABSENT EVERYWHERE?

It may seem easy to play with the idea that the Bible is a book like many other books, or that the story of Sinai is a fairy tale. Yet it is in such playing that we may gamble away our commitment, our tie to God.

Consider what such denial implies. If Moses and Isaiah have failed to find out what the will of God is, who will? If God is not found in the Bible, where should we seek Him?

The question about the Bible is the question about the world. It is an ultimate question. If God had nothing to do with the prophets, then He has nothing to do with mankind. And if God had anything to do with the prophets, then the prophets were neither liars nor impostors.

And yet, we, Philistines, continue to insist upon intellectual clichés, upon setting up our own life as a model and measure of what prophets could possibly attain. We oppose the prophets' word with our claims that God can never reach an ear, God will never stoop to light a word in the mind of man. But this is the principle of fools: what is unattainable to us is unattainable to others. The average man is not the measure. It is not an achievement of man that we are exploring. It is something in which the power of God was active. It is not for us to say that God must conform to our standards. The platitudes of our theories must not decide the greatest issue. There are many things between God and man of which scholars have never dreamt. Does psychology decide the validity of mathematical laws? Does history proceed the way logic predicts?

236

God in search of man

What is the place of the Bible in the world of spirit? What shall the Bible be likened to?

The book that avers:

> Grace is deceitful,
> and beauty is vain

shall it be appraised for its esthetic achievements? Some people hail the Bible as "literature,"[1] as if such juxtaposition were the highest praise, as if "literature" were the climax of spiritual reality. What would Moses, what would Isaiah have said to such praise? Perhaps the same as Einstein would have said, if the manuscript of his Theory of Relativity were acclaimed for its beautiful handwriting. Who but a child would claim that the essence of the ocean is its beauty? Or that the meaning of the stars lies in their charm?

Since the ninth century the Mohammedans have presented as a proof of the divine origin of Islam "the beauty of the Koran," or "the insuperability of the Koranic style."[2] The merit of the claim has always escaped the understanding of non-Mohammedans. It is significant, however, that the esthetic quality of the Bible has never been used as an argument in proving the dogma of revelation. How could Jews and Christians—until recent times—fail to see that the Bible is supreme in form; that never have thoughts been cast in a finer mold; that no man's imagination has ever conceived of a work comparable to it in profound, unvanishing and often unbearable beauty?

We all have a need for beauty and a thirst for noble expression. Beauty and noble expression in varying degrees may be found all over the world. But is the soul in need of beauty and expression alone? The soul, we believe, is in need of consecration; to achieve that goal we must turn to the Bible. There are many literatures, but only one Bible.

The Bible is an answer to the question: how to sanctify life. And if we say we feel no need for sanctification, we only prove that the

237

Bible is indispensable. Because it is the Bible that teaches us how to feel the need for sanctification.

What have the prophets done for the human situation? Let us try to recall but a few out of many things.

The Bible showed man his independence of nature, his superiority to conditions, and called on him to realize the tremendous implications of simple acts. Not only the stars but also the deeds of man travel a course that either reflects or perverts a thought of God. The degree of our appreciation of the Bible is, therefore, determined by the degree of our sensitivity to the divine dignity of human deeds. The insight into the divine implications of human life is the distinct message of the Bible.

The Bible has shattered man's illusion of being alone. Sinai broke the cosmic silence that thickens our blood with despair. God does not stand aloof from our cries; He is not only a pattern, but a power, and life is a response, not a soliloquy.

The Bible shows the way of God with man and the way of man with God. It contains both the complaint of God against the wicked and the shriek of the smitten man, demanding justice of God.

And there dwells also in its pages reminders of man's incredible callousness and obstinacy, of his immense capacity to bring about his doom as well as the assurance that beyond all evil is the compassion of God.

He who seeks an answer to the most pressing question, what is living? will find an answer in the Bible: man's destiny is to be a partner rather than a master. There is a task, a law, and a way: the task is redemption, the law, to do justice, to love mercy, and the way is the secret of being *human and holy*. When we are gasping with despair, when the wisdom of science and the splendor of the arts fail to save us from fear and the sense of futility, the Bible offers us the only hope: history is a circuitous way for the steps of the Messiah.

238

A philosophy of Judaism

There are no words in the world more knowing, more disclosing and more indispensable, words both stern and graceful, heart-rending and healing. A truth so universal: God is One. A thought so consoling: He is with us in distress. A responsibility so overwhelming: His name can be desecrated. A map of time: from creation to redemption. Guideposts along the way: the Seventh Day. An offering: contrition of the heart. A utopia: would that all people were prophets. The insight: man lives by his faithfulness; his home is in time and his substance in deeds. A standard so bold: ye shall be holy. A commandment so daring: love thy neighbor as thyself. A fact so sublime: human and divine pathos can be in accord. And a gift so undeserved: the ability to repent.

The Bible is mankind's greatest privilege. It is so far off and so direct, categorical in its demands and full of compassion in its understanding of the human situation. No other book so loves and respects the life of man. No loftier songs about his true plight and glory, about his agony and joys, misery and hope, have ever been expressed, and nowhere has man's need for guidance and the certainty of his ultimate redemption been so keenly conceived. It has the words that startle the guilty and the promise that upholds the forlorn. And he who seeks a language in which to utter his deepest concern, to pray, will find it in the Bible.

The Bible is not an end but a beginning; a precedent, not a story. Its being embedded in particular historic situations has not deterred it from being everlasting. Nothing in it is surreptitious or trite. It is not an epic about the life of heroes but the story of every man in all climates and all ages. Its topic is the world, the whole of history, containing the pattern of a constitution of a united mankind as well as guidance toward establishing such a union. It shows the way to nations as well as to individuals. It continues to scatter seeds of justice and compassion, to echo God's cry to the world and to pierce man's armor of callousness.

239

When a great poet appears, he does not offer proof of his being a poet. His poetry speaks for itself, creating in us the power to appreciate its novel and exceptional vision of life at the price of abandoning established conceptions. We do not identify his work as poetry by means of preconceived notions. *Genius identifies itself.*

The Bible is not in need of proof of its singularity. It has exercised power over the spirit of man throughout the ages *not* because it was labeled "The Word of God" and was poured into the minds of man through the funnel of a dogma, but because it contained a light that set souls aflame. Had it come down to us without such renown, without such a label, our amazement at its powers would have been even stronger.

Why does the Bible surpass everything created by man? Why is there no work worthy of comparison with it? Why is there no substitute for the Bible, no parallel to the history it has engendered? Why must all who seek the living God turn to its pages?

Set the Bible beside any of the truly great books produced by the genius of man, and see how they are diminished in stature. The Bible shows no concern with literary form, with verbal beauty, yet its absolute sublimity rings through all its pages. Its lines are so monumental and at the same time so simple that whoever tries to compete with them produces either a commentary or a caricature. It is a work we do not know how to assess. The plummet line of scholarship cannot probe its depth nor will critical analysis ever grasp its essence. Other books you can estimate, you can measure, compare; the Bible you can only extol. Its insights surpass our standards. There is nothing greater.

Is it not true that the Bible is the only book in the whole world that can never be replaced, the only book without which our past as well as our future is dark, meaningless and unbearable? None can usurp its place, none can inherit its role. One is afraid to utter its praise.

God in search of man

Other books you can try to account for, but an attempt to explain the Bible is a supreme opportunity to become ridiculous.

Use your imagination and try to conceive of a book that would excel the Bible, and you will admit that the power of the spirit has never gone farther than the Bible. Where is the mind that could express its worth? Endeavoring to appraise it, you discover that the mind is incongruous with the task. It is not a book—it is the limit of the spirit on earth.

Our heart stops when we ponder its terrible greatness. It is the only thing in the world which we may associate with eternity; the only thing in the world which is eternal. The eternal Book. The earth may not be the most important planet, our eon may not be the only one. But in this world, in this eon, the Bible is the most enduring vessel of the spirit.

How are we to comprehend this incomprehensible fact? How and whence did it emerge? What were the circumstances which concurred to permit this incomparable marvel to come to pass? If God was silent while Moses lived, if God did not speak while Moses heard, then Moses was a being whose nature surpassed anything human; then the origin of the Bible is not a mystery but total darkness.

THE OMNIPOTENCE OF THE BIBLE

The omnipotence of God is not always perceptible, but *the omnipotence of the Bible* is the great miracle of history. Like God, it is often misused and distorted by unclean minds, yet its capacity to withstand the most vicious attacks is boundless. The vigor and veracity of its ideas are perceptible under the rust and batter of two millennia of debate and dogma: it does not fade in spite of theology nor collapse under abuse. The Bible is *the perpetual motion of the spirit,* an ocean of meaning, its waves beating against man's abrupt

241

and steep shortcomings, its echo reaching into the blind alleys of his wrestling with despair.

No sadder proof can be given by a man of his own spiritual opacity than his insensitiveness to the Bible. "A ship which looms large in the river seems tiny when on the ocean." The greatness of the Bible becomes more manifest when studied within the framework of universal history, and its majesty increases with the reader's familiarity.

Irrefutably, indestructibly, never wearied by time, the Bible wanders through the ages, giving itself with ease to all men, as if it belonged to every soul on earth. It speaks in every language and in every age. It benefits all the arts and does not compete with them. We all draw upon it, and it remains pure, inexhaustible and complete. In three thousand years it has not aged a day. It is a book that cannot die. Oblivion shuns its pages. Its power is not subsiding. In fact, it is still at the very beginning of its career, the full meaning of its content having hardly touched the threshold of our minds; like an ocean at the bottom of which countless pearls lie, waiting to be discovered, its spirit is still to be unfolded. Though its words seem plain and its idiom translucent, unnoticed meanings, undreamed-of intimations break forth constantly. More than two thousand years of reading and research have not succeeded in exploring its full meaning. Today it is as if it had never been touched, never been seen, as if we had not even begun to read it.

Its spirit is too much for one generation to bear. Its words reveal more than we can absorb. All we usually accomplish is the attempt to appropriate a few single lines so that our spirit becomes synonymous with a passage.

PRECIOUS TO GOD

All flesh is grass,
And all the goodliness thereof is as the flower of the field . . .
The grass withers, the flower fades,
But the word of our God shall stand for ever.

Isaiah 40:6-7,8

242

A philosophy of Judaism

Never before and never since has such a claim been expressed. And who will doubt that the claim has proved true? Has not the word, spoken to the people of Israel, penetrated to all the corners of the world and been accepted as the message of God in a thousand languages? Why did most religions die which were not born of its seed, while every generation welcomes anew the spirit that sprouts from it? Indeed, countless cults, states, empires withered like grass; books by the millions are in the graves; "But the word of our God shall stand for ever." In moments of great crisis they all fail—priests, philosophers, scientists—the prophets alone prevail.

The wisdom, teaching, and counsel of the Bible are not in conflict with the ultimate attainments of the human mind, but, rather, well ahead of our attitudes. The idea of the equality of man, for example, has become a commonplace in our mouths, but how far is it from being an irresistible insight or an honest, ineradicable conviction? The Bible is not behind the times; it is ages ahead of our aspirations.

There is one thing we should try to imagine. In the whirlwind of history the Bible could have been lost; Abraham, Moses, Isaiah retained as vague memories. What would be missing in the world, what would be the condition and faith of man, had the Bible not been preserved?

It is the fountainhead of the finest strivings of man in the Western World. It has elicited more holiness and compassion from mankind than we are able to comprehend. Most of what is noble and just is derived from its spirit. It has given birth and shape to a myriad of precious things in the lives of individuals and peoples.

Free of any tinge of vested interests, of class or nation; free of any regard for persons, be it Moses, the highest of prophets, be it David, the most revered of kings; unconstrained by false deference to any institution, be it the state of Judah or the temple in Jerusalem; it is a book which can conceivably be precious not only to man but to God. Its aim is not to record history but rather to record the encounter of the divine and the human on the level of concrete living. Incomparably more important than all the beauty or wisdom that it bestows upon our lives is the way it opens to man an understanding of what God means, of attaining holiness through justice, through simplicity of soul, through choice. Above all it never ceases to proclaim that worship of God without justice to man is an abomination; that while man's problem is God, God's problem is man.

The Bible is *holiness in words*. To the man of our age nothing is as familiar and trite as words. Of all things they are the cheapest, most abused and least esteemed. They are the objects of perpetual defilement. We all live in them, feel in them, think in them, but, failing to uphold their independent dignity, to respect their power and weight, they turn waif, elusive—a mouthful of dust.[3] When placed before the Bible, the words of which are like dwellings made of rock, we do not know how to find the door.

Some people may wonder: why was the light of God given in the form of language? How is it conceivable that the divine should be contained in such brittle vessels as consonants and vowels? This question betrays the sin of our age: to treat lightly the ether which carries the light-waves of the spirit. What else in the world is as capable of bringing man and man together over the distances in space and in time? Of all things on earth, words alone never die. They have so little matter and so much meaning.

The Bible does not deal with divinity but with humanity. Addressing human beings about human affairs, whose language should be employed if not man's? And yet, it is as if God took these Hebrew words and breathed into them of His power, and the words became a live wire charged with His spirit. To this very day they are hyphens between heaven and earth.

What other medium could have been employed to convey the divine? Pictures enameled on the moon? Statues hewn out of the Rockies? What is wrong with the human ancestry of scriptural vocabulary?

244

God in search of man

If the Bible were a *temple,* equal in majesty and splendor to the simple grandeur of its present form, its divine language might have carried the sign of divine dignity with more undeniable force to most people. But man would have worshiped His work rather than His will . . . and this is exactly what the Bible has tried to prevent.

Just as it is impossible to conceive of God without the world, so it is impossible to conceive of His concern without the Bible.

If God is alive, then the Bible is His voice. No other work is as worthy of being considered a manifestation of His will. There is no other mirror in the world where His will and spiritual guidance is as unmistakably reflected. If the belief in the immanence of God in nature is plausible, then the belief in the immanence of God in the Bible is compelling.

ISRAEL AS EVIDENCE

Judaism is not a prophetic religion but a people's religion. Prophets were found among other nations as well. Unique was the entrance of holiness into the life of all Israel and the fact of prophecy being translated into concrete *history* rather than remaining a private experience of individuals. Biblical revelation took place not for the benefit of the prophets but for the sake of Israel and all men.

In almost every cult and religion certain beings, things, places or actions were considered to be holy. However, the idea of the holiness of an entire people, Israel as a holy people, is without parallel in human history. Holiness is the most precious word in religion and was only used to describe what was believed to be an undeniable manifestation in a certain being of a startling, supernatural quality. Only extraordinary, supernatural events in the life of all of Israel would have made the usage of the term "a holy people" possible.

Had Israel never received a revelation, the puzzle would have been greater. How, of all nations, did an obscure, politically insignificant people acquire the power to speak for the souls of all men in the Western World?

245

The wonder of Israel, the marvel of Jewish existence, the survival of holiness in the history of Israel is a continuous verification of the marvel of the Bible. Revelation to Israel became a revelation through Israel.

Christian Fürchtegott Gellert, when asked by Frederick the Great: "Herr Professor, give me a proof of the Bible, but briefly, for I have little time," answered: "Majesty, the Jews."[4]

HOW TO SHARE THE CERTAINTY OF ISRAEL

Our attitude to the Bible is more than a problem of isolated individual faith. It is as members of the community of Israel that our ultimate decision must be made. Estranged from the community of Israel and its continuous response, who could understand the voice? We are close to the people reprimanded, to the situation in which the words were said, as well as to the prophets. As Jews we are the prophet's spiritual contemporaries.

It is not the rejection of a dogma that would sever us from the Bible but the tearing of the bonds which tie us with the people that lived with the voice.

Our problem, then, is how to share the certainty of Israel that the Bible contains that which God wants us to know and to hearken to; how to attain a collective sense for the presence of God in the Biblical words. In this problem lies the dilemma of our fate, and in the answer lies the dawn or the doom.

NOT BECAUSE OF PROOF

He who cannot make up his mind, who will not introduce his soul to the Bible until the reasons for its divine dignity have gone all the way to meet his mind, is like a person who refuses to look at a painting before he can decipher the name of the artist signed at its corner. He does not realize it is the work which identifies the signature. Signatures may be forged, a work of art must be created.

246

A philosophy of Judaism

We easily forget that reasons, too, are in need of reasons; that no proof is ultimate or self-supporting.

The Bible is its own witness. The evidence for its unique origin is that of *self-evidence*. It has in the course of the ages identified itself as a voice of God. If there is anything in the world that ever deserved the attribute of the divine, it is the Bible. There are many books about God: the Bible is the book of God. Disclosing the love of God for man, it opened our eyes to see the unity of that which is meaningful to mankind and that which is sacred to God, showing us how to make a nation, not only the life of an individual, holy. It always holds out new promise to failing, honest souls, while those who discard it court disaster.

We do not accept the word of God because of proof one, two, three. . . . We accept it because in approaching it our splendid ideas turn pale, because even indisputable proofs appear vulgar at the sound of prophetic words. We do not decide to turn to the Bible because of reasons; we turn to the Bible in order to find a meaning for existence that gives firmness to all reasons.

But our insights may be wrong. Is it not possible that we have all been deceived? Indeed, everything is conceivable, but in such case we must not forget what such a possibility implies.

To deny the divine origin of the Bible is to brand the entire history of spiritual efforts and attainments in Judaism, Christianity and Islam as the outgrowth of a colossal lie, the triumph of a deception which captured the finest souls for more than two thousand years. Yet, an assertion such as this would be such a formidable shock as to have repercussions upon our very ability to make such a statement. If the finest souls are so frail, how can we claim to attain knowledge about the prophets' self-deception? What would remain for us except to despair? The Bible has either originated in a lie or in an act of God. If the Bible is a deception, then the devil is almighty and there is no hope of ever attaining truth, no reliance on the spirit; our very thinking would be useless and our efforts futile. Ultimately, then, we do not accept the Bible because of reasons, but because if the Bible is a lie all reasons are a fake.

247

1 The theory that the Bible is literature was, indeed, maintained by the contemporaries of Ezekiel. The prophet is charged by the Lord to say to "the forest": "Hear the word of the Lord: Thus says the Lord God: Behold I will kindle a fire in thee and it shall devour every green tree in thee . . . and all faces from the south to the north shall be seared thereby. And all flesh shall see that I the Lord have kindled it; it shall not be quenched." But the prophet knew what his people were going to maintain, and he said to the Lord: "Ah, Lord God! They say of me: Is he not a maker of parables?" (Ezekiel 21:1-5). "Alas for the man who regards the Torah as a mere book of tales and everyday matters! If that were so, we, even we, could compose a Torah dealing with everyday affairs and *of even greater excellence.* Nay, the princes of the world possess *books of greater worth* which we could use as a model for composing some such torah." *Zohar* III 152a. An appreciation of the Bible's literary qualities is found, however, in Moses Ibn Ezra, *Shirat Israel.*

2 See Tor Andrae, *Die Person Muhammeds,* Stockholm, 1918, p. 97, and Gustave E. von Grunebaum, *Medieval Islam,* Chicago, 1946, p. 94ff. On the Mutazilites' reservations, see I. Goldizher *Vorlesungen ueber den Islam,* Heidelberg, 1910, p. 102.

3 A. J. Heschel, *Man's Quest for God,* p. 25.

4 A. Jeremias, *Juedische Froemmigkeit,* p. 57.

26 Faith with the Prophets

FAITH WITH THE PROPHETS

Faith in the prophets is not the only basis for what we think about the Bible. This might have been the case if all we had were their reports about their experiences. The fact is that we are being challenged not only by those reports but by what came out in those experiences. The Bible itself is given for all men to absorb. Indeed, this is the way: from the ability to have faith in the faith of the prophets to the ability to share the faith of the prophets in the power of God to speak.

What begins—theoretically—as *faith in the prophets* moves and grows to be *faith with the prophets*. The Bible enables us to hear something of what they have heard, though not in the manner they heard.

The soul of the prophet is a mirror to God. To share the faith of a prophet means more than perceiving what common sense fails to perceive; it means *being* what common people fail to be: a mirror to God. To share the faith of a prophet means rising toward the level of his existence.[1]

The voice of God is incongruous with the ear of man. Symbolically, it is not said of the people at Sinai, the whole people *heard* the voice, but rather, the whole people *saw* the voice (Exodus 20:18).

The Baal Shem offered a simile. A musician was playing on a very beautiful instrument, and the music so enraptured the people that they were driven to dance ecstatically. Then a deaf man who

249

knew nothing of music passed by, and seeing the enthusiastic dancing of the people he decided they must be insane. Had he been wise he would have sensed their joy and rapture and joined their dancing.[2]

We do not *hear* the voice. We only *see* the words in the Bible. Even when we are deaf, we can see the rapture of the words.

ORIGIN AND PRESENCE

He who wishes to ponder what is *beyond* the Bible must first learn to be sensitive to what is *within* the Bible. We do not have to believe Moses and the prophets on their word alone. More decisive than *the origin of the Bible in God* is *the presence of God in the Bible*. It is the sense for the presence that leads us to a belief in its origin.

The way to perceive the presence of God in the words of the Bible is not by inquiring whether the ideas they designate are in perfect agreement with the achievements of our reason or the common sense of man. Such agreement, granted that it could be established, would, indeed, prove that the Bible is the product of common sense or that the spirit in which it originated has nothing more to say than what reason is able to proclaim. What we must ask is whether there is anything in the Bible that is beyond the reach of reason, beyond the scope of common sense; whether its teaching is compatible with our sense of the ineffable, with the idea of unity, helping us to go beyond reason without denying reason, helping man to go beyond himself without losing himself. This is the distinction of the Bible: on the highest level of radical amazement, where all expression ends, it gives us the word. Revelation is an issue that must be decided on the level of the ineffable.

We must ask whether its content speaks to us in moments of spiritual perspicuity, when all our knowing becomes dim in the light of our unknowing and our life is felt to be an overflowing of something greater than ourselves, the excess of a spirit not our own. If the Bible held an appeal to man's everyday understanding,

250

then, indeed, it would be a work that could come into being every day, in the age of Sinai as well as in the age of Hollywood. What we must ask is whether there is anything about the Bible which is beyond the times.

Revelation is a cloudburst, a downpour, yet we live in a dry and weary land, where heaven is as iron and the air as dust. Most of us are like moles, burrowing, and whatever stream we meet is underground. Few are able at rare moments to rise above their own level. Yet, it is at such moments, when discovering that *the essence of human existence* is in the fact of *its being suspended between heaven and earth,* that we begin to comprehend the essence of the prophets' claim.

The sense of our being suspended between heaven and earth is as necessary to being moved by God as the hold of the Archimedean point is to moving the earth. Radical amazement is to the understanding of the realness of God what clarity and distinctness are to the comprehension of mathematical ideas. It is not enough to think *about* the prophets; we must think *through* the prophets. It is not enough to read the Bible for its wisdom; we must *pray the Bible* to comprehend its claim.

Much has happened to destroy our contact with the world of the prophets. Today the way to the Bible is littered with heaps of clichés and preconceptions, and on arriving at its words the mind is blind with shallow knowing. Certainly the first prerequisite for understanding the prophets is trained sensibility to what they stand for. The way remains closed to those to whom God is less real than "a consuming fire," to those who know answers but no wonder. Those who look for a way to the Bible will have to unthink many thoughts and to recall the innate sense of wonder, systematically extirpated by false wisdom.

Abstract reasons could never have persuaded us, if God Himself had not entreated us. He has a stake in our attitude toward His word, and *His will that we believe* may work in ways not accessible to our own will to believe. And, indeed, there is a way of our receiving indirectly what the prophets received *directly.*

251

It is not given to all men to identify the divine. His light may shine upon us, and we may fail to sense it. Devoid of wonder, we remain deaf to the sublime. We cannot sense His presence in the Bible except by being responsive to it. Only living with its words, only sympathy with its pathos, will open our ear to its voice. Biblical words are like musical signs of a divine harmony which only the finest chords of the soul can utter. It is the sense of the holy that perceives the presence of God in the Bible.

We can never approach the Bible alone. It is to *man with God* that the Bible opens itself.

THE FRONTIER OF THE SPIRIT

The divine quality of the Bible is not on display, it is not apparent to an inane, fatuous mind; just as the divine in the universe is not obvious to the debaucher. When we turn to the Bible with an empty spirit, moved by intellectual vanity, striving to show our superiority to the text; or as barren souls who go sight-seeing to the words of the prophets, we discover the shells but miss the core. It is easier to enjoy beauty than to sense the holy. To be able to encounter the spirit within the words, we must learn to crave for an affinity with the pathos of God.

To sense the presence of God in the Bible, one must learn *to be present* to God in the Bible. Presence is not a concept, but a situation. To understand love it is not enough to read tales about it. One must be involved in the prophets to understand the prophets. One must be inspired to understand inspiration. Just as we cannot test thinking without thinking, we cannot sense holiness without being holy. Presence is not disclosed to those who are unattached and try to judge, to those who have no power to go beyond the values they cherish; to those who sense the story, not the pathos; the idea, not the realness of God.

The Bible is the frontier of the spirit where we must move and live in order to discover and to explore. It is open to him who gives himself to it, who lives with it intimately.

252

We can only sense the presence by being responsive to it. We must learn to respond before we may hear; we must learn to fulfill before we may know. *It is the Bible that enables us to know the Bible.* It is through the Bible that we discover what is in the Bible. Unless we are confronted with the word, unless we continue our dialogue with the prophets, unless we respond, the Bible ceases to be Scripture.

We are moving in a circle. We would accept the Bible only if we could be sure of the presence of God in its words. Now, to identify His presence we must know what He is, but such knowledge we can only derive from the Bible. No human mind, conditioned as it is by its own perspectives, relations and aspirations, is able on its own to proclaim for all men and all times "This is God and nothing else." Thus we must accept the Bible in order to know the Bible; we must accept its unique authority in order to sense its unique quality. This, indeed, is the paradox of faith, the paradox of existence.

In our daily experience words are used as means to convey meaning. In the Bible to speak is to act, and the word is more than an instrument of expression; it is a vessel of divine power, the mystery of creation. The prophetic word creates, shapes, changes, builds, and destroys (see Jeremiah 1:10).

When man speaks, he tries to communicate some particular meaning; when the prophet speaks, he uncloses the source of all meaning. The words of the Bible are sources of spirit. They carry fire to the soul and evoke our lost dignity out of our hidden origins. Illumined, we suddenly remember, we suddenly recover the strength of endless longing to sense eternity in time.

"He who prays speaks to God; but he who reads the Bible God speaks to him, as it is said (Psalms 119:99), *Thy statutes are Thy converse with me.*"[3]

Just as there were events at particular moments of time, there is a word pleading with all men at all times.

The Bible is an eternal expression of a continuous concern; God's cry for man; not a letter from one who sent out a message and remained indifferent to the attitude of the recipient. It is not a book to be read but a drama in which to participate; not a book about events but itself an event, the continuation of the event, while our being involved in it is the continuation of the response. The event will endure so long as the response will continue. When we open it as if it were a book, it is silent; as a spiritual power it is a voice

". . . calling men day by day to herself in love. . . . The Torah lets out a word and emerges for a little from her sheath, and then hides herself again. But she does this only for those who understand and obey her. She is like unto a beautiful and stately damsel, who is hidden in a secluded chamber of a palace and who has a lover of whom no one knows but she. Out of his love for her he constantly passes by her gate, turning his eyes towards all sides to find her. She, knowing that he is always haunting the palace, what does she do? She opens a little door in her hidden palace, for a moment discloses her face to her lover, then swiftly hides it again. None but he notices it; but his heart and soul, and all that is in him are drawn to her, knowing as he does that she has revealed herself to him for a moment because she loves him. It is the same with the Torah, which reveals her hidden secrets only to those who love her. She knows that he who is wise of heart daily haunts the gates of her house. What does she do? She shows her face to him from her palace, making a sign of love to him, and straightway returns to her hiding place again. No one understands her message save he alone, and he is drawn to her with heart and soul and all his being. Thus the Torah reveals herself momentarily in love to her lovers in order to awaken fresh love in them."[4]

254

A philosophy of Judaism

The word was not given to the prophets for their own sake. We were all faced by God when the prophets were faced by Him. We were all addressed, when the prophets were spoken to. Our faith is derived from *our perceptiveness to the word that has gone out to all of us.*

The people of Israel came to trust in Moses not on the evidence of the miracles he performed; such feats could have been accomplished by Egypt's magicians. What enabled them to trust in Moses was the fact that they shared for a moment a degree of his suggestibility to God. What is true of them applies to us. Our passionate appreciation of the Bible is not primarily due to any particular test of the veracity of the prophets; it is a degree of the prophetic sense that enables us to say: Here is the presence of God.

"CAST ME NOT AWAY"

There is a grain of the prophet in the recesses of every human existence. "I call heaven and earth for witnesses that every man, whether gentile or Jew, whether man or woman, whether manservant or maidservant, according to the measure of his good deeds, the spirit of holiness rests upon him."[5] The holy spirit rests upon those who live within the Covenant.[6]

Just as in the words of the Bible history became Scripture, so in the life of Israel Scripture became history. The Bible was a revelation of God to Israel, Jewish history has been a revelation of Israel's holiness to God.

It is not as individuals but as the people Israel that we can find an approach to the prophets. The Bible lives within those who live within the Covenant. The community of Israel lives by His promise: "And as for me, this is My Covenant with them, says the Lord: *My spirit which is upon you,* and My words which I have put in your mouth, *shall not depart* out of your mouth, or out of the mouth of your children, or out of the mouth of your children's children, says the Lord, from this time forth and for evermore."[7] The individual, however, may forfeit the spirit. This is why we

255

pray: "Cast me not away from Thy presence, and take not Thy holy spirit from me."[8]

The way to understand the meaning of *torah min hashamayim* ("the Bible is from heaven") is to understand the meaning of *hashamayim min hatorah* ("heaven is from the Bible). Whatever taste of "heaven" we have on earth is in the Bible.

NOTES FOR CHAPTER 26

[1] "He who accepts even one single mitsvah with true faith is worthy that the Holy Spirit should rest upon him" *Mechilta,* to 14:31, ed, Lauterbach, I, p. 252.

[2] *Degel Mahneh Ephraim,* Yitro.

[3] *Yosippon,* ed. D. Guenzburg, Berditshev, 1913, p. 22.

[4] *Zohar,* vol. II, 99a; see vol. III, 58a.

[5] *Seder Eliahu Rabba,* IX, ed. M. Friedmann, Wien, 1902, p. 48.

[6] Hillel said: "Leave Israel alone. The holy spirit rests upon them. Though not being prophets, they are disciples of prophets." *Tosefta Pesahim* 4,8.

[7] Isaiah 59:21. "For prophecy will never depart from you," Rabbi David Kimchi, *Commentary,* ad locum.

[8] Isaiah 51:13. See Targum and Rashi ad locum. This petition is a part of the liturgy of the penitential season.

27 The Principle of Revelation

Prophetic inspiration may be dealt with on two levels, on the level of faith and on the level of belief or creed. Faith is the relation to the prophetic event; belief, or creed, is the relation to the date of the Biblical books.

It is a serious misunderstanding to reduce the problem of revelation to a matter of chronology. Thus it is frequently assumed that the authority and sanctity of the Pentateuch depend upon the fact that it was written down in its entirety in the time of Moses; that to assume that even a few passages were added to it after the death of Moses is to deny the principle of revelation.

Does the sanctity of the Bible depend on the amount of time that elapsed between the moment of revelation and the moment of committing its content to parchment? If God had wished that certain portions of the Pentateuch which were revealed to Moses be written down by Joshua, would that have detracted from its sanctity? And assuming that the soul of Moses returned to this world after it had departed from the body of Moses, and living in a new incarnation has been inspired to add some lines to the Pentateuch, would that make the Pentateuch less Mosaic?[1] Is it proper to treat the divine dignity of the Bible as if it were a *chronological problem,* as if its authenticity could be verified by a notary public?

The meaning of revelation is given to those who are mystery-minded, not to those who are literal-minded, and decisive is not the chronological but the theological fact; decisive is that which happened between God and the prophet rather than that which happened between the prophet and the parchment. We accept the authority of the Pentateuch not because it is Mosaic, but because Moses was a prophet.

The dogma of revelation in regard to the Pentateuch consists of two parts: the divine inspiration and the Mosaic authorship. The first part refers to a mystery, the second to a historic fact. The first part can only be alluded to and expressed in terms of grandeur and amazement; the second may be analyzed, examined, and conveyed in terms of chronological information.

Philosophy of religion must deal with the first part. Its concern is not whether the Pentateuch was written down in its entirety during the forty years of Israel's sojourn in the desert, but rather to understand the meaning and the validity of the claim that the will of God reached the understanding of man, and that the Pentateuch is a mirror of God's reaching man; the second part is the concern of theology which must define the dogma of revelation and offer an answer to historical questions.[2]

The essence of our faith in the sanctity of the Bible is that its words contain that which God wants us to know and to fulfill. How these words were written down is not the fundamental problem. This is why the theme of Biblical criticism is not the theme of faith, just as the question of whether the lightning and thunder at Sinai were a natural phenomenon or not is irrelevent to our faith in revelation. The assumption of some commentators that the Decalogue was given on a rainy day does not affect our conception of the event.[3]

The act of revelation is a mystery, while the record of revelation is a literary fact, phrased in the language of man.

THE TEXT AS IT IS

Are the words of Scripture coextensive and identical with the words of God?

In the eyes of those who experience daily their inability to grasp

A philosophy of Judaism

fully the meaning of a Scriptural verse, such a question represents an attempt to compare the hardly known with the totally unknown.

Granted that the text of Scripture as handed down to us consists of gems of God and diamonds quarried out of prophetic souls, all set in a human frame. Yet who shall presume to be an expert in discerning what is divine and what is but "a little lower" than divine? What is the spirit of God and what the phrase of Amos? The spirit of God is set in the language of man, and who shall judge what is content and what is frame? Certainly those who presume most are qualified least. There are more things between heaven and earth which will not submit themselves to our judgment than we are willing to admit.

Revelation lasted a moment; the text is permanent in time and space. Revelation happened to the prophet; the text is given to all of us. "The Torah is not in heaven"; we are guided by the word, and it is the word, the text, which is our guide, our light in the darkness of platitudes and errors. We must neither reduce revelation to a matter of fact nor spiritualize the Bible and destroy its factual integrity.

In its present form the Bible is the only object in the world which is not in need of either praise or sanctification. In its present form the Bible is the only point in the world from which God will never depart. This is the book to which Israel deferred; we must tremble to tamper with it.

REVELATION IS NOT A MONOLOGUE

By insisting upon the objective revelational character of the Bible, dogmatic theology has often lost sight of the profound and decisive share of man.

The prophet is not a passive recipient, a recording instrument, affected from without without participation of heart and will, nor is he a person who acquires his vision by his own strength and labor. The prophet's personality is rather a unity of inspiration and experience, invasion and response. For every object outside him, there is a feeling inside him, for every event of revelation to him, there is a reaction by him; for every glimpse of truth he is granted, there is a comprehension he must achieve.

Even in the moment of the event he is, we are told, an active partner in the event. His response to what is disclosed to him turns revelation into a dialogue. In a sense, prophecy consists of a revelation of God and *a co-revelation of man.* The share of the prophet manifested itself not only in what he was able to give but also in what he was unable to receive.

Revelation does not happen when God is alone. The two classical terms for the moment at Sinai are *mattan torah* and *ḳabbalat torah,* "the giving of the Torah" and "the acceptance of the Torah." It was both an event in the life of God and an event in the life of man. According to rabbinic legend, the Lord approached every tribe and nation and offered them the Torah, before He gave it to Israel. The wonder of Israel's acceptance was as decisive as the wonder of God's expression. God was alone in the world until Israel became engaged to Him. At Sinai God revealed His word, and Israel revealed the power to respond. Without that power to respond, without the fact that there was a people willing to accept, to hear, the divine command, Sinai would have been impossible. For Sinai consisted of both a divine proclamation and a human perception. It was a moment in which *God was not alone.*

The Bible contains not only records of what transpired in moments of prophetic inspiration; it also records acts and words of man. It is incorrect to maintain that all words in the Bible originated in the spirit of God. The blasphemous tirades of Pharaoh, the rebellious utterances of Korach, the subterfuge of Ephron, the words of the soldiers in the camp of Midian, emanated from the spirit of man. What the prophet says to God when addressed by Him is not considered less holy than what God says to the prophet in addressing him.

Thus the Bible is more than the word of God: it is the word of God *and* man; a record of both revelation and response; the drama

God in search of man

of covenant between God and man. The canonization and preservation of the Bible are the work of Israel.

THE VOICE ACCORDING TO MAN

No man is able to hear the voice of God as it is. But "God thunders marvelously with His voice" (Job 37:5) on Sinai. "The voice went forth—coming to each person with a force adjusted to his individual receptivity—to the old according to their strength, and to the young according to theirs . . . and even to Moses according to his strength, as it is said: *Moses spoke, and God answered him by a voice* (Exodus 19:19), that is, with a voice which he could endure. Similarly it says: *The voice of the Lord is with power* (Psalms 29:4), namely with the power of each individual. This is why the Decalogue begins *I am the Lord thy God,* in the second person singular, rather than in the second person plural: God addressed every individual according to his particular power of comprehension."[4]

This does not imply subjectivism. It is precisely the power of the voice of God to speak to man according to his capacity. It is the marvel of the voice to split up into seventy voices, into seventy languages, so that all the nations should understand.

WISDOM, PROPHECY, AND GOD

God does not reveal Himself; he only reveals His way. Judaism does not speak of God's self-revelation, but of the revelation of His teaching for man. The Bible reflects God's revelation of His relation to history, rather than of a revelation of His very Self. Even His will or His wisdom is not completely expressed through the prophets. Prophecy is superior to human wisdom, and God's love is superior to prophecy. This spiritual hierarchy is explicitly stated by the Rabbis.

"They asked *Wisdom:* What should be the punishment of a sinner? And Wisdom said: *Misfortune pursues sinners* (Proverbs 13:21). They asked *prophecy:* What should be the punishment of a sinner? And prophecy said: *The soul that sins shall die* (Ezekiel 18:4.20). They asked *the Holy One,* blessed be He: What should be the punishment of a sinner? And He said: *Let him repent, and he will be atoned for."*[5]

God is infinitely more sublime than what the prophets were able to comprehend, and the heavenly wisdom is more profound than what the Torah contains in its present form.

"There are five incomplete phenomena (or unripe fruits). The incomplete experience of death is sleep; an incomplete form of prophecy is dream; the incomplete form of the world to come is the Sabbath; the incomplete form of the heavenly light is the orb of the sun; the incomplete form of heavenly wisdom is the Torah."[6]

THE UNREVEALED TORAH

The word Torah is used in two senses: the supernal Torah, the existence of which preceded the creation of the world,[7] and the revealed Torah. Concerning the supernal Torah the Rabbis maintained: "The Torah is hidden from the eyes of all living. . . . Man knows not the price thereof."[8] "Moses received Torah"—but not all of the Torah—"at Sinai."[9] And not all that was revealed to Moses was conveyed to Israel; the meaning of the commandments is given as an example.[10] Together with the gratitude for the word that was disclosed, there is a yearning for the meaning yet to be disclosed. "The Lord gave Israel the Torah and spoke to them face to face, and the memory of that love is more delightful to them than any other joy. They have been promised that He will return to them once more in order to reveal the secret meaning of the Torah and its concealed content. Israel implores Him to fulfill this promise. This is the meaning of the verse: *Let Him kiss me with the kisses of His mouth—for Thy love is better than wine."*[11]

There is a theory in Jewish literature containing a profound parabolical truth which maintains that the Torah, which is eternal in spirit, assumes different forms in various eons. The Torah was known to Adam when he was in the Garden of Eden, although not

262

A philosophy of Judaism

in its present form. Commandments such as those concerning charity to the poor, the stranger, the orphan, and the widow, would have been meaningless in the Garden of Eden. In that eon the Torah was known in its spiritual form.[12] Just as man assumed a material form when he was driven out of the Garden of Eden, so has the Torah assumed a material form. If man had retained "the garments of light," his spiritual form of existence, the Torah, too, would have retained its spiritual form.[13]

THE TORAH IS IN EXILE

God is not only in heaven but in this world as well. But in order to dwell in this world, the divine must assume a form which this world could bear, "shells" in which the light is concealed. The Torah, too, in order to enter the world of history, is encased in "shells," since it could not exist or be fulfilled in its perfect form in a world which is stained with imperfections.[14]

Just as the *Shechinah* is in exile, so is the *Torah in exile*. Adjusting itself to the condition of man, "the Torah assumed for our eon a strange garb and shells of no beauty or comeliness, such as chapter thirty-six of the Book of Genesis or Deuteronomy 2:23 and many others. To the same class belong many agadic passages in Rabbinic literature which are unsavory and objectionable, and yet contain in concealed form mysteries of the Torah. All this is due to the necessity of veiling the light of knowledge in the garb of the *kelipah* and the unclean powers. God, Torah, and Israel will remain in exile until the spirit will be poured upon us from on high to bring back the captivity for the sake of His Torah and His Name and the good and the holy will be purified from the evil and the shells. . . ."[15]

Boldly Rabbi Simeon ben Lakish declared: "There are many verses which to all appearances ought to be burnt like the books of the heretics, but are really essential elements in the Torah." As examples are cited *And the Avvim that dwell in villages as far as Gaza* (Deuteronomy 2:23). *For Heshbon was the city of Sihon the king of the Amorites who had fought against the former king of Moab* (Numbers 21:26).[16]

In its present form, the Torah deals with matters that concern the material relations between man and man. In the messianic eon, a wisdom higher than the one now found in it will be revealed in the Torah. Now we have the Torah, in the messianic eon we will have the crown of the Torah. Thus the wisdom open to us in this eon is but the beginning of its revelation.[17]

"For if a man live many years let him rejoice (Ecclesiastes 11:8) in the joy of the Torah and *remember the days of darkness,* these are the days of evil, *for they shall be many.* The Torah which a man learns in this world *is vanity* in comparison with the Torah [which will be learnt in the days] of the Messiah."[18]

Isaiah's prediction for the days to come, "With joy shall ye draw water out of the wells of salvation" (12:2), is explained by Rashi in the following way: "Ye shall receive new teaching, for the Lord will widen your understanding. . . . The mysteries of the Torah that were forgotten during the exile in Babylonia because of the distress Israel suffered, will be revealed to them."

The words of Scripture are the only lasting record of what was conveyed to the prophets. At the same time they are neither identical with, nor the eternally adequate rendering of, the divine wisdom. As a reflection of His infinite light, the text in its present form is, to speak figuratively, one of an endless number of possible reflections. In the end of the days, it was believed, countless unknown rearrangements of the words and letters and unknown secrets of the Torah would be made known. Yet in its present form the text contains that which God wishes us to know.[19]

IDEA AND EXPRESSION

There is another aspect to the part played by the prophet. According to the Rabbis, *"The same idea* is revealed to many prophets, but *no* two prophets use *the same expression."* The fact that the four hundred prophets of King Ahab employed *the same* phrases was regarded as proof that they were not divinely inspired.[20] When in the court of justice two people testifying to the same event use identical language, they are suspected of having conspired to bear false witness.[21] The prophets bear witness to an event. The event is divine, but the formulation is done by the individual prophet. According to this conception, the idea is revealed; the expression is coined by the prophet.[22] The expression "the word of God" would not refer to the word as a sound or a combination of sounds. Indeed, it has often been maintained that what reached the ear of man was not identical with what has come out of the spirit of the eternal God. For "Israel could not possibly have received the Torah as it came forth from the mouth of the Lord, for the word of the Lord is fire and the Lord is 'a fire that consumes fire.' Surely man would flash into blaze, if he were exposed to the word in itself. Therefore, the word became clothed before it entered the world of creation. And so the Psalmist speaks of revelation as 'coals that flamed forth from Him' (Psalms 18:9). The word of God in itself is like a burning flame, and the Torah that we received is merely a part of the coal to which the flame is attached. And yet, even in this form it would have remained beyond our comprehension as long as we are mortals. The word had to descend further and to assume the form of darkness ('arafel) in order to become perceptible to man."[23]

Out of the experience of the prophets came the words, words that try to interpret what they perceived. To this very day, these words make present what happened in the past. As the meaning and wonder of the event inspired the spiritual comprehension of the prophet, the meaning and wonder of the Biblical words continue to inspire the understanding of man.

The Bible reflects its divine as well as its human authorship. Expressed in the language of a particular age, it addresses itself to all ages; disclosed in particular acts, its spirit is everlasting. The will of God is in time and in eternity. God borrowed the language of man and created a work such as no men had ever made. It is the task of faith to hold fast to that work, to treasure its mixture of timeliness and eternity and to continually understand the polarity of its contents.

We have spoken above of the presence of God in the Bible and characterized its quality as holiness in words. However, there are a few passages in the Bible which lead one to feel that God is not present in them; passages either too commonplace or too harsh to reflect the spirit of God.

We shall discuss the problem presented by both kinds of passages.

The question has been asked. "If it is not dignified for a king of flesh and blood to engage in common talk, much less to write it down, is it conceivable that the most high King, the Holy One, blessed be He, was short of sacred subjects with which to fill the Torah, so that He had to collect such commonplace topics as the anecdotes of Esau, and Hagar, Laban's talks to Jacob, the words of Balaam and his ass, those of Balak, and of Zimri, and such-like, and make of them a Torah? If so, why is it called the 'Torah of truth'? Why do we read 'The Torah of the Lord is perfect. . . . The testimony of the Lord is sure. . . . The ordinances of the Lord are true. . . . More to be desired are they than gold, yea, than much fine gold' (Psalms 19:8-11)?"[24]

The answer seems to be that the Bible has more than one level of meaning. While most of it is open to unambiguous understanding, much of it remains locked to the literal-minded.

"David prayed: Master of the universe, it is Thy will that I keep Thy words, so 'open my eyes, that I may behold wondrous things out of Thy Torah' (Psalms 119:18). If Thou wilt not open my eyes, how would I know? For *though my eyes are open, I know nothing.*"[25]

"Said Rabbi Simeon: 'Alas for the man who regards the Torah as a book of mere tales and everyday matters! If that were so, we, even we could compose a torah dealing with everyday affairs and of even greater excellence. Nay, even the princes of the world possess books of greater worth which we could use as a model for composing some such torah. The Torah, however, contains in all its words supernal truths and sublime mysteries. Observe the perfect balancing of the upper and the lower worlds. Israel here below is balanced by the angels on high, of whom it says. 'Who makest thy angels into winds' (Psalms 114:4). For the angels in descending on earth put on themselves earthly garments, as otherwise they could not stay in this world, nor could the world endure them. Now if thus it is with the angels, how much more so must it be with the Torah—the Torah that created them, that created all the worlds and is the means by which these are sustained. Thus had the Torah not clothed herself in garments of this world the world could not endure it. The stories of the Torah are thus only her outer garments and whoever looks upon that garment as being the Torah itself, woe to that man—such a one will have no portion in the next world. David thus said: 'Open thou mine eyes that I may behold wondrous things out of Thy Torah' (Psalms 119:18); to wit, the things that are beneath the garment. Observe this. The garments worn by a man are the most visible part of him, and senseless people looking at the man do not seem to see more in him than the garments. But in truth the pride of the garments is the body of the man, and the pride of the body is the soul. Similarly the Torah has a body made up of the precepts of the Torah, called *gufe torah* (main principles of the Torah) and that body is enveloped in garments made up of worldly narrations. The senseless people see only the garment, the mere narrations; those who are somewhat wiser penetrate as far as the body; but the really wise, the servants of the most high King, those who stood on Mount Sinai, penetrate right through to the soul, the root principle of all, to the real Torah. In the future the same are destined to penetrate even to the supersoul (soul of the soul) of the Torah. Observe that in a similar way in the supernal world there is garment, body, soul, and supersoul. All these are interlocked within each other. Woe to the sinners who consider the Torah as mere worldly tales, who only see its outer garment; happy are the righteous who fix their gaze on the Torah itself. Wine cannot be kept save in a jar; so the Torah needs an outer garment. These are the stories and narratives, but it behooves us to penetrate beneath them."[26]

HARSH PASSAGES

We encounter an even more serious problem in a number of passages which seem to be incompatible with our certainty of the compassion of God.

In analyzing this extremely difficult problem, we must first of all keep in mind that the standards by which those passages are criticized are impressed upon us by the Bible, which is the main factor in ennobling our conscience and in endowing us with the sensitivity that rebels against all cruelty.

We must, furthermore, realize that the harsh passages in the Bible are only contained in describing actions which were taken *at particular moments* and stand in sharp contrast with the compassion, justice and wisdom of the laws that were legislated *for all times.*

As said above, we must not equate prophecy with God. Prophecy is superior to human wisdom, and God's love is superior to prophecy. Not every utterance contained in the Bible is to be regarded as a norm or a standard of behavior. We are told that Moses, Elijah, Isaiah were reproved by the Lord for uttering harsh words about the people,[27] though these words are a part of the Bible (Exodus 4:1; I Kings 19:14; Isaiah 6:5).

An outstanding mark of Biblical writing is its *ruthless honesty.* None of the prophets is pictured as faultless, none of the heroes is impeccable. The Glory is enveloped in a cloud, and redemption is attained at the price of exile. There is neither perfection nor sweetness nor sentimentality in the Bible's approach. Abraham has the courage to exclaim, "The judge of all the earth shall not act justly?" And Job dares to question the fairness of the Almighty. Accusing his friends who offer apologies for God as being "plasterers of lies," Job pleads:

Will you speak falsely for God,
And talk deceitfully for Him?

Will you show partiality toward Him,
Will you plead the case of God?
Will it be well with you when He searches you out?
Or can you deceive Him, as one deceives a man?
He will surely rebuke you,
If in secret you show partiality.

Job 13:7-10

Resignation and acceptance of the inscrutable will of God are expressions of normal piety. In contrast, though *not* in contradiction, stands the prophet who, instead of being unquestioning and submissive in the face of God, dares to challenge His judgment, to remind Him of His covenant and to plead for His mercy. In the spirit of piety, Jew and Christian will accept evil as well as good, and pray, "Thy will be done,"[28] while the prophet will plead, "Turn from Thy fierce wrath and repent this evil against Thy people" (Exodus 32:12).

Abraham challenged the intention of the Lord to destroy Sodom. In the name of God's mercy, we too have the right to challenge the harsh statements of the prophets. Two examples follow:

"Behold, I call upon heaven and earth to witness that the Lord did not say unto Moses that which Moses said in the gate of the camp— 'Who is on the Lord's side, come unto me . . . ! Thus saith the Lord God of Israel: Put every man his sword on his side' (Exodus 32: 27)—But rather Moses the pious one deduced it from his own reason. He thought, if I command the people—'Slay every man his brother, his companion, his neighbor'—the people will protest—Did you yourself not teach us that a court that condemns to death even one person in seventy years is to be considered bloodthirsty? How can you, then, order the killing of three thousand in one day?—Therefore Moses ascribed his order to the authority of the Lord and said, 'Thus saith the Lord.' Indeed, in stating that the Levites carried out the order, Scripture says: and the sons of Levi did according to the word of Moses."[29]

The independence of human understanding and its power to challenge a prophet's claim may be further illustrated by the following legend:

"When Hezekiah fell ill, the Holy One, blessed be He, said to Isaiah, *Set thy house in order, for thou shalt die and not live* (Isaiah 38:1). Said Hezekiah: It is customary that a person, when visiting the sick should say, 'May mercy be shown upon you from Heaven.' When the physician comes, he tells the sick, 'Eat this and do not eat that, drink this and do not drink that.' Even when he sees him near to death he does not say to him, 'Set thy house in order' because this might upset him. You, however, tell me, *Set thy house in order for thou shalt die and not live!* I pay no attention to what you say, nor will I listen to your advice. I hold on to nothing else than what my ancestor said, *For through the multitude of dreams and vanities there are also many words, but fear thou God* (Ecclesiastes 5:6)."[30]

THE BIBLE IS NOT A UTOPIA

The primordial light is hidden. Had the Torah demanded perfection, it would have remained a utopia. The laws of the Torah ask of each generation to fulfill what is within its power to fulfill. Some of its laws (for example Exodus 21:2 ff),[14] do not represent ideals but compromises, realistic attempts to refine the moral condition of ancient man.

The supreme aspiration of David, a great and an anointed King, was to build a Temple for the Lord which was to be "exceedingly magnificent, of fame and glory throughout all lands." While he was engaged in abundant preparations, "the word of the Lord came to him saying: Thou hast shed much blood and hast waged great wars; thou shalt not build a house to my name" (I Chronicles 22:8; 28:3). Thus the Bible had to deal with the ugly laws of war, though it was aware of the ugliness of war. *The Torah, too, is in exile.*[31]

We must always remember that the Bible is not a book composed for one age, and its significance cannot be assessed by the particular

A philosophy of Judaism

moral and literary standards of one generation. Passages that were considered outdated by one generation have been a fountain of comfort to the next. Many of us once considered Jeremiah's outcry: "Pour out Thy wrath upon the nations that know Thee not, and upon families that call not on Thy name; for they have devoured Jacob, yea they have devoured him, consumed him, and have laid waste his habitation" (10:25), to be primitive. But what other words could there be to recite when mothers saw how their infants were sent to the gas chambers of Nazi extermination camps? Shall we presume to sit in judgment in the name of morality over those who taught the world what justice means?

There is no simple solution to the problem. We must never forget that there is a higher truth than the one we are able to comprehend at first sight.

While the people of Israel sojourned in the wilderness, Moses was commanded by the Lord to send men to spy out Canaan, the promised land. So Moses chose twelve distinguished men and said to them: Go up and see what the land is, and whether the people who dwell in it are strong or weak, few or many. So they went up and searched the land. At the end of forty days they returned and reported: "We came to the land to which you sent us; it flows with milk and honey. Yet the people who dwell in the land are strong, and the cities fortified and very large. We are not able to go up against this people; for they are stronger than we. There we saw the giants; and we seemed to ourselves like grasshoppers, and so we seemed to them" (Numbers 13).

The spies were condemned, and their report characterized as slanderous. But why? Their observations were correct; their report was honest.

To say the obvious is not yet to speak truth. When the obvious and the Word stand in conflict, truth is the refusal to rest content with the facts as they seem. Truth is the courage to fathom the facts in order to see how they relate to the Word.[32]

These were the last words of Job.

Who is this that hideth counsel without knowledge?
Therefore have I uttered that which I understood not,
Things too wonderful for me, which I knew not.
Hear, I beseech Thee, and I will speak;
I will demand of Thee, and declare Thou unto me.
I had heard of Thee by the hearing of the ear;
But now mine eye seeth Thee;
Wherefore I abhor my words, and repent,
Seeing I am dust and ashes.

Job 42:3-6

The words in Job 28:13, *Man does not know its order,* refer to the Torah. "Disarranged are the paths of the Torah." If people knew its true order they would know how to revive the dead, how to work wonders, the Rabbis believed.[33]

"I am a neophyte in the earth, hide not Thy commandments from me" (Psalms 119:19). "Was David a neophyte? But this is what is meant: just as a neophyte comprehends nothing of the Torah, so does man, though his eyes are open, comprehend nothing at all of the Torah. If David, the composer of all the songs and psalms, said I am a neophyte and know nothing, how much more does it apply to us. . . . For we are neophytes before Thee and sojourners, as all our fathers were (I Chronicles 29:16)."[34]

In our encounter with the Bible we may take either a fundamentalist attitude which regards every word as literally valid, making no distinction between the eternal and the temporal, and allowing no place for personal or historic understanding, or for the voice of the conscience. Or we may take a rationalist attitude which, taking science as the touchstone of religion, regards Scripture as a poetic product or myth, useful to men of an inferior civilization and therefore outdated at any later period of history.

Philosophy of religion has to carry on a battle on two fronts, trying to winnow false notions of the fundamentalist, and to dampen the over-confidence of the rationalists. The ultimate task is to lead us to a higher plane of knowledge and experience, to attachment through understanding.

We must beware of the obscurantism of a mechanical deference to the Bible. The prophetic words were given to us to be understood, not merely to be mechanically repeated. The Bible is to be understood by the spirit that grows with it, wrestles with it, and prays with it.

The prophets make us partners of an existence meant for us. What was revealed to them was not for their sake but intended to inspire us. The word must not freeze into habit; it must remain an event.

To disregard the importance of *continuous understanding* is an evasion of the living challenge of the prophets, an escape from the urgency of responsible experience of every man, a denial of the deeper meaning of "the oral Torah."

CONTINUOUS UNDERSTANDING

The Bible is not an intellectual sinecure, and its acceptance should not be like setting up a talismanic lock that seals both the mind and the conscience against the intrusion of new thoughts. Revelation is not *vicarious thinking*. Its purpose is not to substitute for but to extend our understanding. The prophets tried to extend the horizon of our conscience and to impart to us a sense of the divine partnership in our dealings with good and evil and in our wrestling with life's enigmas. They tried to teach us how to think in the categories of God: His holiness, justice and compassion. The appropriation of these categories, far from exempting us from the obligation to gain new insights in our own time, is a challenge to look for ways of translating Biblical commandments into programs required by our own conditions. The full meaning of the Biblical words was not disclosed once and for all. Every hour another aspect is unveiled. The word was given once; the effort to understand it must go on for ever. It is not enough to accept or even to carry out the commandments. To study, to examine, to explore the Torah is a form of worship, a supreme duty. For the Torah is an invitation to perceptivity, a call for *continuous understanding*.

Taken as vicarious thinking, the Bible becomes a stumbling block.

273

He who says, I have *only* the Torah, does not even have the Torah. The Karaites claimed to adhere to a purely Biblical religion. However, Judaism is not a purely Biblical religion. Moses was not the founder of Judaism. Long before he was born the children of Israel cherished traditions that dated back to the days of Abraham. The oral Torah is, in parts, older than the written Torah. The Sabbath, we are told, was known to Israel before the event at Sinai took place.[35] Not all of the Mosaic teachings were incorporated in the Pentateuch. Numerous principles and rules remained "oral teaching" handed down from generation to generation. And it was concerning both the written and the "oral teaching" that the covenant at Sinai was concluded.

We approach the laws of the Bible through the interpretation and the wisdom of the Rabbis. Without their interpretation the text of the laws is often unintelligible. Thus Judaism is based upon a minimum of revelation and a maximum of interpretation, upon the will of God and upon the understanding of Israel. For that understanding we are dependent upon Israel's unwritten tradition. The prophets' inspirations and the sages' interpretations are equally important. There is a partnership of God and Israel in regard to both the world and the Torah: He created the earth and we till the soil; He gave us the text and we refine and complete it. "The Holy One, blessed be He, gave the Torah unto Israel like wheat from which to derive fine flour, or like flax from which to make a garment."[36]

The Bible is a seed, God is the sun, but we are the soil. Every generation is expected to bring forth new understanding and new realization.

The word is the word of God, and its understanding He gave unto man. The source of authority is not the word as given in the text but Israel's understanding of the text. At Sinai we received both the word and the spirit to understand the word. The savants are heirs to the prophets; they determine and interpret the meaning of the word. There is much liberty and much power in the insights of the sages: they have the power to set aside a precept of the Torah

A philosophy of Judaism

when conditions require it. Here on earth, their opinion may over-rule an opinion held in heaven.

Some of that original understanding and response of Israel was poured into words, conveyed from mouth to mouth, entrusted to writing, but much, of which words were only a reflection, remained unsaid, unwritten, a tradition transmitted from soul to soul, inherited like the power to love, and kept alive by constant communion with the Word, by studying it, by guarding it, by living it and by being ready to die for it. In the hands of many peoples it becomes a *book;* in the life of Israel it remained a *voice,* a Torah within the heart (Isaiah 51:7).

For Israel's understanding of the word was not cheaply or idyllically won. It was acquired at the price of a millennia of wrestling, of endurance and bitter ordeals of a stubborn people, of unparalleled martyrdom and self-sacrifice of men, women and children, of loyalty, love and constant study. What modern scholar could vie with the intuition of such a people? The Torah is not only our mother, it is "our life and the length of our days; we will meditate (on her words) day and night" (Evening liturgy).

Without our continuous striving for understanding, the Bible is like paper money without security. Yet such understanding requires austere discipline and can only be achieved in attachment and dedication, in retaining and reliving the original understanding as expressed by the prophets and the ancient sages.

There is always the danger of trying to interpret the Bible in terms of paganism. As there is *false prophecy,* there is *false understanding.* It is possible to commit murder in the name of the Torah; one may be a scoundrel and act within the letter of the law (Nahmanides). There has, indeed, been so much pious abuse that the Bible is often in need of being saved from the hands of its admirers.

THE ORAL TORAH WAS NEVER WRITTEN DOWN

For centuries the prohibition of writing down "the oral teaching" was regarded as a basic tenet. "Those who write down the halacha are like those who burn the Torah."[37] He "who writes down the agada loses his share in the world to come."[38] Then the Rabbis decided to submit "the oral teaching" to the written form. In justification of the bold reform, they interpreted the verse in Psalms 119: 126 to mean: "There comes a time when you may abrogate the Torah in order to do the work of the Lord." Hence, the Rabbis maintained, it is better that one part of the Torah shall be abrogated than the whole Torah be forgotten.[39] The accumulation of the vast amount of learning, the scattering of Jewish communities, and the weakening of memory militated against the oral system.

Rabbi Mendel of Kotsk asked: How could the ancient Rabbis abolish the fundamental principle of Judaism, not to write down what is to be kept as an oral tradition, on the basis of a single verse in the book of Psalms? The truth is that the oral Torah was never written down. The meaning of the Torah has never been contained by books.

NOTES FOR CHAPTER 27

The author intends to publish elsewhere a detailed study of what the principle of revelation meant in Jewish tradition.

[1] Compare the statement by Rabbi Moshe Cordovero, quoted in Rabbi Abraham Azulai, *Or Hachama*, Przemsyl, 1897, vol. II, p. 145d-146a.

[2] Maimonides discusses the second claim in his *Commentary* on the Mishnah, while in *The Guide of the Perplexed* he discusses the first claim.

[3] "A tradition is current among our people that the day of the revelation on Mount Sinai was misty, cloudy, and a little rainy." Maimonides, *The Guide of the Perplexed*, Book III, ch. 9. Compare Rabbi Isaac Caro (a Spanish Talmudist and Bible commentator who flourished in the second half of the fifteenth and the first half of the sixteenth century. He was an uncle of Rabbi Joseph Caro), *Toldot Yizhak*, Amsterdam, 1708, p. 65a.

[4] *Exodus Rabba*, 5, 9.

[5] *Jerushalmi Makkot*, II, 31d.

[6] *Genesis Rabba*, 17, 5.

[7] It is equated with Wisdom, which says of itself, "The Lord created me at the beginning of His way, before His works of old," Proverbs 8:22. See *Sirach*, 1:4; *Wisdom of Solomon* 9:9. Compare Louis Ginzberg, *The Legends of the Jews*, Vol. V, pp. 4 and 132f.

[8] *Shevuot*, 5a.

[9] Rabbi Yehuda Loew ben Bezalel (Maharal), *Derech Hayim*, Warsaw, 1833, p. 8d. See also above, p. 15.

[10] Compare *Pesikta de Rabbi Kahana*, 4, ed. Buber, p. 39a and *Sanhedrin* 21b.

God in search of man

[11] Rashi, *Commentary* on *The Song of Songs* 1:2. See *Tanhuma*, Balak, 14; *Numbers Rabba*, 20, 20.

[12] Rabbi Moshe Cordovero, *Pardes Rimonim*, XXI, 6; Korets, 1786, p. 165a.

[13] Rabbi Isaiah Horowitz, *Shne Luhot Haberit*, p. 59a.

[14] Rabbi Abraham Azulai, *Hesed Leavraham, mayan* 2, *nahar* 12. In regard to the law of Deuteronomy 21:10-14, the Talmud remarks, "The Torah considered the fact of passion." *Kiddushin* 21b.

According to Maimonides, the sacrifices were included in the law because the people of that time would not have been able to dipsense with the sacrificial form of worship to which they and all other peoples of that time were accustomed. *The Guide of the Perplexed*, Book III, 32. 46. This motivation is perhaps indicated in Leviticus 17:7, and expressly stated in *Leviticus Rabba* 22,5. see *Zohar*, vol. III, 224a. The sacrifical cult is not mentioned in the Decalogue. It was introduced only after the children of Israel worshiped the Golden Calf. See Abravanel, *Commentary* on Jeremiah 7:22, and Seforno, *Commentary*, introduction to Leviticus. See Zev Yaavets, *Toldot Israel*, vol. I, Berlin, 1925, pp. 154-160.

[15] *Leshem Shevo Veahlamah, Pietrkov*, 1911, vol. II, p. 305b.

[16] *Hullin* 60b.

[17] *Toameha Hayim Zahu*, Jerusalem, 1924, vol. III, p. 40.

[18] *Ecclesiastes Rabba*, ad locum.

[19] See *Temunah*, Koretz, 1784, pp. 27a, 30a-31a; Rabbi Moshe ben Joseph di Trani (1505-1585), *Bet Elohim*, Venice, 1576, p. 58b; Rabbi Abraham Azulai, *Hesed Leavraham, mayan* 2, *nahar* 11; Rabbi Gedaliah of Luninec, *Teshuot Hen*, in the name of the Baal Shem.

[20] *Sanhedrin*, 89a. The word *signon* is used in two senses, meaning both idea and expression. See Husik's remark in his edition of Albo's *Ikkarim*, III, p. 84.

[21] Rabbi Samuel Edels, *Commentary* to *Sanhedrin* 89b.

[22] The Decalogue is given in the Pentateuch in two versions (Exodus 20:2-17 and Deuteronomy 5:6-18) that exhibit some variants. The Rabbis solved the difficulty by assuming that both versions were of identical divine origin, and were uttered miraculously at one and the same time *(Mechilta* to 20:8). Ibn Ezra, however, holds that these and many similar variants in the Bible are due to the fact that to Moses the meaning of revelation was essential rather than the word. "Know that the words are like bodies, and meanings like souls; and the body is a vessel for the soul. This is the reason why scholars . . . are careful about meanings but think nothing of changing or using different words if the meaning remains the same." Introduction to the Decalogue in his *Commentary* to Exodus 20; see his *Commentary* to Deuteronomy 5:5. Compare Ibn Adret, *Responsa*, 1, 12; Nahmanides, *Commentary* on Numbers 2:4 and on Genesis 1:4; Ibn Zimra, *Responsa*, III, 149; Shem Tov, *Commentary* on *The Guide of the Perplexed*, II, 29; Rabbi Shneur Zalman of Ladi, *Tanya*, ch. 21.

[23] Rabbi Yaakov Yosef of Ostrog, *Rav Yevi* on Psalms 18. The idea is discussed by Rabbi Moshe Alshech, Commentary on Leviticus 9:2. According to the Rabbis, all prophets beheld a vision of God through a dim speculum, while Moses beheld a vision through a lucid speculum. The difference, according to Rashi, was that the prophets believed that they had seen God but did not, whereas Moses, who looked through a lucid speculum, knew that he did not see Him! *Yebamot*, 45b. See Joseph Albo, *Ikkarim*, part 3, 9.

[24] *Zohar,* vol. III, p. 52a.
[25] *Midrash Tehillim,* 119, 9, ed. Buber, p. 493.
[26] *Zohar,* vol. III, p. 152a.
[27] *Shabbat* 97a; *Song of Songs Rabba* 1,39. Compare *Shabbat* 89b; *Yebamot* 49b; *Baba Kamma* 38a; *Sanhedrin* 111b; *Midrash Tehillim* 7,1.3.
[28] *Tosefta Berachot* 3, 7.
[29] *Seder Eliahu Rabba,* ch. 4, ed M. Friedmann, Vienna, 1902, p. 17.
[30] *Ecclesiastes Rabba,* 5,4.
[31] *Leshem Shevo Veahlemah,* vol. II, p. 305b. See above, note 15.
[32] Rabbi Mendel of Kotsk.
[33] *Midrash Tehillim* 3,1.
[34] *Midrash Tehillim* on 119:19.
[35] See I. Reicher, *Torat Harishonim,* Warsaw, 1926; S. Gandz, *The Dawn of Literature,* Osiris, vol. VII, 1939, p. 438f.
[36] *Seder Eliahu Zuta,* ch. 2, ed. Friedmann, p. 172.
[37] *Temurah,* 14b.
[38] *Jerushalmi Shabbat,* XVI, 1.
[39] *Temurah,* 14b; *Gittin,* 60a.

3. RESPONSE

28 A Science of Deeds

Knowledge of God is knowledge of living with God. Israel's religious existence consists of three inner attitudes: engagement to the living God to whom we are accountable; engagement to Torah where His voice is audible; and engagement to His concern as expressed in mitsvot (commandments).

Engagement to God comes about in acts of the soul. Engagement to Torah is the result of study and communion with its words. Engagement to His concern comes about through attachment to the essentials of worship. Its meaning is disclosed in acts of worship.

If God were a theory, the study of theology would be the way to understand Him. But God is alive and in need of love and worship. This is why thinking of God is related to our worship. In an analogy of artistic understanding, we sing to Him before we are able to understand Him. We have to love in order to know. Unless we learn how to sing, unless we know how to love, we will never learn how to understand Him.

Jewish tradition interprets the words that Israel uttered at Sinai, "all that the Lord has spoken, we shall do and we shall hear" (Exodus 24:7), as a promise to fulfill His commands even before hearing them, as the *precedence of faith over knowledge.* "When at Sinai Israel said *we shall do and we shall hear* (instead of saying, we shall hear and we shall do), a heavenly voice went forth and exclaimed, "Who has revealed to My children this *mystery,* which the ministering angels enact, to fulfill His word before they hear the voice."[1]

A heretic, the Talmud reports, chided the Jews for the rashness in which he claimed they persisted. "First you should have listened; if the commandments were within your power of fulfillment, you should have accepted them; if beyond your power, rejected them." Indeed, Israel's *supreme acquiescence* at Sinai was an inversion, turning upside down the order of attitudes as conceived by our abstract thinking. Do we not always maintain that we must first explore a system before we decide to accept it? This order of inquiry is valid in regard to pure theory, to principles and rules, but it has limitations when applied to realms where thought and fact, the abstract and the concrete, theory and experience are inseparable. It would be futile, for example, to explore the meaning of music and abstain from listening to music. It would be just as futile to explore the Jewish thought from a distance, in self-detachment. Jewish thought is disclosed in Jewish living. This, therefore, is the way of religious existence. We do not explore first and decide afterwards whether to accept the Jewish way of living. We must accept in order to be able to explore. At the beginning is *the commitment, the supreme acquiescence.*

A LEAP OF ACTION

In our response to His will we perceive His presence in our deeds. His will is revealed in our doing. In carrying out a sacred deed we unseal the wells of faith. *As for me, I shall behold Thy face in righteousness* (Psalms 18:15).

There is a way that leads *from piety to faith*. Piety and faith are not necessarily concurrent. There can be acts of piety without faith. Faith is vision, sensitivity and attachment to God; piety is an attempt to attain such sensitivity and attachment. The gates of faith are not ajar, but the mitsvah is a key. By living as Jews we may attain our faith as Jews. We do not have faith because of deeds; we may attain faith through sacred deeds.

282

A philosophy of Judaism

A Jew is asked to take a *leap of action* rather than a *leap of thought*. He is asked to surpass his needs, to do more than he understands in order to understand more than he does. In carrying out the word of the Torah he is ushered into the presence of spiritual meaning. Through the ecstasy of deeds he learns to be certain of the hereness of God. Right living is a way to right thinking.

The sense of the ineffable, the participation in Torah and Israel, the leap of action—they all lead to the same goal. Callousness to the mystery of existence, detachment from Torah and Israel, cruelty and profanity of living, alienate the Jew from God. Response to the wonder, participation in Torah and Israel, discipline in daily life, bring us close to Him.

What commitments must precede the experience of such meaning? What convictions must persist to make such insights possible? Our way of living must be compatible with our essence as created in the likeness of God. We must beware lest our likeness be distorted and even forfeited. In our way of living we must remain true not only to our sense of power and beauty but also to our sense of the grandeur and mystery of existence. The true meaning of existence is disclosed in moments of living in the presence of God. The problem we face is: how can we live in a way which is in agreement with such convictions?

THE DEED IS THE RISK

How should man, a being created in the likeness of God, live? What way of living is compatible with the grandeur and mystery of living? It is a problem which man has always been anxious to ignore. Upon the pavement of the Roman city of Timgat an inscription was found which reads: "To hunt, to bathe, to gamble, to laugh, that is to live." Judaism is a reminder of the grandeur and earnestness of living.

In what dimension of existence does man become aware of the grandeur and earnestness of living? What are the occasions in which he discovers the nature of his own self? The necessity to diagnose and to heal the condition of the soul? In the solitude of self-reflection the self may seem to be a fountain of beautiful thoughts and ideals. Yet thought may be a spell, and ideals may be worn like borrowed diadems.

It is in *deeds* that man becomes aware of what his life really is, of his power to harm and to hurt, to wreck and to ruin; of his ability to derive joy and to bestow it upon others; to relieve and to increase his own and other people's tensions. It is in the employment of his will, not in reflection, that he meets his own self as it is; not as he should like it to be. In his deeds man exposes his immanent as well as his suppressed desires, spelling even that which he cannot apprehend. What he may not dare to think, he often utters in deeds. The heart is revealed in the deeds.

The deed is the test, the trial, and the risk. What we perform may seem slight, but the aftermath is immense. An individual's misdeed can be the beginning of a nation's disaster. The sun goes down, but the deeds go on. Darkness is over all we have done. If man were able to survey at a glance all he has done in the course of his life, what would he feel? He would be terrified at the extent of his own power. To bind all we have done to our conscience or to our mind would be like trying to tie a torrent to a reed. Even a single deed generates an endless set of effects, initiating more than the most powerful man is able to master or to predict. A single deed may place the lives of countless men in the chains of its unpredictable effects. All we own is a passing intention, but what comes about will outlive and surpass our power. Gazing soberly at the world man is often overcome with a fear of action, a fear that, without knowledge of God's ways, turns to despair.

OUR ULTIMATE EMBARRASSMENT

The seriousness of doing surpasses the sensitivity of our conscience. Infinite are the consequences of our actions, yet finite is our wisdom. When man stands alone, his responsibility seems to vanish like a drop in the ocean of necessity. It is superhuman to be responsible for all that we do and for all that we fail to do, to answer for all the causalities of one's activities. How should we reconcile infinite responsibility with finite wisdom? How is responsibility possible?

Infinite responsibility without infinite wisdom and infinite power is our ultimate embarrassment.

Not things but deeds are the source of our sad perplexities. Confronted with a world of things, man unloosens a tide of deeds. The fabulous fact of man's ability to act, *the wonder of doing,* is no less amazing than the marvel of being. Ontology inquires: what is *being?* What does it mean to be? The religious mind ponders: what is *doing?* What does it mean to do? What is the relation between the doer and the deed? between doing and being? Is there a purpose to fulfill, a task to carry out?

"A man should always regard himself as though he were half guilty and half meritorious; if he performs one good deed, blessed is he for he moves the scale toward merit; if he commits one transgression, woe to him for he moves the scale toward guilt." Not only the individual but the whole world is in balance. One deed of an individual may decide the fate of the world. "If he performs one good deed, blessed is he for he moves the scale both for himself and for the entire world to the side of merit; if he commits one transgression, woe to him for he moves to the side of guilt himself and the whole world."[2]

A META-ETHICAL APPROACH

What ought we to do? How ought we to conduct our lives? These are basic questions of ethics. They are also questions of religion. Philosophy of religion must inquire: why do we ask these questions? Are they meaningful? On what grounds do we state them? To ethics, these are man's questions, necessitated by the nature of human existence. To religion, these are God's questions, and our answer to them concerns not only man but God.

"What ought I to do?" is according to Kant the basic question in ethics. Ours, however, is a more radical, a meta-ethical approach. The ethical question refers to particular deeds; the meta-ethical question refers to all deeds. It deals with doing as such; not only what ought we to do, but what is our right to act at all? We are endowed with the ability to conquer and to control the forces of nature. In exercising power, we submit to our will a world that we did not create, invading realms that do not belong to us. Are we the kings of the universe or mere pirates? By whose grace, by what right, do we exploit, consume and enjoy the fruits of the trees, the blessings of the earth? Who is responsible for the power to exploit, for the privilege to consume?

It is not an academic problem but an issue we face at every moment. By the will alone man becomes the most destructive of all beings. This is our predicament: our power may become our undoing. We stand on a razor's edge. It is so easy to hurt, to destroy, to insult, to kill. Giving birth to one child is a mystery; bringing death to millions is but a skill. It is not quite within the power of the human will to generate life; it is quite within the power of the will to destroy life.

In the midst of such anxiety we are confronted with the claim of the Bible. The world is not all danger, and man is not alone. God endowed man with freedom, and He will share in our use of freedom. The earth is the Lord's, and God is in search of man. He endowed man with power to conquer the earth, and His honor is upon our faith. We abused His power, we betrayed His trust. We cannot expect Him to say, Though thou betrayest me, yet will I trust in thee.

Man is responsible for His deeds, and God is responsible for man's responsibilty. He who is a life-giver must be a lawgiver. He shares in our responsibility. He is waiting to enter our deeds through our loyalty to His law. He may become a partner to our deeds.

God and man have a task in common as well as a common and mutual responsibility. The ultimate embarrassment is not a problem of solitary man but an intimate problem for both God and man. What is at stake is the meaning of God's creation, not only the meaning of man's existence. Religion is not a concern for man alone but a plea of God and a claim of man, God's expectation and man's aspiration. It is not an effort solely for the sake of man. Religion spells a task within the world of man, but its ends go far beyond. This is why the Bible proclaimed a law not only for man but for both God and man.

For Thou wilt light my lamp (Psalms 18:29). "The Holy One said to man: Thy lamp is in My hand, My lamp in Thine. Thy lamp is in Mine—as it is said: *The lamp of the Lord is the soul of man* (Proverbs 20:27). My lamp is in thine hand, to kindle the perpetual lamp. The Holy One said: If thou lightest My lamp, I will light thine."[3]

THE PARTNERSHIP OF GOD AND MAN

Just as man is not alone in what he *is,* he is not alone in what he *does.* A mitsvah is an act which God and man *have in common.* We say: "Blessed art Thou, Lord our God, King of the universe, who has sanctified us with *His* mitsvot." They oblige Him as well as us. Their fulfillment is not valued as an act performed in spite of "the evil drive," but as an act of *communion* with Him. The spirit of mitsvah is *togetherness.* We know, He is a partner to our act.

The oldest form of piety is expressed in the Bible as walking *with God.* Enoch, Noah, walked with God (Genesis 5:24; 6:9) "It has been told thee, O man, what is good, and what the Lord doth require of thee: only to do justly, to love mercy and *to walk humbly with thy God"* (6:8). Only the egotist is confined to himself, a spiritual recluse. In carrying out a good deed it is impossible to be or to feel alone. To fulfill a mitsvah is to be a partisan, to enter into fellowship with His Will.

WAYS, NOT LAWS

The moral imperative was not disclosed for the first time through Abraham or Sinai. The criminality of murder was known to men before; even the institution to rest on the seventh day was, according to tradition, familiar to Jews when still in Egypt. Nor was the idea of divine justice unknown. What was new was the idea that justice is an obligation to God, *His way* not only His demand;[4] that injustice is not something God scorns when done by others but that which is the very opposite of God; that the rights of man are not legally protected interests of society but the sacred interests of God. He is not only the guardian of moral order, "the Judge of all the earth," but One who cannot act injustly (Genesis 18:25). His favorite was not Nimrod, "the first man on earth to be a hero" (Genesis 10:9), but Abraham: "I have chosen him that he may charge his sons and his household after him to keep the way of the Lord, to do righteousness and justice" (Genesis 18:19). The Torah is primarily *divine ways* rather than *divine laws.* Moses prayed: "Let me know Thy ways" (Exodus 33:13). All that God asks of man was summarized: "And now, Israel, what doth the Lord thy God require of thee . . . but to walk in all His ways" (Deuteronomy 10: 12).

What does it mean, asked Rabbi Hama, son of Rabbi Hanina, when said: "Ye shall walk after the Lord your God"? (Deuteronomy 13:5). "Is it possible for a human being to walk after the *Shechinah;* has it not been said: For the Lord thy God is a devouring fire? But the meaning is to walk in the ways of the Lord. As He clothes the naked so do thou also clothe the naked; as He visited the sick, so do thou also visit the sick; as he comforted mourners, so do Thou also comfort mourners" (*Sotah* 14a).

THE DIVINITY OF DEEDS

Not particular acts but all acts, life itself, can be established as a link between man and God. But how can we presume that the platitudes of our actions have meaning to Him? How do we dare to say that deeds have the power to throng to Him? that human triteness can become attached to eternity?

The validity of science is based upon the premise that the structure of events in nature is intelligible, capable of being observed and described in rational terms. Only because of the analogy of the structure of the human mind to the inner structure of the universe is man able to discover the laws that govern its processes. What about events in the inner and moral life of man? Is there any realm to which they correspond? The prophets who knew how to take the divine measure of human deeds, to see the structure of the absolute light in the spectrum of a single event, sensed that correspondence. What a man does in his darkest corner is relevant to the Creator. In other words, as the rationality of natural events is assumed by science, so is the divinity of human deeds assumed by prophecy.*

Thus beyond the idea of the imitation of divinity goes the conviction of *the divinity of deeds.* Sacred acts, mitsvot, do not only imitate; they represent the Divine. The mitsvot are of the essence of God, more than worldly ways of complying with His will. Rabbi Simeon ben Yohai states: "Honor the mitsvot, for the mitsvot are My deputies, and a deputy is endowed with the authority of his principal. If you honor the mitsvot, it is as if you honored Me; if you dishonor them, it is as if you dishonored Me."[5]

The Bible speaks of man as having been created in the likeness of God, establishing the principle of *an analogy of being.* In his very being, man has something in common with God. Beyond the analogy of being, the Bible teaches the principle of *an analogy in acts.* Man may act in the likeness of God. It is this likeness of acts— "to walk in His ways"—that is the link by which man may come close to God. To live in such likeness is the essence of imitation of the Divine.

TO DO WHAT HE IS

In other religions, gods, heroes, priests are holy; to the Bible not only God but "the whole community is holy" (Numbers 16:3). "Ye shall be unto me a kingdom of priests, a holy people" (Exodus

* See above, p. 104.

19:6), was the reason for Israel's election, the meaning of its distinction. What obtains between man and God is not mere submission to His power or dependence upon His mercy. The plea is not to obey what He wills but to *do* what He *is*.

It is not said: Ye shall be full of awe for I am holy, but: Ye shall be holy, for I the Lord your God am holy (Leviticus 19:2). How does a human being, "dust and ashes," turn holy? Through doing His mitsvot, His commandments. "The Holy God is sanctified through righteousness" (Isaiah 5:16). A man to be holy must fear his mother and father, keep the Sabbath, not turn to idols . . . nor deal falsely nor lie to one another . . . not curse the deaf nor put a stumbling-block before the blind . . . not be guilty of any injustice . . . not be a tale-bearer . . . not stand idly by the blood of your neighbor . . . not hate . . . not take vengeance nor bear any grudge . . . but love thy neighbor as thyself (Leviticus 19:3-18).

We live by the conviction that acts of goodness reflect the hidden light of His holiness. His light is above our minds but not beyond our will. It is within our power to mirror His unending love in deeds of kindness, like brooks that hold the sky.

LIKENESS IN DEEDS

Mitsvot, then, are more than reflections of a man's will or transcripts of his visions. In carrying out a sacred task we disclose a divine intention. With a sacred deed goes more than a stir of the heart. In a sacred deed, we echo God's suppressed chant; in loving we intone God's unfinished song. No image of the Supreme may be fashioned, save one: our own life as an image of His will. Man, formed in His likeness, was made to imitate His ways of mercy. He has delegated to man the power to act in His stead. We represent Him in relieving affliction, in granting joy. Striving for integrity, helping our fellow men; the urge to translate nature into spirit, volition into sacrifice, instinct into love; it is all an effort to represent Him.

290

A philosophy of Judaism

To fulfill the will of God in deeds means to act *in the name* of God, not only *for the sake* of God; to carry out in acts what is potential to His will. He is in need of the work of man for the fulfillment of His ends in the world.

Human action is not the beginning. At the beginning is God's eternal expectation. There is an eternal cry in the world: *God is beseeching man* to answer, to return, to fulfill. Something is asked of man, of all men, at all times. In every act we either answer or defy, we either return or move away, we either fulfill or miss the goal. Life consists of endless opportunities to sanctify the profane, opportunities to redeem the power of God from the chain of potentialities, opportunities to serve spiritual ends.

As surely as we are driven to live, we are driven to serve spiritual ends that surpass our own interests. "The good drive" is not invented by society but is something which makes society possible; not an accidental function but of the very essence of man. We may lack a clear perception of its meaning, but we are moved by the horror of its violation. We are not only in need of God but also in need of serving His ends, and these ends are in need of us.

Mitsvot are not ideals, spiritual entities for ever suspended in eternity. They are commandments addressing every one of us. They are the ways in which God confronts us in particular moments. In the infinite world there is a task for me to accomplish. Not a general task, but a task for me, here and now. Mitsvot are *spiritual ends,* points of eternity in the flux of temporality.

ENDS IN NEED OF MAN

Man and spiritual ends stand in a relation of mutuality to each other. The relation in regard to selfish ends is one-sided: man is in need of eating bread, but the bread is not in need of being eaten. The relation is different in regard to spiritual ends: justice is something that ought to be done, justice is in need of man. The sense of obligation expresses a situation, in which an ideal, as it were, is waiting to be attained. Spiritual ends come with a claim upon the person. They are imperative, not only impressive; demands, not abstract ideas. Esthetic values are experienced as objects of enjoyment, while religious acts are experienced as objects of commitments, as answers to the certainty that something is asked of us, expected of us. Religious ends are *in need of our deeds*.

A SCIENCE OF DEEDS

Judaism is not a science of nature but a science of what man ought to do with nature. It is concerned above all with the problem of living. It takes deeds more seriously than things. Jewish law is, in a sense, *a science of deeds*. Its main concern is not only how to worship Him at certain times but how to live with Him at all times. Every deed is a problem; there is a unique task at every moment. All of life at all moments is the problem and the task.

NOTES FOR CHAPTER 28

[1] *Shabbat* 88a. See also the passage from *Midrash Hazita,* quoted in *Man is Not Alone,* p. 93.
[2] *Kiddushin* 40b.
[3] *Leviticus Rabba* 31, 4.
[4] "The ways of God differ from those of man; whereas man directs others to do a thing whilst he does nothing, God only tells Israel to do and to observe those things which He himself does." *Exodus Rabba* 30, 9. See *Jerushalmi Rosh Hashanah* 1,3, 7a.
[5] *Tanhuma* to Genesis 46:28.

29 More than Inwardness

The claim of Judaism that religion and law are inseparable is difficult for many of us to comprehend. The difficulty may be explained by modern man's conception of the essence of religion. To the modern mind, religion is a state of the soul, inwardness; feeling rather than obedience, faith rather than action, spiritual rather than concrete. To Judaism, religion is not a feeling for something that is, but *an answer* to Him who is asking us to live in a certain way. It is in its very origin a consciousness of total commitment; a realization that all of life is not only man's but also God's sphere of interest.

"God asks for the heart."[1] Yet does he ask for the heart only? Is the right intention enough? Some doctrines insist that love is the sole condition for salvation (Sufi,[2] Bhakti-marga), stressing the importance of inwardness, of love or faith, to the exclusion of good works.

Paul waged a passionate battle against the power of law and proclaimed instead the religion of grace. Law, he claimed, cannot conquer sin, nor can righteousness be attained through works of law. A man is justified "by faith without the deeds of the law."[3]

That salvation is attained by faith alone was Luther's central thesis. The antinomian tendency resulted in the overemphasis of love and faith to the exclusion of good works.

The Formula of Concord of 1580, still valid in Protestantism, condemns the statement that good works are necessary to salvation and rejects the doctrine that they are harmful to salvation. According to Ritschl, the doctrine of the merit of good deeds is an intruder in the domain of Christian theology; the only way of salvation is justification by faith. Barth, following Kierkegaard, voices Lutheran thoughts, when he claims that man's deeds are too sinful to be good. There are fundamentally no human deeds, which, because of their significance in this world, find favor in God's eyes. God can be approached through God alone.

THE ERROR OF FORMALISM

In trying to show that justice is not identical with our predilection or disposition, that it is independent of our interest and consent, we should not commit the common error of confounding the relation of man to justice with the relation of justice to man. For although it is true that we ought to do justice for its own sake, justice itself is for the sake of man. To define justice as that which is worth doing for its own sake is to define the motive, not the purpose. It is just the opposite: the good, unlike play, is never done for its own sake, but for a purpose. To think otherwise is to make an idol of an ideal; it is the beginning of fanaticism. Defining the good by the motive alone, equalizing the good with the good intention and ignoring the purpose and substance of the good action, is a half-truth.

Those who have only paid attention to the relation of man to the ideals, disregarding the relation of the ideals to man, have in their theories seen only the motive but not the purpose of either religion or morality. Echoing the Paulinian doctrine that man is saved by faith alone, Kant and his disciples taught that the essence of religion or morality would consist in an absolute quality of the soul or the will, regardless of the actions that may come out of it or the ends that may be attained. Accordingly, the value of a religious act would be determined wholly by the intensity of one's faith or by the rectitude of one's inner disposition. The intention, not the deed, the *how*, not the *what* of one's conduct, would be essential, and no motive

294

A philosophy of Judaism

other than the sense of duty would be of any moral value. Thus acts of kindness, when not dictated by the sense of duty, are no better than cruelty, and compassion or regard for human happiness as such is looked upon as an ulterior motive. "I would not break my word even to save mankind!" exclaimed Fichte. His salvation and righteousness were apparently so much more important to him than the fate of all men that he would have destroyed mankind to save himself. Does not such an attitude illustrate the truth of the proverb, "The road to hell is paved with good intentions"? Should we not say that a concern with one's own salvation and righteousness that outweighs the regard for the welfare of one human being cannot be qualified as a good intention?

Judaism stresses the relevance of human deeds. It refuses to accept the principle that under all circumstances the intention determines the deed. However, the absence of the right intention does not necessarily vilify the goodness of a deed of charity.[4] The good deeds of any man, to whatever nation or religion he may belong,[5] even when done by a person who has never been reached by a prophet and who therefore acts on the basis of his own insight,[6] will be rewarded by God.

NO DICHOTOMY

The cause of nearly all failures in human relations is this—that while we admire and extol the tasks, we fail to acquire the tools. Neither the naked hand nor the soul left to itself can effect much. It is by instruments that work is done. The soul needs them as much as the hand. And as the instruments of the hand either give motion or guide it, so the instruments of the soul supply either suggestions or cautions. The meaningfulness of the mitsvot consists in their being vehicles by which we advance on the road to spiritual ends.

Faith is not a silent treasure to be kept in the seclusion of the soul, but a mint in which to strike the coin of common deeds. It is not enough to be dedicated in the soul, to consecrate moments in the stillness of contemplation.

The dichotomy of faith and works which presented such an important problem in Christian theology was never a problem in Judaism. To us, the basic problem is neither what is the right action nor what is the right intention. The basic problem is: what is right living? And life is indivisible. The inner sphere is never isolated from outward activities. Deed and thought are bound into one. All a person thinks and feels enters everything he does, and all he does is involved in everything he thinks and feels.

Spiritual aspirations are doomed to failure when we try to cultivate deeds at the expense of thoughts or thoughts at the expense of deeds. Is it the artist's inner vision or his wrestling with the stone that brings about a work of sculpture? Right living is like a work of art, the product of a vision and of a wrestling with concrete situations.

Judaism is averse to generalities, averse to looking for meaning in life detached from doing, as if the meaning were a separate entity. Its tendency is to make ideas convertible into deeds, to interpret metaphysical insights as patterns for action, to endow the most sublime principles with bearing upon everyday conduct. In its tradition, the abstract became concrete, the absolute historic. By enacting the holy on the stage of concrete living, we perceive our kinship with the divine, the presence of the divine. What cannot be grasped in reflection, we comprehend in deeds.

SPIRITUALITY IS NOT THE WAY

The world needs more than the secret holiness of individual inwardness. It needs more than sacred sentiments and good intentions. God asks for the heart because He needs the lives. It is by lives that the world will be redeemed, by lives that beat in concordance with God, by deeds that outbeat the finite charity of the human heart.

Man's power of action is less vague than his power of intention. And an action has intrinsic meaning; its value to the world is independent of what it means to the person performing it. The act of giving food to a helpless child is meaningful regardless of whether or not the moral intention is present. God asks for the heart, and we must spell our answer in terms of deeds.

It would be a device of conceit, if not presumption, to insist that purity of the heart is the exclusive test of piety. Perfect purity is something we rarely know how to obtain or how to retain. No one can claim to have purged all the dross even from his finest desire. The self is finite, but selfishness is infinite.

God asks for the heart, but the heart is oppressed with uncertainty in its own twilight. God asks for faith, and the heart is not sure of its own faith. It is good that there is a dawn of decision for the night of the heart; deeds to objectify faith, definite forms to verify belief.

The heart is often a lonely voice in the marketplace of living. Man may entertain lofty ideals and behave like the ass that, as the saying goes, "carries gold and eats thistles." The problem of the soul is how to live nobly in an animal environment; how to persuade and train the tongue and the senses to behave in agreement with the insights of the soul.

The integrity of life is not exclusively a thing of the heart; it implies more than consciousness of the moral law. The innermost chamber must be guarded at the uttermost outposts. Religion is not the same as spiritualism; what man does in his concrete, physical existence is directly relevant to the divine. Spirituality is the goal, not the way of man. In this world music is played on physical instruments, and to the Jew the mitsvot are the instruments on which the holy is carried out. If man were only mind, worship in thought would be the form in which to commune with God. But man is body and soul, and his goal is so to live that both "his heart and his flesh should sing to the living God."

But how do we know what the right deeds are? Is the knowledge of right and wrong to be derived by reason and conscience alone?

There are those who are ready to discard the message of the divine commands and call upon us to rely on our conscience. Man, we are told, is only under obligation to act in conformity with his reason and conscience, and must not be subjected to any laws except those which he imposes upon himself. Moral laws are attainable by reason and conscience, and there is no need for a lawgiver. God is necessary merely as a guarantee for the ultimate triumph of the moral effort.

The fallacy of the doctrine of autonomy is in equating man with "the good drive," and all of his nature with reason and conscience. Man's capacity for love and self-denial ("the good drive") does not constitute the totality of his nature. He is also inclined to love success, to adore the victors and to despise the vanquished. Those who call upon us to rely on our inner voice fail to realize that there is more than one voice within us, that the power of selfishness may easily subdue the pangs of conscience. The conscience, moreover, is often celebrated for what is beyond its ability. The conscience is not a legislative power, capable of teaching us what we ought to do but rather a preventive agency; a brake, not a guide; a fence, not a way. It raises its voice after a wrong deed has been committed, but often fails to give us direction in advance of our actions.

The individual's insight alone is unable to cope with all the problems of living. It is the guidance of tradition on which we must rely, and whose norms we must learn to interpret and to apply. We must learn not only the ends but also the means by which to realize the ends; not only the general laws but also the particular forms.

Judaism calls upon us to listen *not only* to the voice of the conscience but also to the norms of a heteronomous law. The good is not an abstract idea but a commandment, and the ultimate meaning of its fulfillment is in its being *an answer* to God.

298

A philosophy of Judaism

Man had to be expelled from the Garden of Eden; he had to witness the murder of half of the human species by Cain out of envy;
experience the catastrophy of the Flood; the confusion of the languages; slavery in Egypt and the wonder of the Exodus, to be ready
to accept the law.

We believe that the Jew is committed to a divine law; that the
ultimate standards are beyond man rather than within man. We
believe that there is a law, the essence of which is derived from
prophetic events, and the interpretation of which is in the hands of
the sages.

We are taught that God gave man not only life but also a law. The
supreme imperative is not merely to believe in God but to do the
will of God. The classical code, *Turim,* begins with the words of
Judah ben Tema: "Be bold as a leopard, light as an eagle, swift as a
deer, and strong as a lion *to do* the will of your Father who is in
heaven."[7]

What is *law?* A way of dealing with the most difficult of all problems: life. The law is a problem to him who thinks that life is a
commonplace. *The law is an answer* to him who knows that *life
is a problem.*

In Judaism allegiance to God involves a commitment to Jewish
law, to a discipline, to specific obligations. These terms, against
which modern man seems to feel an aversion, are in fact a part of
civilized living. Every one of us who acknowledges allegiance to the
state of which he is a citizen is committed to its law, and accepts
the obligations it imposes upon him. His loyalty will on occasion
prompt him to do even more than mere allegiance would demand.
Indeed, the word loyalty is derived from the same root as legal, *ligo*
which means "to be bound." Similarly, the word obligation comes
from the Latin *obligo,* to bind, and denotes the state of being bound
by a legal or moral tie.

The object of the prophets was to guide and to demand, not only
to console and to reassure. Judaism is meaningless as an optional

attitude to be assumed at our convenience. To the Jewish mind life is a complex of obligations, and the fundamental category of Judaism is *a demand* rather than *a dogma,* a *commitment* rather than a feeling. *God's will* stands higher than *man's creed.* Reverence for the authority of the law is an expression of our love for God.

However, beyond His will is His love. The Torah was given to Israel as a sign of His love. To reciprocate that love we strive to attain *ahavat Torah.*

A degree of self-control is the prerequisite for creative living. Does not a work of art represent the triumph of form over inchoate matter? Emotion controlled by an idea? We suffer from the illusion of being mature as well as from a tendency to overestimate the degree of human perfectibility. No one is mature unless he has learned to be engaged in pursuits which require discipline and self-control, and human perfectibility is contingent upon the capacity for self-control.

When the mind is sore from bias and presumption, from its inability to halt the stream of overflowing vanity, from the imagination clawing in darkness toward silliness and sin, man begins to bless the Lord for the privilege of serving in faith and in agreement with His will. Time is never idle; life is running out; but the law takes us by our hand and leads us home to an order of eternity.

There are positive as well as negative mitsvot, actions as well as abstentions. Indeed, the sense for the holy is often expressed in terms of restrictions, just as the mystery of God is conveyed *via negationis,* in *negative theology* which claims we can never say what He is; we can only say what He is not. Inadequate would be our service if it consisted only of rituals and positive deeds which are so faulty and often abortive. Precious as positive deeds are, there are times when the silence of sacred abstentions is more articulate than the language of deeds.[8]

God in search of man

A SPIRITUAL ORDER

There is a sure way of missing the meaning of the law by either atomization or generalization, by seeing the parts without the whole or by seeing the whole without the parts.

It is impossible to understand the significance of single acts, detached from the total character of a life in which they are set. Acts are components of a whole and derive their character from the structure of the whole. There is an intimate relation between all acts and experiences of a person. Yet just as the parts are determined by the whole, the whole is determined by the parts. Consequently, the amputation of one part may affect the integrity of the entire structure, unless that part has outlived its vital role in the organic body of the whole.

Some people are so occupied collecting shreds and patches of the law, that they hardly think of weaving the pattern of the whole; others are so enchanted by the glamor of generalities, by the image of ideals, that while their eyes fly up, their actions remain below.

What we must try to avoid is not only the failure to observe a single mitsvah, but the loss of the whole, the loss of belonging to the spiritual order of Jewish living. The order of Jewish living is meant to be, not a set of rituals but an order of all man's existence, shaping all his traits, interests, and dispositions; not so much the performance of single acts, the taking of a step now and then, as the pursuit of a way, being on the way; not so much the acts of fulfilling as the state of being committed to the task, the belonging to an order in which single deeds, aggregates of religious feeling, sporadic sentiments, moral episodes become a part of a complete pattern.[9]

It is a distortion to reduce Judaism to a cult or system of ceremonies. The Torah is both the detail and the whole. As time and space are presupposed in any perception, so is the totality of life implied in every act of piety. There is an objective coherence that holds all episodes together. A man may commit a crime now and teach mathematics effortlessly an hour later. But when a man prays, all he has done in his life enters his prayer.

A THEOLOGICAL EXAGGERATION

Jewish tradition does not maintain that every iota of the law was revealed to Moses at Sinai. This is an unwarranted extension of the rabbinic conception of revelation. "Could Moses have learned the whole Torah? Of the Torah it is said, *Its measure is longer than the earth and broader than the sea* (Job 11:9); could then Moses have learned it in forty days? No, it was only the principles thereof (*klalim*) which God taught Moses."[10]

The Rabbis maintain that "things not revealed to Moses were revealed to Rabbi Akiba and his colleagues."[11] The role of the sages in interpreting the word of the Bible and their power to issue new ordinances are basic elements of Jewish belief, and something for which our sages found sanction in Deuteronomy 17:11. The Torah was compared to "a fountain which continually sends forth water, giving forth more than it absorbs. In the same sense, you can teach (or say) more Torah than you received at Sinai."[12]

In their intention to inspire greater joy and love of God, the Rabbis expanded the scope of the law, imposing more and more restrictions and prohibitions. "There is no generation in which the Rabbis do not add to the law."[13] In the time of Moses, only what he had explicitly received at Sinai [the written law] was binding, plus several ordinances which he added for whatever reasons he saw fit. [However] the prophets, the Tannaim, and the rabbis of every generation [have continued to multiply these restrictions].[14]

The industrial civilization has profoundly affected the condition of man, and vast numbers of Jews loyal to Jewish law feel that many of the rabbinic restrictions tend to impede rather than to inspire greater joy and love of God.

In their zeal to carry out the ancient injunction, "make a hedge about the Torah," many Rabbis failed to heed the warning, "Do not consider the hedge more important than the vineyard." Excessive regard for the hedge may spell ruin for the vineyard.[15] The vineyard is being trodden down. It is all but laid waste. Is this the time to insist upon the sanctity of the hedges? "Were the Torah given as a rigid immutable code of laws, Israel could not survive. . . . Moses exclaimed: Lord of the universe, let me know what is the law. And the Lord said: Rule by the principle of majority. . . . The law will be explained, now one way, now another, according to the perception of the majority of the *sages*."[16]

A great Jewish authority offers the following remarks on our theme:

How did the generations prior to Sinai attain spiritual integrity? How can we say that the patriarchs stood as high or higher than the community of Israel, since in their time the commandments were not yet given and so all their acts of piety could be voluntary service but not commandments? The Rabbis have taught that history can be divided into three periods: the age of chaos, the age of Torah, and the prelude of the Messiah. The patriarchs lived in an age of chaos during which His holy presence could only be found in a very veiled form. Yet despite the darkness and the barriers they were able to discern seven commandments. He who attains a little under such difficulties is counted as having as much merit as one who attains much in a time of plenty. Whoever was able to perceive and maintain the seven commandments of Noah during the age of chaos did as much as one who keeps all the Torah in a time when God's word was more full.

The power to observe depends on the situation. So in this age, we are not obligated to fulfill the laws of the Temple, and the little that we do is counted as equal with the observance of those who were able to fulfill the laws that were possible in the time of the Temple.

In the time of Abraham, it was not amiss to neglect the commandments, for the time for their fulfillment had not yet come. Each word and each deed of the law has its own time in which it can and must be kept.[17]

303

[1] *Sanhedrin* 106b.

[2] Ignaz Goldziher, *Vorlesinger ueber den Islam,* Heidelberg, 1910, pp. 167 ff; D. S. Margoliouth, "The Devil's Delusion of Ibn Al-Jauzi," *Islamic Culture,* x, (1936), p. 348. "The Brethren of the Free Spirit," who emerged in the thirteenth century, taught that God could best be served in freedom of spirit and that the sacraments and ordinances of the Church were not needed. "As man is essentially divine and is able through contemplation and withdrawal from things of sense to know himself united with God, he can in his freedom do what God does, and must act as God works in him. There is, therefore, for the free man neither virtue nor vice. God is all, and all is God, and all is His." "Such is the virtue of love and charity that whatever was done in their behalf could be no sin. . . . Have charity and do what thou pleasest." J. Herkless, *Encyclopedia of Religion and Ethics,* vol. II, pp. 842f; H. Ch. Lea, *A History of the Inquisition,* N. Y. 1909, vol. II, p. 321.

[3] Romans 3:28. "By the deeds of the law there shall no flesh be justified in his sight; for by the law is knowledge of sin." On the theological implications of the whole problem, see Z. La B. Cherbonnier, *Hardness of Heart,* New York, 1955, ch. XI.

[4] Said Rabbi Eleazar ben Azariah: "Scripture says (Deuteronomy 24:19), 'When you reap your harvest in your field, and have forgotten a sheaf in the field, you shall not go back to get it; it shall be for the stranger, for the fatherless and the widow.' You see, it states immediately afterwards, 'that the Lord your God may bless you.' Scripture thus gives the assurance of a blessing to one through whom a meritorious deed came about (the feeding of the stranger), though he had no knowledge of what he was doing (since he forgot to remove the sheaf from the field). You must now admit that if a Sela (a coin) was tied up in the skirt of one's garment and it fell from it and a poor man finds it and supports himself by it, the Holy One, blessed be He, gives the assurance of blessing to the man who has lost the Sela." *Sifra* to 5:17, ed. Weiss, p. 27a.

[5] Halevi, *Kuzari* 1, III.

[6] Maimonides, *The Guide of the Perplexed,* Book III, 17; see, however, *Mishnah Torah,* Melachim 8, 11.

[7] *Abot* 5, 20.

[8] A. J. Heschel, *The Sabbath,* p. 15.

[9] A. J. Heschel, *Man's Quest for God,* ch. 4.

[10] *Exodus Rabba* 41,6. Rabbi Simon ben Lakish did claim that the entire content of the Jewish lore was given to Moses at Sinai, *Berachot* 5a. However, Maimonides, in discussing the dogma of the Oral Law, maintains merely that the general forms of observing the Biblical laws, such as *sukkah, lulav, shofar, tsitsit,* originated in Moses, but not the countless details which arise in exceptional cases and which are extensively discussed in rabbinic literature.

[11] *Pesikta Rabbati,* ed. M. Friedmann, Wien, 1880, p. 64b; *Numbers Rabba,* 19. According to a medieval scholar, everyone who labors in the Torah for its own sake may discover meanings and laws "which were not given even to Moses at Sinai." Alfred Freimann, Yehiel, the father of Rabbenu Asher, on the study of the Torah, in *Louis Ginzberg Jubilee Volume,* New York, 1945, (Hebrew), p. 360.

[12] *Pirke de Rabbi Eliezer,* ch. 21.

[13] Rabbi Yom Tov Lipmann Heller, *Tosefot Yom Tov,* preface.

[14] Rabbi Isaiah Horovitz, *Shne Luhot Haberit,* p. 25b. See Rabbi Moshe Cordovero, *Pardes Rimonim,* 23, *sub humra.*

[15] *Genesis Rabba* 19, 3.

[16] *Jerushalmi Sanhedrin* IV, 22a. See *Pne Moshe,* ad locum; also *Midrash Tehillim,* ch. 12.

[17] Rabbi Moshe Cordovero, *Shiur Komah,* Warsaw. 1885, p. 45f.

30 The Art of Being

ONLY DEEDS AND NOTHING ELSE?

Life arranged according to halacha looks like a mosaic of external deeds, and a superficial view may lead one to think that a person is judged exclusively by how many rituals or deeds of kindness he performs, by how strictly he observes the minutiae of the law, rather than by qualities of inwardness and devotion.

Does Judaism glorify outward action, regardless of intention and motive? Is it action it calls for rather than devotion? Is a person to be judged by what he *does* rather than by what he *is?* Is conduct alone important? Have the mitsvot nothing to say to the soul? Has the soul nothing to say through the mitsvot? We are commanded to carry out specific rituals, such as reciting twice a day "Hear O Israel . . ." or setting of the *tefillin* on arm and head. Are we merely commanded *to recite "Hear* O Israel . . . God is One," and not *to hear?* Is one's setting of the *tefillin* on head and arm merely a matter of external performance?

No religious act is properly fulfilled unless it is done with a willing heart and a craving soul. You cannot worship Him with your body, if you do not know how to worship Him in your soul.[1] The relationship between deed and inner devotion must be understood, as we shall see, in terms of polarity.

A CRY FOR CREATIVITY

Observance must not be reduced to external compliance with the law. Agreement of the heart with the spirit, not only with the

306

A philosophy of Judaism

letter of the law, is itself a requirement of the law. The goal is to live beyond the dictates of the law; to fulfill the eternal suddenly; to create goodness out of nothing, as it were.

The law, stiff with formality, is *a cry for creativity;* a call for nobility concealed in the form of commandments. It is not designed to be a yoke, a curb, a strait jacket for human action. Above all, the Torah asks for *love: thou shalt love thy God; thou shalt love thy neighbor.* All observance is training in the art of love. To forget that love is the purpose of all *mitsvot* is to vitiate their meaning. "Those who think that the performance is the main thing are mistaken. The main thing is the heart; what we do and what we say has only one purpose: to evoke the devotion of the heart. This is the essence and purpose of all mitsvot: to love Him wholeheartedly."[2]

"All ye do should be done out of love."[3] The end of our readiness to obey is the ability to love. The law is given to be cherished, not merely to be complied with.

Jewish observance, it must be stressed, takes place on two levels. It consists of acts performed by the body in a clearly defined and tangible manner, and of acts of the soul carried out in a manner that is neither definable nor ostensible; of the right intention and of putting the right intention into action. Both body and soul must participate in carrying out a ritual, a law, an imperative, a mitsvah. Thoughts, feelings ensconced in the inwardness of man, deeds performed in the absence of the soul, are incomplete.

Judaism stresses the importance of a fixed pattern of deeds as well as that of spontaneity of devotion, quantity as well as quality of religious living, action as well as kavanah. A good deed consists not only in *what* but also in *how* we do it. Even those mitsvot which require for their fulfillment a concrete object and an external act call for inner acknowledgement, participation, understanding and the freedom of the heart.

It is true that the law speaks always of external performance and rarely of inner devotion. It does not rigorously insist upon kavanah. There is wisdom in this reticence. The Rabbis knew that man may be commanded to act in a certain way, but not to feel in a certain

307

way; that the actions of man may be regulated, but not his thoughts or emotions.

There are, therefore, no detailed laws of kavanah, and kavanah may, indeed, run dry in the mere halacha. To maintain the flow of kavanah we must keep alive the sense of the ineffable, that which lies beyond kavanah.

GOD ASKS FOR THE HEART

Jewish observance may be divided into two classes: into duties that call for both external performance and an act of the soul, and into duties that call only for an act of the soul. Thus the mind and the heart are never exempted from being engaged in the service of God. The number of precepts which call for external performance as well as for an act of the soul is limited; whereas the number of precepts which are exclusively duties of the heart to be carried out in the soul is endless.

We exalt the deed; we do not idolize external performance. The outward performance is but an aspect of the totality of a deed. Jewish literature dilates on the idea that every act of man hinges and rests on the intention and hidden sentiments of the heart, that the duties of the heart take precedence over the duties to fulfill the practical precepts. They are binding upon us "at all seasons, in all places, every hour, every moment, under all circumstances, as long as we have life and reason."[4]

No other area of observance required such strict adherence to formalities as the ritual at the Temple in Jerusalem. The description of the rules and customs according to which the ceremonies of sacrifice were conducted occupies almost a whole section of the Mishnah. Significantly, however, the two main tractates of that section begin with a statement about the inner attitude of the priest, stressing the principle that the validity of the ceremony depends first of all upon what goes on in the mind of the priest. Having set forth all the minutiae of the priest's performance, the editor of the Mishnah resumes the original principle and concludes the

308

second tractate with a statement that almost sounds like a proclamation: "It amounts to the same, whether one offers much or little—provided one directs his heart to heaven." The good Lord may pardon every one that directed his heart to seek God . . . though he was not cleansed according to the purification of the sanctuary. (II Chronicles 30:18-19.)[4a]

To the ancient Rabbis the pursuit of learning, of Torah, was one of the highest goals.[5] Did that conception imply that in the eyes of God the scholar in the house of learning stood higher than the peasant in the field? It was a favorite saying of the scholars in Yavneh:

> I am a creature of God,
> My neighbor is also a creature of God;
> My work is in the city,
> His work is in the field;
> I rise early to my work,
> He rises early to his.
> Just as he is not overbearing in his calling,
> So am I not overbearing in my calling.
> Perhaps thou sayest:
> I do great things and he does small things!
> We have learnt:
> It matters not whether one does much or little,
> If only he directs his heart to heaven.[6]

There is much that Judaism has to say to the mind and to the soul, and there is much that the mind and the soul must give to Judaism. There is no Judaism without love and fear, wonder and awe, faith and concern, knowledge and understanding.

"God asks for the heart," not only for deeds; for insight, not only for obedience; for understanding and knowledge of God, not only for acceptance.

Impersonal obedience is not what the Bible requires. The harshest words of the Book of Deuteronomy are directed against him who did not serve the Lord "with joyfulness, and with gladness of heart" (28:47). The ways of the Torah are "ways of pleasantness, and all

309

her paths are peace. She is a tree of life to them that lay hold upon her, and happy is everyone that holds her fast" (Proverbs 3:17-18). Must we not learn how to taste the joy, the pleasantness, the peace and the happiness that emanate from the Torah?

The main function of observance is not in imposing a discipline but in keeping us spiritually perceptive. Judaism is not interested in automatons. In its essence obedience is a form of imitating God. *That* we observe is obedience; *what* we observe is imitation of God.[7]

WHY KAVANAH?

If a deed is good in itself, why should it be considered imperfect if done without the participation of the soul? Why is kavanah necessary?

A moral deed unwittingly done may be relevant to the world because of the aid it renders unto others. Yet a deed without devotion, for all its effects on the lives of others, will leave the life of the doer unaffected. The true goal for man is *to be* what he *does*. The worth of a religion is the worth of the individuals living it. A mitsvah, therefore, is not mere doing but an act that embraces both the doer and the deed. The means may be external, but the end is personal. Your deeds be pure, so that ye shall be holy.

A hero is he who is greater than his feats, and a pious man is he who is greater than his rituals. The deed is definite, yet the task is infinite.

It is a distortion to say that Judaism consists exclusively of performing ritual or moral deeds, and to forget that the goal of all performing is in *transforming* the soul. Even before Israel was told in the Ten Commandments what *to do* it was told what *to be: a holy people.* To perform deeds of holiness is to absorb the holiness of deeds. We must learn how to be one with what we do. This is why in addition to halacha, *the science of deeds,* there is agada, *the art of being.*

A philosophy of Judaism

TO DO IN ORDER TO BE

Man is not for the sake of good deeds; the good deeds are for the sake of man. Judaism asks for more than works, for more than the *opus operatum*. The goal is not that a ceremony be *performed;* the goal is that man be *transformed;* to worship the Holy in order to be holy. The purpose of the mitsvot is *to sanctify* man.

The more we do for His sake, the more we receive for our sake. What ultimately counts most is not the scope of one's deeds but their impact upon the life of the soul. "He who does a mitsvah lights a lamp before God and endows his soul with more life."[8]

Man is more than what he does. What he does is spiritually a minimum of what he is. Deeds are outpourings, not the essence of the self. They may reflect or refine the self, but they remain the functions, not the substance of inner life. It is the inner life, however, which is our most urgent problem.

The Pentateuch consists of five books. The Code of Law *(Shulchan Aruch)* consists of only four books. Where is the missing part of the law? Answered Rabbi Israel of Rushin: the missing part is the person. Without the living participation of the person the law is incomplete.

The Torah has no glory if man remains apart. The goal is for man to be an incarnation of the Torah;[9] for the Torah to be in man, in his soul and in his deeds.

THE IMMANENCE OF GOD IN DEEDS

Where is the presence, where is the glory of God to be found? It is found in the world ("the whole earth is full of His glory"), in the Bible, and in a sacred deed.

Do only the heavens declare the glory of God? It is deeply significant that Psalm 19 begins, "The heavens declare the glory of God," and concludes with a paean to the Torah and to the mitsvot. The world, the word, as well as the sacred deed are full of His glory. God is more immediately found in the Bible as well as in acts of kindness and worship than in the mountains and forests. It is more meaningful for us to believe in the *immanence of God in deeds* than in the immanence of God in nature. Indeed, the concern of Judaism is primarily not how to find the presence of God in the world of things but how to let Him enter the ways in which we deal with things; how to be with Him in time, not only in space. This is why the mitsvah is a supreme source of religious insight and experience. The way to God is a way of God, and the mitsvah is a way of God, a way where the self-evidence of the Holy is disclosed. We have few words, but we know how to live in deeds that express God.

God is One, and His glory is One. And oneness means wholeness, indivisibility. His glory is not partly here and partly there; it is all here and all there. But here and now, in this world, the glory is concealed. It becomes revealed in a sacred deed, in a sacred moment, in a sacrificial deed. No one is lonely when doing a mitsvah, for a mitsvah is where God and man meet.

We do not meet Him in the way in which we meet things of space. To meet Him means to come upon an inner certainty of His realness, upon an awareness of His will. Such meeting, such presence, we experience in deeds.

TO BE PRESENT

The presence of God is a majestic expectation, to be sensed and retained and, when lost, to be regained and resumed. Time is the presence of God in the world.[10] Every moment is His subtle arrival, and man's task is *to be present.* His presence is retained in moments in which *God is not alone,* in which we try to be present in His presence, to let Him enter our daily deeds, in which we coin our thoughts in the mint of eternity. The presence is not one realm and the sacred deed another; the sacred deed is the divine in disguise.[11]

The destiny of man is to be a partner of God and a mitsvah is an act in which man is present, an act of participation; while sin is an act in which God is alone; an act of alienation.

God in search of man

Such acts of man's revelations of the divine are acts of redemption. The meaning of redemption is to reveal the holy that is concealed, to disclose the divine that is suppressed. Every man is called upon to be a redeemer, and redemption takes place every moment, every day.[12]

The meaning of Jewish law is disclosed when conceived as sacred prosody. The divine sings in our good deeds, the divine is disclosed in our sacred deeds. Our effort is but a counterpoint in the music of His will. In exposing our lives to God we discover the divine within ourselves and its accord with the divine beyond ourselves.

NOTES FOR CHAPTER 30

[1] Bahya Ibn Paquda, *The Duties of the Heart*, ed. Haymson, New York, 1925, vol. I, p. 4.

[2] Hachayim, ms. Munich, in *Otsar Hasafrut*, vol. III, p. 66.

[3] *Sifre* to Deuteronomy 11:13.

[4] See Paquda, *The Duties of the Heart*, ed. Haymson, vol. I, p. 7.

[4a] According to *Moed Katan* 9a, the Day of Atonement was not observed in the year in which Solomon's Temple was inaugurated, because the people were engaged in the joyous festivities of the consecration of the Temple. When the people felt perturbed because of their failure to observe the holy day, a voice from heaven came forth and announced: "All of you are destined for the life in the world to come."

[5] *Mishnah Kiddushin* 4:14.

[6] *Berachot* 17a. Yavneh was the seat of a famous academy of Talmudic learning, established by Rabban Yohanan ben Zakkai after the destruction of the Second Temple in the year 70.

[7] The Talmud condemns the Pharisee who says, "What is my duty that I may perform it?" *Sotah* 22b. "God is not satisfied with deeds done merely in a spirit of obedience to a command; He wants mainly that the heart should be pure and aim to attain true worship. The heart is king and guide of the organs of the body. Hence, if the heart cannot persuade itself to worship God, the worship rendered by the other members of the body can have but little worth. Hence the verse, *My son, give me thy heart* (Proverbs 23:26)." M. H. Luzzatto, *Mesillat Yesharim*, ed. M. M. Kaplan, p. 140.

[8] *Exodus Rabba* 36, 3.

[9] "The divine Torah should become the very essence of man, so that a person can no longer be conceived as man without Torah, as little as he can be conceived as man without having life." Rabbi Moshe Almosnino, *Tefillah Lemoshe*, p. 11a.

[10] A. J. Heschel, *The Sabbath*, p. 100.

[11] "Shechinah is the mitsvah," *Tikkune Zohar*, VI; see *Zohar*, vol. I, p. 21a.

[12] See above, p. 50.

313

31 Kavanah

What is meant by the term kavanah? In its verbal form the original meaning seems to be: to straighten, to place in a straight line, to direct. From this it came to mean to direct the mind, to pay attention, to do a thing with an intention. The noun, kavanah, denotes meaning, purpose, motive and intention.

Kavanah, then, includes, first of all, what is commonly called *intention,* namely the direction of the mind toward the accomplishment of a particular act, the state of being aware of what we are doing, of the task we are engaged in. In this sense, kavanah is the same as *attentiveness.*

Does attentiveness express all that the term kavanah implies? Does kavanah mean nothing but presence of mind? Is it not obvious that a sacred act may be performed in full participation of the mind and yet be little more than a perfunctory affair, a task discharged for the sake of getting through a duty? Moreover, if kavanah were only an attitude of the mind, it would be achieved easily by a mere turn of the mind. Yet the pious men of old felt that they had to meditate for an hour in order to attain the state of kavanah.[1]

Attentiveness is a formal concept; it expresses the direction, not the goal of the mind. But what is it we ought to be attentive to in placing the mezuzah on the doorpost or in uttering a prayer? Is it the physical aspect of the act: that the mezuzah be placed in the right spot or that the words be pronounced according to the requirements of Hebrew phonetics?

A philosophy of Judaism

To have kavanah means, according to a classical formulation, "to direct the heart to the Father in heaven." The phrasing does not say direct the heart to the "text" or to the "content of the prayer." Kavanah, then, is more than paying attention to the text of the liturgy or to the performance of the mitsvah. Kavanah is attentiveness to God. Its purpose is to direct the heart rather than the tongue or the arms. It is not an act of the mind that serves to guide the external action, but one that has meaning in itself.

APPRECIATION

Mitsvah means commandment. In doing a mitsvah our primary awareness is the thought of carrying out that which He commanded us to do, and it is such awareness which places our action in the direction of the divine. Kavanah in this sense is not the awareness of being commanded but the awareness of Him who commands; not of a yoke we carry but of the Will we remember; the awareness of God rather than the awareness of duty. Such awareness is more than an attitude of the mind; it is an act of valuation or *appreciation* of being commanded, of living in a covenant, of the opportunity to act in agreement with God.

Appreciation is not the same as reflection. It is an attitude of the whole person. It is one's being drawn to the preciousness of an object or a situation. To sense the preciousness of being able to listen to an imperative of God; to be perceptive of the unique worth of doing a mitsvah, is the beginning of higher kavanah.

It is in such appreciation that we realize that to *perform* is to lend *form* to a divine theme; that our task is to set forth the divine in acts, to express the spirit in tangible forms. For a mitsvah is like a musical score, and its performance is not a mechanical accomplishment but an artistic act.

The music in a score is open only to him who has music in his soul. It is not enough to play the notes; one must *be* what he *plays.* It is not enough to do the mitsvah; one must *live* what he *does.* The goal is to find access to the sacred deed. But the holiness in the mitsvah is only open to him who knows how to discover the holiness in his own soul. To do a mitsvah is one thing; to partake of its inspiration another. And in order to partake we must learn how to bestow.

Those who dwell exclusively on the technicalities of performance fail to be sensitive to the essence of the task. When the soul is dull, the mitsvah is a shell. "The dead cannot praise God" (Psalms 115:17). The mitsvot do not always shine by their own light. When we open our inner life to a mitsvah, songs rise up in our souls.

INTEGRATION

The presence of God demands more than the presence of mind. Kavanah is direction to God and requires the redirection of the whole person. It is the act of bringing together the scattered forces of the self; the participation of heart and soul, not only of will and mind; the integration of the soul with the theme of the mitsvah.

It is one thing to be *for* a cause and another thing to be *in* a cause. It is not enough to help thy neighbor; "Thou shalt love thy neighbor." It is not enough to serve thy God; you are asked "to serve Him with all your heart and with all your soul" (Deuteronomy 11:13). It is not enough to love Him: "thou shalt love . . . with all thy heart, and with all thy soul, and with all thy might" (Deuteronomy 6:5-6).

BEYOND KAVANAH

What we feel primarily is our inability to feel adequately. Human inadequacy is not an inference of humility; it is the truth of existence. A mitsvah is neither a substitute for thought nor an expression of kavanah. A mitsvah is an act in which we go beyond the scope of our thought and intention. He who plants a tree rises beyond the level of his own intention. He who does a mitsvah plants a tree in the divine garden of eternity.

With a sacred deed goes a cry of the soul, inarticulate at times, that is more expressive of what we witness, of what we sense than words.

A pious man is usually pictured as a sort of bookworm, a person who thrives among the pages of ancient tomes, and to whom life with its longing, sadness, and tensions, is but a footnote in a scholarly commentary on the Bible. The truth is that a religious man is like a salamander, that legendary animal that originates from a fire of myrtlewood kept burning for seven years.

Religion is born of fire, of a flame, in which the dross of the mind and soul is melted away. Religion can only thrive on fire. "The Lord spoke unto Moses. . . . This they shall give . . . half a shekel for an offering to the Lord" (Exodus 30:13). Said Rabbi Meir: "The Lord showed unto Moses a coin of fire, saying: This is what they shall give."[2] A life of religion is an altar. "Fire shall be kept burning upon the altar continually; it shall not go out" (Leviticus 6:6).

Man cannot live without acts of exaltation, without moments of trembling and revering, without being transported by grandeur. For weeks and months he may be confined to the routine of sensible interests, until an hour arrives when all his habits burst under the strain. Common sense may sign a decree that life be kept under the lock of average conceptions, but much in our lives is made to be burned up in a holy flame or it will rot in monstrous deeds, in evil thoughts. To satisfy his need for exaltation, man will plunge into rage, wage wars; he will set the city of Rome afire.

When superimposed as a yoke, as a dogma, as a fear, religion tends to violate rather than to nurture the spirit of man. Religion must be an altar upon which the fire of the soul may be kindled in holiness.[3]

NOTES FOR CHAPTER 31

[1] *Mishnah Berachot* 1, 5.

[2] *Tanhuma*, ed. Buber, ad locum; *Jerushalmi Shekalim* I, 46b.

[3] There is an ancient controversy among scholars of Jewish law whether the presence of kavanah—of the right intention in carrying out one's duty—is absolutely required for the performance of all religious acts. The question, for

example, arose whether one who has accidentally heard the sounding of the Shofar on the first day of Tishri (the New Year's day) without thinking of the Biblical command (Numbers 29:1) may be considered as having satisfied the law.

A classical precedent is found in the Temple cult. According to the law, the priest who performs the ritual of (slaughtering) a sacrificial offering must act *with proper intention,* e.g., in the awareness of performing the ritual for the sake of God, or in the awareness of acting in the name of the owner of the offering (the person whose offering the priest administers). See *Mishnah Zebahim* 4, 6. However, if the officiating priest has performed the ceremony *with improper intention* (e.g., he offered it for a person other than the one whose offering it was), the offering does not acquit the owner of his obligation, and the owner must bring anew the offering that was due from him. See *Mishnah Zebahim* 1, 1. (Even though the first offering retains its original sanctity and all subsequent rites must be performed.) If performed with a certain kind of improper intention—e.g., when the priest performs with the intention of eating or burning the sacrifice at the improper time (*piggul*)—the offering is considered foul, sacrilegious or sinful. See *Mishnah Zabahim* 3, b. On the other hand, if *no intention* at all was in the mind of the priest (he acted without being mindful of the purpose of the performance), the offering acquits the owner of his obligation, the principle being: no intention is considered as if there were proper intention (*Zebahim* 2b). The objective circumstances indicate the purpose of the act. The intention is implicitly present.

To summarize: the presence of proper intention is required for the act; the presence of improper intention (in some cases) invalidates the act; the lack or absence of intention, proper or improper, while not desirable, does not invalidate the act.

Another precedent. There is a rule that a Deed of Divorce must from its inception have been intended expressly for the woman who is to receive it. Thus if a Deed of Divorce was written out without mentioning any name and the name was later inserted, the Deed is invalid. The principle is: the writing must be done with specific intention; it must be done for the sake of the woman for whom it is intended. Here, unlike the case of sacrifice, the absence of intention invalidates the act. The reason being: the Deed of Divorce, if no name is mentioned in it, is not in itself related to any particular woman, whereas an offering stands implicitly in a relation to the will of God, for whose sake it is administered, even though at the moment of administering the priest may not be explicitly mindful of it.

The question arises whether all religious acts should be regarded as analogous to the sacrifice or as analogous to the Deed of Divorce.

Rabbinic authorities are divided on the question. Some maintain that proper intention is absolutely required for the fulfillment of a commandment and that religious acts must be repeated if performed without such intention. This is why in later times it became customary to declare when one was about to perform a religious act: "I am ready and prepared to fulfill the divine command of . . ." Others maintain that while proper intention is desirable the validity of religious acts does not depend upon the intention with which they are performed. Intention is indispensable only when the fulfillment of the commandment consists of an oral act. Whenever the fulfillment includes an external act,

A philosophy of Judaism

the act is relevant even when there is no proper intention. See Rabbenu Yonah, *Berachot* 12a.

The latter opinion, however, does not imply that no kavanah is required. It only means that the deed without the kavanah is considered as if it had been done with kavanah, for where no intention is consciously entertained, it may still be assumed that the deed was done for its proper purpose. Consequently in the case of improper intention, wherein that assumption cannot be maintained, the deed is not valid because of the absence of kavanah. See Engel, *Athvan Deoraitha*, Lemberg, 1891, ch. 23.

32 Religious Behaviorism

RELIGIOUS BEHAVIORISM

It is important that we analyze a popular misunderstanding of Judaism which may be called "religious behaviorism." It signifies an attitude toward the law as well as a philosophy of Judaism as a whole. As an attitude toward the law, it stresses the external compliance with the law and disregards the importance of inner devotion. It maintains that, according to Judaism, there is only one way in which the will of God need be fulfilled, namely, outward action; that inner devotion is not indigenous to Judaism; that Judaism is concerned with deeds, not with ideas; that all it asks for is obedience to the law. It is a Judaism that consists of laws, deeds, things; it has two dimensions; depth, the personal dimension, is missing. Accordingly, religious behaviorists speak of discipline, tradition, observance, but never of religious experience, of religious ideas. You do not have to believe, but you must observe the law; as if all that mattered is how men behaved in physical terms; as if God were not concerned with the inner life; as if faith were not indigenous to Judaism, but *orthopraxis* were. Such a conception reduces Judaism to a sort of sacred physics, with no sense for the imponderable, the introspective, the metaphysical.

As a personal attitude religious behaviorism usually reflects a widely held theology in which the supreme article of faith is *respect for tradition*. People are urged to observe the rituals or to attend services out of deference to what has come down to us from our ancestors. The *theology of respect* pleads for the maintenance of the inherited and transmitted customs and institutions and is characterized by a spirit of conformity, excessive moderation and disrespect of spontaneity.

Wise, important, essential, and pedagogically useful as the principle "respect for tradition" is, it is grotesque and self-defeating to make of it the supreme article of faith. We do not adhere to the specific forms of observance because of their antiquity. Antics of the past are hardly more venerable than vagaries of the present. Is the archaic a mark of vital preference? Is unconditional respect for the past the essence of Judaism? Did not Judaism begin when Abraham broke with tradition and rejected the past? Religious behaviorism is guilty of a total misunderstanding of the nature of man. Is it psychologically true that religious deeds can be performed in a spiritual vacuum, in the absence of the soul? Is respect without reason, ancestral loyalty without faith, or group-consciousness without personal conviction compatible with the life of a free man?

Let us analyze the origin as well as the basic assumptions of religious behaviorism in the light of Jewish thinking.

SPINOZA AND MENDELSSOHN

The theory of Judaism as a system of religious behaviorism goes back to Spinoza and Moses Mendelssohn.

Spinoza advanced the theory that the Israelites were distinguished from other nations neither in knowledge nor in piety. "Of God and nature they had only very primitive ideas," above which not even the prophets were able to rise.

"Scriptural doctrine contains no lofty speculations nor philosophic reasoning, but only very simple matters, such as could be understood by the slowest intelligence." "I should be surprised if I found [the prophets] teaching any new speculative doctrine which was not a commonplace to . . . Gentile philosophers." "It, therefore, follows that we must by no means go to the prophets for knowledge, either of natural or spiritual phenomena." "The Israelites knew scarcely anything of God, although he was revealed to them." It is

hardly likely that they "should have held any sound notions about
the Deity, or that Moses should have taught them anything beyond
a rule of right living. . . . Thus the rule of right living, the worship
and the love of God, was to them rather a bondage than the true
liberty, the gift and grace of the Deity." What the Bible contains is
not a religion but a law, the character of which was political rather
than religious.[1]

Spinoza's insistence upon the intellectual irrelevance and spiritual
inferiority of the Bible has proved to be of momentous importance,
and has shaped the minds of subsequent generations in their attitude to the Bible. Kant, Fichte, Hegel, and the thinkers of the
romantic school, even when rejecting his views about metaphysics,
adopted his views about the Bible.[2]

It is one of the ironies of Jewish history that Moses Mendelssohn,
a zealous opponent of Spinoza's metaphysical theories and profoundly different from him in motivation and intention, has nevertheless embraced Spinoza's view of the essential nature of the Bible.[3]

Mendelssohn believed that ultimate religious verities cannot be
communicated from the outside, for our mind would not understand them if they were not already known to us. Ultimate verities
have their origin in the mind rather than in revelation. The Jewish
belief in one God is not a revelation but part of a natural religion
at which all men can arrive by the exercise of reason. With Spinoza,
he maintains that Judaism asks for obedience to a law but not acceptance of doctrines. "Judaism is no revealed religion in the usual
sense of the term, but only *revealed legislation,* laws, commandments and regulations, which were supernaturally given to the Jews
through Moses." It demands no faith, no specific religious attitudes.
"The spirit of Judaism is freedom in doctrine and conformity in
action."[4]

JUDAISM AND LEGALISM

In the spirit of Spinoza and Moses Mendelssohn, many of those who
take the law seriously, as well as those who pay lip service to it,

A philosophy of Judaism

maintain that the science of law is the only authentic expression of Judaism; that agada—in the strict sense of the non-legal rabbinic literature and in the wider sense of all post-rabbinic attempts to interpret the non-legal ideas and beliefs of our faith—is not "within the mainstream of Judaism." Theology, it is claimed, is alien to Judaism; the law, "An ox who gores a cow," is Jewish theology, for Judaism is law and nothing else. Such *pan-halachic* "theology" claims that in Judaism religious living consists of complying with a law rather than of striving to attain a goal which is the purpose of the law. It is a view that exalts the Torah only because it discloses the law, not because it discloses a way of finding God in life. It claims that obedience is the substance rather than the form of religious existence; that the law is an end, not a way.

This, indeed, has been the contention of those who attacked Judaism that "the law of Moses commands only right action, and says nothing about purity of heart." Albo rejects this as being the opposite of the truth. "For do we not read, *Circumcise therefore the foreskin of your heart* (Deuteronomy 10:16); *And thou shalt love the Lord thy God with all thy heart* (Deuteronomy 10:16); *And thou shalt love thy neighbor as thyself* (Leviticus 19:18); *But Thou shalt fear thy God* (Leviticus 19:14); *Thou shalt not take vengeance, nor bear any grudge against the children of thy people* (Leviticus 19:18). The reason it commands right action is because purity of heart is of no account unless practice is in agreement with it. The most important thing, however, is intention. David says, *Create me a clean heart* (Psalms 51:12)."[5]

Judaism is not another word for legalism. The rules of observance are law in form and love in substance. The Torah contains both law and love. Law is what holds the world together; love is what brings the world forward. The law is the means, not the end; the way, not the goal. One of the goals is "Ye shalt be holy." The Torah is guidance to an end through a law. It is both a vision and a law. Man created in the likeness of God is called upon to re-create the world in the likeness of the vision of God. Halacha is neither the ultimate nor the all-embracing term for Jewish learning and living.

The Torah is more than a system of laws; only a portion of the Pentateuch deals with law. The prophets, the Psalms, agadic midrashim, are not a part of halacha. The Torah comprises both halacha and agada. Like body and soul, they are mutually dependent, and each is a dimension of its own.

Agada is usually defined negatively as embracing all non-legal or non-halachic parts of rabbinic literature,[6] whether in the form of a tale or an explanation of scripture; an epigram or a homily. Significantly, though the Bible, like rabbinic literature, embraces both legal and non-legal teachings, the distinction between halacha and agada was never applied to it.[7] The fact remains that, central as is law, only a small part of the Bible deals with the law. The narratives of the Bible are as holy as its legal portions.[8] According to one rabbi, "the conversation of the servants of the patriarchs is more beautiful than even the laws of the later generations."[9]

THE FUNDAMENTAL IMPORTANCE OF AGADA

The preciousness and fundamental importance of agada is categorically set forth in the following statement of the ancient Rabbis: *"If you desire to know Him at whose word the universe came into being, study agada for hereby will you recognize the Holy One and cleave unto His ways."*[10] It is by means of agada that the name of God is sanctified in the world.[11] To those who did not appreciate the value of agada, the Rabbis applied the verse, "They give no heed to the works of the Lord, nor to the acts of His hands."[12]

In the Tannaitic period, agada was an organic part of Jewish learning. It was said that just as the written Torah consists of three parts, the Pentateuch, the Prophets, and the Hagiography, the oral Torah consists of midrash, halacha, and agada.[13]

The collections of agada that have been preserved contain an almost inexhaustible wealth of religious insight and feeling, for in the agada the religious consciousness with its motivations, difficulties, perplexities, and longings, came to immediate and imaginative expression. And a Jew was commanded to study not only halacha but also agada.[14]. On the Day of Judgment one would be held accountable for having failed to study agada.[15] According to a decision of a later authority, one is obliged to devote a third of one's studies to the field of agada.[16]

Jewish enlightenment, however, showed little appreciation of agada.[17] In a study on Jewish education in which all aspects of classical Jewish literature were recommended as topics of instruction, the author strongly inveighs against including agada in the curriculum.[18]

TORAH IS MORE THAN LAW

The translators of the Septuagint committed a fatal and momentous error when, for lack of a Greek equivalent, they rendered Torah with *nomos*, which means *law*, giving rise to a huge and chronic misconception of Judaism and supplying an effective weapon to those who sought to attack the teachings of Judaism. That the Jews considered Scripture as teaching is evidenced by the fact that in the Aramaic translations Torah is rendered with *oraita* which can only mean teaching, never law.

In the Avesta, religion is called law *(daêna)*, and the Persians had no way of distinguishing between religion and law.[19] In Judaism even the word *Torah* is not all-inclusive. "A man who has Torah but no *yirat shamayim* (awe and fear of God) is like a treasurer who was given the keys to the inner chamber but not the keys to the outer chamber."[20] Nor does the term *mitsvot*, commandments, express the totality of Judaism. The acceptance of *God* must precede, and is distinguished from, the acceptance of the commandments.[21]

At the head of the Decalogue stand the words, *I am the Lord thy God*. The Rabbis offered a parable. "The Emperor extended his reign over a new province. Said his attendants to him: Issue some decrees upon the people. But the emperor replied: Only after they will have accepted my *kingship*, will I issue *decrees*. For if they do not accept my kingship, how will they carry out my decrees? Likewise, God said to Israel, *I am the Lord thy God—Thou shalt have no other gods.* I am He whose kingship you have taken upon yourselves in Egypt. And when they said to Him: Yes, yes, He continued, *Thou shalt have no other gods beside me.*"[22]

Through sheer punctiliousness in observing the law one may become oblivious of the living presence and forget that the law is not for its own sake but for the sake of God. Indeed, the essence of observance has, at times, become encrusted with so many customs and conventions that the jewel was lost in the setting. Outward compliance with externalities of the law took the place of the engagement of the whole person to the living God. What is the ultimate objective of observance if not to become sensitive to the spirit of Him, is whose ways the mitsvot are signposts?

Halacha must not be observed for its own sake but for the sake of God. The law must not be idolized. It is a part, not all, of the Torah. We live and die for the sake of God rather than for the sake of the law.

We are told, *Ye shall keep my Sabbaths, and reverence My sanctuary* (Leviticus 19:30). One might think that we are commanded to pay homage to the sanctuary. The Talmud exhorts us: "Just as one does not revere the Sabbath but Him who commanded the observance of the Sabbath, one is not to revere the sanctuary but Him who gave the commandment concerning the sanctuary."[23]

The glorification of the law and the insistence upon its strict observance, did not lead the Rabbis to a deification of the law. "The Sabbath is given unto you, not you unto the Sabbath." The ancient Rabbis knew that excessive piety may endanger the fulfillment of the essence of the law. "There is nothing more important, according to the Torah, than to preserve human life. . . . Even when there is the slightest possibility that a life may be at stake one may disregard every prohibition of the law." One must sacrifice mitsvot for the sake of man, rather than sacrifice man for the sake of mitsvot. The purpose of the Torah is "to bring life to Israel, in this world and in the world to come."[24]

A philosophy of Judaism

The ultimate requirement is to act beyond the requirements of the law. Torah is not the same as law, as *din*. To fulfill one's duties is not enough. One may be a *scoundrel* within the limits of the law.[25] Why was Jerusalem destroyed? Because her people acted according to the law, and did not act beyond the requirements of the law.[26]

Halacha stresses uniformity, agada represents the principle of inflection and diversity. Rules are generalizations. In actual living, we come upon countless problems for which no general solutions are available. There are many ways of applying a general rule to a concrete situation. There are evil applications of noble rules. Thus the choice of the right way of applying a general rule to a particular situation is "left to the heart,"[27] to the individual, to one's conscience.

> "Where is the sage that would understand it?
> Where is the prophet who is able to declare it?
> Wherefore is the land perished and laid waste like a wilderness?"

"This question was asked of the sages, but they could not answer it; it was asked of prophets, but they could not answer it. Until God Himself resolved it.

"And the Lord said: Because they have forsaken My Torah.

"Said Rav Judah in Rav's name: It means that they did not approach the Torah with a blessing."[28]

This interpretation that the land of Israel was destroyed because of the wrong inner attitude rather than because of a literal abandonment of the Torah was praised by Rabbenu Yonah the saint. "For if the verse meant that the people had forsaken the Torah literally and that they were not devoted to it at all, then why were the prophets and sages unable to explain the destruction of the land? Why couldn't they cite this clear and simple reason?

"The truth is that the people actually kept the Torah and that they never forsook the task of studying it. Therefore the prophets and sages were perplexed until God Himself came to explain. He, who knows the depths of the human heart, could see that though they studied Torah [as a duty], they did not bless it. He saw that though they performed the Torah, they did not consider it to be a blessing." They did not sense its preciousness. They failed to fulfill it "for its own sake," for the sake of God. The land was destroyed because there was no kavanah, no inner devotion.[29]

It was in the spirit of such a radical demand for inner purity that the word of the Psalmist (119:113), *I hate those who are of a divided mind,* was applied to those who serve the Lord out of fear rather than out of love.[30] We must always remember the words of Isaiah 29:13. "This people draw near with their mouth and honor Me with their lips, while their hearts are far from Me, and their fear of Me is a commandment of men learned by rote."

PAN-HALACHISM

The rendering of Torah with *nomos* was not done thoughtlessly. It is rather an example of a tendency toward legalism or *pan-halachism* which regards halacha as the only authentic source of Jewish thinking and living. Both in the Rabbinic period and in the Middle Ages there were people who took a negative attitude toward agada[31] and would even "reject and ridicule" some of its statements.[32]

The outstanding expression of the anti-agadic attitude is contained in a classical rabbinic question with which Rashi opens his famous commentary on the Book of Genesis. "Rabbi Isaac said: The Torah [which is the law book of Israel] should have commenced with chapter 12 of Exodus," since prior to that chapter hardly any laws are set forth.[33]

The premise and implications of this question are staggering. The Bible should have omitted such non-legal chapters as those on creation, the sins of Adam and Cain, the flood, the tower of Babel, the lives of Abraham, Isaac, and Jacob, the lives of the twelve tribes, the suffering and miracles in Egypt!

God in search of man

The exponents of religious behaviorism claim that Judaism is a religion of law, not a religion of faith, that faith "was never regarded by Judaism as something meritorious in itself." This, of course, would be valid, if Abraham's willingness to sacrifice his only son, or Job's avowal, "though He slay me, yet will I trust in Him" (13:15), could be disregarded. What if not the power of faith, is the motive behind the injunction of the Mishnah, "A man is obliged to bless God for the evil things that come upon him as he is obliged to bless God for the good things that come to him?"[34] "If there is anything sure, it is that the highest motives which worked through the history of Judaism are the strong belief in God and the unshaken confidence that at last this God, the God of Israel, will be the God of the whole world; or, in other words, Faith and Hope are the two most prominent characteristics of Judaism."[35]

In the Bible, unbelievers are rebuked again and again, while belief is praised in such lofty words as, "Thus saith the Lord, I remember the affection of thy youth, thy love as a bride when thou wentest after Me in the wilderness, in a land that was not sown" (Jeremiah 2:2). The Rabbis are inclined to ascribe sin to a defect in, or a lack of, faith in God. "No man speaks slanderously of another . . . no man deals fraudulently with his neighbor, unless he has first denied (or disbelieved in) the Root of all (namely, God)."[36]

Faith is so precious that Israel was redeemed from Egypt as a reward for their faith. The future redemption is contingent upon the degree of faith shown by Israel.[37] The Rabbis denied a share in the life to come not to those who were guilty of wrong deeds, but to those who asserted views that contradicted fundamental beliefs.[38]

In justification of their view, exponents of religious behaviorism cite the passage in which the Rabbis paraphrased the words of Jeremiah (16:11), *They have forsaken Me and have not kept My Torah* in the following way: "Would that they had forsaken Me and kept My Torah."[39] However, to regard this passage as a declaration of the primary if not exclusive importance of studying Torah over

329

concern for God is to pervert the meaning of the passage. Such perversion is made possible by overlooking the second part of the passage which reads as follows: "since by occupying themselves with the Torah, the light which she contains would have led them back *to Me*."[40] It was not an ideal that the Rabbis envisaged but a last resort. Having forsaken all commandments, if the people had at least continued to study Torah, the light of the Torah would have brought them back to God.

DOGMAS ARE NOT ENOUGH

It is true, as said above, that the essence of Judaism is a demand rather than a creed, that by faith alone we do not come close to Him. But the first demand of Judaism is to have faith in God,[41] in Torah, and in the people Israel. It is by faith and love of God that find expression in deeds that we live as Jews. Faith is attachment, and to be a Jew is to be attached to God, Torah, and Israel.

Unquestionably, Judaism stands for verities not only for laws, expecting us to cherish certain thoughts and to be loyal to certain beliefs, not only to perform certain actions. It is both a way of thinking and a way of living, a doctrine and a discipline, faith and action.[42]

We deny the exclusive primacy of dogmas not because we think that Judaism has no beliefs or that Judaism is merely a system of laws and observances, but because we realize that what we believe in surpasses the power and range of human expression.

Moreover, underlying the doctrines of dogmas is an intellectualism which claims that right and correctly expressed thinking is the most important thing. To Jewish tradition, however, right living is what counts most. Follow the pattern of the right living, even though you do not know how to formulate adequately its basic theory.

A dogma is something that is carried out totally in the mind by an act of belief. The mind, however, is but a part of man; the capital

330

of the human realm, not the whole realm. A dogma, therefore, can only be a partial representation of the religious situation.

The danger of dogmas lies in their tendency to serve as *vicarious faith,* as if all we had to do were to accept on authority a fixed set of principles without the necessity of searching for a way of faith. But dogmas, if they are to serve any purpose at all, should be a summary or an epitome of faith rather than a substitute for it.

Not the confession of belief, but the active acceptance of the kingship of God and its order is the central demand of Judaism. Asserting "I believe in . . ." will not make a person a Jew, just as asserting "I believe in the United States of America" will not make a person an American. A citizen is he who accepts the allegiance to the Constitution, its rights and obligations. Thus our relation to God cannot be expressed in a belief but rather in the accepting of an order that determines all of life.

THE FOUR CUBITS

Another statement which seems to express an anti-agadic spirit is that of the Babylonian Amora Ula. "Since the day the Temple in Jerusalem was destroyed all that is left to the Holy One are the four cubits of halacha";[43] as if God were not present outside the realm of halacha. Those who quote this passage as a statement of disparagement of agada fail to notice that the passage is hardly an expression of jubilation. Its intention rather is to convey profound grief at the fact that man's attentiveness to God became restricted to matters of halacha; that God is absent in world affairs, in matters that lie outside the limits of halacha.[44] This, indeed, is why we pray for redemption.

In contrast to that passage is a statement that "all that the Holy One has in this world is the awe and fear of God."[45]

Certain ritual actions if performed by a person who has no faith are considered invalid. To cite an example: "It is forbidden to burn or otherwise destroy any of the Sacred Scriptures, their commentaries or expositions. . . . This rule only applies to Scriptures written

331

hy a person who is conscious of their sanctity. But if a disbeliever wrote a scroll of the Torah, it is to be burnt with all the names of God contained therein. The reason is that he does not believe in the sanctity of the divine name and did not write it for its sake, but regarded it like to any other writing. This being his attitude, the Divine Name, which he wrote, never became sanctified."[46]

"A priest who does not believe in the sacrificial service—who says in his heart that the Temple sacrifices are pure vanity; that the Lord has not commanded them and that Moses invented them—has no share in the priesthood."[47]

The cleavage between the Saducees and the Pharisees was partly caused by differences in doctrine. Scripture is the only authority, asserted the Saducee; Scriptures and tradition, asserted the Pharisee. "The fiercest of all conflicts between Pharisee and Saducee concerned the doctrine of the resurrection."[48] The Pharisee believed in the survival of the soul, the revival of the body, the great judgment, and the life in the world to come, while the Saducee rejected these beliefs.

The anti-Maimonidean controversy did not revolve around matters of the law. The authority of Maimonides' *halachic* decisions was never questioned. It was his views concerning angels, prophecy, miracles, resurrection, and creation, that provoked the indignation of many orthodox rabbis.[49]

The bitter antagonism of the Gaon of Vilna to the hasidic movement was caused primarily not by differences in custom but by differences in doctrine, such as the right understanding of God's immanence in all things, of the doctrine of "the redemption of the sparks" and the doctrine of the *tsimtsum*.[50]

NOTES FOR CHAPTER 32

[1] *Tractatus Theologica-Politicus,* III, IV, XIII.

[2] Kant owed his knowledge of Judaism partly to Spinoza's *Tractatus* and partly to Mendelssohn's *Jerusalem.* He maintained that Judaism is *"eigenllich gar keine Religion."* Compare Hermann Cohen, "Spinoza uber Staat und Religion, Judentum and Christentum," *Juedische Schriften,* Berlin, 1924, vol. III, pp. 290-372, and vol. I, p. 284f. The same applies to Hegel, compare Hegel, *Early Theological Writings,* Chicago, 1948, p. 195f.

God in search of man

[3] That Spinoza's *Tractatus* served in more than one respect as the model for Mendelssohn's *Jerusalem* was proved by Julius Guttmann, *Mendelssohn's Jerusalem und Spinozas Theologisch Pulitischer Traktat*, Berlin, 1931. See also Guttmann, *Die Philosophie des Judentums*, Munich, 1933, p. 312f. For a critical view, compare Isaac Heinemann's study on Mendelssohn's philosophy in *Metsudah*, 1954, p. 205ff.

[4] *Jerusalem*, ch. 2. See Hermann Cohen, *Die Religion der Vernunft*, p. 415ff.

[5] Joseph Albo, *Ikkarim*, Part 3, ch. 25.

[6] Rabbi Samuel Hanagid, *Mevo Hatalmud*.

[7] On the basis of *Genesis Rabba* 44, 8, it was suggested that originally the term agada was also applied to the narrative portions of the Bible, including the Pentateuch. See M. Guttmann, *Clavis Talmudis*, I, 453.

[8] Compare *Genesis Rabba* 85, 2.

[9] *Genesis Rabba* 60, 8.

[10] *Sifre*, Deuteronomy, 49, to 11:22.

[11] *Yalkut Shimoni*, Psalms, 672.

[12] *Midrash Tehillim* 28, 5. According to Maimonides, *Commentary on Abot*, end, *kaddish* is recited after *agada* only; see, however, *Mishneh Torah*, *Ahavah*, end, and *Magen Avrahan*, 54, 3.

[13] *Jerushalmi Shekalim*, V, beginning. Agada was one of the treasures which were promised to Israel at Marah (*Mechilta* to 15:26), and which Moses received during the forty days he spent in heaven, *Exodus Rabba* 47:1; see Ibn Zimra, *Responsa*, IV, 232. Unlike the First Tablets of the Covenant, the Second Tablets contained agada as well (*Exodus Rabba* 46:1). On the belief in the divine origin of agada, see *Leviticus Rabba* 22:1; *Jerushalmi Megillah* 4, 1.

[14] *Sifre*, Deuteronomy, 48; *Kiddushin* 30a.

[15] *Midrash Mishle*, to 10:3.

[16] Rabbi Shneur Zalman of Ladi, *Shulchan Aruch*, Talmud Torah, ch. 2, par. 1-2.

[17] See Maimonides. *Commentary on the Mishnah, Sanhedrin* X, introduction. Abraham Geiger ascribed to the Rabbis *"ein getruebtes exegetisches Bewusstsein."* See Michael Sachs, *Die Religiose Poesie der Juden in Spanien*, Berlin, 1845, p. 160.

[18] Elijah Morpurgo, in Asaf, *Mekorot Letoldot Hachinuch Beisrael*, Vol. II, p. 231.

[19] Eduard Lehmann, Die Perser, in "Chantepie de la Saussaye," *Lehrbuch der Religionsgeschichte*, edited by Alfred Bertholet and Eduard Lehmann, Tuebingen, 1925, Vol. II, p. 246.

[20] *Shabbat* 31a-b.

[21] "Rabbi Joshua ben Karha said: Why does in our liturgy the section *Hear O Israel* precede the section *And it shall come to pass if ye shall hearken* (which deals with the observance)? So that a man shall first receive upon himself the yoke of the kingship of heaven, and afterwards receive upon himself the yoke of the commandments." *Mishneh Berachot*, II, 2.

[22] *Mechilta* to 20:3. According to *Mechilta de Rabbi Simon ben Jochai*, Frankfurt a. M., 1905, p. 103, the "I am the Lord thy God" is a part of every commandment of the law, for without faith in the reality of God there are no commandments; see David Hoffmann's comment.

[23] *Yebamot* 6a-6b.

[24] A. J. Heschel, *The Sabbath*, p. 17.

25 Nahmanides, *Commentary* on Leviticus 19:2.

26 *Baba Metsia* 30b.

27 See *Kiddushin* 32b.

28 *Nedarim* 81a; the quotations are from Jeremiah 9:11f, slightly paraphrased.

29 R. Nisim to *Nedarim* 81a.

30 *Midrash Tehillim* 119:13

31 See, for example, *Sotah* 40a. In studying the Talmud, the main subject of Jewish learning for many centuries, the agadic parts were often neglected. Due to the unbroken tradition in the study of halacha, knowledge of its ancient sources has been preserved to this day. The lack of a similar tradition in the study of *agada* has deprived us of much of the understanding of agadic sources. Some teachers would omit the *agadic* portions. Bahya complained that the study of "the duties of the heart" was neglected, "although they form the foundation of all precepts." Bahya, *The Duties of the Heart*, vol. II, p. 49; also vol. I, p. 14. See also Rabbi Isaac Aboab, *Menorat Hamaor*, introduction. Rabbenu Yonah, *Shaare Teshuvah*, 3, 20. Rabbi Abraham, the son of Maimonides, *Milhamot Hashem*, Jerusalem, 1953, p. 49. Rabbi Joseph Ibn Kaspi, in I. Abrahams, *Hebrew Ethical Wills*, II, p. 153f. Luzatto, *Mesillat Yesharim*, preface. Rabbi Chayim of Volozhin, *Nefesh Hachayim*, 4,1.

32 See Maimonides, *The Guide of the Perplexed*, Book III, p. 43. The sharp reprobation of agada by Rabbi Zeira (*Jerushalmi Maaserot* III, 51a), himself a prominent agadist, must have been directed not to agada generally but to its abuse; see A. Marmorstein, *The Old Rabbinic Doctrine of God*, London, 1937, pp. 137ff. In this connection one might recall that Rabbi Zeira spent one hundred days in fasting in order to forget the dialectic method of instruction of the Babylonian schools. See *Baba Metsia* 85a.

33 Nahmanides, in his commentary, was very much puzzled by this question. "It was certainly necessary to begin with the story of creation; creation is the most fundamental belief, and he who denies it is an atheist *(kofer ba-ikkar)* and has no share in the Torah." However, Nahmanides justifies the question by saying that the story of creation remains a mystery in spite of what is said about it in the Book of Genesis. Whatever understanding of the mystery distinguished individuals possess, is derived exclusively from tradition. For the ordinary people, therefore, the reference to creation contained in the Decalogue would have been sufficient.

34 *Mishnah Berachot* 9, 5.

35 S. Schechter, *Studies in Judaism*, First Series, p. 151.

36 *Jerushalmi Peah* 16a. To the question of a philosopher, who is the most hateful of all? a Rabbi replied, "He who denies his Creator." See *Tosefta Shevuot* 3,6.

37 *Mechilta* to Exodus 14:31.

38 *Mishnah Sanhedrin* 10,1.

39 *Lamentations Rabba*, 2, proemium. According to S. Abramson, *Leshonenu,* xiv, p. 122-125, the original reading is not *meor* but *seor* in the sense of "essence."

40 See the reading in *Pesikta de Rabbi Kahana*, ed. Buber, Lyck, 1868, and *Jerushalmi Hagigah*, 1, 7, 76c. In *Pesikta* the passage is followed by the statement that one ought to study Torah even if it is not for her sake, for in studying one learns how to study Torah for her own sake.

A philosophy of Judaism

[41] According to Maimonides, Halevi, Nahmanides and others, the first words of the Decalogue contain the command to believe in the existence of God.

[42] On the relation of creed and faith, see *Man Is Not Alone*, p. 167f.

[43] *Berachot* 8a.

[44] Compare the suggestion of Maimonides, *Introduction to the Mishnah*, that halacha in this passage is employed in a wider meaning than elsewhere. The passage was extremely puzzling to Maimonides. "If you take it literally, it is very far from being true, for it would imply that the four cubits of halacha were the only kind of knowledge we ought to acquire, whereas all other kinds of wisdom and science were to be rejected. Does it mean that in the age of Shem and Eber (prior to the time of Abraham) in which halacha was unknown, God had no share whatsoever in this world?"

[45] *Shabbat* 31b.

[46] *Mishneh Torah, Yesode Hatorah*, vi, 8.

[47] *Hullin* 132b, and Rashi's comment. If he does believe in sacrifices, although he is not conversant with their laws, he is entitled to a portion in the distribution of priestly gifts.

[48] Louis Finkelstein, *The Pharisees*, Philadelphia, 1938, p. 145.

[49] See Julius Guttmann, *Die Philosophie des Judentums*, Muenchen, 1935, p. 206f; Joseph Sarachek, *Faith and Reason*, Williamsport, Pa., 1935.

[50] See D. Z. Hilman, *Iggrot Baal Hatanya*, Jerusalem, 1953, p. 97; M. Teitelbaum, *Harav Meladi*, Warsaw, 1914, vol. II, p. 87ff.

33 The Problem of Polarity

There is a general assumption that the Rabbis were naive, simple-minded, and unreflective people. How such an assumption can be generalized in regard to such a galaxy of men whose subtle and profound judgments in halacha have remained an intellectual challenge to all future students is difficult to see. It is refuted by any unbiased analysis of their agadic sayings, which clearly indicate that their inner life was neither simple nor idyllic. Their thinking can only be adequately understood in terms of a contest between receptivity and spontaneity, between halacha and agada.

Halacha represents the strength to shape one's life according to a fixed pattern; it is a form-giving force. Agada is the expression of man's ceaseless striving which often defies all limitations. Halacha is the rationalization and schematization of living; it defines, specifies, sets measure and limit, placing life into an exact system. Agada deals with man's ineffable relations to God, to other men, and to the world. Halacha deals with details, with each commandment separately; agada with the whole of life, with the totality of religious life. Halacha deals with the law; agada with the meaning of the law. Halacha deals with subjects that can be expressed literally; agada introduces us to a realm which lies beyond the range of expression. Halacha teaches us how to perform common acts; agada tells us how to participate in the eternal drama. Halacha gives us knowledge; agada gives us aspiration.

336

God in search of man

Halacha gives us the norms for action; agada, the vision of the ends of living. Halacha prescribes, agada suggests; halacha decrees, agada inspires; halacha is definite; agada is allusive.

When Isaac blessed Jacob he said: "God give thee the dew of heaven, the fat of the earth, and plenty of corn and wine." Remarked the Midrash: "Dew of heaven is Scripture, the fat of the earth is mishnah, corn is halacha, wine is agada."[1]

Halacha, by necessity, treats with the laws in the abstract, regardless of the totality of the person. It is agada that keeps on reminding that the purpose of performance is to transform the performer, that the purpose of observance is to train us in achieving spiritual ends. "It is well known that the purpose of all mitsvot is to purify the heart, for the heart is the essence."[2] The chief aim and purpose of the mitsvot performed with our body is to arouse our attention to the mitsvot that are fulfilled with the mind and heart, for these are the pillars on which the service of God rests.[3]

To maintain that the essence of Judaism consists exclusively of halacha is as erroneous as to maintain that the essence of Judaism consists exclusively of agada. The interrelationship of halacha and agada is the very heart of Judaism.[4] Halacha without agada is dead, agada without halacha is wild.

QUANTITY AND QUALITY

Halacha thinks in the category of quantity; agada is the category of quality. Agada maintains that he who saves one human life is as if he had saved all mankind. In the eyes of him whose first category is the category of quantity, one man is less than two men, but in the eyes of God one life is worth as much as all of life. Halacha speaks of the estimable and measurable dimensions of our deeds, informing us how *much* we must perform in order to fulfill our duty, about the size, capacity, or content of the doer and the deed. Agada deals with the immeasurable, inward aspect of living, telling us *how* we must think and feel; *how* rather than *how much* we must do to fulfill our duty; the manner, not only the content, is important. To halacha the quantity decides; agada, for which quality is the ultimate standard, is not dazzled by either the number or the magnitude of good deeds but stresses the spirit, *kavanah,* dedication, purity. Agada therefore looks for inwardness rather than for the outer garments.

HALACHA WITHOUT AGADA

To reduce Judaism to law, to halacha, is to dim its light, to pervert its essence and to kill its spirit. We have a legacy of agada together with a system of halacha, and although, because of a variety of reasons, that legacy was frequently overlooked and agada became subservient to halacha, halacha is ultimately dependent upon agada. Halacha, the rationalization of living, is not only forced to employ elements which are themselves unreasoned; its ultimate authority depends upon agada. For what is the basis of halacha? The statement "Moses received the Torah from Sinai." Yet this statement does not express a halachic idea. For halacha deals with what man ought to do, with that which man can translate into action, with things which are definite and concrete, and anything that lies beyond man's scope is not an object of halacha. The event at Sinai, the mystery of revelation, belongs to the sphere of agada. Thus while the content of halacha is subject to its own reasoning, its authority is derived from agada.

Halacha does not deal with the ultimate level of existence. The law does not create in us the motivation to love and to fear God, nor is it capable of endowing us with the power to overcome evil and to resist its temptations, nor with the loyalty to fulfill its precepts. It supplies the weapons, it points the way; the fighting is left to the soul of man.

The code of conduct is like the score to a musician. Rules, principles, forms may be taught; insight, feeling, the sense of rhythm must come from within. Ultimately, then, the goal of religious life is quality rather than quantity, not only *what* is done, but *how* it is done.

338

A philosophy of Judaism

Obedience to the letter of the law regulates our daily living, but such obedience must not stultify the spontaneity of our inner life. When the law becomes petrified and our observance mechanical, we in fact violate and distort its very spirit. He who does not know that observance of the law means constant decision is a *foolish pietist*. "What is a foolish pietist? A woman is drowning in the river, and he says: It is improper for me to look upon her and rescue her."[5]

Halacha is an *answer* to a question, namely: What does God ask of me? The moment that question dies in the heart, the answer becomes meaningless. That question, however, is agadic, spontaneous, personal. It is an outburst of insight, longing, faith. It is not given; it must come about. The task of religious teaching is to be a midwife and bring about the birth of the question. Many religious teachers are guilty of ignoring the vital role of the question and condoning spiritual sterility. But the soul is never calm. Every human being is pregnant with problems in a preconceptual form. Most of us do not know how to phrase our quest for meaning, our concern for the ultimate. Without guidance, our concern for the ultimate is not thought through and what we express is premature and penultimate, a miscarriage of the spirit.

The question is not immutable in form. Every generation must express the question in its own way. In this sense agada may be employed as denoting all religious thinking in the tradition of Judaism.

It would be a fatal error to isolate the law, to disconnect it from the perplexities, cravings, and aspirations of the soul, from spontaneity and the totality of the person. In the spiritual crisis of the modern Jew the problem of faith takes precedence over the problem of law. Without faith, inwardness and the power of appreciation, the law is meaningless.

AGADA WITHOUT HALACHA

To reduce Judaism to inwardness, to agada, is to blot out its light, to dissolve its essence and to destroy its reality. Indeed, the surest way to forfeit agada is to abolish halacha. They can only survive in symbiosis. Without halacha agada loses its substance, its character, its source of inspiration, its security against becoming secularized.

By inwardness alone we do not come close to God.* The purest intentions, the finest sense of devotion, the noblest spiritual aspirations are fatuous when not realized in action. Spiritualism is a way for angels, not for man. There is only one function that can take place without the aid of external means: dreaming. When dreaming, man is almost detached from concrete reality. Yet spiritual life is not a dream and is in constant need of action. Action is the verification of the spirit. Does friendship consist of mere emotion? Of indulgence in feeling? Is it not always in need of tangible, material means of expression? The life of the spirit too needs concrete actions for its actualization. The body must not be left alone; the spirit must be fulfilled in the flesh. The spirit is decisive; but it is life, all of life, where the spirit is at stake. To consecrate our tongue and our hands we need extraordinary means of pedagogy.

It is impossible to decide whether in Judaism supremacy belongs to halacha or to agada, to the lawgiver or to the Psalmist. The Rabbis may have sensed the problem. Rab said: The world was created for the sake of David, so that he might sing hymns and psalms to God. Samuel said: The world was created for the sake of Moses, so that he might receive the Torah.[6]

A view of the supremacy of agada is reflected in the following tradition: It is said of Rabbi Yohanan ben Zakkai that his studies included all fields of Jewish learning, *great matters or small matters.* *Great matters* mean *ma'aseh merkabah* (mystical doctrines), *small matters* the discussions of *Abaye* and *Raba* (legal interpretations).[7] Here the study of the law is called "a small matter" compared with the st dy of mystical wisdom.[8]

Maimonides, one of the greatest scholars of the law of all times, declares: "It is more precious to me to teach some of the fundamentals of our religion than any of the other things I study."[9]

* See above, pp. 293-97.

God in search of man

Jewish thinking and living can only be adequately understood in terms of a dialectic pattern, containing opposite or contrasted properties. As in a magnet, the ends of which have opposite magnetic qualities, these terms are opposite to one another and exemplify a *polarity* which lies at the very heart of Judaism, the polarity of ideas and events, of mitsvah and sin, of kavanah and deed, of regularity and spontaneity, of uniformity and individuality, of halacha and agada, of law and inwardness, of love and fear, of understanding and obedience, of joy and discipline, of the good and the evil drive, of time and eternity, of this world and the world to come, of revelation and response, of insight and information, of empathy and self-expression, of creed and faith, of the word and that which is beyond words, of man's quest for God and God in search of man. Even God's relation to the world is characterized by the polarity of justice and mercy, providence and concealment, the promise of reward and the demand to serve Him for His sake. Taken abstractedly, all these terms seem to be mutually exclusive, yet in actual living they involve each other; the separation of the two is fatal to both. There is no halacha without agada, and no agada without halacha. We must neither disparage the body, nor sacrifice the spirit. The body is the discipline, the pattern, the law; the spirit is inner devotion, spontaneity, freedom. The body without the spirit is a corpse; the spirit without the body is a ghost. Thus a mitsvah is both a discipline and an inspiration, an act of obedience and an experience of joy, a yoke and a prerogative. Our task is to learn how to maintain a harmony between the demands of halacha and the spirit of agada.

Since each of the two principles moves in the opposite direction, equilibrium can only be maintained if both are of equal force. But such a condition is rarely attained. Polarity is an essential trait of all things. Tension, contrast, and contradiction characterize all of reality. In the language of the *Zohar,* this world is called *alma deperuda,* "the world of separation." Discrepancy, contention, ambiguity, and ambivalence afflict all of life, including the study of the Torah; even the sages of the Talmud disagree on many details of the law.[10]

THE TENSION BETWEEN HALACHA AND AGADA

There are situations when the relationship between law and inwardness, discipline and delight, becomes gravely unbalanced. In their illustrious fear of desecrating the spirit of the divine command, the Rabbis established a level of observance which, in modern society, is within the reach of exalted souls but not infrequently beyond the grasp of ordinary men. Must halacha continue to ignore the voice of agada?

"It has been foretold in the Bible that someday Ephraim will not be jealous of Judah and Judah will not harass Ephraim (Isaiah 11: 13). These two types (tribes) are always in conflict. Ephraim has been appointed by God to concentrate himself on the law and to be devoted to the commandments. This is why the prophet warns the people of Israel to observe the law strictly, 'Lest he break out like fire in the house of Joseph' (Amos 5:6).

"Judah has been appointed to concentrate on God and to be attached to Him in all his ways. Therefore Judah is not satisfied to know the mere law but looks for God to reveal to him the depths of truth beyond the law itself. (For it is possible in law for a verdict to be correct according to the information which is available to the judges and yet to go against the truth. Cf. *Shevuot* 29a, for example).

"Judah refuses to be content with routine observance or perfunctory faith. Not content to do today what he did yesterday, he desires to find new light in His commandments every day. This insistence on fresh light sometimes drives Judah into doing actions for the sake of God which are against the strict law.

"But in the future, we have been promised that Ephraim and Judah will no longer contend. God will show Ephraim that Judah's actions, even when they go outside the limits of the law, are always for His sake and not for any impure motive, and then there will be genuine understanding and peace between them."[11]

342

A philosophy of Judaism

The tension between regularity and spontaneity, between the fixed pattern of the law and the inwardness of the person, has often been a source of embarrassment and agony. We are not always ready to rise to a level from which we could respond, for example, to the grandeur of our liturgy. But the law expects us to confront that grandeur thrice daily. The words, the forms, remain the same, yet we are told that a sacred act should be done for the first time, as it were. The voice proclaimed: "These words which I command thee *this day* shall be upon thy heart" (Deuteronomy 6:6). "They are not to be regarded as an old set of ordinances . . . but as new words toward which men eagerly rush to hear them"; new as if they were given *this day, today.*[12]

Trying to remain loyal to both aspects of Jewish living, we discover that the pole of regularity is stronger than the pole of spontaneity, and, as a result, there is a perpetual danger of our observance and worship becoming mere habit, a mechanical performance. The fixed pattern and regularity of our services tend to stifle the spontaneity of devotion. Our great problem, therefore, is how not to let the principle of regularity (keva) impair the power of spontaneity (kavanah). It is a problem that concerns the very heart of religious living, and is as easy to solve as other central problems of existence. It is a part of human freedom to face that challenge and to create an answer in every situation, every day of our life. Palliatives may be found, but no cure to polarity is available in this "world of separation."

The simplest way to obviate the problem is to abrogate the principle of regularity, to worship only when we are touched by the spirit and to observe only what is relevant to our minds. But in abrogating regularity we deplete spontaneity. Our spiritual resources are not inexhaustible. What may seem to be spontaneous is in truth a response to an occasion. The soul would remain silent if it were not for the summons and reminder of the law. There may be mo-

343

ments in which the soul fails to respond, but abiding at the threshold of the holy we are unconsciously affected by its power.

We cannot rely on the inspirations of the heart if we detach ourselves from the inspiration of the prophets. Our own moments of illumination are brief, sporadic and rare. In the long interims the mind is often dull, bare and vapid. There is hardly a soul that can radiate more light than it receives. To perform a mitsvah is to meet the spirit. The spirit, however, is not something we can acquire once and for all but something we must be with. For this reason the Jewish way of life is to reiterate the ritual, to meet the spirit again and again, the spirit in oneself and the spirit that hovers over all beings.

The spirit rests not only on our achievement, on our goal, but also on our effort, on our way. This is why the very act of going to the house of worship, every day or every seventh day, is a song without words. When done in humility, in simplicity of heart, it is like a child who, eager to hear a song, spreads out the score before its mother. All the child can do is to open the book.[13]

The way to kavanah is through the deed; the way of faith is a way of living. Halacha and agada are correlated: halacha is the string, agada is the bow. When the string is tight the bow will evoke the melody. But the string may jar in the fumbler's hand.

THE VALUE OF HABIT

Being bound to an order and stability of observance, to a discipline of worship at set hours and fixed forms is a celestial routine. Nature does not cease to be natural because of its being subject to regularity of seasons. Loyalty to external forms, dedication of the will is itself a form of worship. The mitsvot sustain their halo even when our minds forget to light in us the attentiveness to the holy. The path of loyalty to the routine of sacred living runs along the borderline of the spirit; though being outside, one remains very close to the spirit. Routine holds us in readiness for the moments in which the soul enters into accord with the spirit.

While love is hibernating, our loyal deeds speak. It is right that the good actions should become a habit, that the preference of justice should become our second nature; even though it is not native to the self. A good person is not he who does the right thing, but he who is in the habit of doing the right thing.

The absence of understanding at the moment of performing a ritual act does not vitiate the meaningfulness of the act. A father laboring to earn a living for his children fulfills the good regardless of whether his mind is constantly bent upon the moral intention of his deeds. Once a person decides to feed a child every day, his daily act is good regardless of whether it is always accompanied by an awareness of its moral implication. What lends meaning to the acts of ritual is not only the particular intention which is co-temporal with the acts but primarily the decision of faith to accept the ritual way of living. It is that decision—*the general intention,* the basic kavanah—and the accumulated insight throughout many moments of religious experience that bestows devotional meaning upon all ritual acts of our life.

ACTIONS TEACH

It is true that a person may know the acts of loving-kindness, without always knowing the spirit of loving-kindness. Yet it also is true that acts are a challenge to the soul. Indeed, one must be deliberately callous to remain forever deaf to the spirit of the acts he is engaged in performing day after day, year after year. How else can one learn the joy of loving-kindness, if not by enacting it?

Deeds not only follow intention; they also engender kavanah. There is no static polarity of kavanah and deed, of devotion and action. The deed may bring out what is dormant in the mind, and acts in which an idea is lived, moments which are filled with dedication make us eloquent in a way which is not open to the naked mind. Kavanah comes into being with the deed. Actions teach.

"Man is affected by all his actions; his heart and all his thoughts follow the deeds which he does, whether good or bad. Though one be altogether wicked at heart and all his inclinations be always evil, if he makes a valiant effort to continually study the Torah and follow its commandments, even if not out of pure motives, he will in course of time incline toward the good, and, despite his engaging in religious pursuits out of impure motives, he will come to follow them for their own sake. . . . On the other hand a perfectly righteous person, whose heart is upright and sincere, who takes delight in the Torah and its commandments, but engages in offensive matters— say, for example, that the king compelled him to pursue an evil occupation—if he devotes himself to that business all the time, he will ultimately turn from his righteousness and become wicked."[14]

This explains why the problem of particular kavanah is *secondary* to the problem of *general piety*. Love and fear at all times decide the value of every particular act.

Insistence upon receiving the prize of stimulation in return for what we are doing would be a misleading notion. True riches are not required *quid pro quo*. To do the holy is its own reward. We receive all when we ask for nothing.

Inspiration is a gift. It cannot be willed into existence nor coerced into being. Piety is unconditional loyalty to the holy. The pious man is he who seeks attachment to the holy. Inspiration is a promise unto man. The holy when done wholeheartedly bestows light on a person, but it may also remain hidden.

"Happy are the mass of believers . . . who do not seek to be too clever in their relation to God, but follow the law of God with simplicity."[15]

NOTES FOR CHAPTER 33

[1] *Genesis Rabba* to 27:28.
[2] *Kad Hakemach,* Shavuot.
[3] Bahya Ibn Paquda, *Duties of the Heart,* ed. Haymson, v. IV, p. 91.
[4] Rabbi Samuel Edels composed two separate commentaries, one dealing with the legal and the other with the agadic portions of the Talmud. In his preface, however, he expressed regret at having divorced the two, for both are aspects of the one Torah.
[5] *Sotah* 21b.
[6] *Sanhedrin* 98b.
[7] *Sukkah* 28a.

A philosophy of Judaism

8 This is definitely the meaning of the passage as understood by Maimonides, *Mishneh Torah, Yesode Hatorah,* iv, 3. See also Maimonides, *The Guide of the Perplexed,* Book III, ch. 51; A. J. Heschel, *Maimonides,* Berlin, 1935, ch. IX; Ibn Adret, in *'En Jacob,* Wilna, 1883, on *Sukkah* 28a, and *Responsa,* I, 93.

9 *Commentary on the Mishnah, Berachot,* 9, 5.

10 "God has also set one thing against the other; the good against the evil, and the evil against the good; good from good and evil from good; the good marks out the evil and the evil marks out the good; good is reserved for the good ones and evil is reserved for the evil ones." *Yetsirah,* vi, 6. The passage in Ecclesiastes 7:14, "God has made the one as well as the other," inspired a medieval Jewish author to compose a treatise (*Temurah*) for the purpose of proving that contrast and contradiction are necessary to existence. "All things cleave to one another, the pure and the impure. There is no purity except through impurity; a mystery which is expressed in the words: *a clean thing out of an unclean.* (Job 14:4). The brain is contained in a shell, a shell which will not be broken until that time when the dead shall rise again. Then will the shell be broken and the light shine out into the world from the brain, without any covering on it." *Zohar,* vol. II, p. 69b. There is a polarity in everything except God. For all tension ends in God. He is beyond all dichotomies.

11 Rabbi Mordecai Joseph of Isbitsa, *Me Hashiloah,* Vienna, 1860, pp. 14d-15a.

12 *Sifre,* ad locum.

13 A. J. Heschel, *Man's Quest for God,* p. 107.

14 Rabbi Aaron Halevi of Barcelona, *Sefer Hachinuch,* mitsvah 20.

15 Albo, *Ikkarim* III, 27.

34 The Meaning of Observance

ORIGIN AND PRESENCE

A serious difficulty is the problem of the meaning of Jewish observance. The modern Jew cannot accept the way of static obedience as a short cut to the mystery of the divine will. His religious situation is not conducive to an attitude of intellectual or spiritual surrender. He is not ready to sacrifice his liberty on the altar of loyalty to the spirit of his ancestors. He will only respond to a demonstration that there is meaning to be found in what is expected of him. His primary difficulty is not in his inability to comprehend *the divine origin* of the law; his essential difficulty is in his inability to sense *the presence of divine meaning* in the fulfillment of the law.

THE MEANING OF OBSERVANCE

It is an ancient topic of Jewish speculation: what are the reasons, the rational grounds, for Jewish observance?

There are many perspectives from which observance may be judged. The sociological: does it contribute to the good of society or to the survival of the people? The esthetic: does it enhance our sense of form and beauty? The moral: does it help us to realize the good? There is also the dogmatic: observance is the will of God and no other justification is called for. Since Jewish observance embraces the totality of existence, a *synoptic approach* would bring forth its

348

relevance in terms of all higher values, and would open a comprehensive view of its meaning.

Judaism is concerned with the happiness of the individual as well as with the survival of the Jewish people, with the redemption of all men and with the will of one God. It claims, however, that happiness is contingent upon faithfulness to God; that the unique importance of the survival of the people is in its being a partner to a covenant with God; that the redemption of all men depends upon their serving His will. The perspective, therefore, from which the individual, the community and all mankind are judged is that of religious insight and conviction. Without minimizing the profound relevance of other perspectives, we will analyze the problem of the meaning of observance from the point of view developed in the previous sections of this book and try to answer the question of how observance is related to religious insight.

As said above, some of the basic theological presuppositions of Judaism cannot be completely justified in terms of human reason. Its conception of the nature of man as having been created in the likeness of God, its conception of God and history, of prayer and even of morality, defy some of the realizations at which we have honestly arrived at the end of our analysis and scrutiny. The demands of piety are a mystery before which man is reduced to reverence and silence. In a technological society, when religion becomes a function, piety too is an instrument to satisfy man's needs. We must therefore be particularly careful not to fall into the habit of looking at religion as if it were a machine or an organization which can be run according to one's calculations.

The problem of how to live as a Jew cannot be solved in terms of common sense and common experience. The order of Jewish living is a spiritual one; it has a spiritual logic of its own which cannot be apprehended unless its basic terms are lived and appreciated. Its meaning can be better comprehended in personal response than in detached definitions. Life must be *earned spiritually,* not only materially. We must keep alive the sense of wonder through deeds of wonder.

349

What kind of meaning do we look for? There is no understanding of meaning as such. Meaning is always related to a system of meanings. The kind of meaning we look for depends on the kind of system we choose. The most common system is that of psychology. A mitsvah is considered to be meaningful when proved to be capable of satisfying a personal need.

However, the essence of religion does not lie in the satisfaction of a human need. As long as man sees religion as a source of satisfaction for his own needs, it is not God whom he serves but his own self.[1] Such satisfaction can be obtained from civilization, which supplies abundant means to gratify our needs.

Indeed, most of our attention is given to the expedient, to that which is conducive to our advantage and which would enhance our ability to exploit the resources of this planet. If our philosophy were a projection of man's actual behavior, we would have to define the value of the earth as a source of supply for our industries, and the ocean as a fish pond. However, as we have seen, there is more than one aspect of nature that commands our attention. We go out to meet the world not only by the way of expediency but also by the way of wonder. In the first we accumulate information in order to dominate; in the second we deepen our appreciation in order to respond. Power is the language of expediency; poetry the language of wonder.

He who goes to pray is not intent upon enhancing his store of knowledge; he who performs a ritual does not expect to advance his interests. Sacred deeds are designed to make living *compatible with our sense of the ineffable*. The mitsvot are forms of expressing in deeds the appreciation of the ineffable. They are terms of the spirit in which we allude to that which is beyond reason. To look for rational explanations, to scrutinize the mitsvot in terms of common sense is to quench their intrinsic meaning. What would be the value of proving that the observance of the dietary laws is helpful in the promotion of health, that keeping the Sabbath is conducive to hap-

A philosophy of Judaism

piness? It is not *utility* that we seek in religion but *eternity*. The criterion of religion is not in its being in agreement with our *common sense* but in its being compatible with our *sense of the ineffable*. The purpose of religion is not to satisfy the needs we feel but to create in us the need of serving ends, of which we otherwise remain oblivious.

SPIRITUAL MEANING

The problem of ethics is, what is the ideal or principle of conduct that is *rationally* justifiable? To religion the problem of living is, what is the ideal or principle of living that is *spiritually* justifiable? The legitimate question concerning the forms of Jewish observance is the question: Are they spiritually meaningful?

We should, therefore, not evaluate the mitsvot by the amount of rational meaning we may discover at their basis. Religion is not within but beyond the limits of mere reason; its task is not to compete with reason, to be a source of speculative ideas, but to aid us where reason is of little aid. Its meaning must be understood in terms compatible with the sense of the ineffable. Frequently, where concepts fail, where rational understanding ends, the meaning of observance begins. Its purpose is not to serve hygiene, happiness or the vitality of man; its purpose is to add holiness to hygiene, grandeur to happiness, spirit to vitality.

Spiritual meaning is not always limpid; transparency is the quality of glass, while diamonds are distinguished by refractive power and the play of prismatic colors.

Indeed, any reason we may advance for our loyalty to the Jewish order of living merely points to one of its many facets. To say that the mitsvot have meaning is less accurate than saying that they lead us to wells of emergent meaning, to experiences which are full of hidden brilliance of the holy, suddenly blazing in our thoughts.

Those who, in order to save the Jewish way of life, bring its meaning under the hammer, sell it in the end to the lowest bidder. The highest values are not in demand and are not saleable on the marketplace. In spiritual life some experiences are like a camera obscura, through which light has to enter in order to form an image upon the mind, the image of ineffable intelligibility. Insistence upon explaining and relating the holy to the relative and functional is like lighting a candle in the camera.

Works of piety are like works of art. They are functional, they serve a purpose, but their essence is intrinsic. A mitsvah is the perpetuation of an insight or an act of bringing together the passing with the everlasting, the momentary with the eternal.

If insights of the individual are to be conveyed to others and to become a part of social life, or even if they are to be stored up effectively for one's own future understanding, they must assume the forms of deeds, of mitsvot.

Religion without mitsvot is an experience without the power of expression, a sense of mystery without the power of sanctification; a question without an answer. Without the Torah we have only deeds that dream of God; with the Torah we have mitsvot that utter God in acts.

When Rabbi Yohanan ben Zakkai asked his disciples, "Which is the worst quality a man should shun?" Rabbi Simeon answered, *"One who borrows and does not repay.* It is the same whether one borrows from man or from God."[2] Perhaps this is the essence of human misery: to forget that life is a gift as well as a trust.

AN ANSWER TO THE MYSTERY

"How can I repay unto the Lord all His bountiful dealings toward me?" How to answer the mystery that surrounds us, the ineffable that calls on our souls? This is, indeed, the universal theme of religion. The world is full of wonder. Who will answer? Who will care? Our reverence is no answer. The more deeply we revere the more clearly we realize the inadequacy of mere reverence. Is it enough to praise, to extol that which is beyond all praise? What is the worth of reverence? Faint are all our songs and praises. If

God in search of man

we could only give away all we have, all we are. The only answer to the ineffable is a mode of living compatible with the ineffable.

Human life is a point where mind and mystery meet. This is why man cannot live by his reason alone, nor can he thrive on mystery alone. To surrender to the mystery is fatalism, to withdraw into reason is solipsism. Man is driven to commune with that which is beyond the mystery. The ineffable in him seeks a way to that which is beyond the ineffable.

Israel was taught how to accost Him who is beyond the mystery. Beyond the mind is mystery, but beyond the mystery is mercy. Out of the darkness comes a voice disclosing that the ultimate mystery is not an enigma but the God of mercy; that the Creator of all is the "Father in Heaven." The ultimate question became a specific commandment. A mitsvah is where mind and mystery mate to create an image of an attribute of God. A sacred deed is where earth and heaven meet.

The heavens are the heavens of the Lord, but the earth hath He given to the children of man (Psalms 115:16). "It is as if a king had decreed that the citizens of Rome should not visit Syria, nor the citizens of Syria visit Rome. Thus when God created the world, He decreed, *'The heavens are the heavens of the Lord; but the earth hath He given to the children of man.'* Yet, when He was about to give the Torah, He rescinded the first decree and said: 'Those who are below shall ascend to those on high, while those who are on high shall descend to those that are below and I will begin,' as it is said, *And the Lord came down upon Mount Sinai* (Exodus 19:20), and later it is written: *And unto Moses he said: Come up unto the Lord* (Exodus 24:11)."[3]

To outsiders the mitsvot may appear like hieroglyphic signs, obscure, absurd, chains of lifeless legalism. To those who do not strive to share in the unexampled and surpassing, observance may become dreary, irksome routine. To those who want to tie their lives to the lasting, the *mitsvot* are an art, pleasing, expressive, full of condensed significance. "Thy statutes have been my songs," said the Psalmist (119:54), statutes, *huqim,* traditionally denoting precepts for which no reasons can be found. In the Jewish mind the action sings and regularity of fulfillment is the rhythm by which we utter our tunes. Our dogmas are allusions, intimations; yet our actions are definitions.

Explanations for the mitsvot are like insights of art criticism; the interpretation can never rival the creative acts of the artist. Reason in the realm of religion is like a whetstone that makes iron sharp, as the saying goes, though unable itself to cut.

There is only one way to appraise the mitsvot: to relate the adventures of one's soul among the thoughts and deeds of eternal Israel rather than to guess oneself into the original and essential intentions of the law.

Explanations of the mitsvot come and go; theories change with the temper of the age, but the song of the mitsvot continues. Explanations are translations; they are both useful and inadequate. A translator of the Iliad into German once remarked, "Dear reader, study Greek and throw my translation into the fire."[4] The same applies to the holy: explanations are not substitutes.

Significantly, the Hebrew term for the explanation of the mitvsot is *ta'am,* or *ta'ame hamitsvot.*[5] Yet *ta'am* means also taste, or flavor. It is the flavor that a person perceives in doing a mitsvah which communicates its meaning.

The true meaning is not to be found in a stagnant concept, fixed and determined once and for all. The exclusive meaning-flavor is not something formulations can convey. It is born with the act of fulfillment, and our appreciation grows with our experience.

Mitsvot are not only expressions of meanings given once and for all, but ways of evoking new meaning again and again. They are acts of inspiration rather than acts of compliance. They are the songs that express our wonder.

A philosophy of Judaism

In the words of Rabbi Yohanan, "If one reads Scripture without a melody or repeats the Mishnah without a tune, of him Scripture says, *Wherefore I gave them also statutes that were not good* (Ezekiel 20:25)."[6] A mitsvah without a melody is devoid of soul; Torah without a tune is devoid of spirit. Kavanah is the art of setting a deed to inner music. "Come before His presence with singing" (Psalms 100:2). In singing we enter His presence.

What is a noble deed? A hungry soul on the rise. To some the act is fresh and precious, though its meaning is partly here, partly beyond the stars. To others it is like disposing of a burden, leaving a wake of regret and frustration. The test of *kavanah* is in the joy it calls forth, in the happiness it incurs. "Rejoice the soul of thy servant, for unto Thee O Lord do I lift up my soul" (Psalms 86:4). He who knows how to lift up his soul above the pettiness of momentary meaning will indeed receive the blessing of joy.

What we accomplish is infinitely humble, moving but an inch toward a distant goal. But what we attempt is noble: to lend a sacred aura to common deeds. What is a mitsvah? A deed in the form of a prayer. Jewish observance is a liturgy of deeds.

It is sacrilege to grieve when the task calls, and God is grateful in advance for the service we shall render unto Him. The fruition of a sacred deed is in the joy the soul reveals. The Psalmist (100:2) proclaims: "Serve Him with joy." His service and joy are one and the same.

To meet a mitsvah is to discover His presence as it is meant for me, and in His presence is "fullness of joy." What is piety? "A song every day, a song every day."[7] Every morning we begin with a prayer: "Make sweet, we beseech Thee, O Lord our God, the words of Thy Torah in our mouth."

There is a fountain in a sacred deed. It plays an eternal tune to the soul that washes its own wilderness away.

The deed and the reward must come together. "Be not like servants who serve the master for the sake of receiving a reward, but be like servants who serve the master without the expectation of receiving a reward."[8] The reward of a mitsvah is eternity. But do not be like those who expect eternity to follow the deed: in the life to come. Eternity is in the deed, in the doing.[9] The reward of a mitsvah is the mitsvah itself.[10]

REMINDERS

As said above, the Jewish way of living is an answer to a supreme human problem, namely: How must man, a being who is in essence the likeness of God, think, feel and act? How can he live in a way compatible with the presence of God? Unless we are aware of the problem, we are unable to appreciate the answer.

All mitsvot are means of evoking in us the awareness of living in the neighborhood of God, of living in the holy dimension. They call to mind the inconspicuous mystery of things and acts, and are reminders of our being the stewards, rather than the landlords of the universe; reminders of the fact that man does not live in a spiritual wilderness, that *every act* of man is an encounter of the human and the holy.

All mitsvot first of all express reverence. They are indications of our awareness of God's eternal presence, celebrating His presence in action. The benedictions are in the present tense. We say, "Blessed be Thou Who *creates* . . . Who *brings forth*." To say a benediction is to be aware of His continuous creation.

What are all prophetic utterance if not an expression of God's anxiety for man and His concern with man's integrity? A reminder of God's stake in human life; a reminder that there is no privacy? No one can conceal himself, no one can be out of His sight. He dwells with the Israel "in the midst of their uncleanness" (Leviticus 16:16). Living is not a private affair of the individual. Living is what man does with God's time, what man does with God's world.

To the vulgar mind, a deed consists of the self trying to exploit the non-self. To the pious man, a deed is an encounter of the human and the holy, of man's will and God's world. Both are hewn from the same rock and destined to be parts of one great mosaic.

There is no dichotomy between the happiness of man and the designs of God. To discover the absence of that dichotomy, to live that identity, is the true reward of religious living. God shares man's joy, if man is open to God's concern. The satisfaction of a human need is a dedication to a divine end.

The world is torn by conflicts, by folly, by hatred. Our task is to cleanse, to illumine, to repair. Every deed is either a clash or an aid in the effort of redemption. Man is not one with God, not even with his true self. Our task is to bring eternity into time, to clear in the wilderness a way, to make plain in the desert a highway for God. "Happy is the man in whose heart are the highways" (Psalm 84:6).

What is the motive behind Jewish living? It is, perhaps, the yearning to establish an accord of the self and His will, a going through a wasteland toward the only flower on the distant peak. It is as if I were the only man on the globe and God, too, were alone, waiting for me.

ATTACHMENT TO THE HOLY

Before fulfilling a mitsvah we pray: "Blessed be Thou . . . Who hast sanctified us with His mitsvot . . ." The meaning of a mitsvah is in its power of sanctification.

What is a sacred deed? An encounter with the divine; a way of living in fellowship with God; a flash of holiness in the darkness of profanity; the birth of greater love; endowment with deeper sensibility.

The mitsvot are formative. The soul grows by noble deeds. The soul is illumined by sacred acts. Indeed, the purpose of all mitsvot is to refine man.[11] They were given for the benefit of man: to protect and to ennoble him, to discipline and to inspire him. We ennoble the self by disclosing the divine. God is hiding in the world and our task is to let the divine emerge from our deeds.

It has been observed that the last two letters of the word mitsvah are the same as the last two of the Tetragrammaton, the Ineffable Name, and that its first two letters are interchangeable, in the alphabetic order of A-T, B-Sh, with the first two letters of the Tetragrammaton. A mitsvah is the Ineffable Name. His name is both concealed and revealed in our deeds.

The purpose of observance is not to give expression to what we feel or what we think. In giving expression to a thought or a feeling we delegate to words what we bear in our souls. Expressions are substitutions, vicarious acts. We say, and we part from what we say. The purpose of observance is not to express but to *be* what we feel or think, to unite our existence with that which we feel or think; to be close to the reality that lies beyond all thought and feeling; to be attached to the holy.

THE ECSTASY OF DEEDS

To do a mitsvah is to outdo oneself, to go beyond one's own needs and to illumine the world. But whence should come fire to illumine the world? Time and again we discover how blank, how dim and abrupt is the light that comes from within. There is not enough strength within our power to transcend ourselves, to ensoul our deeds. Our strenuous effort is too feeble to outsoar the petty movements of the ego.

But there is *an ecstasy of deeds,* luminous moments in which we are raised by overpowering deeds above our own will; moments filled with outgoing joy, with intense delight. Such exaltation is a gift. To him who strives with heart and soul to give himself to God and who succeeds as far as is *within his power,* the gates of greatness break open and he is able to attain that which is *beyond his power.*[12]

The gift of greatness does not come to those who do not toil to shatter their own smallness. The mitsvah does not conjure holiness out of nothing, it only adds to what man contributes. Nothing will light the wonder in us, when our craving is dormant and our heart both dim and content. We must render kindness to acquire goodness; we must do the good to attain the holy.

The following may be used as an illustration of this thought. "A man planted trees, trimmed their roots, cleared the soil of thorns and weeds, watered the trees when necessary, and applied fertilizers to them; then he prays to God that the trees should yield fruit. But if he neglects tending them and looking after them, he does not deserve that the Creator, blessed be He, should give him fruit from them."[13]

The mitsvah is compared to a lamp (Proverbs 6:23). The purpose of lighting a lamp does not lie in the act itself nor in its immediate effects, namely in the consumption of the oil and the burning of the wick. The real purpose is to produce light. In the same sense, the purpose of performing a mitsvah is in the meaning, in the light which emanates from it. The act is performed by man, but the light emanates from God.[14] Every mitsvah adds holiness to Israel.[15]

The spark of man may be enhanced and inflamed by a flash of God. "If a man sanctifies himself a little, he becomes greatly sanctified. If he sanctify himself below, he becomes sanctified from above."[16] Holiness is not exclusively the product of the soul but the outcome of moments in which God and soul meet in the light of a good deed.

Religion is not given to us once and for all as something to be preserved in a safe-deposit box. It must be re-created all the time. Mitsvot are forms; *to fulfill* a mitsvah means *to fill it with meaning.*

The Psalmist prays:

> The Lord send forth Thy help from holiness,
> And support thee out of Zion.
>   Psalms 20:3

Help comes from holiness. But where is holiness? Is it embodied somewhere in space, in a celestial sphere? This is how the Rabbis interpreted the verse: "The Lord send forth thy help *from the holiness of the deeds* which thou hast done, and support thee out of Zion (*mitsiyon*), from thy distinction in deeds; from the sanctification of the name, from thy sanctifications of deeds which is within thee."[17]

The preciousness that loyalty to the mitsvot bestows upon the life of the individual or the community cannot be fully expressed. Jewish observance gives us cleanliness and what is more: compassion. It gives us health and what is more: holiness. It gives us strength and what is more: an inner world. A world that is often wretched and appalling becomes gentle and enchanting.

NOTES FOR CHAPTER 34

[1] See *Man is Not Alone*, pp. 232ff.
[2] *Abot* 2, 14.
[3] *Exodus Rabba* 12, 3; *Tanhuma* to Exodus 9:22.
[4] Friedrich Leopold von Stollberg, quoted by Franz Rosenzweig, *Jehuda Halevi*, p. 153.
[5] For a history of such attempts, see Isaac Heinemann, *Ta'ame Hamitsvot Besafrut Israel*, Jerusalem, 1942.
[6] *Megillah* 32a.
[7] Compare Rabbi Akiba's statement in *Sanhedrin* 99b.
[8] *Abot* 1, 3.
[9] Rabbi Nahum of Tschernobil, *Meor 'Ainayim*.
[10] *Abot* 4, 2.
[11] *Genesis Rabba*, 44.
[12] Bahya, vol. IV, p. 91.
[13] Bahya, vol. IV, pp. 91-92.
[14] Albo, *Ikkarim*, III, 28.
[15] See *Mekilta* to 22:30; *Sifre* to Numbers 15:40.
[16] *Yoma* 39a.
[17] *Leviticus Rabba* 24, 4.

35 Mitsvah and Sin

If the frequency and intensity with which a word is used may serve as an index of its importance to the mentality of a people, than the word mitsvah is one of supreme importance. Indeed, the role of the term mitsvah in both Hebrew and Yiddish is almost without parallel. Just as salvation is the central concept in Christian piety, so does mitsvah serve as a focus of Jewish religious consciousness. It is, next to Torah, the basic term of Judaism, serving as a general name for both positive and negative rules, for both directives and restrictions.

A definition or paraphrase of the word mitsvah is difficult to frame. In other languages there are separate words for the different meanings which in Hebrew are conveyed by the single word mitsvah. It denotes not only commandment, but also *the law,* man's *obligation* to fulfill the law, and *the act* of fulfilling the obligation or the deed, particularly an act of benevolence or charity.

Its meanings range from the acts performed by the high priest in the Temple to the most humble gesture of kindness to one's fellow man, from acts of external performance to inner attitudes, in relation to others as well as in relation to oneself. It is often used in the wide sense of *religion* or *religious.*[1] It combines all levels of human and spiritual living. Every act done in agreement with the will of God is a mitsvah.[2]

But the scope of meaning of the word mitsvah is even wider. Beyond the meanings it denotes—namely commandment, law, obligation, and deed—it connotes numerous attributes which are implied in addition to its primary meanings. It has the connotation of goodness, value, virtue, meritoriousness, piety, and even holiness. Thus while it is possible to say a good, virtuous, valuable, meritorious, pious, or holy deed, it would be a tautology to say a good, meritorious, pious, or holy mitsvah.

In Hebrew we speak of the mitsvah as if it were endowed with sensible properties, as if it were a concrete entity, a thing. We say, for example, "to appropriate mitsvot," "to acquire mitsvot," "to pursue mitsvot," "to be well-laden with mitsvot";[3] "even the ignorant men are replete with mitsvot as a pomegranate (is replete with grains)";[4] "Adorn thyself with mitsvot before Him."[5] Every mitsvah brings "a good angel into being." Mitsvot are "man's friends,"[6] his true "offspring," his defenders in the world to come,[7] his garments, his form. Without mitsvot one is naked.[8] It is because of the unique conception of the mitsvah as an almost concrete entity that it is hard to find an equivalent for it in other languages. Three translations of the verse in Proverbs 10:8 will illustrate the point. It says: "The wise in heart *yiḳah* mitsvot." The two Hebrew words are rendered in King James "will receive commandments," in Moffatt "defers to authority," in the American Translation "obeys the laws," in the Revised Standard Version "will heed commandments." The Rabbis retained the sense for the concreteness and understood the verse to mean, "the wise in heart will *acquire* mitsvot."

The basic term of Jewish living, therefore, is mitsvah rather than law (*din*). The law serves us as a source of knowledge about what is and what is not to be regarded as a mitsvah. The act itself, what a person does with that knowledge, is determined not only by what the law describes but also by that which the law cannot enforce: the freedom of the heart.

The supreme dignity of mitsvah is of such spiritual power that it gained a position of primacy over its antonym, namely, sin or *averah*. Even the sin of Adam was described as a loss of a mitsvah. After the forbidden fruit, we are told, their eyes were unclosed and

362

A philosophy of Judaism

"they knew that they were naked" (Genesis 3:7). "One mitsvah was entrusted to them, and they had stripped themselves of it."[9]

To the mind of the Jew mitsvah bears more reality and is a term more frequently and more prominently used than *averah*. In the Christian vocabulary the frequency and importance of the two terms is just the reverse. Christianity has not taken over the idea of mitsvah and, as we have seen, there is no precise equivalent for it in Western languages. On the other hand, the term "sin" has assumed the connotation of something substantial, a meaning not implied in *averah*.

Life revolves around the right and the wrong deed, but we have been trained to be more *mitsvah-conscious* than *averah* or sin-conscious.[10]

In Yiddish, the idioms of which are revealing of the Jewish way of thinking, to do a mitsvah means to acquire a spiritual gain. *Gib mir a gloss vasser vest hobn in mir a mitsvah* means: give me a glass of water, you will acquire a spiritual gain. To do an *averah* means to waste, to expend to no purpose. *Du redst tsu a toybn s'iz an aveyre (averah) di reid* means you talk to a deaf person—you are wasting words.

"FOR WE HAVE SINNED"

Both poles, mitsvah and sin, are real. We are taught to be *mitsvah-conscious* in regard to the present moment, to be mindful of the constant opportunity to do the good. We are also taught to be *sin-conscious* in regard to the past, to realize and to remember our failures and transgressions. The power of both mitsvah and sin must be fully apprehended. The exclusive fear of sin may lead to a deprecation of works; the exclusive appreciation of mitsvah may lead to self-righteousness. The first may result in a denial of the relevance of history, in an overly eschatological view; the second in a denial of Messianism, in a secular optimism. Against both deviations Judaism warns repeatedly.

Two things must always be present to our minds: God and our

own sins (Psalms 16:8; 51:5). Three times daily we pray, *Forgive us, our Father, for we have sinned; pardon us, our King, for we have transgressed*. According to a Talmudic saying, every soul when about to be born into this world, is admonished: "Be righteous, and be never wicked; and even if all the world tells you, 'you are righteous' consider yourself wicked."[11] Indeed, "who can say: I have made my heart clean, I am pure from my sin?" (Proverbs 20:9).

The burden of sins is light to those who are oblivious. It was not light to him who said, "Out of the depths have I called Thee, O Lord. . . . If Thou shouldst mark iniquities, who could stand?" (Psalms 130:1,3).

Twice daily we are told, "Do not follow after your own heart and your own eyes, which you are inclined to go after wantonly" (Numbers 15:39). The house of Israel says, "Our transgressions and our sins are upon us, and we waste away because of them; how, then, can we live?" (Ezekiel 33:10). Indeed, "we are neither so arrogant nor so hardened as to say before Thee, O Lord our God and God of our fathers, 'we are righteous and have not sinned'; verily, we have sinned" (The liturgy of the Day of Atonement).

"THE EVIL DRIVE"

We fail and sin not only in our deeds. We also fail and sin in our hearts. Evil in the heart is the source of evil in deeds. The envy of Cain, the greed of the generation of the Flood, the pride of those who built the Tower of Babel brought misery upon mankind. "Envy, greed, and pride destroy the lives of man."[12] Indeed, this is the diagnosis of the human situation: "The Lord saw that the wickedness of man was great in the earth, and that every drive of the thought of his heart was only evil continually" (Genesis 6:5).

"The wickedness of man" may refer to sinful deeds, but the central part of the diagnosis, repeated in Genesis 8:21, refers to "the drive of the heart." The only one of the Ten Commandments which is said twice and with which they are concluded is: Thou shalt not covet.

Daily we pray, *My God, the soul which Thou hast placed within me is pure.* What must we do to keep it pure? How shall we maintain our integrity in a world where power, success, and money are valued above all else? How shall we control "envy, greed, and pride"? "Thou hast given me a holy soul, but through my deeds I have defiled it," exclaimed Ibn Gabirol.[13]

The soul which we receive is clean, but within it resides a power for evil, "a strange god,"[14] "that seeks constantly to get the upper hand over man and to kill him; and if God did not help him, he could not resist it, as it is said, the wicked watches the righteous, and seeks to slay him."[15] "While men have a strong desire to attain evil ends, they are negligent in the pursuit of what is noble. They are tardy in seeking the good but dally in the paths of frivolity and pleasure. If a vision of greed appears and beckons to them, they invent falsehoods so that they may turn to it. They bolster up arguments to make its obliquities upright, its weaknesses strong, its looseness firm and compact. But when the lamp of truth invitingly shines before them, they frame idle pretexts for refraining from turning to it. They argue against it, declare its courses misleading and contradict its assertions, so as to make it appear inconsistent and thus have an excuse for keeping away from it."[16]

"The Holy One, blessed be He, says to the soul: 'All that I have created in the six days of creation I have created for thy sake alone, and thou goest forth and sinnest!' "[17] "See, I am pure, My abode is pure, My ministers are pure, and the soul I have given thee is pure; if thou returnest it to Me as I am giving it to thee, it will be well, but if not, I shall throw it away."[18]

"THERE IS BUT ONE STEP"

The emphasis upon the consciousness of mitsvah must not in any way weaken our attentiveness to the fact that we are always ready to betray Him, that even while engaged in a righteous act we are exposed to sin. "Be not sure of thyself till the day of thy death," said Hillel.[19] We have been taught that man may be impregnated with the spirit of the holy all the days of his life, yet one moment of carelessness is sufficient to plunge him in the abyss. *There is but one step between me and death* (I Samuel 20:3).

Life is lived on a spiritual battlefield. Man must constantly struggle with "the evil drive," "for man is like unto a rope, one end of which is pulled by God and the other end by Satan." "Woe to me for my *yotser* [Creator], woe to me for my *yetser* [the evil drive]," says a Talmudic epigram.[20] If a man yield to his lower impulses, he is accountable to his Creator; if he obey his Creator, then he is plagued by sinful thoughts.

NOTES FOR CHAPTER 35

[1] *Devar mitsvah* is contrasted with *devar reshut*. Compare *Shabbat* 25b: "Neither an obligation nor a mitsvah but a religiously neutral act."
[2] Rabbi Nahman of Braslav, *Likkute Maharan*, II, 5, 10.
[3] *Sanhedrin* 17a.
[4] *Sanhedrin* 37a.
[5] *Shabbat* 133b.
[6] *Pirke de Rabbi Eliezer*, ch. 34.
[7] *Avoda Zara* 2a.
[8] *Genesis Rabba* 3,7.
[9] *Genesis Rabba*, 19, 17.
[10] Characteristic is the term "replete with mitsvot"; see above, note 4.
[11] *Niddah* 30b.
[12] *Abot* 4, 28.
[13] *Selected Religious Poems*, p. 113.
[14] *Shabbat* 105b.
[15] *Sukkah* 52b.
[16] Bahya Ibn Paguda, *The Duties of the Heart*, vol. I, p. 14.
[17] *Leviticus Rabba*, 4,2.
[18] *Leviticus Rabba*, 18,1; see *Niddah* 30b; *Baba Metsia* 107a.
[19] *Abot* 2, 5.
[20] *Berachot* 61a, see Rashi; *Erubin* 18a.

36 The Problem of Evil

There are those who sense the ultimate question in moments of wonder, in moments of joy; there are those who sense the ultimate question in moments of horror, in moments of despair. It is both the grandeur and the misery of living that makes man sensitive to the ultimate question. Indeed, his misery is as great as his grandeur.

How did Abraham arrive at his certainty that there is a God who is concerned with the world? Said Rabbi Isaac: Abraham may be "compared to a man who was traveling from place to place when he saw *a palace in flames.* Is it possible that there is no one who cares for the palace? he wondered. Until the owner of the palace looked at him and said, 'I am the owner of the palace.' Similarly, Abraham our father wondered, 'Is is conceivable that the world is without a guide?' The Holy One, blessed be He, looked out and said, 'I am the Guide, the Sovereign of the world.' "[1]

The world is in flames, consumed by evil. Is it possible that there is no one who cares?

"INTO THE HANDS OF THE WICKED"

Was the Biblical man unaware of the dreadful turmoil of world history, of the horrible cruelty of man, as many theologians have consistently maintained? A careful study will hardly sustain such a view.[2] With the exception of the first chapter of the Book of

367

Genesis, the rest of the Bible does not cease to refer to the sorrow, sins, and evil of this world. When the prophets look at the world, they see "distress and darkness, the gloom of anguish" (Isaiah 8:22). When they look at the land, they find it "full of guilt against the Holy One of Israel" (Jeremiah 51:5). "O Lord, how long shall I cry for help and Thou wilt not hear? Or cry to Thee 'violence' and Thou wilt not save? Why dost Thou make me see wrongs and look upon trouble? Destruction and violence are before me; strife and contention arise. So the law is slacked and justice never goes forth. For the wicked surround the righteous, so justice goes forth perverted" (Habakuk 1:2-4). This is a world in which the way of the wicked prosper and "all who are treacherous thrive" (Jeremiah 12:1); a world which made it possible for some people to maintain that "Everyone who does evil is good in the sight of the Lord, and He delights in them," and for others to ask, "Where is the God of justice?" (Malachi 2:17).

The Psalmist did not feel that this was a happy world when he prayed, "O God, do not keep silence; do not hold peace or be still, O God. For, lo, Thy enemies are in uproar; those who hate Thee have raised their heads" (Psalms 83:2-3).

The terror and anguish that came upon the Psalmist were not caused by calamities of nature but by the wickedness of man, by the evil in history.

> Fearfulness and trembling come upon me,
> Horror has overwhelmed me.
> And I said, O that I had wings like a dove,
> Then would I fly away, and be at rest.
> Psalms 55: 6-7

There is one line that expresses the mood of the Jewish man throughout the ages: "The earth is given into the hand of the wicked" (Job 9:24).

How does the world look in the eyes of God? Are we ever told: the Lord saw that the righteousness of man was great in the earth? That He was glad to have made man on the earth? The general

tone of the Biblical view of history is set after the first ten genera
tions: "The Lord saw the wickedness of man was great in the
earth . . . And the Lord was sorry that He had made man on the
earth, and it grieved Him to His heart" (Genesis 6.5-6, cf. 8:21).
One great cry resounds throughout the Bible: The wickedness of
man is great on the earth.

The experience of the easy and endless opportunities for evil and
the awareness of the dreadful danger, threatens to outweigh all
delight of living. The answer to that danger is either despair or the
question: God, where art Thou? "Where is the God of justice?"
(Malachi 2:17).[3]

This essential predicament of man has assumed a peculiar
urgency in our time, living as we do in a civilization where factories
were established in order to exterminate millions of men, women,
and children; where soap was made of human flesh. What have we
done to make such crimes possible? What are we doing to make
such crimes impossible?

Modern man may be characterized as a being who is callous to
catastrophies. A victim of enforced brutalization, his sensibility is
being increasingly reduced; his sense of horror is on the wane. The
distinction between right and wrong is becoming blurred. All that
is left to us is our being horrified at the loss of our sense of horror.

THE CONFUSION OF GOOD AND EVIL

Even more frustrating than the fact that evil is real, mighty and
tempting is the fact that it thrives so well in the disguise of the
good, that it can draw its nutriment from the life of the holy. In
this world, it seems, the holy and the unholy do not exist apart,
but are mixed, interrelated and confounded. It is a world where
idols may be rich in beauty, and where the worship of God may be
tinged with wickedness.

It was not the lack of religion but the perversion of it that the
prophets of Israel denounced. "Many an altar has Ephraim raised,
altars that only serve for sin" (Hosea 8:11). "The priests said not:

Where is the Lord? And they that handle the law knew Me not" (Jeremiah 2:8). The greater the man, the more he is exposed to sin.[4] Piety is at times evil in disguise, an instrument in the pursuit of power. "The tragedies in human history, the cruelties and fanaticisms, have not been caused by the criminals . . . but by the good people . . . by idealists who did not understand the strange mixture of self-interest and ideals which is compounded in all human motives." The great contest is not "between God-fearing believers and unrighteous unbelievers." Biblical religion has emphasized "the *inequality of guilt* just as much as the equality of sin." "Especially severe judgments fall upon the rich and the powerful, the mighty and the noble, the wise and the righteous."[5] Indeed the most horrible manifestation of evil is when it acts in the guise of good. "Such monstrous evil deeds could religion urge man to commit" (Lucretius).[6]

Ezekiel saw in his great vision, "a stormy wind came out of the north, and a great cloud, with brightness *(nogah)* around about it, and fire flashing forth continually" (1:4). He first beheld the powers of unholiness. *A great cloud* represents "the power of destruction," "it is called *great,* on account of its darkness, which is so intense that it hides and makes invisible all the sources of light, thus overshadowing the whole world. The *fire flashing forth* indicates the fire of rigorous judgment that never departs from it. *With brightness (nogah) around about it* . . . that is, although it is the very region of defilement, yet it is surrounded by a certain brightness . . . it possesses an aspect of holiness, and hence should not be treated with contempt, but should be allowed a part in the side of holiness."[7] Thus there is a holy spark of God even in the dark recesses of evil. If not for that spark, evil would lose its power and reality, and would turn to nothingness. Even Satan contains a particle of sanctity. In doing his ugly work as the seducer of man, his intention is to act "for the sake of heaven," for it is for the purpose of seducing man that he was created.

The great saint, Rabbi Hirsh of Zydatshov, once remarked to his disciple and nephew: Even after I had reached the age of forty—

A philosophy of Judaism

"the age of understanding"—I was not sure whether my life was not immersed in that mire and confusion of good and evil *(nogah)*. . . . My son, every moment of my life I fear lest I am still caught in that confusion [8]

The dreadful confusion, the fact that there is nothing in this world that is not a mixture of good and evil, of holy and unholy, of silver and dross, is, according to Jewish mysticism, the central problem of history and the ultimate issue of redemption. The confusion goes back to the very process of creation.

"When God came to create the world and reveal what was hidden in the depths and disclose the light out of darkness, they were all wrapped in one another, and therefore light emerged from darkness, and from the impenetrable came forth the profound. So, too, from good issues evil and from mercy issues judgment, and all are intertwined, the good impulse and the evil impulse. . . ."[9]

THE ATONEMENT FOR THE HOLY

The awareness of evil's intrusion into the sphere of the good and the holy has, in our tradition, often come to expression. It may have been the meaning of one of the great acts that took place annually at the Temple in Jerusalem. At the ritual of the Day of Atonement the High Priest would cast lots upon two goats: one lot for the Lord and the other lot for Azazel. The purpose of the ritual of the goat on which the lot fell for Azazel was *to atone for the evil.* The High Priest would lay both his hands upon the head of the goat, "and confess over him all the iniquities of the children of Israel, all their transgressions, all their sins." While the purpose of the goat upon which the lot fell for the Lord was *to atone for the holy,* "to make atonement *for the holy place,* because of the uncleannesses of the children of Israel, and because of their transgressions, even all their sins; and so shall he do for the tent of meeting, that dwells with them in the midst of their uncleannesses."[10] On the most sacred day of the year the supreme task was *to atone for the holy.*

371

It preceded the sacrifice, the purpose of which was to atone for the sins.

Let us labor under no illusions. There are no easy solutions for problems that are at the same time intensely personal and universal, urgent and eternal. Technological progress creates more problems than it solves. Efficiency experts or social engineering will not redeem humanity. Important as their contributions may be, they do not reach the heart of the problem. Religion, therefore, with its demands and visions, is not a luxury but a matter of life and death. True, its message is often diluted and distorted by pedantry, externalization, ceremonialism, and superstition. But this precisely is our task: to recall the urgencies, the perpetual emergencies of human existence, the rare cravings of the spirit, the eternal voice of God, to which the demands of religion are an answer.

The power to make distinctions is a primary operation of intelligence. We distinguish between white and black, beautiful and ugly, pleasant and unpleasant, gain and loss, good and evil, right and wrong. The fate of mankind depends upon the realization that the distinction between good and evil, right and wrong, is superior to all other distinctions. As long as such realization is lacking, pleasantness in alliance with evil will be preferred to unpleasantness in alliance with good. To teach humanity the primacy of that distinction is of the essence to the Biblical message.

After the Lord had created the universe, He took a look at His creation. What was the word that conveyed His impression? If an artist were to find a word describing how the universe looked to God at the dawn of its existence, the word would be sublime or beautiful. But the word that the Bible has is *good*. Indeed, when looking through a telescope into the stellar space, the word that comes to our mind is grandeur, mystery, splendor. But the God of Israel is not impressed with splendor; He is impressed with goodness.

Good and evil are not values among other values. Good is life, and evil is death. "See I have set before thee this day life and good, death and evil . . . choose life" (Deuteronomy 30:15.19). Good and evil are not values among other values. The distinction between good and evil counts as much as the distinction between life and death.

"Justice has always appeared as obligatory, but for a long time it was an obligation like other obligations. It met, like the others, a social need; and it was the pressure of society on the individual which made justice obligatory. This being so, an injustice was neither more nor less shocking than any other breach of the rules. There was no justice for slaves, save perhaps a relative, almost an optional, justice. Public safety was not merely the supreme law, as indeed it has remained, it was furthermore proclaimed as such; whereas today we should not dare to lay down the principle that it justifies injustice, even if we accept any particular consequence of that principle.

"Let us dwell on this point, put to ourselves the famous question: 'What should we do if we heard that for the common good, for the very existence of mankind, there was somewhere a man, an innocent man, condemned to suffer eternal torment?' Well, we should perhaps agree to it on the understanding that some magic philter is going to make us forget it, that we shall never hear anything more about it; but if we were bound to know it, to think of it, to realize that this man's hideous torture was the price of our existence, that it was even the fundamental condition of existence in general, no! a thousand times no! Better to accept that nothing should exist at all! Better let our planet be blown to pieces.

"Now what has happened? How has justice emerged from social life, within which it had always dwelt with no particular privilege, and soared above it, categorical and transcendent? Let us recall the tone and accents of the Prophets of Israel. It is their voice we hear when a great injustice has been done and condoned. From the depths of the centuries they raise their protest. They imparted to justice the violently imperative character which it has kept, which it has since stamped on a substance grown infinitely more extensive. Could it have been brought about by mere philosophy? There is nothing more instructive than to see how the philosophers have skirted round it, touched it, and yet missed it."[11]

But how is such a supremacy possible? Is not our sense of beauty and ugliness, of gain and loss, more acute than our sense of good and evil?

HOW TO FIND AN ALLY

The ego is a powerful rival of the good. When coupled with gain, when virtue pays, the good has a chance to prevail. When the good is to be realized at a loss, with no reward, it is easily defeated. Now, since it is of the essence of virtue that the good is not to be done for the sake of a reward, what is the chance of the good ever to prevail over the interests of the ego? Who is our help in the struggle with evil?

Does not goodness tend to turn impotent in the face of temptations? Crime, vice, sin offer us rewards; while virtue demands self-restraint, self-denial. Sin is thrilling and full of excitement. Is virtue thrilling? Are there many mystery stories that describe virtue? Are there many best-selling novels that portray adventures in goodness?

THE TORAH IS AN ANTIDOTE

If the nature of man were all we had, then surely the outlook would be dim. But we also have the aid of God, the commandment, the mitsvah. The central Biblical fact is *Sinai,* the covenant, the word of God. Sinai was superimposed on the failure of Adam. The fact that we were given the knowledge of His will is a sign of some

374

A philosophy of Judaism

ability to cope with evil. The voice is more than a challenge. It is powerful enough to shake the wilderness of the soul, to strip the ego bare, to flash forth His will like fire.

To the Jew, Sinai is at stake in every act of man, and the supreme issue is not good and evil but God, and His commandment to love good and to hate evil; not the sinfulness of man but the commandment of God.

"The Lord created the evil inclination in man and He created the Torah to temper it."[12] The life of man was compared with "a lonely settlement which was kept in disorder by invading bands. What did the king do? He appointed a commander to protect it." The Torah is a safeguard, the Torah is an antidote.[13]

We are never alone in our struggle with evil. A mitsvah, unlike the concept of duty, is not anonymous and impersonal. To do a mitsvah is to give an answer to His will, to respond to what He expects of us. This is why an act of mitsvah is preceded by a prayer: "Blessed be Thou . . ."

What is a mitsvah? A prayer in the form of a deed. And to pray is to sense His presence. "In all thy ways thou shalt know Him." Prayer should be part of all our ways. It does not have to be always on our lips; it must always be on our minds, in our hearts.

In the light of the Bible, the good is more than a value; it is a *divine concern,* a way of God. This is the profound implication of the oneness of God: all deeds are relevant to Him. He is present in all our deeds. "The Lord is good to all and His compassion is over all that He has made" (Psalms 145:10). There is no reverence for God without reverence for man. Love of man is the way to the love of God. The fear lest we hurt a poor man must be as deep as the fear of God, for *He that oppresses the poor blasphemes his maker, but he who is gracious unto the needy honors Him* (Proverbs 14:31).

IS THE GOOD A PARASITE?

What we are discussing as a moral issue is but an aspect of the larger metaphysical problem about the relation of good and evil.

375

Which of the two is self-subsistent? Is good ultimately a parasite on the body of evil? Or is it just the opposite: is it evil that lives as a parasite on the body of the good?

In our intellectual climate there seems to be only one answer to that problem. Ideals have a high mortality rate in our generation. Contemporary thinking looks like a graveyard of discredited ideals. With his moral efforts man, it is felt, can build castles in the air. All our norms are nothing but desires in disguise.

He who accepts this world as the ultimate reality will, if his mind is realistic and his heart sensitive to suffering, tend to doubt that the good is either the origin or the ultimate goal of history. To the Jewish mind, evil is an instrument rather than an iron wall; a temptation, an occasion, rather than an ultimate power.

The words of the Psalmist, *Depart from evil, and do good* (34:15), contain the epitome of right living. Yet, it seems that Jewish tradition believes that the right way of departing from evil is to do good; it puts the accent on the second half of the sentence.

EVIL IS NOT THE ULTIMATE PROBLEM

Evil is not man's ultimate problem. Man's ultimate problem is his relation to God. Evil entered history as a result of man's disobedience to God, as a result of his having forfeited the only mitsvah he had (not to eat the fruit of the tree of knowledge). The Biblical answer to evil is not the good but the *holy*. It is an attempt to raise man to a higher level of existence, where man is not alone when confronted with evil. Living in "the light of the face of God" bestows upon man a power of love that enables him to overcome the powers of evil. The seductiveness of vice is excelled by the joys of the mitsvah. "Ye shall be men of holiness unto Me" (Exodus 22:30). How do we receive that quality, that power? "With every new mitsvah which God issues to Israel, He adds holiness to them."[14]

We do not wage war with evil in the name of an abstract concept of duty. We do the good not because it is a value or because of expediency, but because we owe it to God. God created man, and

376

what is good "in His eyes" is good for man. Life is human as well as divine. Man is a child of God, not only a value to society. We may explore things without God; we cannot decide about values without Him.

We do not conceive of values as absolute essences which are laid up in heaven, to use the language of Plato. Values are not eternal ideas, existing independently of God and man. If not for the will of God, there would be no goodness; if not for the freedom of man, goodness would be out of place in history. Greek philosophy is concerned with *values;* Jewish thought dwells on *mitsvot.*

GOD AND MAN HAVE A TASK IN COMMON

Evil is not only a threat, it is also a challenge. Neither the recognition of the peril nor faith in the redemptive power of God is sufficient to solve the tragic predicament of the world. We cannot stem the tide of evil by taking refuge in temples, by fervently imploring the restrained omnipotence of God.

The mitsvah, the humble single act of serving God, of helping man, of cleansing the self, is our way of dealing with the problem. We do not know how to solve the problem of *evil,* but we are not exempt from dealing with *evils.* The power of evil does not vitiate the reality of good. Significantly, Jewish tradition, while conscious of the possibilities of evil in the good, stresses the possibilities of further good in the good. Ben Azzai said, "Be eager to do a minor mitsvah, and flee from transgression; for one mitsvah leads to (brings on) another mitsvah, and one transgression leads to another transgression; for the reward of a mitsvah is a mitsvah, and the reward of a transgression is a transgression."[15]

At the end of days, evil will be conquered by the One; in historic times, evils must be conquered one by one.[16]

Jewish tradition, though conscious of the perils and pitfalls of existence, is a constant reminder of the grand and everlasting opportunities to do the good. We are taught to love life in this world because of the possibilities of charity and sanctity, because of the

377

many ways open to us in which to serve the Lord. "More precious, therefore, than all of life in the world to come is a single hour of life on earth—an hour of repentance and good deeds."[17]

True, this world is only "a vestibule to the world to come," where we must prepare ourselves before we enter "the banquet hall."[18] Yet, in the eyes of God, the endeavor and the preparation are greater than the achievement and perfection.

THE ABILITY TO FULFILL

In stressing the fundamental importance of the mitsvah, Judaism assumes that man is endowed with the ability to fulfill what God demands, at least to some degree. This may, indeed, be an article of prophetic faith: the belief in our ability to do His will. "For this commandment (mitsvah) which I command thee this day, it is not too hard for thee, neither is it far off. . . . But the word is very nigh unto thee, in thy mouth and in thy heart, that thou mayest do it" (Deuteronomy 30:11-14). Man's actual failures rather than his essential inability to do the good are constantly stressed by Jewish tradition. In spite of all imperfection, the worth of good deeds remains in all eternity.

The idea with which Judaism starts is not the realness of evil or the sinfulness of man but rather the wonder of creation and the ability of man to do the will of God. There is always an opportunity to do a mitsvah, and precious is life because at all times and in all places we are able to do His will. This is why despair is alien to Jewish faith.

It is true that the commandment to be holy is exorbitant, and that our constant failures and transgressions fill us with contrition and grief. Yet we are never lost. We are the sons of Abraham. Despite all faults, failures, and sins, we remain parts of the Covenant. His compassion is greater than His justice. He will accept us in all our frailty and weakness. "For He knows our drive [yetser], He remembers that we are dust" (Psalms 103:14).

Judaism would reject the Kantian axiom, "I ought, therefore I

378

can"; it would claim, instead, "Thou art commanded, therefore thou canst." Judaism, as we have said, claims that man has the resources to fulfill what God commands, at least to some degree. On the other hand, we are continually warned lest we rely on man's own power and the belief that man, by his power alone, is capable of redeeming the world. Good deeds alone will not redeem history; it is the obedience to God that will make us worthy of being redeemed by God.[19]

If Judaism had relied exclusively on the human resources for the good, on man's ability to fulfill what God demands, on man's power to achieve redemption, why did it insist upon the promise of messianic redemption? Indeed, messianism implies that any course of living, even the supreme human efforts, must fail in redeeming the world. It implies that history for all its relevance is not sufficient to itself.

IN NEED OF REDEMPTION

There are two problems: the particular sins, the examples of breaking the law, and the general and radical problem of "the evil drive" in man. The law deals with the first problem; obedience to the law prevents evil deeds. Yet, the problem of the evil drive is not solved by observance. The prophets' answer was eschatological. "Behold, the days come, saith the Lord, when I will make a new covenant with the house of Israel . . . not like the covenant which I made with their fathers . . . I will put my law within them, and I will write it upon their hearts" (Jeremiah 31:31-34). "A new heart I will give you, and a new spirit I will put within you; and I will take out of your flesh the heart of stone and give you a heart of flesh. And I will put My spirit within you, and cause you to walk in My statutes and be careful to keep My ordinances" (Ezekiel 36:26-27).

"A definite period was set for the world to spend in darkness. What is the proof? It is written, He sets an end to darkness and searches out to the utmost end the stones of thick darkness and of the shadow of death (Job 28:3). For as long as the evil drive exists in the world, thick darkness and the shadow of death are in the world; when the evil drive will be uprooted from the world, thick darkness and the shadow of death will pass away from the world."[20]

The world is in need of redemption, but the redemption must not be expected to happen as an act of sheer grace. Man's task is to make the world worthy of redemption. His faith and his works are preparations for *ultimate redemption.*

NOTES FOR CHAPTER 36

[1] *Genesis Rabba,* ch. 39. See above, p. 113, n. 7.

[2] It was Schopenhauer who made popular the idea that the Bible had no awareness of the problem of evil. See *Die Welt Als Wille und Vorstelling,* II, ch. 48; *Parerga und Paralipomena,* Gusbach ed., II, p. 397; *Sämtliche Werke,* Frauenstadt ed., III, p. 712f. On his hostility to the Bible, see Isak Unna, Die Stellung Schopenhauers zum Judentum, in *Juedische Schriften* Josef Wohlgemuth zu seinem sedizigsten geburtstage . . . gewidmet, Berlin, 1928, p. 103f.

[3] What the Rabbis thought about the situation of man may be shown in the following comment. We read in Habakuk 1:14 "And Thou makest man as the fishes of the sea, and as the creeping things, that have no ruler over them?" "Why is man here compared to the fishes of the sea? Just as among fishes of the sea, the greater swallow up the smaller ones, so with men, were it not for fear of government, men would swallow each other alive. This is just what we have learnt: Rabbi Hanina, the Deputy High Priest, said, Pray for the welfare of the government, for were it not for fear thereof, men would swallow each other alive." *Avodah Zarah* 3b-4a and *Abot* 3, 2.

"In the time to come the Holy One, blessed be He, will bring the evil drive (the *yetser hara*) and slay it in the presence of the righteous and the wicked. To the righteous the evil *yetser* will appear as huge as a mountain; to the wicked it will seem thin as a hair. Both the former and the latter will weep. The righteous will marvel that they could overcome so great a power; the wicked will be amazed that they succumbed to so slight a force. And the Holy One, blessed be He, will marvel with them, as it is said, *Thus says the Lord of Hosts. If it be marvelous in the eyes of the remnant of this people in those days, it shall also be marvelous in My eyes"* (Zecharaiah 8:6). *Sukkah* 52a.

[4] *Sukkah* 52a. See the interpretation of Isaiah 64:5 in *Baba Metsia* 32b.

[5] Reinhold Niebuhr, *The Nature and Destiny of Man,* vol. I, p. 222f.

[6] The power of images and idols which man is prone to worship is due to their being endowed with a tinge of the holy. *Pesel,* the Hebrew word for image, is associated in the *Zohar* with *pesolet,* meaning "refuse." Idols are the refuse of holiness. See *Zohar,* vol. II, p. 91a.

[7] *Zohar,* vol. II, pp. 203a-203b; see pp. 69a-69b. The *kelipot* or the forces of the unholy are unclean and harmful from the aspect of man. However, from the aspect of the holy, they exist because of the will of the Creator and for His

God in search of man

sake. A spark of holiness abides in them and maintains them. Rabbi Abraham Azulai, *Or Hahamah*, Przemishl, 1897, vol. II, p. 218a.

[8] *Zohar Hai*, Lemberg, 1875, vol. I, p. 2.

[9] *Zohar*, vol. III, p. 80b.

[10] Leviticus 16:6f. See *Sifra, Aahare* ch 4, ed Weiss, p. 81c. According to Ezekiel 45:18-20 atonement for the Temple is to be made twice a year.

[11] Henri Bergson, *The Two Sources of Morality and Religion*, New York, 1935, p. 67f.

[12] *Sifre*, Deuteronomy, 45; *Kiddushin* 30b.

[13] *Leviticus Rabba*, 35, 5.

[14] *Mechilta*, ad locum.

[15] *Abot* 4, 2.

[16] "Israel said to the Holy One, blessed be He: Sovereign of the universe! Thou knowest the power of the evil drive, how strong it is! Said the Holy One, blessed be He, to them: You dislodge it a little in this world and I will remove it from you in the future. . . . In the world to come I shall put it out of you by the roots." *Numbers Rabba* 15, 16.

[17] *Abot* 4:17.

[18] *Abot* 4:16.

[19] Compare Reinhold Niebuhr, *An Interpretation of Christian Ethics*, p. 65.

[20] *Genesis Rabba*, 89,1. The evil drive is often called "a stone" see Theodor, ad locum.

37 The Problem of the Neutral

The weakness of many systems of moral philosophy is in their iso-lationism, in the tacit assumption that the good is unrelated to the morally neutral deeds. However, there is an interrelatedness be-tween the moral and all other acts of man, whether in the realm of theory or in the realm of esthetic or technical application, and the moral person must not be thought of as if he were a professional magician, behaving morally in some situations and remaining neutral in others.

Consequently, the moral problem cannot be solved as a moral problem. It must be dealt with as part of the total issue of man. The supreme problem is all of life, not good and evil. We cannot deal with morality unless we deal with all of man, the nature of existence, of doing, of meaning.

Man lives in three realms: the animal, the rational and the spiritual. The animal realm is spiritually neutral, and neutrality breeds peril. There is dross in the natural state of living and much that is untidy, crude and cruel. Who will tame the brute in us when passion overwhelms the mind? Who will teach us that the good is worth the price of self-denial? It is not in a single debate between happiness and mercy, between pleasure and justice that the latter would triumph. Unless we place all of life under the law of holiness, the outcome of temptation is doubtful.

Neutrality is an illusion. At the end of his days man always

A philosophy of Judaism

emerges either as a priest or as a pirate. The life we leave behind as we march along the road of time is full of guideposts to a sanctuary or ruins of a vision. The vision of God is to see "a kingdom of priests, a holy people." Every home can be a temple, every table an altar, and all of life a song to God.

Every act—thought or deed—is an exemplification of the totality of existence. The spirit that flickered even once at a distant moment of existence will illumine every act, so that almost every act will be touched with the quiet nobility of devotion. At the same time, the cruelty and callousness to which a person succumbs at some moments of his life may break out even in his rapturous acts of devotion.

HOW TO DEAL WITH THE NEUTRAL

The problem of living does not begin with the question of how to take care of the rascals, of how to prevent delinquency or hideous crimes. The problem of living begins with the realization that all of us blunder in our dealings with our fellow men. The silent atrocities, the secret scandals, which no law can prevent, are the true seat of moral infection. The problem of living begins, in fact, in relation to our own selves, in the handling of our emotional functions, in the way we deal with envy, greed, and pride. What is first at stake in the life of man is not the fact of sin, of the wrong and corrupt, but the neutral acts, the needs. Our possessions pose no less a problem than our passions. The primary task, therefore, is not how to deal with the evil, but *how to deal with the neutral,* how to deal with needs.

The only safeguard against constant danger is constant vigilance, constant guidance. Such guidance, such vigilance is given to him who lives by the light of Sinai; whose weeks, days, hours, are set in the rhythm of *ḳeva* and *ḳavanah.*

Thrice daily we remind ourselves that in the light of His face He gave "the Torah of life and the love of kindness." All day long we must learn how to see a situation in the light of His face.

383

"In all Thy ways know Him, and He will straighten out thy paths" (Proverbs 3:6). Upon these words everything depends.[1]

Worship and living are not two separate realms. Unless living is a form of worship, our worship has no life. Religion is not a reservation, a tract of time reserved for solemn celebrations on festive days. The spirit withers when confined in splendid isolation. What is decisive is not the climax we reach in rare moments, but how the achievements of rare moments affect the climate of the entire life. The goal of Jewish law is to be the grammar of living, dealing with all relations and functions of living. Its main theme is the person rather than an institution.

Religion is not made for extraordinary occasions, such as birth, marriage, and death. Religion is trying to teach us that no act is trite, every moment is an extraordinary occasion.

The highest peak of spiritual living is not necessarily reached in rare moments of ecstasy; the highest peak lies wherever we are and may be ascended in a common deed. There can be as sublime a holiness in performing friendship, in observing dietary laws day by day, as in uttering a prayer on the Day of Atonement.

It is not by the rare act of greatness that character is determined, but by everyday actions, by a constant effort to rend our callousness. It is constancy that sanctifies. Judaism is an attempt to place all of life under the glory of ultimate significance, to relate all scattered actions to the One. Through the constant rhythm of prayers, disciplines, reminders, joys, man is taught not to forfeit his grandeur.

ALL JOY COMES FROM GOD

As said above, one of our problems is to endow virtue with vitality. Sin is thrilling and full of excitement. But is virtue thrilling? Do passion and virtue go together?

We believe that the ego can become converted to a friend of the spirit. "The evil drive" may become the helpmate of "the good drive." But such conversion does not come about in moments of despair, or by accepting our moral bankruptcy, but rather through the realization of our ability to answer God's question. We must learn how to endow "the good drive" with more power, how to lend beauty to sacred deeds. The power of evil can be consumed in the flames of joy. It may be true that not all joys lead to God, yet all joys come from God. Even lowly merriment has its ultimate origin in holiness.

Perhaps this is one of the goals of Jewish education: to learn how to sense the ineffable delight of good deeds. It has been said that the joy with which a deed is done is more precious than the deed itself. The good without the joy is a good half done; and the love and delight with which we do the good and the holy are the test of our spirit. "Thy Torah is my delight. . . . Oh, how I love Thy Torah" (Psalms 119:77,97).

"Morality inevitably involves pain. There can be no bliss in the good—there can only be bliss beyond good and evil."[2] In contrast, Jewish experience is a testimony to *simhah shel mitsvah,* to "the joy in doing a mitsvah."[3] Everyone knows that out of suffering goes a way that leads to Him. Judaism is a reminder that joy is a way to God. The mitsvah and the holy spirit are incompatible with grief or despair.

The experience of bliss in doing the good is the greatest moment that mortals know. The discipline, sacrifice, self-denial, or even suffering which are often involved in doing the good do not vitiate the joy; they are its ingredients.

Daily we pray: "Happy are we! How good is our destiny, how pleasant our lot, how beautiful our heritage." There is joy in being a Jew, in belonging to Israel, to God, in being able to taste heaven in a sacred deed. There is joy in being a link to eternity, in being able to do His will. A rabbinic principle states that "the mitsvot were not given for the purpose of affording pleasure."[4] Yet pleasure is not the same as joy.

"I am pleased with an object when it gratifies some interest of mind or some instinctive impulse. It gives me pleasure because it fulfills my need. It is a pleasure in relation to my sensibility or to

385

my activity. And we speak correctly of the pleasures of sense and movement. But joy is not self-centered like pleasure. No doubt there is pleasure in it, for all our emotions are toned by pleasure or pain, but such pleasure is but the pleasure of the joy. There is also a self-enlargement in joy, but this is not of its essence. The joy itself attaches not to the subject but to the object, and to have joy in an object is to value it for its own sake. Joy is thus an active disinterestedness, and its instinctive impulse is not only to maintain its object, but to surrender itself to it and rest freely in it as in something of intrinsic value and promise.

"To have joy in an object is to respect its individuality. This is implied in the very idea of delighting in it for its own sake. To have joy in what is real is to subordinate individual opinion wholeheartedly to the truth of the matter; to have joy in what is beautiful is to trust to the inspiration of beauty and not to the contrivance of artifice. The interests of the object dictate at each step the line of advance."[5]

NOTES FOR CHAPTER 37

[1] *Berachot* 63a.
[2] N. Berdyaev, *The Destiny of Man,* p. 30.
[3] *Shabbat* 30b. See *Midrash Tehillim,* 112, 1. Maimonides, *Mishne Torah, Lulav,* 8, 15.
[4] *Mitsvot lav lehanot nitnu, Erubin* 31a; *Rosh Hashanah* 28a. Rashi: "but as a yoke."
[5] W. R. Boyce Gibson, *Encyclopaedia of Religion and Ethics,* vol. VIII, p. 152a.

38 The Problem of Integrity

The *mitsvah,* we have said, is our instrument in dealing with evil. But do we employ the instruments adequately? If *ƙavanah* is as intrinsic to the service of God as impartiality of judgment is to scientific investigation; if, in other words, it is not only essential what one does but also what one is motivated by, the possibility of true service, of genuine piety may be questioned.

Depth-psychology has made it clear to us that the springs of human action are complex, that the subrational either dominates or at least affects the conscious life, that the power and the drive of the ego penetrate all our attitudes and decisions. We may assume that we love God, while in truth it is the ego we care for.

Psychologically it seems inconceivable a person should be able to love God wholeheartedly, to do the good for its own sake, regardless of reward and expediency. We do not have to use a divining rod in order to come upon deep layers of vested interests beneath the surface of our immediate motivations. Anyone capable of self-examination knows that the regard for the self is present in every cell of our brain; that it is extremely hard to disentangle oneself from the intricate plexus of selfish interests.

Thus, not only our evil deeds, but also our good deeds precipitate a problem. Assuming that our good deeds are well done, are they also well meant? Do we serve Him for His sake? Are we capable of serving Him in purity?

387

Moreover, assuming that man has succeeded in his effort to embark upon a good deed out of a pure and single motive, will he succeed in protecting himself against the intrusion of vanity during the moments of carrying out the deed?

Consciousness abides in the company of self-consciousness. With any perception or apprehension comes the awareness of my possessing it, which is dangerously close to vanity. The ego, with its characteristic lack of reserve or discretion, is prone to interfere obtrusively even in acts which had been initiated behind its back. Such interference or "alien thoughts"—alien to the spirit of the act—which was absent from the original motive constitute a problem of its own.

In addition to our being uncertain of whether our motivation prior to the act is pure, and to our being embarrassed during the act by "alien thoughts," one is not even safe after the act. We are urged by Jewish tradition to conceal from others our acts of charity;[1] but are we able to conceal them from ourselves? Are we able to overcome the danger of pride, self-righteousness, vanity, and the sense of superiority, derived from what are supposed to be acts of dedication to God?

It is easier to discipline the body than to control the soul. The pious man knows that his inner life is full of pitfalls. The ego, "the evil drive," is constantly trying to enchant him. The temptations are fierce, yet his resistance is unyielding. And so he proves his spiritual strength and stands victorious, unconquerable. Does not his situation look glorious? But then the "evil drive" employs a more subtle device, approaching him with congratulations: what a pious man you are!—He begins to feel proud of himself. And there he is caught in the trap.[2]

THE ESCAPE TO SUSPICION

The problem of integrity concerns not only the character of our moral deeds but also the integrity of our thinking. It is not only difficult for us to conceive of man doing the good for its own sake; we also question his ability to comprehend the good unsoiled and unconditioned. The prerequisite of impartial judgment is to be unbiased, to discount oneself. But we are beginning to wonder whether to discount oneself is not something man can never achieve. Psychological (and sociological) research has disclosed not only how the motivations of our conduct are entangled in the functions of instinctual desires, but also how the vested interests of the ego penetrate not only moral motivations but also acts of cognition.

The discovery of this tragic predicament is a most painful blow to man's sense of spiritual security. What lesson is to be drawn from it if not the advice that suspicion is the shortest way to the understanding of human nature. This it seems is the modern version of the Golden Rule: *Suspect thy neighbor as thyself.* Thus, the predicament of modern man may be characterized as an escape to suspicion. There is a tabu on the idea of objective validity, of sacredness or supremacy of a value. It is our implicit belief that there is a vicious underground beneath all action, that ulterior motives are the humus of all virtue, and righteousness is a camouflage of evil. There is no depth to virtue, no reality to integrity. All we can do is to graft goodness upon selfishness, to use truth as a pragmatic pretext and to relish self-indulgence in all values. In a world such as this, close as it is to being pandemonium, honesty must be held to be wishful thinking; purity the squaring of the circle of human nature; and the notions of objective validity, sacredness or supremacy of any value must be considered hypocrisy or superstition.

The hysteria of suspicion holds many of us in its spell. It has not only affected our understanding of others but also made us unreliable to ourselves, making it impossible for us to trust either our aspirations or convictions.

The self-suspicious man shrinks from the light. He is often afraid to think as he feels, afraid to admit what he believes, afraid to love what he admires. Going astray, he blames others for his failure and becomes more evasive, smooth-tongued and deceitful. Living in fear, he thinks that ambush is the normal dwelling-place of all men.

It is the new perception of evil that drives man to despair. For what is ghastly about evil is not so much its apparent might as its cryptic ubiquity, its ability to camouflage.

Self-suspicion looms as a more serious threat to faith than doubt, and "anthropodicy," the justification of man, is today as difficult a problem as theodicy, the justification of God. Is there anything pure and untinged with selfishness in the soul of man? Is integrity at all possible? Can we trust our own faith? Is piety ever detached from expediency?

THE TEST OF JOB

Self-examination was not inaugurated by analytical psychology. Austere soul-searching is an essential feature of piety, and the pious man is prone to suspect that his reverence and devotion may be furtive attachments to selfish purposes.

Time and again the Bible calls upon us to worship Him "with all thy heart." "Walk before me, and be wholehearted" (Genesis 17:1). "Thou shalt be wholehearted with the Lord Thy God" (Deuteronomy 18:13). "And thou shalt love the Lord thy God with all thy heart, with all thy soul, and with all thy might" (Deuteronomy 6:5). And yet it seems that the Biblical man was disturbed by the problem of whether man is at all capable of serving God wholeheartedly.

An entire book in the Bible is, in a sense, dedicated to its exploration: *the Book of Job*. From the perspective of this world the theme of the Book of Job is *theodicy*, the vindication of God in view of the existence of evil. From the perspective of heaven its theme is *anthropodicy*, the vindication of man. In the opening scene of the book we hear that the issue between God and Satan is whether Job served God "out of fear" or "out of love." The Lord says to Satan: "Hast thou considered my servant Job? There is no one like him on earth, a wholehearted and upright man, one who fears God and shuns evil." Answers the Satan: "But is it for nothing that Job fears God? Hast Thou not made a hedge about him, about his

390

A philosophy of Judaism

house and about all he has? Thou hast blessed the work of his hands, and his flocks are teeming on the land. Only put out Thy hand, touch whatever he possesses, surely he will blaspheme Thee to Thy face" (1:8 11).

It is significant of how serious and basic the problem was to the Biblical man if the author considered it fair to let Job undergo the most dreadful forms of suffering in order to prove that man is capable of selfless piety.

The prophet complained, "They never put their heart into their prayers, but howl away for corn and wine beside their altars" (Hosea 7:14). According to the Book of Proverbs (11:20), "they that are perverse in the heart are an abomination to the Lord." Yet the prophet seems to have realized how hard it is not to be perverse, not to be an abomination.

> The heart is deceitful above all things,
> It is exceedingly weak—who can know it?
> Jeremiah 17:9

"A DIADEM WITH WHICH TO BOAST"

There are many passages in Jewish literature enjoining self-detachment and just as many bewailing the difficulty of attaining it. The first scholar of whom Pharisaic tradition has preserved not only the name but also a saying is Antigonos of Socho, who lived about the first half of the third century before the common era. His maxim was: "Be not like servants who wait upon their master in the expectation of receiving a reward, but be like the servants who wait upon their master in no expectation of receiving reward."[3] Vital, precious, and holy as dedication to Torah is, it is pernicious to study Torah for selfish ends, to study it so that we may be called rabbis, in order to obtain reward either here or in the life to come,[4] to make of the Torah "a diadem with which to boast," "a spade with which to dig." According to Hillel, "he who uses the crown of Torah to his own advantage will perish; he who derives a profit for himself from the words of the Torah takes his own life."[5]

The Rabbis continue to warn us: "He who studies the Torah for its own sake, his learning becomes an elixir of life to him . . . but he who studies the Torah not for its own sake, it becomes to him a deadly poison."[6] "If you fulfill the words of the Torah for their own sake, they bring you life; but if you fulfill the words of the Torah not for their own sake they will kill you."[7]

In rabbinic literature Abraham is the only person of whom it is said that he served God "out of love."[8] The fact that Abraham was the only one to be singled out[9] indicates an awareness of how imperfect was the spirit of all other prophets and saints.

DISGUISED POLYTHEISM

One may observe all the laws and still be practicing *a disguised polytheism*. For if in performing a religious act one's intention is to please a human being whom he fears or from whom he hopes to receive benefit, then it is not God whom he worships but a human being. "Such a person is worse than an idol-worshiper. . . . The latter, paying homage to the stars, worships an object that does not rebel against God, whereas the former worships beings some of whom rebel against God. The former only worships one object, but there is no limit to the number of human beings whom the perverse in religion may worship. Finally the inner attitude of the idolator is apparent to everybody; people can guard themselves from him— his denial of God is public knowledge. The hypocrite's denial, however, is unnoticed. . . . This makes him the worst of the universal evils."[10]

Disguised polytheism is also the religion of him who combines with the worship of God the devotion to his own gain, as it is said, *There shall be no strange god in thee* (Psalms 81:10), on which our teachers remarked that it meant the strange god in the very self of man.[11]

THE FAILURE OF THE HEART

God asks for the heart. Yet, our greatest failure is in the heart. Who can be trustful of good intentions, knowing that under the cloak of kavanah may hide a streak of vanity? Who can claim to have fulfilled even one mitsvah with perfect devotion? Said Rabbi Elimelech of Lizhensk to one of his disciples: "I am sixty years old, and I have not fulfilled one mitsvah."[12] *There is not a single mitsvah which we fulfill perfectly* . . . except circumcision and the Torah that we study in our childhood,[13] for these two acts are not infringed upon by "alien thoughts" or impure motivations.

"I saw that wherever there is justice there is also wickedness, that wherever there is righteousness there is also wickedness." God will, therefore, judge not only the wicked but also the righteous (Ecclesiastes 3:16-17). *For God shall bring every deed into judgment . . . whether it be good or whether it will be evil* (12:14). "Every deed" refers, according to Rabbi Judah, to "mitsvot and good deeds."[13a]

For there is not a righteous man upon earth, that does good and sins not (Ecclesiastes 7:20). The commentators take this verse to mean that even a righteous man sins on occasion, suggesting that his life is a mosaic of perfect deeds with a few sins strewn about. The Baal Shem, however, reads the verse: *For there is not a righteous man upon earth that does good and there is no sin in the good.* "It is impossible that the good should be free of sin and self-interest."[14] Empirically, our spiritual situation looks hopeless.

> We are all as an unclean thing, and all our deeds
> of righteousness are as filthy rags.
> Isaiah 64:5

"Even our good deeds are not pleasing but revolting, for we perform them out of the desire for self-aggrandizement and pride, and in order to impress our neighbors."[15]

The mind is never immune to "alien thoughts," and there is no easy way of weeding them out. A hasidic rabbi, asked by his disciples in the last hours of his life whom they should choose as their master after his passing away, said: "If someone should give you advice on how to eradicate alien intentions, know he is not your master."

According to one legend, the last words which the Baal Shem uttered before he departed from this world were, "Lord of the World, save me from pride and ulterior motives." According to another legend, his last words were, "Let not the foot of pride come upon me" (Psalms 36:12).

We do not know with what we must serve until we arrive there (Exodus 10:26). "All our service, all the good deeds we are doing in this world, we do not know whether they are of any value, whether they are really pure, honest, or done for the sake of heaven,—until we arrive there—in the world to come, only there shall we learn what our service was here."[16]

Moses' saying to Israel, "I stand between God and you" (Deuteronomy 5:5), was allegorically interpreted by Rabbi Michael of Zlotshov to mean: *The "I" stands between God and man.*[17]

NOTES FOR CHAPTER 38

[1] We are told that in every city in Palestine there was a place called "the chamber of the silent" in which people deposited their charitable donations in secrecy, and that with equal privacy the impoverished members of self-respecting families would receive their support. *Mishnah Shekalim*, 5,6; *Tosefta Shekalim*, 2, 16.

[2] Rabbi Raphael of Bersht.

[3] *Abot* 1:5. See Louis Ginzberg, in *Jewish Encyclopedia*, 1, 629. Commenting on Psalms 112:1, "Blessed is the man who fears the Lord and in His commandments delights greatly", Rabbi Eliezer said, "In His commandments and not in the reward of His commandments." *Abodah Zarah* 19a.

[4] *Sifre*, Deuteronomy, 41 (to 11:13).

[5] *Abot* IV, 7.

[6] *Taanit* 7a.

[7] *Sifre*, Deuteronomy, 306. Compare the views of Rabbi Joshua ben Levi and Rabbi Jonathan in *Yoma* 72b, and of Rabba in *Shabbat* 88b.

[8] To act "out of love" means to study or to fulfill the Torah "for its own sake" (*Sifre Deuteronomy*, 48; *Nedarim* 62a), "for the sake of heaven" (compare *Abot* II, 17, with *Sifre Deuteronomy*, 41).

[9] According to Rabban Yohanan ben Zakkai, it was Rabbi Joshua ben Hyrcanus who subsequently claimed the same distinction for Job. See *Mishnah Sotah* V, 5.

A philosophy of Judaism

[10] Bahya, *The Duties of the Heart*, yihud hamasseh, ch. 4.

[11] Bahya, ibid., shaar hayihud, ch. 10. See Schechter, *Some Aspects of Rabbinic Theology*, p. 69.

[12] Rabbi Yaakob Aaron of Zalshin, *Bet Yaakov*, Pietrkov, 1899, p. 144.

[13] *Midrash Tehillim*, 6, 1. According to some Rabbis, even at the moment when our forefathers stood at Sinai, proclaiming, *All that the Lord has spoken will we do and obey* (Exodus 24:7), which according to tradition was a moment in which Israel reached the highest stage in man's spiritual development (*Shabbat* 88a), they did not fully mean what they said. *They beguiled Him with their mouth, and lied unto Him with their tongue. Their heart was not steadfast with Him, neither were they faithful in His covenant* (Psalms 78: 36-37). According to Rabbi Meir, at that very moment their heart was directed to idolatry. See *Mechilta, mishpatim* 13; *Tosefta, Baba Kamma* 7,9; *Tanhuma*, ed. Buber, 1,77; *Exodus Rabba* 42, 6; *Leviticus Rabba* 6,1; *Deuteronomy Rabba* 7,10.

[13a] *Ecclesiastes Rabba* 11, end.

[14] *Toldot Yaakov Yosef*, Lemberg 1863, p. 150d. "There is no possibility of perfect kavanah in this world." Rabbi Zadok, *Resyse Laylah*, Warsaw, 1902, at the beginning.

[15] David Kimhi, *Commentary on Isaiah* ad locum. Similarly, S. D. Luzatto in his commentary. Compare Rabbi N. J. Berlin, Commentary on *Sheeltoth*, section 64, p. 420. See also Rashi, *Baba Batra* 9b. Compare Eliezer ben Jehuda, *Thesaurus*, vol. IX, p. 4328.

Isaiah's saying, against the scope and spirit of the prophet, was often applied to impugn the "good works." On the antinomian and anti-Biblical implications of such a conception, see E. La B. Cherbonnier, *Hardness of Heart*, p. 94f. In contrast, Rabbi Hanina thought that the intention of the prophet was to praise good works, inadequate as they may be. "Just as in a garment every thread united with the rest to form a whole garment, so every farthing given to charity united with the rest to form a large sum." *Baba Batra* 9b.

[16] Rabbi Isaac Meir of Ger.

[17] Quoted by Rabbi Kalonymus Kalman Epstein, *Maor Vashamesh*, Lemberg, 1859, p. 29b.

39 The Self and the non-Self

Is it true, as we asked above, that our religious beliefs are nothing but attempts to satisfy subconscious wishes? That our moral norms are nothing but desires in disguise? That desire is the measure of all things?

If it is never a norm that guides our actions but a selfish desire, we must give up our efforts to find ultimate norms for our conduct and instead concentrate on the psychology of desires. Our principle would be: desire is the father of all values; what is desirable is valuable.

Is it true that promoting his own prosperity is all man can do? That a psychology of desires would be able to define intentions and aims as well as to codify an all-comprehensive standard of behavior? In spite of the tempting flavor of such a view, the enthusiasm of those who think and live it through in scrutinizing human life as a study in desires turns at the end to disgust and despair. But why should the idea be repellent that humanity be a stench of greediness rising to the sky? Moreover, why must a civilization glittering with fortunes and vested interests run out in nausea? Why does the mind decay when the roots of values begin to rot? What is wrong with living in a jungle of incitements? With living in voracity? Why must disgust be the aftermath of greed?

Despair and disgust, which the foul odor of a life dedicated to self-indulgence evokes in our hearts—should they, too, be explained

396

as self-indulgence in disguise? Theories may, indeed, try to dispose of such reactions as vague, as logically meaningless, as egotism in a dialectical disguise. But such theories disregard unquestionable empirical facts of human consciousness.

There is, indeed, a perpetual tension in man between the focus of the self and the goal that lies beyond the self. Animal life is a state of living driven by forces regardless of examined goals. Animal in man is the drive to concentrate on the satisfaction of needs; spiritual in man is the will to serve higher ends, and in serving ends he transcends his needs. To say that the yearning to be free of selfish interests is as selfish as any other interest is semantic confusion. The difference is in the intention or direction of the act. Selfish interests are centripetal; freedom from selfish interests is centrifugal, a turning away from the self. The essence of man, his uniqueness, is in his power to surpass the self, to rise above his needs and selfish motives. To ignore the seriousness of that tension is to live in a fool's paradise; to despair of the power to deal with it is to move into the cynic's inferno. But how should the battle for integrity be fought?

THE CONVERSION OF NEEDS

A living organism cannot be defined by the number of cells it contains, and a human personality cannot be defined by the number of its needs, nor its life considered as an interplay of need and satisfaction. Needs are not essences but responses to objects, coming into being in concrete situations. The art of living is an art of dealing with needs, and man's character is shaped and revealed by the way in which he shapes his passions and desires. Many people may have a mother-fixation, but essential is that one turns to poetry, the other to social work and another one to crime.

The distinguishing feature of man is his capacity for the *conversion of needs*. He knows not only how to expand and to satisfy but also how to modify his needs; to defy, not only to relish desire and delight. His creative achievements come about by conscious alteration, by acts of selection and interchange of conflicting aims rather than by outright ruthless suppression.

In biology we speak of heterogenesis as a mode of reproduction in which the parent produces offsprings that differ from itself in structure and habits, but which after one or more generations revert to the parent form. A similar phenomenon is possible within the inner life of man. While we cannot arrest the expansion of needs nor successfully suppress human passion, it is given us to convert needs and to redirect passion towards goals of our own choosing. Thus, selfish needs may become the occasions for the attainment of universal ends.

Yet, does the technique of conversion solve the problem of selfishness? Is it right to assume that by conversion of needs man is capable of changing not only patterns of behavior but also trends of motivation? Do we not conceal rather than change selfish needs? Evil in concealment is a greater threat than evil in display; perverted interests may be more vicious than original needs. Does not the conversion of needs amount to offering a safe retreat to motives which we mean to subdue? Is it at all possible to overcome selfish motives?

SELF-EFFACEMENT

The discovery of a failure to educate desire brings with it an impulse to suppress it. Self-effacement seems to us then to be the only way of redemption from the enslavement to the ego. Yet self-effacement as such is an escape by which we may rush to worse corruption. Elimination of the self is in itself no virtue. To give up life or the right to satisfaction is not a moral requirement. If self-effacement were virtuous in itself, suicide would be the climax of moral living. It is Moloch that demands the sacrifice of life; it is militarism that glorifies death in battle as the highest aspiration. The prophets of Baal rather than the prophets of Israel indulged in self-mortification.

In fact, only he who truly understands the justice of his own rights is capable of rendering justice to the rights of others. Moral

398

training consists in deepening one's passionate understanding for the rights and needs of others in a manner equal to the passionate understanding of one's own rights and needs.

The value of sacrifice is determined, not only by what one gives away, but also by the goal to which it is given. The Hebrew word for the verb to sacrifice means literally to come near, to approach. Our task is not to renounce life but to bring it close to Him. What we strive for are not single moments of self-denial but sober constant affirmation of other selves, the ability to feel the needs and problems of our fellow men. Never call such an attitude self-effacing or being spiteful to the soul. What is effaced is an offensiveness, an oppressiveness which at good moments the soul detests, wishing it away.

The self may be turned into a friend of the spirit if one is capable of developing a persistent perception of the non-self, of the anxiety and dignity of fellow beings.

Self-centeredness is the tragic misunderstanding of our destiny and existence. For man, to be human is an existential tautology. In order to be a man, man must be more than a man. The self is spiritually immature; it grows in the concern for the non-self. This is the profound paradox and redeeming feature of human existence. There is no joy for the self within the self. Joy is found in giving rather than in acquiring; in serving rather than in taking.

We are all endowed with talents, aptitudes, facilities; yet talent without dedication, aptitude without vocation, facility without spiritual dignity end in frustration. What is spiritual dignity? The attachment of the soul to a goal that lies beyond the self, a goal not within but beyond the self.

This, indeed, is the mystery of the self, not explicable in terms of psychological analysis. Just as our sense of the ineffable goes beyond all words, so does the coercion for wholeheartedness, the power for self-transcendence, go beyond all interests and desires.

In dealing with the problem of the self one must abstain from any overstatement. Regard for the self is not evil. It is when arrogating to the self what is not its due, enhancing one's interests at the expense of others or setting up the self as an ultimate goal that evil comes into being. Thus, assuming that man is conscious of the good he is doing and even derives joy from what he is doing, is it wrong? Is it a sin to enjoy a good deed? Is an act not to be considered good unless it is performed automatically? Must we not say that a just man is a person to whom that which is *required* is also *desired* rather than a person who does the good in spite of his own will? The right relationship of the self to the good is not that of tension but that of inner agreement and accord. In terms of Biblical thinking, the association of the self with the deed and even the attainment of a reward are considered desirable.

The fact that men "censure injustice fearing that they may be the victims of it and not because they shrink from committing it"[1]; the fact that in defending justice we may subconsciously be moved by selfish interest does not refute the intrinsic, absolute significance of justice. It only shows that justice is so entrenched in our concrete social setting that it speaks to us as a requirement for survival, not only as a command of ethics or religion. It is, of course, conceivable that a society might be established in which murder would be considered right. But the fact that such a society would eventually provoke the hostility of other groups; the fact that in the name of their own safety those groups would rise to destroy that society; the fact that the survival of mankind as a whole is incompatible with evil, is a sign that the requiredness of justice is stronger than our conscious relation to it.[2]

NOTES FOR CHAPTER 39

[1] Plato, *Republic*, 344c.
[2] See *Man is Not Alone*, p. 224f.

40 The Deed Redeems

Is the idea of integrity a flight of fancy? The word of Moses, *Thou shalt love the Lord thy God with all thy heart, with all thy soul, with all thy might;* the word of Joshua, *Fear the Lord, and serve Him in sincerity and in truth* (Joshua 24:14); the word of Samuel, *Fear the Lord, and serve in truth with all your heart* (I Samuel 12:24); cannot be dismissed as utopian. The prophets would not demand to love Him wholeheartedly, if such love were utterly beyond the realm of possibility.

This is how we must begin in our effort to purify the self: *to become aware of our inner enslavement* to the ego, to detect the taints in our virtues, the tinge of idolatry in our worship of God.

There is great merit in knowing our subtle hypocrisies, in our having no absolute faith in our faith, in our sense of shame and contrition. The sting of shame is the only pain the ego cannot bear and the only blow that may cause its forces to shrink and to retreat, and contrition is the saving feature of our soul. Remorse stands higher than sacrifice.

> Thou carest not for sacrifice,
> Else I would give it;
> Thou hast no pleasure in burnt offerings.
> The sacrifices of God are a broken spirit;
> A broken and contrite heart,
> O God, Thou will not despise.
>   (Psalms 51:18-19)

401

Unto Thee, O Lord, belongs righteousness, but unto us shame-facedness (Daniel 9:7). "Why is this so? Said Rabbi Nehemiah: Because even when we perform righteousness, we survey our actions and are filled with shame."[1]

And man shall question all his ways. For no one is righteous in His eyes. Yet it is the awareness of our inner enslavement that is the first sign of help.

MOMENTS OF PURITY

The less willing we are to resign ourselves to our being enchained to the ego and the more deeply we understand that ultimate meaning is found in deeds composed on the margin of the self, the greater is the chance of release at least *for a moment.* And it is the moment that counts most.

There are moments when we all awake to the grandeur of cosmic reality, in the face of which the unworthiness of self-centered thinking, the speciousness of rewards, and the eagerness of vanity fill us with shame. There is so much wisdom in wood, so much kindness in the soil, and not a trace of insolence. We become aware of our true plight, of our position on the pendulum of duty and escape, and of the fact that there is no escape, that even death is no way out. Shamed, shocked at the misery of an overloaded ego, we seek to break out of the circle of the ego.

CONTRITION

Comforting as the reliance upon moments of pure devotion is, the anxiety remains. After all our efforts and attempts to purify the self, we discover that envy, vanity, pride continue to prowl in the dark. Whence cometh our help? The moments of ecstatic self-forgetfulness pass quickly. What, then, is the answer?

Should we, then, despair because of our being unable to retain perfect purity? We should, if perfection were our goal. However, we are not obliged to be perfect once and for all, but only to rise again and again beyond the level of the self. Perfection is divine, and

402

to make it a goal of man is to call on man to be divine. All we can do is to try to wring our hearts clean in *contrition*. Contrition begins with a feeling of shame at our being incapable of disentanglement from the self. To be contrite at our failures is holier than to be complacent in perfection.

GOD IS FULL OF COMPASSION

In the world of Jewish piety two voices may be heard. One voice is severe, uncompromising: good deeds done out of impure motives are entirely inadequate.[2] The other voice is one of moderation: good deeds are precious even if their motivation is not pure.[3]

What are the facts? Even the finest intention is not strong enough to fill all corners of the soul which at all sides is open to intrusions of the ego. Judged by the severe, uncompromising standard of total purity of intention, who could stand? It is, indeed, the voice of moderation that has generally prevailed. Thus we are taught to believe that "alien thoughts" or even improper motives do not vitiate the value of a sacred deed.

The soul is frail, but God is full of compassion for the distress of the soul, for the failure of the heart. It is said in the Talmud: "There are some who desire [to help others] but have not the means; whilst others have the means [and help] but have not the desire [to help]." Yet both kinds of people are holy in the eyes of God.[4]

ENDS PURIFY MOTIVES

Judaism insists upon the deed and hopes for the intention. Every morning we pray:

> Make sweet, we beseech thee, O Lord our God, the words of Thy Torah in our mouth . . . so that we study Thy Torah *for its own sake*.

While constantly keeping the goal in mind, we are taught that one must continue to observe the law even when one is not ready to fulfill it "for the sake of God." For the good, even if it is not done for its own sake, will teach us eventually how to act for the sake of God. We must continue to perform the sacred deeds even though we may be compelled to bribe the self with human incentives. Purity of motivation is the goal; constancy of action is the way. It is useless endeavor to fight the ego in the open; like a wounded hydra, it produces two heads for every one cut off. We must not indulge in self-scrutinization; we must not concentrate upon the problem of egocentricity. The way to purify the self is to avoid dwelling upon the self and to concentrate upon the task.

THE DEED REDEEMS

Any religious or ethical teaching that places the main emphasis upon the virtues of inwardness such as faith and the purity of motivation must come to grief. If faith were the only standard, the effort of man would be doomed to failure. Indeed, the awareness of the weakness of the heart; the unreliability of human inwardness may perhaps have been one of the reasons that compelled Judaism to take recourse to actions instead of relying upon inward devotion. Perhaps this is the deeper meaning of the Rabbis' counsel: one should always do the good, even though it is not done for its own sake. It is the act that teaches us the meaning of the act.

The way to pure intention is paved with good deeds. The good is carried out in acts, and there is an intense fascination that comes from a good deed counteracting the pressure and ardor of the ego. The ego is redeemed by the absorbing power and the inexorable provocativeness of a just task which we face. It is the deed that carries us away, that transports the soul, proving to us that the greatest beauty grows at the greatest distance from the center of the ego.

Deeds set upon ideal goals, deeds performed not with careless ease and routine but in exertion and submission to their ends are stronger than the surprise and attack of caprice. Serving sacred goals may change mean motives. For such deeds are exacting.

404

God in search of man

Whatever our motive may have been prior to the act, the act itself demands undivided attention. Thus the desire for reward is not the driving force of the poet in his creative moments, and the pursuit of pleasure or profit are not the essence of a religious or moral act.

At the moment in which an artist is absorbed in playing a concerto the thought of applause, fame or remuneration is far from his mind. His complete attention, his whole being is involved in the music. Should any extraneous thought enter his mind, it would arrest his concentration and mar the purity of his playing. The reward may have been on his mind when he negotiated with his agent, but during the performance it is the music that claims his complete concentration.

Man's situation in carrying out a religious or moral deed is similar. Left alone, the soul is subject to caprice. Yet there is power in the deed that purifies desires. It is the act, life itself, that educates the will. The good motive comes into being while doing the good.

If the initial motive is strong and pure, obtrusive intentions which emerge during the act may even serve to invigorate it, for the initial motive may absorb the vigor of the intruder into its own strength. Man may be replete with selfish motives but a deed and God are stronger than selfish motives. The redemptive power discharged in carrying out the good purifies the mind. The deed is wiser than the heart.

A disciple of the Rabbi Mendel of Kotsk complained to his master of his inability to worship God without becoming self-conscious and tinged with a sense of pride. Is there a way of worship in which the self does not intrude? he asked.

—Have you ever encountered a wolf while walking alone in the forest?

—I did, he retorted.

—What was on your mind at that moment?

—Fear, nothing but fear and the will to escape.

—You see, in such a moment you were in fear without being

conscious or proud of your fear. It is in such a way that we may worship God.

Though deeply aware of how impure and imperfect all our deeds are, the fact of our doing must be cherished as the highest privilege, as a source of joy, as that which endows life with ultimate preciousness. We believe that moments lived in fellowship with God, acts fulfilled in imitation of God's will, never perish; the validity of the good remains regardless of all impurity.

"SERVE HIM WITH JOY"

Traditionally, the Jew is taught to feel delight in being able to fulfill the law, albeit imperfectly, rather than to feel anxiety because of his being unable to fulfill it perfectly. "Serve Him with joy; come before His presence with singing" (Psalms 100:2).

Israel feels a certain ease and delight in the fulfillment of the law which to a hired servant is burdensome and perplexing. For "the son who serves his father serves him with joy, saying, Even if I do not entirely succeed [in carrying out His commandments], yet, as a loving father, He will not be angry with me. In contrast, a hired servant is always afraid lest he may commit some fault, and therefore serves God in a condition of anxiety and confusion."[5] Indeed, when Israel feels uneasy because of their having to stand in judgment before God, the angels say unto them, "Fear ye not the judgment. . . . Know ye not Him? He is your next of kin, He is your brother, and what is more, He is your father."[6]

"WE SPOIL AND HE RESTORES"

The eternal command, like a saw, is trying to cut the callousness of hearts. In spite of all efforts, the callousness remains uncut. What, then, is the meaning of all endeavor? Rabbi Tarfon said: "You are not called upon to complete the task, yet you are not free to evade it." Whatever we do is only a partial fulfillment; the rest is completed by God.

406

A philosophy of Judaism

Alone we have no capacity to liberate our soul from ulterior motives. This, however, is our hope: God will redeem where we fail; He will complete what we are trying to achieve. It is the grace of God that helps those who do everything that lies within their power to achieve that which is beyond their power.

Rabbi Nahman of Kossov told a parable. A stork fell into the mud and was unable to pull out his legs until an idea occurred to him: Does he not have a long beak? So he stuck his beak into the mud, leaned upon it, and pulled out his legs. But what was the use? His legs were out, but his beak was stuck. So another idea occurred to him. He stuck his legs into the mud and pulled out his beak. But what was the use? The legs were stuck in the mud. . . .

Such is the condition of man. Succeeding in one way, he fails in another. We must constantly remember: *we spoil and God restores.* How ugly is the way in which we spoil, and how good and how beautiful is the way in which He restores.

Out of the depth we cry for help. We believe that we are able to overcome ulterior motives, since otherwise no good would be done, and no love would be possible. Yet "to attain purity of heart we are in need of divine help."[7] This is why we pray:

> Purify our hearts so that we may worship Thee in honesty.
> The Sabbath Liturgy

All is inadequate: our actions as well as our abstentions. We cannot rely on our devotion, for it is tainted with alien thoughts, conceit, and vanity. It requires a great effort *to realize before Whom we stand,* for such realization is more than having a thought in one's mind. It is a knowledge in which the whole person is involved; the mind, the heart, body, and soul. To know it is to forget everything else, including the self. At best, we can only attain it for an instant, and only from time to time.

What then is left for us to do except *to pray for the ability to pray,* to bewail our ignorance of living in His presence? And even if such prayer is tainted with vanity, His mercy accepts and redeems our feeble efforts. It is the continuity of trying to pray, the unbroken loyalty to our duty to pray, that lends strength to our fragile worship; and it is the holiness of the community that bestows meaning upon our individual acts of worship. These are the three pillars on which our prayer rises to God: our own loyalty, the holiness of Israel, the mercy of God.

NOTES FOR CHAPTER 40

[1] *Exodus Rabba* 41:1. See Will Herberg, *Judaism and Modern Man*, New York, 1951, p. 149f.

[2] In one particular case, the Rabbis call a person who performs a commandment without the proper intention a transgressor. *(Nazir* 23a see Albo, *Ikkarim III*, ch. 28). One rabbi maintained that "he who does not fulfill the Torah for its own sake, it were better had he not been born." Raba's saying, *Berachot* 17b. While this extreme view was rejected by most Jewish theologians, it was to some degree upheld by others. According to Bahya, "All works done for God's sake must have as their roots purity of heart and singleness of mind. Where the motive is tainted, good deeds, however numerous and even though practiced continuously, are not accepted." *The Duties of the Heart*, introduction.

[3] *Hullin* 7a. See *Tosefot* ad locum. God does not withhold the reward of any creatures; even the wicked are rewarded for what good they may do. He does not withhold the reward even for a decorous word. See *Pesahim* 118a; *Nazir* 23b. Abstention from work on the Sabbath motivated by indolence rather than by reverence for the Sabbath, is still considered meritorious.

[4] *Hullin* 7b.

[5] *Tanhuma*, Noah 19.

[6] *Midrash Tehillim*, 118, 10. See Schechter, *Some Aspects of Rabbinic Theology*, p. 55f.

[7] Rabbenu Yonah, Commentary on Alfasi, *Berachot*, 5, 1. Compare Psalms 51:12 "Create in me a clean heart, O God, and renew a right spirit within me," and Jeremiah 32:40, "I will put the fear of Me in their hearts." See above, chapter 12, n. 2.

41 Freedom

We have said that the grand premise of religion is that man is able to surpass himself. Such ability is the essence of freedom. According to Hegel, the history of the world is nothing more than the progress of the consciousness of freedom. Now, what gives us the assurance that freedom is not a *specious* concept? By the term freedom we mean the will's independence of antecedent conditions, psychological and physiological. Yet is the will ever independent of the character of the person or the circumstances of the environment? Is not every action the result of an antecedent factor? Is not the present moment in which a decision is made loaded with the pressure of the past? The ability of the mind to compare the reasons for and against a certain action and to prefer one against the other does not extend beyond the scope of those reasons which are conscious and apparent. Yet these reasons are derived from other reasons which in turn have an infinite genealogy. Whatever the genesis of the original reasons may have been, facing the descendants is not an act of unbiased, undetermined thinking. Can we really claim to possess the power over the determinations of our own will?

Who is to be regarded as free? Free is not always he whose actions are dominated by his own will, since the will is not an ultimate and isolated entity but rather determined in its motivations by forces which are beyond its control. Nor is he free who *is* what he wants to be, since what a person wants to be is obviously determined by factors outside him. Is he who does good for its own sake to be

409

considered free? But how is it possible to do good for its own sake?

How then is personal freedom possible? Its nature is a mystery,[1] and the formidable array of cumulative evidence for determinism makes it very difficult for us to believe in freedom. And yet, without such a belief there is no meaning left to the moral life. Without taking freedom seriously, it is impossible to take humanity seriously.

From the viewpoint of naturalism, human freedom is an illusion. If all facts in the physical universe and hence also in human history are absolutely dependent upon and conditioned by causes, then man is a prisoner of circumstances. There can be no free, creative moments in his life, since they would presuppose a vacuum in time or a break in the series of cause and effect.

Man lives in bondage to his natural environment, to society, and to his own "character"; he is enslaved to needs, interests, and selfish desires. Yet to be free means to transcend nature, society, "character," needs, interests, desires. How then is freedom conceivable?

FREEDOM IS AN EVENT

The reality of freedom, of the ability to think, to will, or to make decisions beyond physiological and psychological causation is only conceivable if we assume that human life embraces both *process and event.** If man is treated as a process, if his future determinations are regarded as calculable, then freedom must be denied. Freedom means that man is capable of expressing himself in events beyond his being involved in the natural processes of living.

To believe in freedom is to believe in events, namely to maintain that man is able to escape the bonds of the processes in which he is involved and to act in a way not necessitated by antecedent factors. Freedom is the state of going out of the self, an act of *spiritual ecstacy,* in the original sense of the term.

Who, then, is free? The creative man who is not carried away by the streams of necessity, who is not enchained by processes, who is not enslaved to circumstances.

* See above, p. 209 f.

A philosophy of Judaism

We are free at rare moments. Most of the time we are driven by a process; we submit to the power of inherited character qualities or to the force of external circumstances. Freedom is not a continual state of man, "a permanent attitude of the conscious subject."[2] It *is* not, it *happens*. Freedom is an act, an event. We all are endowed with the potentiality of freedom. In actuality, however, we only act freely in rare creative moments.

Man's ability to transcend the self, to rise above all natural ties and bonds, presupposes further that every man lives in a realm governed by law and necessity as well as in a realm of creative possibilities. It presupposes his belonging to a dimension that is higher than nature, society, and the self, and accepts the reality of such a dimension beyond the natural order. Freedom does not mean the right to live as we please. It means the power to live spiritually, to rise to a higher level of existence.

Freedom is not, as is often maintained, a principle of uncertainty, the ability to act without motive. Such a view confounds freedom with chaos, free will with a freak of unmotivated volition, with subrational action.

Nor is freedom the same as the ability to choose between motives. Freedom includes an act of choice, but its root is in the realization that the self is no sovereign, in the discontent with the tyranny of the ego. Freedom comes about in the moment of transcending the self, thus rising above the habit of regarding the self as its own end. *Freedom is an act of self-engagement of the spirit, a spiritual event.*

FREEDOM AND CREATION

The basic issue of freedom is how we can be sure that the so-called events are not disguised aspects of a process, or that creative acts are not brought upon by natural developments of which we are not aware. The idea of creative possibilities and the possibility of living spiritually depend upon the idea of creation and man's being more than the product of nature.

The ultimate concept in Greek philosophy is the idea of cosmos, of order; the first teaching in the Bible is the idea of *creation*. Translated into eternal principles, cosmos means fate, while creation means freedom. The essential meaning of creation is not the idea that the universe was created at a particular moment in time. The essential meaning of creation is, as Maimonides explained, the idea that the universe did not come about by necessity but as a result of freedom.

Man is free to act in freedom and free to forfeit freedom. In choosing evil he surrenders his attachment to the spirit and forgoes the opportunity to let freedom happen. Thus we may be free in employing or in ignoring freedom; we are not free in having freedom. We are free to choose between good and evil; we are not free in having to choose. We are in fact compelled to choose. Thus all freedom is a situation of God's waiting for man to choose.

DIVINE CONCERN

The decisive thought in the message of the prophets is not the presence of God to man but rather the presence of man to God. This is why the Bible is God's anthropology rather than man's theology. The prophets speak not so much of man's concern for God as of God's concern for man. At the beginning is God's concern. It is because of His concern for man that man may have a concern for Him, that we are able to search for Him.

In Jewish thinking, the problem of being can never be treated in isolation but only in relation to God. The supreme categories in such ontology are not being and becoming but law and love (justice and compassion, order and pathos). Being, as well as all beings, stands in a polarity of divine justice and divine compassion.

To most of us, the abstract static principle of order and necessity is an ultimate category and one which is inherent in the very concept of being (or of our consciousness of being). To the Jewish mind, order or necessity is not an ultimate category but an aspect of the dynamic attribute of divine judgment. Jewish thinking, furthermore, claims that being is constituted (created) and main-

412

tained not only by necessity but also by freedom, by God's free and personal concern for being.

The divine concern is not a theological afterthought but a fundamental category of ontology. Reality seems to be maintained by the necessity of its laws. Yet, when we inquire: why is necessity necessary? there is only one answer: the divine freedom, the divine concern.

The question may be asked: Is it plausible to believe that the eternal should be concerned with the trivial? Should we not rather assume that man is too insignificant to be an object for His concern? The truth, however, is that nothing is trivial. What seems infinitely small in our eyes is infinitely great in the eyes of the infinite God. Because the finite is never isolated; it is involved in countless ways in the course of infinite events. And the higher the level of spiritual awareness, the greater is the degree of sensibility to, and concern for, others.

We must continue to ask: what is man that God should care for him? And we must continue to remember that it is precisely God's care for man that constitutes the greatness of man. *To be* is to *stand for,* and what man stands for is the great mystery of being His partner. *God is in need of man.*[3]

NOTES FOR CHAPTER 41

[1] See W. James, *The Will to Believe.*
"On the basis of ethical arguments, personal freedom must be recognized as a necessary constituent of moral being. . . . The question accordingly is not whether personal freedom is possible, but the more difficult one: how is it possible? . . . . Freedom of the will on its ontological side does not permit 'proof,' in the strict sense. Moreover, its actual possibility can be entertained only within the limits of hypothetical certainty. What still remains to be done is in truth the most important part of the work; but today we are far from being able to do it. We can only take one or two steps toward cleaning up the problem. The nature and the actuality of personal freedom are beyond the limits of human reason." N. Hartmann, *Ethics,* vol. III, p. 205f; the German edition, p. 69b f.
[2] W. James, *Personal Idealism.*
[3] *Man is Not Alone,* p. 25, p. 241f.

42 The Spirit of Judaism

Religion becomes sinful when it begins to advocate the segregation of God, to forget that the true sanctuary has no walls. Religion has always suffered from the tendency to become an end in itself, to seclude the holy, to become parochial, self-indulgent, self-seeking; as if the task were not to ennoble human nature but to enhance the power and beauty of its institutions or to enlarge the body of doctrines. It has often done more to canonize prejudices than to wrestle for truth; to petrify the sacred than to sanctify the secular. Yet the task of religion is to be a challenge to the stabilization of values.

Deep in our hearts there is a perpetual temptation to worship the imposing; to make an idol of things dear to us. It is easy to adore the illustrious. It is easy to appreciate beauty, and hard to see through the masquerade of the ostentatious. Had a poet come to Samaria, the capital of the Northern Kingdom, he would have written songs exalting its magnificent edifices, its beautiful temples and monuments of worldly glory. But Amos of Tekoa upon his visit to Samaria did not speak of the splendor of the "house of ivory" nor sing the praise of the palaces. Looking at them he saw nothing but moral confusion and oppression. Instead of being fascinated, he was appalled. "I abhor the pride of Jacob and hate his palaces," he cried out in the name of the Lord. Was Amos not sensitive to beauty?

414

A philosophy of Judaism

We must not regard any human institution or object as being an end in itself. Man's achievements in this world are but attempts, and a temple that comes to mean more than a reminder of the living God is an abomination.

What is an idol? A thing, a force, a person, a group, an institution or an ideal, regarded as supreme. God alone is supreme.

The prophet abhors idolatry. He refuses to regard the instrumental as final, the temporal as ultimate. We must worship neither mankind nor nature, neither ideas nor ideals. Even evil should not be idolized, but instrumentalized. The evil urge does not spell doom; it can be integrated in the service of God. It was possible for Rabbi Meir to remark: "And God saw it was very good—very good is the evil urge."

Even the laws of the Torah are not absolutes.[1] Nothing is deified: neither power nor wisdom, neither heroes nor institutions. To ascribe divine qualities to all of these, to anything, sublime and lofty as it may be, is to distort both the idea it represents and the concept of the divine which we bestow upon it.

Having passed the abyss of paganism, Judaism is often a lonely, unperceived voice raised against man's converting instrumentals into finals. We are a challenge to the sovereignty of any one value: whether it be the ego, the state, nature, or beauty. Judaism has disturbed the inflexibility and isolationism of values, lifting the natural to the moral, dissolving the esthetic in the sacred, seeking to shape the human in the pattern of the divine. It has not only detested beauty when produced at the price of justice; it has rejected the ritual when performed by the morally corrupted. Even religion itself, worship, was not considered to be an absolute. "Your prayers are an abomination," said Isaiah to the exploiters of the poor. Stay away from the synagogue, wrote the Gaon of Wilna to his household, if you cannot abstain from envy and gossiping about the dresses of your fellow attendants.

Nothing exists for its own sake, nothing is valid by its own right. What seems to be a purpose is but a station on the road. All is set in the dimension of the holy. All is endowed with bearing on God.

415

To be a Jew is to renounce allegiance to false gods; to be sensitive to God's infinite stake in every finite situation; to bear witness to His presence in the hours of His concealment; to remember that the world is unredeemed. We are born to be an answer to His question. Our way is either a pilgrimage or a flight. We are chosen to remain free of infatuation with worldly triumphs, to retain independence of hysteria and deceptive glories; never to surrender to splendor, even at the price of remaining strangers to fashion.

This is what we mean by the term *spiritual*: It is the reference to the transcendent in our own existence, the direction of the Here toward the Beyond. It is the ecstatic force that stirs all our goals, redeeming values from the narrowness of being ends in themselves, turning arrivals into new pilgrimages, new farings forth. It is an all-pervading trend that both contains and transcends all values, a never-ending process, the upward movement of being. The spiritual is not something we own, but something we may share in. We do not possess it; we may be possessed by it. When we perceive it, it is as if our mind were gliding for a while with an eternal current, in which our ideas become knowledge swept beyond itself.

It is impossible to grasp spirit in itself. Spirit is a *direction,* the turning of all beings to God: *theotropism.* It is always more than— and superior to—what we are and know.

THE SPIRIT OF JUDAISM

Is there a unique expression for the spirit of Judaism? Is there a term that would convey its singular nature?

Let us turn to the text of the Ten Commandments, the most representative monument of Jewish teaching, and see whether such a term can be found. The Ten Commandments have been translated into all tongues, and its vocabulary has become part of the literature of all nations. Reading that famous text in any translation, Greek, Latin or English, we are struck by a surprising fact. All words of the Hebrew text have been easily rendered by English equivalents. There is a word for *pesel:* a graven image; there are words for

416

shamayim, for example, and *erets:* heaven and earth. The whole text has been faithfully translated into English and yet it reads as if it were originally written in English. But, lo and behold! There is one Hebrew word for which no English equivalent has been found and which remained untranslated: *Sabbath.* "Remember the Sabbath Day." In the Greek of the Septuagint we read *Sabbaton;* in the Latin of the Vulgate *Sabbatum;* in Aramaic *Shabbatha;* in the King James version the *Sabbath.*

Perhaps Sabbath is the idea that expresses what is most characteristic of Judaism.

What is the Sabbath?[2] A reminder of every man's royalty; an abolition of the distinction of master and slave, rich and poor, success and failure. To celebrate the Sabbath is to experience one's ultimate independence of civilization and society, of achievement and anxiety. The Sabbath is an embodiment of the belief that all men are equal and that equality of men means the nobility of men. The greatest sin of man is to forget that he is a prince.

The Sabbath is an assurance that the spirit is greater than the universe, that beyond the good is the holy. The universe was created in six days, but the climax of creation was the seventh day. Things that come into being in the six days are good, but the seventh day is holy. The Sabbath is *holiness in time.*

What is the Sabbath? The presence of eternity, a moment of majesty, the radiance of joy. The soul is enhanced, time is a delight, and inwardness a supreme reward. Indignation is felt to be a desecration of the day, and strife the suicide of one's additional soul. Man does not stand alone, he lives in the presence of the day.

THE ART OF SURPASSING CIVILIZATION

Lift up your eyes and see: who created these. Six days a week we are engaged in conquering the forces of nature, in the arts of civilization. The seventh day is dedicated to the remembrance of creation and the remembrance of redemption, to the liberation of Israel from Egypt, to the exodus from a great civilization into a wilderness where the word of God was given. By our acts of labor during the six days we participate in the works of history; by sanctifying the seventh day we are reminded of the acts that surpass, ennoble and redeem history.

The world is contingent on creation, and the worth of history depends on redemption. To be a Jew is to affirm the world without being enslaved to it; to be a part of civilization and to go beyond it; to conquer space and to sanctify time. Judaism is *the art of surpassing civilization,* sanctification of time, sanctification of history.

Civilization is on trial. Its future will depend upon how much of the Sabbath will penetrate its spirit.

The Sabbath, as experienced by man, cannot survive in exile, a lonely stranger among days of profanity. It needs the companionship of the other days. All days of the week must be spiritually consistent with the seventh day. Even if we cannot reach a plane where all our life would be a pilgrimage to the seventh day, the thought and appreciation of what the day may bring to us should always be present in our minds. The Sabbath is the counterpoint of living; the melody sustained throughout all agitations and vicissitudes which menace our conscience; our awareness of God's presence in the world. It teaches us to sense the delights of spirit, the joys of the good, the grandeur of living in the face of eternity.

What the Sabbath is among the days, the consecrated man, the *talmid chacham,* is among us, the common people. The consecrated man is he who knows how to sanctify time. Not deceived by the splendor of space, he remains attentive to the divine tangent at the whirling wheel of living.

The Sabbath is more than a day, more than a name for a seventh part of the week. It is eternity within time, *the spiritual underground of history.*

In the language of the Jew, living *sub specie aeternitatis* means living *sub specie Sabbatis.* Every Friday eve we must kindle the lights in the soul, enhance our mercy, deepen our sensitivity.

The Sabbath is one day, *Shabbesdikeit* is what should permeate

A philosophy of Judaism

all our days. *Shabbesdikeit* is spirituality, the epitome and spirit of Judaism.

The great dream of Judaism is not to raise priests, but a people of priests; to consecrate all men, not only some men.

"And why was not the tribe of Levi granted a share in the land of Israel? . . . Because it was dedicated to the worship of God and His ministry. The vocation of the tribe of Levi was to teach the multitude the upright ways of the Lord and His righteous judgments. . . . But not the tribe of Levi alone was consecrated thus. Every human being born into this world whose spirit stirs him and whose intellect guides him to dedicate himself to the Lord in order to minister to Him and worship Him and to come to know Him, and who acts in conformity with God's design and disembarrasses himself of the devious ways which men have sought out, becomes sanctified with supreme sanctity."[3]

NOTES FOR CHAPTER 42

[1] See above, p. 326.
[2] Compare A. J. Heschel, *The Sabbath.*
[3] Maimonides, *Mishneh Torah,* Shemitah ve-Yobel, 13, 12-13.

43 The People Israel

There is a high cost of living to be paid by a Jew. He has to be exalted in order to be normal in a world that is neither propitious for nor sympathetic to his survival. Some of us, tired of sacrifice and exertion, often wonder: Is Jewish existence worth the price? Others are overcome with panic; they are perplexed, and despair of recovery.

The meaning of Jewish existence, the major theme of any Jewish philosophy, is baffling. To fit it into the framework of personal intellectual predilections or current fashions of our time would be a distortion. The claim of Israel must be recognized *before* attempting an interpretation. As the ocean is more than what we know about it, so Judaism surpasses the content of all philosophies of it. We have not invented it. We may accept or reject, but should not distort it.

It is as an individual that I am moved by an anxiety for the meaning of my existence as a Jew. Yet when I begin to ponder about it, my theme is not the problem of one Jew but of all Jews. And the more deeply I probe, the more strongly I realize the scope of the problem: It embraces not only the Jews of the present but also those of the past and those of the future, the meaning of Jewish existence in all ages.

What is at stake in our lives is more than the fate of one generation. In this moment *we,* the living, are Israel. The tasks begun by the patriarchs and prophets, and carried out by countless Jews of the past, are now entrusted to us. No other group has superseded them. We are the only channel of Jewish tradition, those who must save Judaism from oblivion, those who must hand over the entire past to the generations to come. We are either the last, the dying, Jews or else we are those who will give new life to our tradition. Rarely in our history has so much depended upon one generation. We will either forfeit or enrich the legacy of the ages.

THINKING COMPATIBLE WITH OUR DESTINY

Understanding Judaism cannot be attained in the comfort of playing a chess-game of theories. Only ideas that are meaningful to those who are steeped in misery may be accepted as principles by those who dwell in safety. In trying to understand Jewish existence a Jewish philosopher must look for agreement with the men of Sinai as well as with the people of Auschwitz.

We are the most challenged people under the sun. Our existence is either superfluous or indispensable to the world; it is either tragic or holy to be a Jew.

It is a matter of immense responsibility that we here and Jewish teachers everywhere have undertaken to instill in our youth the will to be Jews today, tomorrow and for ever and ever. Unless being a Jew is of absolute significance how can we justify the ultimate price which our people was often forced to pay throughout its history? To assess Judaism soberly and farsightedly is to establish it as a good to be preferred, if necessary, to any alternative which we may ever face.

The task of Jewish philosophy today, is not only to describe the essence but also to set forth the universal relevance of Judaism, the bearings of its demands upon the chance of man to remain human. Bringing to light the lonely splendor of Jewish thinking, conveying the taste of eternity in our daily living is the greatest aid we can render to the man of our time who has fallen so low that he is not even capable of being ashamed of what happened in his days.

We were not born by mere chance as a by-product of a migration of nations or in the obscurity of a primitive past. God's vision of Israel came first and only then did we come into the world. We were formed according to an intention and for the sake of a purpose. Our souls tremble with the echo of unforgettable experiences and with the sublime expectation of our own response. To be a Jew is to be committed to the experience of great ideas. The task of Jewish philosophy is to formulate not only these ideas but also the depth of that commitment in vivid, consistent thinking. The task of Jewish philosophy is *to make our thinking compatible with our destiny*.

Life appears dismal if not mirrored in what is more than life. Nothing can be regarded as valuable unless assessed in relation to something higher in value. Man's survival depends on the conviction that there is something that is worth the price of life. It depends upon a sense of the supremacy of what is lasting. That sense of conviction may be asleep, but it awakens when challenged. In some people it lives as a sporadic wish; in others it is a permanent concern.

What we have learned from Jewish history is that if a man is not more than human then he is less than human. Judaism is an attempt to prove that in order to be a man, you have to be more than a man, that in order to be a people we have to be more than a people. Israel was made to be a "holy people." This is the essence of its dignity and the essence of its merit. Judaism is a link to eternity, kinship with ultimate reality.

A sense of contact with the ultimate dawns upon most people when their self-reliance is swept away by violent misery. Judaism is the attempt to instill in us that sense as an everyday awareness. It leads us to regard injustice as a metaphysical calamity, to sense the divine significance of human happiness, to keep slightly above the twilight of the self, enabling us to sense the eternal within the temporal.

We are endowed with the consciousness of being involved in a history that transcends time and its specious glories. We are taught to feel the knots of life in which the trivial is intertwined with the sublime. There is no end to our experience of the spiritual grandeur, of the divine earnestness of human life. Our blossoms may be crushed, but we are upheld by the faith that comes from the core of our roots. We are not deceived by the obvious, knowing that all delight is but a pretext for adding strength to that which is beyond joy and grief. We know that no hour is the last hour, that the world is more than the world.

ISRAEL—A SPIRITUAL ORDER

Why is our belonging to the Jewish people a sacred relation? Israel is a *spiritual order* in which the human and the ultimate, the natural and the holy enter a lasting covenant, in which kinship with God is not an aspiration but a reality of destiny. For us Jews there can be no fellowship with God without the fellowship with the people Israel. Abandoning Israel, we desert God.

Jewish existence is not only the adherence to particular doctrines and observances, but primarily the living *in* the spiritual order of the Jewish people, the living *in* the Jews of the past and *with* the Jews of the present. It is not only a certain quality in the souls of the individuals, but primarily the existence of the community of Israel. It is neither an experience nor a creed, neither the possession of psychic traits nor the acceptance of a theological doctrine, but the living in a holy dimension, in a spiritual order. Our share in holiness we acquire by living in the Jewish community. What we do as individuals is a trivial episode, what we attain as Israel causes us to grow into the infinite.

The meaning of history is to be a sanctuary in time, and every one of us has his part in the great ritual. The ultimate meaning of human deeds is not restricted to the life of him who does these deeds and to the particular moment in which they occur.

Religious living is not only a private concern. Our own life is a movement in the symphony of ages. We are taught to pray as well as to live in the first person plural. We do a mitsvah "in the name of all Israel." We act both as individuals and as the community of Israel. All generations are present, as it were, in every moment.

Israel is the tree, we are the leaves. It is the clinging to the stem that keeps us alive. There has perhaps never been more need of Judaism than in our time, a time in which many cherished hopes of humanity lie crushed. We should be pioneers as were our fathers three thousand years ago. The future of all men depends upon their realizing that the sense of holiness is as vital as health. By following the Jewish way of life we maintain that sense and preserve the light for mankind's future visions.

It is our destiny to live for what is more than ourselves. Our very existence is an unparalleled symbol of such aspiration. By being what we are, namely Jews, we mean more to mankind than by any particular service we may render.

We have faith in God and faith in Israel. Though some of its children have gone astray, Israel remains the mate of God. We cannot hate what God loves. Rabbi Aaron the Great used to say: "I wish I could love the greatest saint as the Lord loves the greatest rascal."

Israel exists not in order to be, but in order to cherish the vision of God. Our faith may be strained but our destiny is anchored to the ultimate. Who can establish the outcome of our history? Out of the wonder we came and into the wonder we shall return.

THE DIGNITY OF ISRAEL

Belonging to Israel is in itself a spiritual act. It is utterly inconvenient to be a Jew. The very survival of our people is a *kiddush hashem*. We live in spite of peril. Our very existence is a refusal to surrender to normalcy, to security and comfort. Experts in assimilation, the Jews could have disappeared even before the names of modern nations were known. Still we are patient and cherish the will to perpetuate our essence.

We are Jews as we are men. The alternative to our existence as Jews is spiritual suicide, disappearance. It is *not* a change into something else. Judaism has allies but no substitutes. Jewish faith consists of attachment to God, attachment to Torah, and attachment to Israel.

There is a unique association between the people and the land of Israel. Even before Israel becomes a people, the land is preordained for it. What we have witnessed in our own days is a reminder of the power of God's mysterious promise to Abraham and a testimony to the fact that the people kept its promise, "If I forget thee, O Jerusalem, let my right hand wither" (Psalms 137:5). The Jew in whose heart the love of Zion dies is doomed to lose his faith in the God of Abraham who gave the land as an earnest of the redemption of all men.

The people of Israel groaned in distress. Out of Egypt, the land of plentiful food, they were driven into the wilderness. Their souls were dried away; there was nothing at all: no flesh to eat, no water to drink. All they had was a promise: to be led to the land of milk and honey. They were almost ready to stone Moses. "Wherefore hast thou brought us up out of Egypt, to kill us and our children and our cattle with thirst?" they cried. But, after they had worshipped the golden calf—when God had decided to detach Himself from His people, not to dwell any more in their midst, but to entrust an angel with the task of leading them out of the wilderness to the Promised Land—Moses exclaimed: "If Thou Thyself dost not go with us, take us not out of the wilderness" (Exodus 33:15). This, perhaps, is the secret of our history: *to choose to remain in the wilderness rather than to be abandoned by Him.*

Israel's experience of God has not evolved from search. Israel did not discover God. Israel was discovered by God. Judaism is *God's quest for man.* The Bible is a record of God's approach to His people. More statements are found in the Bible about God's love for Israel than about Israel's love for God.

We have not chosen God; He has chosen us. There is no concept of a chosen God but there is the idea of a chosen people. The idea of a chosen people does not suggest the preference for a people based upon a discrimination among a number of peoples. We do not say that we are a superior people. The "chosen people" means a people approached and chosen by God. The significance of this term is genuine in relation to God rather than in relation to other peoples. It signifies not a quality inherent in the people but a relationship between the people and God.

Harassed, pursued with enmity and wrong, our fathers continued to feel joy in being Jews. "Happy are we. How good is our destiny, how pleasant our lot, how beautiful our heritage." What is the source of that feeling?

The quest for immortality is common to all men. To most of them the vexing question points to the future. Jews think not only of the end but also of the beginning. As parts of Israel we are endowed with a very rare, a very precious consciousness, the consciousness that we do not live in a void. We never suffer from harrowing anxiety and fear of roaming about in the emptiness of time. We own the past and are, hence, not afraid of what is to be. We remember where we came from. We were summoned and cannot forget it, as we wind the clock of eternal history. We remember the beginning and believe in an end. We live between two historic poles: Sinai and the Kingdom of God.

> Upon thy walls, O Jerusalem,
> I have set watchmen,
> All the day and all the night
> They shall never be silent.
> Ye that stir the Lord to remember,
> Take no rest,
> And give Him no rest
> Till He establishes Jerusalem,
> And makes it a praise in the earth.
>
> Isaiah 62:6-7

Acknowledgment

The present volume is a continuation and application of some of the ideas in *Man Is Not Alone*.

For valuable suggestions, the author is grateful to Professor Maurice Friedman, to Professor Fritz Kaufmann, and to Rabbi Jacob Riemer who have read all or parts of the manuscript. For the warm friendship of Mr. Roger W. Straus, Jr., I am deeply indebted.

Index

430

God's quest, 198, 425
Good, the, 11, 17, 21, 82, 90, 103,
    162, 173, 307, 345, 347, 362,
    365, 369, 374, 376, 379, 385,
    387, 389, 393, 404, 406
Good and evil, 26, 273, 369, 372,
    373, 375, 382
Grace, 30, 140, 142
Grandeur, 33, 34, 36, 37, 46, 83, 88,
    90, 91, 92, 95, 97, 98, 105, 115,
    122, 127, 140, 163, 180, 207,
    258, 283, 293, 367, 373, 384,
    402
Greece, 21, 23, 37, 88, 91, 92, 98
Guidance, 164, 169, 239, 383
Guilt, 36, 368

Habit, 3, 343f
Habit, value of, 344
Halacha, 306, 310, 323-342
Happiness, 351, 382, 422
Hellenic (see also Greece), 94
Heart, failure of the, 393
Heart, hardness of, 85
Heart, stubbornness of, 85
Heteronomous, 298
History, 20, 21, 31, 45, 61, 82, 136,
    155, 164, 171f, 200-211, 216,
    231, 236, 238-246, 255, 258,
    261, 349, 363, 368, 369, 370,
    371, 376, 377, 379, 409f, 418,
    422ff
History, religion of, 200
Holiness, 17, 64, 76, 88, 103, 137,
    238, 244f, 260, 266, 273, 290,
    296, 300, 310, 317, 346, 351,
    357, 358, 359, 362, 369, 370,
    371, 376, 378, 385, 391, 408
Holy, atonement for the, 371
Honesty, 229, 389
Honesty, intellectual, 10
Hope, 225, 239
Horror, 367
Humility, 5, 73, 77, 105, 111, 132,
    170, 344
Hypocrisy, 389, 392

Idol, 119, 127, 392
Idolatry, 125, 414f
Ignorance, 57, 74, 140

Illusion, 195, 222f, 235, 238, 300,
    410
Immediacy, 115f
Immortality, 426
Impulse, evil, 371
Inability to believe, 119
Inability to experience, 117
Inclination, evil, 375
Incompatibility, 104
Inconceivability, 130
Indebtedness, 112
Indications, 103, 356
Ineffable, 103f, 106, 116, 120, 137,
    163f, 184, 189
    sense of the, 20, 65, 105, 131, 182,
    250, 308, 350-353, 399
Injustice, 290, 373f, 400, 422
Insanity, product of, 223
Insight, moments of, 114
    preconceptual, 116
    ultimate, 177, 132
Institutions, 293, 389, 415
Intellectualism, 330
Intention, 295f, 306-308, 314, 315,
    316, 322, 403
    general, 345
Integrity, 297, 388, 390, 401
    intellectual, 15
Interests, 294, 301, 385, 397, 410
    vested, 243, 387, 389
Intimation, 113, 114, 131
Intrusion, evil's, 371
Intuition, 8, 14, 74, 75, 106, 148,
    163f, 189, 194, 227
Invention, pedagogical, 227
Involvement, 5
Inwardness, 8, 293, 296, 306, 337,
    339, 343, 404
Isolation, fallacy of, 95
Israel, election of, 65

Joy, 79, 302, 310, 341, 345, 355,
    357, 358, 367, 384-386, 399f,
    400, 406
Judaism, spirit of, 416
Justice, 65, 155, 164, 171, 239, 244,
    273, 288, 291, 294, 341, 345,
    368, 373, 378, 383, 398, 400,
    412

432

Index

433

Situation, 57, 119, 129, 132, 136, 204, 292
  human, 65
Situation, religious, 116, 130
Society, 171, 348, 377, 400f, 410
Solipsism, 353
Soul, simplicity of, 244
Space, 205, 312, 418
  things of, 202
Speculation, 120f, 227
Speculative, 127, 130
Speech, 123, 188
Spirit, 18, 19, 97, 101, 134, 138, 241, 244, 250, 341, 344, 351, 399, 412, 416
Spiritual, 106, 108, 142f
Spirtualism, 340
Spirituality, 296
Spirit, Holy, 385
Spontaneity, 341, 343
Standards, 161, 240, 268
State, 90
Study, 281
Subconscious, 36, 231
Subject, ultimate, 100
Sublime, 33, 36-40, 43, 48, 95, 106, 111, 240, 252
Suffering, 69, 391
Suggestiveness, 106
Superstition, 155, 389
Supreme acquiescence, 282
Survival, 348f, 422
Suspicion, 389
Symbiosis, 340
Symbol, 69, 103, 108, 115, 127, 181, 201
Sympathy, 11, 75, 90, 252
Synagogue, 415

Teaching, oral, 274-276
Temperance, 102
Temple, 245
Teshuvah, 141
Theodicy, 390
Theology, 4, 25, 39, 258, 412
  conceptual, 8
  negative, 186
  pan-halachic, 323
Theotropism, 416
Thinking, 112, 115, 121, 216, 422
  act of, 6, 47, 111

  artistic, 116
  Biblical, 22f, 90, 136
  conceptual, 5
  content of, 6
  creative, 115
  discursive, 117, 121
  ellyptic, 12f
  form of, 46
  Greek way of, 14
  Jewish, 412
  religious, 9, 16, 103, 114, 116, 127, 140
  situational, 5
  vicarious, 273
  way of, 14f, 24, 103, 197
  wishful, 223
Time, 57, 62, 130, 131, 138, 142, 181, 200-205, 214-216, 239, 242, 300, 312, 341, 412, 422, 426
  holiness in, 417
  religion of, 200
  role of, 128, 129, 134
  timeless, 196, 250
Times, 135
Torah, unrevealed, 262
Tradition, 3, 16, 19, 31, 43, 129, 152, 274f, 277, 296, 298, 330, 332, 391
  respect for, 320f
Transcendence, 51, 75, 94, 102, 105, 114, 117, 120, 159, 162, 197, 199, 204, 216, 221, 223, 411, 416
Transforming, 310, 337
Transgression, 285, 377
Truth, 120, 138, 139, 162, 204, 227, 271

Ultimacy, 125
Understanding, 154
  continuous, 275
  false, 275
Understatements, 116, 121, 127, 178, 180, 399
Unique, Uniqueness, 16, 125, 201f, 221, 362, 397
Unity, 250
Universe, 43f, 57, 67, 101, 105, 109, 120, 126, 127, 170, 252, 286, 410, 412
Urgency, 118

436